Also by Bruno Bettelheim

Love Is Not Enough: The Treatment of Emotionally
   Disturbed Children (1950)
Truants from Life: The Rehabilitation of Emotionally
   Disturbed Children (1955)
The Informed Heart: Autonomy in a Mass Age (1960)
Paul and Mary: Two Cases from Truants from Life (1961)
Dialogues with Mothers (1962)
Symbolic Wounds: Puberty Rites and the
   Envious Male (1962)
Co-author (with M. B. Janowitz): Social Change
   and Prejudice (1964)
The Empty Fortress (1967)
Children of the Dream (1969)

A Home for the Heart

Bruno Bettelheim

A Home for the Heart

Alfred A. Knopf | *New York*
1974

40671

Copyright © 1974 by Bruno Bettelheim and Trude Bettelheim as Trustees, and
their successors in trust of the Bruno Bettelheim Trust #1

Library of Congress Cataloging in Publication Data

Bettelheim, Bruno.   A home for the heart.

Bibliography: p.
1. Child psychotherapy—Residential treatment.
2. Schizophrenia in children. 3. Chicago. University.
Sonia Shankman Orthogenic School. I. Title.
[DNLM: 1. Child psychiatry. 2. Hospitals, Psychiatric. ws350 b565h 1974]
RJ504.5.B47 1974   618.9′28′915   73-7295
ISBN 0-394-48377-4

Manufactured in the United States of America

First Edition

Grateful acknowledgment is made to the following for permission to reprint previously published
material:

American Journal of Orthopsychiatry and Fritz Redl: For excerpts from "Strategy and
Techniques of the Life Space Interview," by Fritz Redl, reprinted from American Journal of
Orthopsychiatry, 29, 1959. Copyright © 1959, American Journal of Orthopsychiatry.

American Journal of Orthopsychiatry and Mary Jane Riley Key: For excerpts from "Psychiatric
Consultation in Residential Treatment: The Child Care Worker's View," by M. J. Riley,
reprinted from American Journal of Orthopsychiatry, 28, 1958. Copyright © 1958, American
Journal of Orthopsychiatry.

Basic Books, Inc.: For Figure 4, Chapter 11, "Formal Routes of Oral Communication of Clinical
Information," from The Mental Hospital: A Study of Institutional Participation in Psychiatric
Illness and Treatment by Alfred H. Stanton, M.D., Morris S. Schwartz, Ph.D., copyright © 1954
by Basic Books, Inc., Publishers, New York.

Holt, Rinehart & Winston, Inc.: For specified lines from "Mending Wall," by Robert Frost,
reprinted from The Poetry of Robert Frost, edited by Edward Connery Lathem. Copyright 1930,
1939, © 1969 by Holt, Rinehart & Winston, Inc. Copyright © 1958 by Robert Frost. Copyright
© 1967 by Lesley Frost Ballantine.

International Universities Press, Inc., and Heinz Kohut, M.D.: For an excerpt from
"Introspection, Empathy, and Psychoanalysis," by Heinz Kohut, reprinted from Journal of the
American Psychoanalytic Association, Vol. 7, 1959.

Psychiatry: For an excerpt from "Maternal Care and Infant Behavior in Japan and America," by
William Caudill and Helen Weinstein, from Vol. 32, 1969 (p. 12–43); and for the table "Types
of Institutional Structure," by Jules Henry, from Vol. 20, 1957 (p. 59–60). Copyright © 1957
William Alanson White Psychoanalytic Foundation, Inc.

Science and Behavior Books, Inc.: For excerpts from Inpatient Care of the Psychotic Child by
J. A. Szurek, I. N. Berlin, and M. J. Boatman, Langley Porter Child Psychiatry Series, Science
and Behavior Books, 1971.

Contents

IV | Staff

List of Plates

Foreword

This book took form ever so slowly, over some twenty-five years. It is impossible to recall all the influences that entered into my life's work, to remember all the many people who personally or through their writings contributed to my thoughts. It seems unfair to mention some here and not others; to give individual credit to a few, when so many helped shape my opinions and actions.

To acknowledge all the publications from which thoughts were derived in this book would require a bibliography of many thousand entries. Rather than trying to cite the writings which most deeply influenced my thinking, the Bibliography at the end of the book is restricted only to publications specifically quoted in the book. These pale in significance when compared with many others which remain unnamed.

Even a complete bibliography would still fail to do justice to the innumerable other influences that aided in the creation of the institution here described, the Orthogenic School of the University of Chicago. Practically all staff members and patients, past and present, contributed to it in some fashion; they either taught me directly what a psychiatric institution ought to be like, or indirectly through their actions, which forced me to clarify my thoughts.

Although I am thus unable to give personal thanks to the many who helped create what this book is based on, I wish to name at least those who directly aided in its writing. A year as a fellow at the Center for Advanced Study in the Behavioral Sciences at Stanford in California permitted me to complete a first draft of this volume. I am most grateful to the Center not only for this opportunity, but also for the splendid help given me there. Miriam Gallaher's patient and sensitive understanding of my difficulties in expressing myself, and all her help in preparing the first draft, went way beyond what are usually viewed as the tasks of an editor. Her criticisms as well as her positive suggestions permitted me to clarify much; to add what was needed; and to eliminate the superfluous. Without her I never could have accomplished so much in relatively little time. Nor could I have done without Doris Norgard's generous devotion toward getting this task done.

Conversations with other fellows at the Center were stimulating and enriching. From among them, at least Alan Derschowitz and Robert LeVine should be gratefully mentioned for their help in improving the manuscript.

This book's final form owes much to the careful scrutiny which some friends gave it. They, too, made many important suggestions for its improvement. I am deeply indebted to Marjorie and Al Flarsheim, Jack Getzels, Robert Koff, Paul Kramer, Kathy and Marc Lubin, Jacqui Sanders, Benjamin Wright, and Karen Zelan for their splendid contributions. Much that is good in this book is due to them.

It was a real pleasure to collaborate on the final draft with Joyce Jack, whose understanding care made the book so much more readable. I am also most grateful to Robert Gottlieb for his sensitive editing, which greatly improved the manuscript I submitted to him.

Most of all, thanks are due to the University of Chicago, which provided the Orthogenic School with its home and at all times has supported it generously, with great empathy for its difficult task.

To each and all of these, and those who remain unmentioned, go my heartfelt thanks.

B. B.

A Home for the Heart

Introduction

There was never any proper reason or excuse for the dreadful places where mental patients are kept; nor for the neglect and outright mistreatment that camouflages itself as their therapy. Our mental institutions are shameful, festering sores of society which break shockingly into public awareness, only to be quickly forgotten before they seriously disturb our consciences. Not so long ago the image of the snake pit shook many into realizing how inhumanly we treat the mentally ill (128).* Yet the treatment of these wretched people is no better today, even though every year or two there is this great public outcry when the utter degradation of mental patients is discovered in some institution, as if such conditions were not typical of mental hospitals all over the world.

This can all be explained only as a basic ambivalence in our treatment of the insane, which has its source in our own anxiety about insanity. We want the mentally deranged person to be treated humanely, but we also want to keep thoughts of insanity from disturbing our peace of mind. The way such people are forced to exist upsets us. We cannot sleep well if we keep their fate in our minds, for our dreams are too akin to some of their ravings, and our unconscious desires too like some of their actions. We wish to believe that the insane person is dangerous, but the uncanny feeling we experience when confronted with insanity shows all too clearly that we feel endangered not so much by him, as by the idea that we might be, or become, like him. Our anxious attitude is a modern counterpart of the ancient paradoxical belief that the insane are possessed by, and at the same time sacred to, the gods, but that for the well-being of society they must be cast out.

* The numbers in parentheses refer to the Bibliography.

As long as we permit fear for *our* sanity to dominate our attitudes to insanity nothing will change: we will continue to relegate the mentally unbalanced person to the inferno of the typical mental institution, and occasionally cry out in outrage because he dwells there in complete misery. We will create institutions which offer real hope of restoring the insane to their full humanity only when we can muster the courage to keep our minds focused on the problem of insanity, and the treatment of the insane.

Readily available knowledge would permit us to cure most mental patients, and to provide excellent care for the rest. But we will be able to achieve this only if we believe that it can be done; otherwise, fear for ourselves will continue to induce us to put the whole problem out of our minds. If we could feel certain that the insane person could be well taken care of and successfully guided back to emotional health, then we would not need to repress the knowledge that he is a man much like us. We could concentrate our energy on creating institutions which would do that for him, and, when perchance needed, for us. Only then could hidden anxiety and public apathy about insanity give way to a demand for mental institutions that would be a source of pride in our humanity. Thus we would also be relieved of one of the deepest fears to which we are heir: that we might lose our mind. This book is to show that such institutions are possible if we set our intelligence to it, and how we can create them.

Whatever the setting may be, it is the big events and the small occurrences in their combination that "make our day" or, when negative, undo us. If all things flow essentially in a positive direction, they cannot help supporting us in the unavoidable struggles of life. Cross currents and contradictions confuse us, or if they are too severe, they may cause us to give up in despair (4). If life's events are consistently negative, particularly during our most impressionable years, they are likely to be utterly destructive to the psyche. Therefore, if it were possible to arrange the life of even the most severely disturbed person so that its events consistently carried positive meaning, this should have marked beneficial effects. To live in an institutional setting which protects him against the vagaries of life, and in which, contrary to his past experiences, those people important to him are characterized by a deep commitment to his physical and emotional well-being and to serving his psychological needs—this in a slow process should heal his diseased mind.

The thesis of a total therapeutic milieu sounds convincing, but does it work? I have written three books on the work of the Orthogenic School of the University of Chicago. The first was called *Love*

Is Not Enough (7); its title was meant to suggest that a consistent therapeutic philosophy, with careful thinking, planning, and acting on it, has to underpin that tender care which is necessary if one is to help a psychotic person gain mental health—by inducing him to restructure his personality so that it will successfully protect him and serve his needs. The book illustrated this principle by describing big and small events alike as they followed each other in the course of the day, in the life of those whom the institution served.

The next book, *Truants From Life* (8), contained only a short statement on overall treatment success as of that time; the essential content consisted of four long case histories. It was hoped that these would show how—and why—the personalities of these children unfolded during the years they lived at the institution. From their quite different life histories, and their various pathologies (severe delinquency, anorexia, institutionalism, and childhood psychosis), the reader could see how a unified philosophy, and an institution based on it, is helpful in restoring mental health, even if the disturbances are most severe and their causes and the overt symptoms all quite different. Many years later, *The Empty Fortress* (13) was to present a more complete discussion of therapeutic results of the Orthogenic School for the most severe form of childhood psychosis, infantile autism. These books having described how the day proceeds for the children we cared for at the Orthogenic School, and how they fared over a considerable period of time when living under the conditions we created for them, the most important task still remained: to make this particular form of total therapy useful to others by detailing what it consists of, and by telling the story of the staff, because they are all-important for its success.

Through its earlier publications the Orthogenic School became best known for its work with children. Since this volume postulates that its method can and must be applied to the treatment of all mental patients requiring residential treatment, it should be stressed that in the last two decades the Orthogenic School has extended its scope—first to treating adolescents, and then, in the last fifteen years, also to young adults. With its expanding range of operation, plant, and staff, the School's population slowly increased from about thirty until during the last ten years it has been serving about fifty patients at any given time, with an age range of six to twenty-six and a median age of fifteen and a half.

The Orthogenic School is maintained by the university because of its efforts to explore, and to demonstrate, the possibility of treating disturbances which generally are considered "hopeless," that is, do not respond to other therapeutic methods. Given the severity of the pathologies involved, it takes considerable time to conclude treatment of each patient, easily five years or more. Such sustained efforts have the result wished for: better than 85 per cent of those with whom we worked have been restored to full participation in life. Most of our former patients are by now married and raising children who are doing well. Not all those who leave us do outstanding work; feeling no need to prove themselves in strenuous competition, they are satisfied with living a comfortable life. Among the more than two hundred former patients are pilots of commercial airlines, social workers, journalists, nurses and professors of nursing education, businessmen and bankers, but also some master barbers, construction foremen, and secretaries. An unusually large percentage of former patients, both male and female, have gone into education. One of them, for example, came to us unable to learn in school to the degree that he was classified as feeble-minded. He is now a professor, and dean of one of the colleges of a great university. Ten are classroom teachers; eleven others are college teachers in such fields as education, English, French, and psychology.

No man is an island, entire of itself, even after emotional maturity has been reached; and this is much more true while his personality is still developing. The life of a child cannot be understood independently of that of his parents, or of whoever else is his caretaker. A person who is extremely insecure emotionally, such as the psychotic person, is as dependent psychologically on those who take care of him (in whose power he is) as the child is on his parents.

A therapy that relies on the impact of human relations must consider most carefully all those who engage in it. Even in classical psychoanalysis we have come to recognize the tremendous importance of the so-called countertransference for success or failure of treatment —that is, the impact of the therapist's personality, of his inner attitudes and emotions while he is with the patient. If this applies in the psychoanalytic setting where interaction is quite restricted, it is much more relevant when therapist and patient encounter together all the vagaries of life. If the experience between therapist and patient should become a meaningful one—and unless and until it is, nothing good will come from it—those who enter into it together form a human relation. To be sure, the contribution of the two will be quite different. We, the therapists, will have to nurture the relationship patiently and understandingly for a long time before the patient may come to consider, at first tentatively and with many reservations, the possibility of his relating. But even though we the therapists have a definite goal in mind and go about it in a deliberate, purposeful way, this relationship, like all other true human relationships, must be very meaningful to both partners, each in his own way; the partners must become very important to each other through it. These relationships, and a setting that promotes them, are what this book is all about.

The mental patient lives as if in a deep, dark hole without exit, imprisoned there both by his anxieties and by the insensitivities of others which he views as inimical designs. We have to invent and construct a way out for him—let's say a ladder. We have to build this from our own past; our knowledge; our personality; and our understanding of the patient; but most of all through our empathy that tells us which unique, and uniquely human, ladder will be suitable for this particular patient. Contrary to his old convictions that there is no exit, the patient must first come to believe that on this ladder he can climb out of his prison, and then eventually try to do so. To bring this about, it must be possible for him to watch us work long and hard putting together this ladder, which must be very different from all others that have ever existed before. The patient will try to destroy the ladder, convinced for a long time that we do not fashion it to help him climb to liberty, but only to induce him to move into a worse prison (which we wish him to enter for some unfathomable reason that will benefit us more than him, and which may only project him into more dangers). After all, the patient knows his old prison, as terrible as it is, and somehow has learned to protect himself against its most painful features through his symptoms. These symptoms—his protective devices—he knows we want him to relinquish. How can he trust us who have such evil designs? He also will try to dismantle the ladder in much the same way as the child destroys the toy whose nature he wishes to understand.

We will have to climb down into the hole where the patient vegetates on this ladder of empathic understanding, while the patient tries to destroy it if for no other reason than to test our determination.

If a patient decides that he does not wish to use this avenue of escape offered to him, we must accept and respect such a decision—without stopping our efforts to be with the patient in his now no longer inescapable, but self-chosen abode, so that at least he won't dwell alone in his misery. Any slight suggestion that our way of life is superior to his is but another arrogance on our part—another rejection of the patient, another demonstration that we do not understand him. His mode of life, whatever it is, is indeed superior to ours as far as the patient is concerned, because it offers him much-needed protection, which he did not find in our world.

Our hope is that our taking care of him as well as possible where he desires to be will eventually convince him of our good intentions. This then may induce him to change his mind about wishing to remain permanently in his dark hole. Any impatience on our part, any insistence that he should change the miserable conditions of his life (apart from our improving them for him as much as we can without interfering with his autonomy) is nothing but pushing around a person who has given up functioning already, because he was so overpowered in his past. Again and again it has been our experience that only after our willingness to join the patient where he dwells emotionally has been recognized by him as genuine, will he consider also joining us—for a long time only very tentatively, perhaps only for moments—where and how we wish to live. Actually, what happens is that because of the services we render him, he becomes interested in us and wishes to find out more about us, including why we prefer our way of life for ourselves.

But he will do so only if we as human beings meet him as a human being. At no time can the relation between "him"—the patient—and "us"—the therapists—be muddled by a class distinction, by a sense of superiority on our part.

The message of this book will be lost on the reader who permits himself to think of "patients" as one class of people, and "therapists" as another. These two terms refer to people who are very much individuals, with their own life histories and personalities, but who are also in many respects very much like the rest of us, the author and the reader. The same goes for such terms as "worker" or "staff." There is no such entity as a "staff," but only a varying number of persons who, though they may share similar training or work together for a common goal, do so only in line with their own unique, particular, and sometimes even peculiar personality. My hope is that whenever any one of these words is used in this book, the reader will remember that there is a person hidden behind it.

For the patient, once we can convince him to try climbing our ladder out of his dark hole, it is a long pull, rung by rung, toward self-discovery and rediscovery of the world; most of all toward finding and facing what meaningful, good, and enduring human relations are possible and available to him. But what about all the skills that have to go into the construction of the symbolic ladder by the therapist? Where does one find the material needed and how does one develop the ability to build it? The answer can come from looking at how it is done, step by step, piece by piece.

If we wish to build the unique ladder which will permit this particular patient to use it, we must be able to understand those hidden messages which alone enable us to help persons who suffer from severe emotional disorders. To do so we must pay attention to the minute details of human behavior. Our intentions too are conveyed by the smallest details of our behavior and of the physical environment with which we surround the patients. The underlying concepts which we use both to read correctly their hidden messages, and to convey our intentions to them, are derived from psychoanalytic thinking as it is applied to all aspects of living. As the psychoanalyst considers the smallest deviation in expression a significant clue to understanding what goes on in the patient, so the patient will view any detail of the therapist's behavior as of the greatest importance, because his anxiety about what his therapist may be up to is so great. And, of course, because of the intensity of his fears, he will tend to interpret what he observes in ominous ways. For the same reason, the emotionally disturbed person in residential treatment responds deeply to even the tiniest detail of the physical setting into which those responsible for his treatment project him. This is why no aspect of the physical arrangements of a mental institution is insignificant, and why some will be discussed at length: to serve as examples of what thinking and planning should go into the silent messages which the patient must receive from his surroundings if he is to get well.

Even more significant than professional training for a therapist is a person's ability to use therapeutically not only his particular talents and idiosyncrasies but his own experiences in life. Among these he must be able to distinguish between that which has been meaningful and supportive, and that which has been actually or potentially destructive, so he can make full use of the first and prevent himself from letting the second enter into the therapeutic relation. A person will be of more help to another when his own emotional assets—and sometimes even his emotional problems—match the most pressing therapeutic needs of a particular patient.

Over the years, we found that every person who was truly successful in helping those suffering from the most severe psychiatric disturbances had undergone experiences which, for one reason or another, made this type of work so attractive that he could accept the severe hardships it imposed, and therefore succeed in helping patients recuperate where others might have failed. If this is so, what kinds of past experience made the residential treatment of seriously disturbed persons attractive to us? How can I report on the rest of the staff, without first considering how the residues of my own past were active in motivating my work?

The Informed Heart (11) discussed, among many other issues, what it meant to be incarcerated in a Nazi concentration camp. Often, when comparing my reactions to events with those of my co-workers, I realized that mine were strongly influenced by the experience of having been at the mercy of others who believed they knew how I should live—or rather that I should not live. Lacking this experience, my partners in our common work had much less direct empathy with the inner reactions of a person who is forced by others to change his way of life against his will.

Seeking to enhance their awareness of how hard it is to accept such a situation, I suggested that staff members contemplate how they would feel if they were dependent on someone else who made decisions which would determine how they have to arrange their life's circumstances. At the same time, my deliberate efforts to do away with *any* status hierarchy—whether based on training, experience, or anything else—as well as my concentrated efforts to limit the areas where the staff exercised control over those under their care, had to do with therapeutic convictions which were strongly influenced by the experience of having been so dominated.

In fact, these very personal convictions, which originated in my past and made me unable to accept locking anybody in, brought about my first head-on clash with the staff that had been working at the Orthogenic School before I joined it in 1944. I insisted that the large number of keys and the many locked doors be done away with, whereas the staff felt these were needed to keep things safe.

The camp experience radically changed both my outlook on life and the course of my life, much more than my extended and penetrating psychoanalysis had earlier. The wanton destruction of so many lives, one of which so easily could have been one's own, can lead to a passionate conviction that in the future—as far as one can help it—no single life will be senselessly done away with (14, 86).

What one selects as the particular endeavor through which he tries to counteract these haunting memories depends on chance, talent, and interest. In my own experience, self-examination led to the recognition that the anger I felt at the idea that human lives—those of psychotics, for example—were being wasted when it was possible to save them was an emotional residue of my camp experience. I was determined that they must be given a chance to have a good life. Thus powerful emotions coming from a past experience I could not rid myself of, because of inescapable memories, were set to what turned out to be constructive uses.

As in all human undertakings which are engaged in with fervor, there is the danger that one's emotions may carry one away, and that one may use others to satisfy one's own unconscious needs at their expense, instead of doing justice to their needs. My psychoanalytic training helped to safeguard me against using my work to gratify infantile and megalomanic rescue fantasies, to the satisfaction of which mental patients—and particularly children, whether or not they are mental patients—lend themselves so easily and exquisitely. The camp experience helped me to be aware of such fantasies and to aid staff members in containing and overcoming theirs. The same experience motivated, in part, the title *Love Is Not Enough*—stressing that emotion, even a most positive one such as love, is not sufficient; one must never permit oneself to neglect the most careful rational planning and doing.

These remarks may suggest how the concentration camp experience gave deeper and highly personal meaning to my efforts and infused them with strong and supportive emotions, always in addition to the real validity of the task. Thus fed by such unconscious nutrients, the work could draw on sources of energy which otherwise would not have been available.

The success of our common undertaking at the Orthogenic School depended on the cooperation of many: the entire staff. As I found out, my main contribution was not what I happened to know— for example, about psychiatric disturbances—nor even how well I was able to teach it usefully to others in their day-to-day work. This was only a wedge which opened others to my enthusiasm about our common tasks and allowed it to become contagious. The staff began to feel how my commitment to work, rational as were the courses of actions which followed from it, had its mainspring in unconscious needs not to fail—because failure here would imply a much deeper personal failing than a mere deficiency in a specific type of work. My commitment provided an example that specific "irrational" pressures need not be repressed as being all infantile, unhealthy, damaging, destructive; but that, to the contrary, they can be made to serve the most constructive endeavors.

Activating and using these sources of unconscious energy, which were completely different for each staff member, led all of us to the strong conviction that the work must not collapse. Some were sustained by trying to quiet unanswerable questions such as, Why did my mother become insane? or Why do I have a psychotic brother when I am not?; or questions which, in reality, were easily answerable and had indeed been answered long ago, but in ways which were unacceptable for unconscious reasons, such as: Why did my sister die?

.   .   .

My introduction to severe psychiatric disturbance and its treatment was the most direct possible. Before our own children were born, because of our fascination with child psychoanalysis which had just then begun to develop, my wife and I brought in a child who suffered from infantile autism (a "hopeless" case) in order to find out whether the new discipline could help her. Something within the little girl, and within myself, made me become deeply involved with her. To try to understand what went on in her mind was a fascinating and rewarding challenge; and so was the riddle of how to help her. The experience of living with her eventually made me realize that a normal family would never be able to meet all the needs of such a patient.

As much as the girl improved over the years she lived with us and grew into a charming and most talented adolescent, she had not been helped sufficiently to overcome entirely the remnants of her severe disturbance. This was mostly due to Hitler's sudden invasion of Austria: her therapy, which should have continued for at least a few more years, terminated without any preparation. What had we successfully done for her, and where had we failed? Our work had been both a success and a failure. It left me with the vexing question of how to understand childhood schizophrenia, and how to approach it therapeutically. Was it, as the literature claimed, beyond the reaches of therapy? Or had we simply not been good enough therapists?

This was another remnant of my past which had to be dealt with more fully. It was childhood schizophrenia that brought me to what, late in life, had become my profession. Up to that time, other pursuits had claimed my conscious interests. Why and how had the concentration camp experience in my middle thirties, the turning point in my life, led me to work with psychotic children? Why had I selected this particular field to quiet the question: Why was I spared?

The camp experience permitted me finally to comprehend schizophrenia. I had been unable fully to cope with either of these two experiences in isolation. In time, as I saw their interconnection, I could make better sense of both of them (9).

Working at the Orthogenic School had meaning for everyone connected with it, meaning beyond what we did with and for the children. To translate into everyday institutional practice what we believed to be the best way to conduct the work of a mental institution was a great and continuous challenge. In our more arrogant moments we hoped it could serve as an example for others to learn from, and to improve on. And if this were to happen, then the account would have to be more than a book on just the staff, as originally contemplated.

An institution, like a man, is both a body and a soul; and like a man, it shall be known by its deeds. If body and soul are not in harmony, if one ill serves the other, there will be conflict and frustration.

The soul of an institution is not the institution's philosophy. I have seen beautiful statements of the institutional philosophy of psychiatric hospitals and other mental institutions, but the reality was an abomination. The soul of an institution is its philosophy only as it is practiced by the staff. The deeds by which the Orthogenic School shall be known—that is, how its body and soul function— have been reported in earlier books. What remains is to show in greater detail how it is done, so that others can do the same.

This book consists of four unequal but closely interrelated parts. The first is a discussion of the physical setting within which the institutional life proceeds. The second is an account of total residential therapy as it evolved over some twenty-seven years. The third and fourth parts discuss, in detail, how the staff operates and how its training is carried out.

The material has been collected over many years, but for the most part it was written after my association with the School had officially ended. I hope it is as objective an account as a person can render who has been deeply involved. The Orthogenic School as we conceived it was at all times in the process of becoming. In this sense what is contained in the following pages reflects what it was like at a certain period in its history, approximately at the time when I withdrew from being its director in 1973. At that time my closest associate, Jacqui Sanders, became the director. Before that she had worked for some ten years as a counselor, then for three years she assisted me in directing the Orthogenic School's work. After an absence of seven years spent as a college teacher, she returned permanently to an endeavor which always had been close to her heart. For my last year at the School she was its co-director. The fourteen years of our working intimately together promise that the changes she will make over time will be improvements over what is here described.

Like all the other writings based on the work of the Orthogenic School, this book also owes its existence to those who worked there. While I am enormously in the staff's debt for all the support they have given me, honesty requires the acknowledgment that we both made many errors; but we tried to understand our mistakes fully in order truly to learn from them. The staff helped me to learn from my errors and comprehend their origins; what shortcomings in feeling or thinking caused them; how and why my actions had not produced what I had intended, or what had been needed most. I know the staff learned a great deal about themselves, about the work, even quite a bit about the world, from understanding both their successes and their mistakes. Trying to help the staff learn from their successes and their failures was the agony and the pleasure of my working life. The first is by now long forgotten; for the latter I wish to thank them.

For the rest, I hope that those who read this book will also learn from our achievements and our errors. I have all along believed our relative success came from trying to extract meaning from the consequences of our efforts, both good and bad. I hope the reader too will actively seek this meaning, and that he will not be satisfied with simply accepting what is said to be good about our work, but will ask himself why he should believe it. I hope he will try to discover where I may have gone wrong, but again not be satisfied merely with registering a negative, but try to understand why and how it all could be done better. If he does do this, he will have paid the author the highest compliment possible. For this I wish to thank him.

I | The Idea of the Mental Hospital

1 | *Ambience: Buildings and Their Inhabitants*

Whatever a human activity may be, its success is facilitated by a particular setting; the more so when complex and subtle issues are at stake. The structure of family life, and the nature of the human relations within it, will be quite different in a one-room hovel and in a palace, though either may be less than ideal when the goal is to promote good mental health.

We owe our greatest progress in the treatment of emotional disturbances of individuals to the insights of psychoanalysis. Other types of therapeutic efforts, such as group therapy, became possible only because of these advances. For psychoanalysis to succeed, it requires a unique situation which Freud invented largely by reflecting on what the therapeutic experience requires both from the physical and the psychological environment, taking into account not only what the patient needs but also what the therapist requires to be able to function well. Freud was quite specific in postulating this setting. He found that only within it could patient and therapist engage in a most difficult enterprise, in which the two were unequal but equally important participants.

It is by no means unique to the psychoanalytic situation that the participants in a human enterprise are unequal but equally important. This situation typically pertains wherever planned personality or intellectual development is the goal of the undertaking, for example, in all educational enterprises. But in any psychotherapy, the setting must militate against the therapist's exercising an unwarranted dominance over the patient, and against the patient's falling into the trap of accepting such dominance. The patient may be sorely tempted to do just this because of his weakness, insecurity, and anxiety; but if he does, the result will be further personality disintegration instead of healthy personality growth.

To be successful, the mental hospital needs to be a setting which is as uniquely fitting for its particular task as the psychoanalytic situation is for its methods and goals. To achieve this, the planners of a mental institution must aim to create the specific environment which will best meet the needs of the patients and the requirements of their psychotherapy. This therapy—different from any medical regimen—flows from the understandings, convictions, and feelings, as well as from the actions, of those who take care of the patients all day long.

The therapeutic environment must be a setting designed so that those in charge of the procedures, whatever their status may be—doctor, nurse, attendant—will not become sidetracked, confused, or seduced by the patient's behavior. Whether the patient is submissive or obstreperous, silently withdrawn or threatening violence, fawning or abusive, regressed to infantile behavior or megalomaniacally asserting his superiority, the circumstances must prevent the staff from responding and acting on the basis of their own unexamined unconscious tendencies, which tend to be activated by exposure to such behavior. Instead, the setting must be conducive to their responding to the patient's conscious wishes and unconscious needs, and to their making the right decisions in how to do so.

Freud carefully structured the psychoanalytic situation as the only way he could preclude acting out on the patient some of his own unconscious needs, and also avoid the enticement to dominate the patient, one of the most hazardous temptations to the psychotherapist. But such thinking has hardly touched the psychiatric hospitals, although in the best of them, the staff are now warned against acting out their own unconscious needs or desires on the patients. In the classical psychoanalytic setting, there are many safeguards against giving in to such danger; but the typical psychiatric hospital worker has nothing to support him, to protect him and the patient against such acting out. Therefore, domination of the patient "for his own good" is the rule rather than the exception. How can it be otherwise, as long as we assume that relatively poorly trained persons can function well without institutional safeguards, when even the psychoanalyst cannot do without them? Indeed, most institutional settings render it not only difficult but impossible to do right by the patient.

In this book I am concerned with the many specific arrangements, or conditions of life, characteristic of psychiatric hospitals which do not benefit either patients or staff. These arrangements do not merely make life at best distressing for the patients, and working more difficult and unpleasant for the staff, but are detrimental to all, including society, since they tend to prolong the patient's stay in the hospital and reduce his chance for recovery. Nevertheless, these arrangements survive because nobody seems to question them. My own conviction is that nobody should be put in such places as our present mental institutions, though we may have to continue to use them as long as nothing better is available. People suffering from severe psychiatric difficulties can benefit greatly from living under conditions specifically designed to help them, and, contrary to those who advocate abolishing all mental hospitals, I believe that such special places should be available to them. Unfortunately, at this moment they hardly exist.

The absence of self-respect is a central issue in all functional disturbances. The most important task of therapy is not to have the patient gain insight into his unconscious, but to restore him to a high degree of justified self-esteem. Understanding one's unconscious can be a most important step toward this goal, because then one's "crazy" ideas come to make sense. But it is only a step in which we move from an inability to grasp meanings to understanding them; from the feeling that we have lost our mind to the conviction that we have gained control over it.

This is hardly a new idea. A century and a half ago, Tuke managed the Retreat at York for the Society of Friends. There he did away with the excessive restraints then regarded as essential in the treatment of the insane. He was convinced that "the need for esteem" was most effective in helping mental patients improve their conditions, because it is a "principle in the human mind, which doubtless influences in a great degree, though often secretly, our general manners; and which operates with peculiar force. . . ." To stimulate esteem we can no longer rely mainly on such things as occasional polite tea parties, where the director and staff invite the patients to "dress in their best clothes, and vie with each other in politeness and propriety. The best fare is provided, and the visitors [i.e., patients] are treated with all the attention of strangers" (124). Such intermingling as equals, with the greatest respect for the dignity of the patients, should not be a rare therapeutic device but a matter of course all day long—with the qualification that consideration for the dignity of the other must be required of the staff, but not of the patients. The best possible fare should be the patient's right, and not a rare privilege. From the inception of my work at the Orthogenic School I have been convinced that the restoration of true, as opposed to megalomaniacally distorted, self-esteem must be a main goal of therapy.

Others who have worked intensively with schizophrenics have

come to the same conclusion, to the extent that the schizophrenic process has been viewed as "a failure at being anything that one could respect as worth being" (117). If this is so, and my experience convinces me that it is, then everything that increases the feeling of being a good, worthwhile person is curative; everything that diminishes that feeling aggravates the disturbance and makes it less accessible to therapy.

Let us consider, as a primary example of what is wrong with our current mental hospitals, the buildings in which they are housed. Nearly everybody agrees they are bad, without this having led to an appreciably better design. Even a fairly recent study of psychiatric hospitals, commissioned by the World Health Organization, proposes what are essentially only small improvements superimposed on the old pattern (2). The reason is a failure to analyze specifically what is wrong with the existing institutions and why—beyond such obvious things as too many patients in one ward, or unappealing color on the walls. If we do not know *why* a particular feature forces a certain manner of operating, we will not be in a good position to replace it with one that is better.

The way our mental hospitals are built can be understood only from their history. Beginning in the Middle Ages, the insane were viewed as being possessed by evil spirits. This belief, combined with the potential dangerousness and occasional open violence of the insane, spawned the idea that to protect society the insane must be incarcerated. But beyond rational fear of what the insane might do, the irrational anxiety about having run loose a person inhabited by the "evil one" led to the punitive treatment of the mentally deranged. The point of mistreating the insane was to drive these spirits out of their bodies; and while doing so, to imprison those bodies, the more securely the better. So for centuries in Germany they were confined in a prison-like structure, often the tower of a city gate, and their abode became known as the "Fools' Tower" (*Narrenturm*). Today they are still put into prison-like buildings—not, as is claimed, for their security, but for our own. Again, the rational fear of what harm they might do could never alone lead us to treat them so brutishly. Society can permit this inhumanity only because of the unconscious anxiety that, were they not treated punitively, the example of their regressed, uninhibited, drive-controlled behavior, of their engaging in primary process thinking, would, as if by contagion, threaten our own integration Our need to keep these, our inner, chaotic strivings, under rigid control leads us to impose such controls on the mental patient, though it is only through a very different régime that he could be restored to mental health.

Despite this centuries-old European tradition of imprisoning the insane, it could not have held sway in the face of the rational countervailing influences that began with the Enlightenment, had it not been powerfully reinforced by an Anglo-American tradition. In this country, before the idea of institutions became generally accepted, the poor and the sick were cared for within their own families, while orphans were placed with other families. If, for one reason or another, the poor or the mentally ill could not live with their families, persons were appointed who took them into their own homes. Jails were used to confine criminals only until such time as they were tried and judgment passed on them. All this changed when, during the early part of the last century, it was claimed that for their own and society's good, the sick and the poor had to be reformed, and that this could be achieved only by rigidly controlling and regulating their lives down to the last detail. In consequence, from then on, mental hospitals in the United States were designed to facilitate the enforcement of a strictly ordered life, to help inmates regain their health. Since then this regimen has become known as the "moral treatment" of insanity (102).

The European story was different, since from the Middle Ages the insane there had been locked up in places like Bedlam in London where they served as a public spectacle, to be viewed for a fee, much like animals in a zoo, while the physically sick were cared for if not in monasteries, by religious orders. During the Enlightenment, particularly during the reforms inaugurated by Pinel during the French Revolution, it was realized that the insane were not viciously perverted or possessed by the Devil, but unfortunate human beings in need of therapy. Thereafter, in continental Europe the informed tendency was to treat the insane in hospitals, based on the example of those conducted by religious orders. But before this became widespread, the influence of the U.S. institutions practicing moral therapy changed European thinking on both mental institutions and prisons, and reinforced the strictly regimented, prison-like treatment of the insane, in opposition to the hospital-like therapy suggested by an enlightened minority.

Today, we are still using many of these fortress-like buildings, and so powerful has this model remained that very few new ideas on how to design an institution for the mentally disturbed have even been formulated. Hospital buildings for the physically sick still serve as models for mental institutions. Consequently, "features appropriate to a general medical and surgical institution are transferred and applied thoughtlessly—and very expensively—not because of any particular need but because the medical analogy bears down on the imagination of the architect and the planners of the building" (103). And the irrational imagination of nearly everybody about what the insane person may do explains why prison-like characteristics are added, making the buildings unsuited to the very purposes for which they are created. The very features of an ordinary hospital which have reassuring connotations for the physically sick are ominous for the mentally disturbed person, while the additional prison-like aspects of the mental hospital arouse in the inmates anxiety, anger, and dejection, yet add only little to their feeling of security.

The physically ill person spends most of his days in his room, confined to his bed, neither of which the mental patient should do. Although the rooms of a hospital for the physically ill person are meant to provide the patient with a very temporary abode, the mental patient may spend years in his quarters. While the layout of the hospital room is based on the assumption that the movements of the physically sick are usually restricted for their own benefit, this is most detrimental for the emotionally disturbed person in whom it leads, if not to claustrophobia, to the feeling of being incarcerated.

How physically confined—and hence mentally confining—such a hospital existence is for the mentally ill person can be seen by comparing the amount of space allocated to him with the space we think necessary for comfortable living. Even in the best private psychiatric hospitals, long-term patients have to make do with much less living area per person than is available to the member of an average middle-class family (114). If one compares the living space of the patient with minimal middle-class standards, the patient under the most favorable conditions has about half this space; but when the basis for comparison is the average middle-class apartment or house, it shrinks to only one-fourth. In the typical mental hospital, the ratios are much worse.

But these facts only begin to tell the story. In order to correctly assess how cramped the patient is in even our better mental institutions, we must consider how many hours of the day we are away from home: at work, visiting with friends, shopping, and pursuing a wide variety of other recreational and cultural pursuits. The result is that each day the vast majority of us spend only a few of our waking hours at home. But the psychiatric patient is expected to spend nearly all of his day in an area which is much smaller than we believe to be the minimum needed, and than he was accustomed to before entering the institution.

During the night, conditions are worse, because the patient is expected to spend more hours in bed than do most active persons of his age who live at home. With bedtime at 10 p.m., or even earlier, and being wakened around 7:30 in the morning, the patient has to stay restless in bed for some hours either before falling asleep or before getting up, depending on the sleep rhythm of the individual. This is because the patient's night time does not depend on *his* needs but on the routines of the staff, mostly on the hour at which nurses or attendants leave or begin their shifts. The longer the patient is quiet in bed, the easier the staff's load. Patients do not object more strenuously against such imposition because there are clearly no alternatives for them, so to rebel seems hardly worth it. But they know that their bedtime is not regulated by their needs, but by those of the staff, and they naturally resent it.

In addition, there are hardly any provisions made for the mental patient to spend his sleepless hours anywhere but in bed. Patients in self-defense pester the staff for medication in order to sleep, or they wander aimlessly in the corridors, seeking refuge in the toilets—ways to kill time which are degrading to the patient and annoying to the staff. These conditions are a direct result of both insufficient space and lack of intelligent spatial planning. A different physical design of the mental hospital could easily provide rooms which would at least make such periods less empty and hence more bearable.

Recent studies have shown how noxious the impact of physical crowding is on the behavior of animals (23, 28). Being forced to live restricted in space is injurious to the mental and physical health of human beings as well, unless the necessary inner and outer regulation is available to counteract its effects, so that one can manage to survive. Regulation can either come from internal sources—the ego and superego—or be externally imposed. But mental patients are typically either lacking in inner controls, or have far too many of them. In the first case, their ego and superego are entirely inadequate for mastering life; they cannot possibly manage the additional burden imposed on them, since they cannot activate the requisite inner controls to counteract the destructive impact of crowding. In the second case, the personality has broken down because of excessive superego control; to subject such persons to conditions which require them further to control themselves is about the worst thing one can do to them. In either case, because of lack of space or insensitive use of it, external controls have to be imposed, which seriously reduce the capacity of the psychiatric hospital to help the patient.

All this applies equally to the huge public mental hospitals and to the smaller private psychiatric hospitals. True, there is considerable difference between their daily practice. Large mental institutions are often badly understaffed, particularly as far as professional skills are concerned. Originally, many mental hospitals in this country accepted only "curable" patients, who could be returned to their communities within a reasonably short period, but this changed a long time ago; since then, public mental institutions have become overcrowded and to a considerable degree filled by chronic patients, including mental defectives.

Since a 1966 Federal Court decision which adjudged that a mental hospital patient is entitled to therapy, many institutions have arranged for some kind of treatment for all of their inmates, from the administration of drugs to occupational or group therapy, or similar activities. Unfortunately, such well-meant intentions are poorly set into practice, and fail, because they are not supported by the hospital routines. Individual therapy of relatively high quality is only occasionally available to the patients of larger mental hospitals. On the other hand, private psychiatric hospitals and medical school psychiatric wards by and large accept only "curable" patients and usually provide their patients with individual psychiatric treatment by psychiatrists or residents, and with the services of a well-trained nursing staff.

Living conditions are usually better in these small private psychiatric hospitals, and the ratio of professionally trained staff per patient is much more favorable. But the inner attitude with which patients are treated is not that different. This is understandable since those who administer mental hospitals and work there as psychiatrists have been trained and have gained their most important experiences in relatively small psychiatric wards of teaching hospitals. Thus all shortcomings of the small psychiatric hospital are typically found also in the mental institution, though the latter suffers from many additional ones. In this book, the terms "mental hospital" or "institution" will refer to larger hospitals. When speaking of the smaller and better private settings, the adjective "psychiatric" will be used. As far as the inmates of the smaller psychiatric hospital and the "mental institution" are concerned, both types of institutions serve the same kinds of patients (with the exception of mental defectives), and the terms "psychiatric" and "mental patients" are used interchangeably. For example, closed wards are found in psychiatric hospitals as well as in "mental institutions," pretty much the same type of patient is incarcerated in them, and he receives quite similar treatment. Of course, there are some psychiatric hospitals which are much better than others, and a very few provide excellent services in all respects. While there are also some public mental institutions in which the patients' treatment compares favorably with that of good private psychiatric hospitals.

Whether it is a psychiatric hospital or a mental institution, it is often difficult to decide for whose benefit the existing arrangements are made. If the question of who truly gains from the arrangements is not most carefully considered at all times, the consequence is often the facile belief that whatever makes things easier for the staff is also advantageous for those in their care. This justifies procedures which would never be accepted if it were clear that they are by no means helpful to those who are subjected to them.

During the last decades, tranquilizing drugs have made the management of mental patients much easier. They permit doing away with the frequent use of bodily restraints, but the straitjacket has by no means become a matter of the past, though in some of the best institutions it is replaced by wrapping the patient in a cold pack (53) or the use of such heavy doses of drugs that they equally prevent all freedom of movement or action. All this has made it possible to close some of the worst wards of mental hospitals, wards in which what goes on is so upsetting that it has to be hidden away—not just from the view of visitors but also from the awareness of the staff. Hence they are commonly called the back wards, though their official designation is that of "disturbed" wards, since the patients kept there are assumed to be too disturbed to be able to live in the regular "closed" wards. But is it that the patients are too disturbed to be placed in surroundings which are a bit less desolate, or is it that their behavior—in part the consequence of the conditions they live under—is so unsettling to the staff that they are "put away" physically, as we all put them out of our thoughts psychologically? The reality of typical psychiatric hospitals may be exemplified by one community mental health center recently built with government funds, its operation largely supported by them, to provide the best up-to-date services. It contains a hundred-bed psychiatric hospital, including ten seclusion rooms where the patients are tied down to their beds with heavy leather straps. These rooms are in use much of the time. Thus nearly 10 per cent of all patients in this modern facility, designed to serve as an example, are at any one time in complete restraint. As far as therapy is concerned, 90 per cent of the patients received electroshock treatment (29). If we would permit ourselves to be aware of this reality, surely we could not permit such conditions to go on existing.

Patients in mental hospitals are placed in "open," "closed," and "noisy" or "disturbed" wards, rarely in regard for what is best for the patient but on the basis of what makes the management of the hospital simpler. I am convinced that there is no need for closed wards in which persons are locked up supposedly for their benefit. In fact, it is detrimental to them to be so incarcerated. Closed wards—to say nothing of those disturbed wards where conditions are often worse than those of prisons—become necessary only if patients are not treated correctly, in line with their psychological needs (which is exactly what mental hospitals are for).

Unsuitable as they are, we continue to use the old institutions though we know they are bad, and we even build new ones in their image. This suggests that the continued use of old buildings which by all modern standards are obsolete has other reasons than the usual justification that these edifices are available, and that it would be too expensive to replace them with new ones. Indeed, the expense of maintaining patients in mental hospitals is staggering; and by comparison, the expense of new buildings would be small. If newly designed structures could improve the condition of psychiatric patients so that even a segment of them could sooner take care of themselves or at least in some other way be maintained outside an institution, these savings would far outweigh the cost of razing the old buildings and replacing them. If the average stay of the mental patient in the hospital were shortened by only a small percentage, these savings would repay necessary construction outlays in a few years.

Since it may seem that it would be exorbitantly expensive to erect and equip buildings to best serve the needs of mental patients, and to treat them in the most humane and hence most therapeutic fashion, it should be stressed that to operate the institution which this book describes was not only less expensive throughout its existence than other good institutions, but even cheaper than most public mental hospitals serving the same kind of patients.

In 1970, for example, it cost about $8,000 to maintain a patient for a year at the Orthogenic School, while at that time the yearly patient cost in private institutions offering similar services amounted to $25,000 or more. Public institutions where services were much inferior expended between $10,000 to $14,000 a year for patients of the same age group. The Orthogenic School did not use volunteers (we did not find them satisfactory, since they usually didn't remain for the two or more years needed to learn the work, and for forming those permanent relations which the patients need for their emotional security); and the technical staff was as well paid as everywhere else—secretaries, cooks, maids, janitors, and so on, received union wages which were the same university-wide, identical, for example, with those of the university hospitals. To a large measure this was possible because the professional staff members were well satisfied with re-munerations considerably below those they could easily command in other institutions because they found being part of this particular enterprise exciting and rewarding. Not only those who began their training in this field at the Orthogenic School, but many others who joined it after years of experience in working with mental patients did so at salaries which were a fraction of those they would receive anywhere else because they wanted to be able to work in line with their therapeutic convictions, rather than continuing in settings where they felt patients were not treated as humanely. Most of all they wanted to feel that what they did was creative rather than routine.

Speaking of the expenses to society involved in taking care of psychiatric patients, it ought to be mentioned again that the vast majority of our patients make significant contributions to society after they have left us. Most of these later in their lives returned in taxes alone more to society than the state or private social agencies had spent on them, even though they had been maintained for several years while with us. Most patients suffering from equally severe disturbances treated in other settings, such as public mental hospitals, never became truly self-supporting.

But, of course, such economic arguments are demeaning, since one can neither put a positive price on human happiness, nor a nega-tive on human misery. The misery of psychiatric patients is abysmal. Returning them to a life which they find satisfying would justify vastly greater expenses than those incurred in condemning them to the non-life which is all most mental hospitals do for many of their patients.

The whole building-expense argument certainly doesn't hold water; there are abundant examples to show that once we really be-lieve a building stands in the way of some successful operation, no expense is too great to have it replaced. This is a daily occurrence in the business world. Therefore, we can assume that we still use the old mental hospital because in some ways it still meets our ideas of what should be done with mental patients. We put up with buildings which force a drab and regimented existence on the mental patient because we are tacitly convinced either that he doesn't deserve any better, or that it's necessary for his rehabilitation, or as a deterrent to his continued stay, or as a warning to others who might without it be tempted to enter the hospital. Most likely it is a combination of all of these reasons, even though the first is no longer admitted and the others are camouflaged behind all kinds of convincing-sounding arguments, including psychiatric ones.

The prison and the poorhouse, out of which the mental institution grew (and from which the mental patient was finally separated), were based on the notion that most of these people simply didn't want to do any better or live any differently. Therefore they had to be forced to do so. Lately, the "forced" has been replaced by the nicer-sounding "induced" or "motivated." The rationale is that if life in these places were to be made pleasant, why wouldn't everybody prefer to be taken care of by the community? It is the same basic attitude which unfortunately still motivates our actions in dealing with poverty. Though we have done away with the poorhouse, the spirit which created it is still very much with us: "If the community has to provide funds for maintaining these wretches, let's do it as cheaply as possible." This continues although all evidence now suggests that treating the poor in this way keeps them, and some of their progeny, dependent indefinitely and forces society to continue to maintain them.

The idea that the prison should serve as a deterrent is widely and openly held. That deterrence is also the purpose which the mental institution serves is now openly denied. But there are too many similarities between the two to overlook this common purpose, though each has different ones. Visually and in location the institutions appear very similar; they not only look equally forbidding, but in both the inmates are locked up—if not for their own good, then to benefit society, so they can no longer damage it. The often-used threat, "If you don't mend your ways, if you don't watch out, that's where you'll end up," is applied in regard to both with little discrimination—the jail or the "nuthouse." Clearly, at least in the unconscious of many people, the two institutions have a great deal in common. And what kind of deterrent would either of them be, if conditions in them were to be pleasant?

It is quite possible that both institutions are effective as deterrents, but their large populations (including the many who return after leaving) suggest that while they may deter the rest of us, they do not seem to deter those who are, or may become, their inmates. I am not so sure what the attitude to prisoners might be, but I feel certain that nobody would dare suggest that mental patients be treated with so little regard to what is good for them only as a warning to the rest of us not to lose our mental faculties. No, we are told instead that the regimen to which mental patients are subjected is "good for them." We are told that we must not make the mental patient too comfortable, because then he would not relinquish his insanity.

What has to be carefully considered is the question of whether —since we now treat the psychiatric patient with much less physical cruelty than when we believed the mad to be possessed by the Devil—there has actually been a fundamental change in thinking. Our actions have changed for the better; however, our thinking and our unconscious motivation may have remained the same, and that is why we now must concern ourselves with the psychological abuse of human beings, which is still widespread. Though the method is less crude than physical abuse, the resulting damage to the psyche can be utterly devastating. That is why I believe we have to understand completely the unconscious causes of the cruelty, and to uncover the disguise behind which it tries to hide.

2 | The "Secondary Gain" as Therapy

Our mental institutions are bad and ought to be done away with. To decide this takes little ingenuity and can be readily accepted as a solution, so long as one doesn't concern oneself with what happens to those who need help and are deprived of these institutions. Indeed, one can engage in all kinds of daydreams about what would be better than existing hospitals, since daydreams will not be put to the test and are easier than expending thought and money on creating good institutions which would better serve those who need them.

Some critics, disgusted by the conditions prevailing in psychiatric hospitals, have advocated placing their patients in homes inside their own communities. This has been tried, and is still being done, with devastating results. Conditions of living in these homes in the communities have been summed up in expert reports by the statement: "This is not outplacement care. It is *no care*" (29, emphasis in the original). For example, Dr. Murray C. Brown, Commissioner of Health of the City of Chicago, told a Senate Committee investigating this problem that far in excess of 50 per cent of the seven thousand patients discharged by Illinois state hospitals in 1970 were "sent to nursing and residential care homes in Chicago without adequate provisions that they would receive decent care. Such patients were discharged not only into licensed facilities but into rooming houses, some of which the Chicago Board of Health has never been able to identify or locate." In Washington, D.C., many of these so-called foster homes were found reeking of stench. In some of them, totally disoriented people had been left all alone, completely neglected. There were those who could remember nothing but their names; but poisonous, potentially lethal medications had been entrusted to their own keeping. A Senate Committee found that in many

states, places supposedly providing home or community care were
nothing but "mini snake pits" (125).

There is no indication that we can expect any significant improvements in the foster home care of psychiatric patients who need
residential treatment. Having had first-hand experience for some
seven years of the incredible demands which taking good care of
such a person in a private home makes on those who live with him—
and despite the fact that this was a home where the menial tasks
were performed by a living-in servant—I know that persons who need
residential care are better off even in an average institution than in
most private homes willing to take them.

While many emotionally ill persons can be aided without being
placed in an institution, this is not true for others who are most
seriously disturbed. To serve those others well, we need good institutions. Interestingly enough, some of the "bad" features of existing
institutions which are cited as evidence that inmates should be placed
in communities are features which actually suggest what a good
mental institution ought to be like.

Despite all the shortcomings of mental hospitals, some patients
do manage to extract small, but to them significant, advantages from
living in them. This phenomenon is called the "secondary gain"
which they derive from their illness; it can be readily observed in
physical illness as well as in all types of emotional disturbances. Due
to the patient's wish to hold onto these benefits, real or imagined, he
often does not wish to cooperate with his treatment; his fear of losing
these advantages makes him indifferent to getting well. It has been
argued that the only way to induce the patient to use treatment is to
have him give up these secondary gains—a psychological argument
employed to justify current hospital conditions.

In this enlightened and humanitarian age we need all kinds of
scientific backing to hold onto our prejudices, and to act in accordance with them. Thus the idea that the mental patient, like that
other social deviate, the criminal, should not be treated decently, now
enters through the respectable front door of scientific reasoning. The
mental hospital should not make the patient feel too comfortable;
not because he does not deserve any better, but because it would
interfere with his therapeutic progress. To illustrate this secondary
gain argument, the anecdote is told of the inmate of an asylum who,
when his special privileges were denied, replied indignantly: "Then
what am I nuts for?" (37).

There are many patients who wish to get well in order to leave
the hospital, but there are also many so-called chronic cases ("sta-
bilized schizophrenics"), who have permanently settled down to a

life in the mental hospital because their experiences there failed to restore to them the conviction that they could manage outside in society. Therefore some investigators conclude that keeping them hospitalized serves no good purpose—an argument valid only from a certain point of view and only because of the conditions of the existing institutions. These same investigators remark that the style of life of these patients makes it look as if they were "on a permanent weekend." The feelings which underlie such "objective" studies can be savored from a quotation such as this: "The relationship between the patient and the hospital" has to be viewed "as a function of a hedonistic calculus where the hospital is to be seen as a potential pleasure dome and the patient as an architect of his own personal Shangri-La" (21).

Pleasure dome and Shangri-La indeed! The feeling conveyed is that these patients simply have it too good, it is implied that these seriously ill people are not really sick, they just have a different style of life, and we should recognize it as such.

Sociological studies also arrive at similar conclusions. Lately some sociologists have told us a great deal about "the culture of poverty." It is not that the poor really want to live like the middle classes; they have their own culture, which we must respect. The underlying suggestion is that those who possess a culture must want to hold onto it; that it would be a disadvantage to them to give it up. The result of such reasoning follows: there are considerable advantages to being poor; therefore, the poor want to be poor, and that's why they are poor.

The kernel of truth in these observations is that the poor person, like the mental patient, does the best he can to make his situation endurable. In order to do so he develops certain attitudes, group customs, and methods of dealing with the surrounding world. All of this constitutes neither a specific culture of poverty, nor a "life-of-mental-hospital" culture; it is simply the best adjustment a person is able to make to a miserable situation. As long as he despairs of a better life he will of course hold onto the methods which make some manner of survival possible.

In practice, "advantages" in the mental hospital are such pitiful things as patients sneaking into the barber's room "because if a barber's chair was free, they could sometimes obtain a few minutes of comfortable chair rest," while others "pressed for gym periods because in the basement gym they could sometimes manage to use the relatively soft gym mats for a daytime nap, one of the great passions of hospital life." Patients sneak a second serving of food, or a special diet to which they are not entitled; swindle an extra frankfurter or piece of cheese and bread out of the dining room to make themselves a snack to eat later on. They even wheedle insulin shock treatment because then they "were allowed to lie in bed all morning in the insulin ward, a pleasure impossible in most other wards, and were treated quite like patients by nurses there." These examples are from one of the best and most famous U.S. government mental hospitals (49) but could be duplicated in almost any other.

If we were not looking for excuses to continue condemning mental patients to the kind of life the hospital offers, the conclusions drawn from the observations on secondary gain would be quite different. Contrast, if you will, the anecdote about the person who asked, "Then what am I nuts for?" when he was denied his privileges, with this one: A man, while driving by a mental hospital, had a flat tire and was forced to change it. As he did so, he made an awkward move and knocked all the nuts he had carefully put aside down into a deep and inaccessible ravine. So he asked a patient, who had been observing all this through the fence, how far it was to the next gas station, which turned out to be several miles away. As he started out, the patient asked him why he was walking there. "What else can I do?" said the driver. "I must get some nuts to fasten the spare tire to the car." "No you don't," said the patient. The driver, convinced that he was dealing with an insane individual, was annoyed by this stupid remark, but polite enough to ask "Why not?" The patient then explained that each tire is fastened to the car with five or six nuts, but three or four are sufficient to do some driving. So the simplest thing to do would be to take some nuts off the other wheels, use them to fasten the spare, and drive to the gas station to get the additional nuts. The man proceeded to do this, but couldn't help asking: "Tell me—with such intelligence, why are you the one behind the fence?" To which he received the reply: "I may be crazy, but I'm not stupid."

Since he is not stupid, the patient will use his intelligence to arrange his life as comfortably as he can within the hospital routine. And since there is nothing for him to do that he considers worthwhile—although the staff may think such opportunities are offered to him—he will try to arrange his days as much as he can like nonworking (or weekend) days. But this does not mean he would not prefer an entirely different way of life, *if* he could believe he could manage it, or that there was any real opportunity open to him. Similarly, the patient who cannot believe he will get well will use his intelligence to find opportunities to gain some advantage from his inescapable life of sickness. To counter these attitudes, the paramount need is to instill in the patient the feeling that his situation—contrary to his fears and convictions—is not hopeless at all.

Our problem comes from our failure to consider how the patient sees the world. The therapist knows, or believes he knows, that therapy will help the patient, and he proceeds on the basis of that knowledge, expecting the patient to do likewise. The patient proceeds on the basis of *his* conviction that there is no hope for him. So they are stalemated. The impasse can be broken only if one of the two—and it must be the therapist—begins to respond to the situation on the basis of the convictions of the other, without making them his own.

Unless this is done, a vicious circle of reinforcement is created. The patient holds onto his so-called secondary gains, extracting small advantages from his hospital existence, because he is convinced that nothing better is possible for him. The observer may decide that the patient does not want to get well, and conclude that taking away his secondary gains is therefore called for. But doing this will not induce the patient to hope that he can get well, it will make him only more suspicious of those who try to rob him of the few comforts he has struggled so hard to gain. How can he trust someone who is obviously out to make life even more unpleasant for him? So begins another series of mutually aggravating misunderstandings, which push the patient further away from reality.

What, then, is one to do about the secondary gain which is supposed to stand in the way of therapy? First, I suggest that if we respect the patient's ability to find ways to secure such a secondary gain, by doing so we enhance his self-respect, which should be a major therapeutic goal. By trying to take away, or have him give up these small advantages, we deny him the recognition he deserves for having tried to do something to better his life. If we cannot or do not respect such tangible achievement, he knows that all we want is to have our way; even to have him gain his self-respect our way, not his. Thus, being critical of the secondary gain—not to mention taking it away—is destructive to sound therapy.

Seeking secondary gain is only one of the many types of symptomatic behavior the patient engages in. All of these represent his efforts to do something about his situation *as he sees it*, no matter how unreasonable his view may seem to us. His therapist, therefore, ought to consider carefully the value the symptomatic behavior has for the patient. Even more important, the therapist and the therapeutic institution must deeply respect the patient's symptoms, as well as the reasons why he developed them. Far from viewing the secondary gain as something that stands in the way of therapy, we ought to consider it as something providing the most significant cues to what therapy must consist of, or at least include, if we want the patient to get well. The most important advantages the patient tries to achieve for himself through his efforts to procure secondary gains have been described as "demonstration of one's own helplessness in order to secure external help such as was available in childhood" and "getting special attention by being sick" (37). This is an excellent specification of what the patient needs to get well. The psychiatric patient indeed needs special attention and the kind of help he lost out on in childhood (or received so little of that the pressures and desires for it were carried into an age at which most people no longer crave them to the same degree). If we could give him all the attention he yearns for—or at least attention to what for him are the crucial areas of deficiency in his life—there would be no need for his attempting to secure it through what to the misinformed seem devious means. It would become one of the *primary* gains therapy offers and as such it would eventually satisfy the need, which the surreptitiously secured secondary gain never can. Since secondary gain is wheedled out of the therapist or institution, once obtained it is unsatisfying, even depriving—because one has had to connive for something that is of positive value only when freely and gladly given. Having to steal what we desperately need, even if we succeed in getting away with it, does not change our experience of the world as depriving; nor does it alter our image of ourselves from one unworthy to receive, to one deserving to be given to. Effecting such change is what therapy ought to consist of.

For the patient to feel degraded, to become convinced that we do not want him to become self-reliant, it is not even necessary that his secondary gains be actually taken away. The schizophrenic has an uncanny ability to respond to what we are thinking, even when we do not act on it—provided it is in line with what preoccupies his mind. Many who deal intimately with schizophrenics and are sensitive to their reactions come to believe that they can read our minds. For example, while we are considering adding a new patient to a group, some patient will remark that he expects a new arrival; while we ponder his having a home visit, he suddenly begins to talk about one; not to mention violent reactions when a staff member important to a patient is contemplating leaving the institution, often long before he has definitely made up his mind to do so, or even told anybody about such plans.

Several investigators have remarked on how intensely mental patients react to disagreements among staff which center upon them

(114). What has escaped notice is that schizophrenics respond equally strongly to dissensions which are not at all concerned with them, but have to do only with personal relations between staff members who are important to a patient. If they react to them, this is ascribed to their disturbed minds and not to their heightened sensitivity to what goes on around them. What is equally overlooked is that the schizophrenic's ability to "read our mind" correctly is quite limited. He can do so only in relation to his dominant concerns, anxieties, and delusions. Very important things can be on our minds which schizophrenics do not react to at all, remain extremely insensitive to, or interpret all wrong, because they respond to life only in accordance with their concerns and not with reality.

When they recognize something unusual in our mien, tone of voice, way of moving, or whatever, they may interpret its cause quite inappropriately; that is, inappropriately in regard to reality, but very much in accordance with what preoccupies their thoughts. Thus if when scrutinizing our appearance they observe something out of the ordinary—for example, if we are worried about some member of our family having fallen ill—they will interpret their observations in accord with their own dominant anxiety. If this happens to be anxiety about being deserted, they may express fears about our leaving when we have no intention whatsoever of doing so.

Their ability to thus "read our minds," that is, to draw correct— but also often incorrect—inferences from subliminal cues is not as surprising as it may seem. It is something many people learn to do who find themselves in situations which make it seem necessary to pay keen attention to stimuli the rest of us disregard because we have much better sources of vital information. For example, blind persons learn to find their way in corridors, know where there is a turn, from the echo of their footsteps. Responsive to the sound reverberations coming from the side walls of a corridor, they keep walking equidistantly between them. If every blind person can learn to do that, how natural that the psychiatric hospital patient, whose living conditions deprive him of many of the messages which we receive from direct investigation of our surroundings, develops skills for making deductions from stimuli to which the rest of us have no reason to make ourselves sensitive.

Therefore for things to go wrong over so-called secondary gains, it is sufficient that the patient somehow feels we are opposed to his efforts at wheedling some advantage from his hospital life. To him, we are known not by our words but by our actions, and by what we are silently thinking about matters which he is anxious or guilty about. If we are opposed to his ways of securing a better life for himself at the moment, he concludes we are against his getting a better life, whatever we may say to the contrary; and he gives up trying.

The view that there is no such thing as mental illness, that the chronic schizophrenic is nothing but a person who has settled down to a way of life which is the most appropriate or comfortable for him, is held by so few that it hardly warrants serious discussion. But it permits making a point. To begin with, those who insist that the mental patient is simply one who has developed a different style of life beg the question they pretend to investigate, because they neither ask nor answer what constitutes mental health.

Freud thought that we are all heir to the same anxieties and desires; that our unconscious, and the roots out of which our personality grows, are common to all of us. Plato aphorized that the difference between the virtuous man and the wicked man is that the first only dreams of doing what the other does. According to psychoanalysis, many of the thoughts and feelings of the sane and insane are alike, and the latter have no thoughts or feelings that we could not also find in ourselves. If this is so, if we are so inherently alike, how do we explain the difference in actions? One answer is that we would all be essentially asocial, uninhibited, criminal, even insane, if we had not succeeded, with the help of others and of society, in erecting inner controls which prevent some of our impulses from ending in actions. There is some obvious truth in this, because we know we sometimes have to stop ourselves—inhibit and control doing what we feel driven to. But experience with psychotic persons suggests that while controls are one element, this is hardly the most important one in separating mental health from mental illness. There are mentally ill persons who suffer from too much control.

Freud's criteria for psychological well-being are the ability to love well and to work hard. This is a literal translation, which does not provide the emotional overtones and intellectual connotations his statement had for his German readers at the time he made it. What he thought constitutes mental health can currently be described as the desire for and the ability to form human relations which are both mutually satisfying and permanent, and the ability to find and hold a meaningful place in society. The first would certainly include sexual love; the second, work to which one is committed, and which one hence finds satisfying. Looked at this way, it becomes obvious that the mental patient is sorely deficient in both criteria, and the chronic schizophrenic even more so.

In order to understand both mental health and mental illness, we must know what prevents the mentally ill from living like the healthy. For those interested in therapy, an important question is: How can we assess whether a person is moving in one or the other direction? Do we really have to wait until he finds deep enjoyment in lasting human relations, and meaning as well as satisfaction in his work, before we can know whether he is getting better? With some qualifications I suggest that nothing is more characteristic of mental well-being than a healthy self-respect, a regard for one's body and its functions, and a reasonably optimistic outlook on life. It must be a self-respect and an outlook which are equidistant from depression and from its denial, megalomania or mania. Calling it a "healthy" self-respect indicates that it must co-exist with a sound capacity for self-criticism, against which it is realistically and intelligently tested, in a manner that may lead to short periods of discontent and thus motivate improvement, but never permits despair to set in. It must be a self-respect which does not need to be buttressed by thinking little of, or tearing down, others; and which permits the person to be so secure within himself that he can well afford to recognize the superiority of others if they possess it, without coming to feel inferior as a person (or only in some circumscribed respects which do not endanger his feeling of self-worth). Similarly, a reasonably optimistic outlook on life, particularly one's own, may include doubts about the future—recognizing that it is always uncertain—but it prevents such doubts from "getting one down." A regard for one's body must be equidistant from disgust or neglect on the one hand, and obsessional anxiety about it and its functioning on the other hand.

When mental health and sickness are viewed in this perspective, the basic error becomes apparent in thinking the chronic schizophrenic has simply adopted a different style of life. If self-respect and reasonable optimism are part of the criteria of mental health, then being able to accept one's life as an existence which is devoid of satisfying human relations; deprived of sexual satisfactions; where work does not make any sense other than to kill time; and where one has given up hope for one's future in society—these are not just the signs of serious mental illness, they are the illness itself.

It is not the presence of delusions, of violence, of illogic, or the inability to adjust to a situation which constitute mental illness, but how one feels about oneself, one's body and person, and one's place in the world. The delusions, violence, illogic, and so on, are symptoms of desperate deficiency in positive feeling about oneself and one's place in the world. Therapy must include helping the patient to examine his views and feelings about his body, himself, his relations with others, and his place in the world. As the result of successful therapy, the person should have gained or regained self-respect, and an optimistic outlook about himself and the world he lives in. If he has these, he will be able to form the human relations Freud had in mind when he spoke of love, and to find in society meaningful tasks which he can perform well. For many in our modern technological mass society, this meaningful work may have to be found not in the occupation from which they gain their livelihood, but in free-time pursuits.

Evidence from sociological studies shows that if human beings are utterly downtrodden, in despair of ever being able to improve their conditions, they settle down to accepting their life of misery and become unable to struggle for something better (83). If, on the other hand, by some means they are able to gain inner strength, they soon refuse to live in dependency and strive for greater self-determination. It is usually only after people stop being desperately poor and have gained some hope about themselves that they refuse to continue in their debased condition and begin to fight for something better (32, 48). I am referring here to the Tocquevillean hypothesis according to which the improvement of conditions increases the desire for greater change for the better. And people become able to translate this desire into action when they feel themselves to be stronger and more potent.

It might be objected that this applies only to normal persons and does not hold true for mental patients. The experience of the Orthogenic School proves that in this respect, as in so many others, there is no difference between mental patients and the rest of us. Only after our patients had been subjected for some time to as comfortable and satisfying a life as we could make for them, and when they were no longer feeling desperately deprived, needful, and miserable, did they begin to experience "rising expectations"—and to cooperate with us in a struggle to gain something better for themselves. This struggle they had shunned before, probably because they did not have sufficient strength for it, and did not believe that it could possibly yield results.

In line with what we trusted would be the results when we decided to offer the patients the most advantageous living conditions we could arrange for them, not a single one wanted to continue living in an institution once he had achieved the minimal personality integration needed for living on his own in society. Understandably, quite a few had fears as to how they would be able to make it, living on their own, and hence at times had hesitation about leaving. But none wished to remain in our institution any longer than necessary just because life there was pleasant, as indeed it was. Quite a few left of their own volition even before we thought they were fully ready for it. Their reason: that, despite most pleasant surroundings and a wide variety of other satisfactions, they were living in a psychiatric institution as psychiatric patients.

Many of them said about the same thing: "I know I'll never again have it so easy, but I want to be on my own. I know life will be much harder for me than it was here, but I hope I now can make a go of it." They all were willing to, and most did, pay the price of reduced living conditions and greater emotional difficulties, rather than continue living even in what seemed to them the best of institutions. After their leaving, some longed for what was left behind, but they never considered returning as patients, much as they liked to come back and visit with us from time to time.

It could be argued that while this is true for persons who have achieved a reasonable degree of mental health, it says nothing about those who have not. These would never want to leave an institution where they have it so good. True, but they can't leave it anyway, because they are too disturbed and debilitated to do so. What our experience proves is that, contrary to widespread opinion, comfort and pleasant living aid therapy, and never induce the patient to wish to continue as such.

Anybody who possesses the minimum ability needed for coping with the world prefers to be as fully master of his own fate as possible; willing to run the risks, even to suffer from his own mistakes and all the other vagaries of an independent existence. Without liking the hardships life may impose, he prefers them to existing under conditions of dependency, even if he is handed the most comfortable of lives. However problematic it may be, any person prefers his own life to one prepared for him, as long as he feels confident that he will eventually master its difficulties.

3 | Mental Health, Autonomy, and Need-Satisfaction

At present, since there are no definite and successful models for designing the physical structures and internal organization of a mental institution, the best one can do is try to apply those theories which seem able to offer an understanding of the disturbed mind: what, psychologically speaking, is involved in insanity and in its cure. Psychoanalysis itself is not the treatment method to which patients in need of residential care respond best; if it were, there would be no need for their institutionalization. However, since there is no better body of theory yet available to explain what has gone wrong in the lives and minds of psychiatric patients, and what then is needed to restore them to mental health, it is psychoanalytic understanding of human behavior which has to be the source of our thinking on institutional design.

Not without reason has the name "schizophrenia" (i.e., a splitting in the personality) been given to the syndrome of disturbances which affect a large segment of the population of our mental hospitals. The deterioration of the senile patients, though different in origin, has this feature in common with schizophrenia: it is marked by an inability to cope, as is also the case with those who suffer from organic disturbances. All persons so afflicted have experienced a breakdown of their ego functions. The routine type of life which existing mental institutions impose is based on this fact. Living by routines permits easy predictions; the simpler the routine, the less it demands an ability to cope. This is the pragmatic reason brought forth to justify the operation of psychiatric hospitals: the patient who lives by routines is less bewildered and confused than he would be without them.

Many critics of psychiatric institutions overlook the great service these routines provide to the patient, who benefits from being in a situation where he is still able to cope. Therefore, psychiatric hospital staffs feel justified in paying little attention to those critics who, by railing against all routines, demonstrate that they do not comprehend how much the patient needs them. Such defense of routines is not fashionable and hence is rarely voiced. But without some such controversy, no informed discussion is possible of which routines are beneficial, and why; and which are detrimental, and in what ways. The result is that routines are either uncritically maintained, or equally uncritically all done away with—whereas both alternatives are detrimental to patients.

This is the predicament of the psychiatric hospital: its method of operation permits patients some degree of mastery within its confines despite their reduced capacities, but it does not restore the patient's ability to cope with higher complexity. Criticism of mental institutions should recognize the value of the first, and address itself only to the latter point. Obviously, higher coping can be achieved only under the impact of challenges which are graded, so that each level can be mastered with just a minimum of further effort. If the challenge is too great—as life outside an institution would be to any patient who needs to live in one—it overwhelms the person, who thereby becomes less able to manage than before. This is why the good mental institution has to help the patient, small step by small step, learn to cope.

The inability to cope is, to a large measure, the consequence of an inner disorganization of the personality, of which the splitting off (schizophrenia) is only one possible form. The mental patient "cannot make sense," is "out of touch," "can't get hold" of himself and life. He cannot order and integrate into a consistent whole all the sensations and impressions which overpower him. Psychoanalysis speaks of the "need for internalization and integration" which eventually enables the patient to bring order into what would otherwise be an inner chaos. We must stop our id, ego, and superego warring within ourselves and tearing us apart. We can do this as we internalize values and ways of behaving so that they are no longer alien to us. These internalizations are among the most important emotional experiences in our life.

If we have to behave as others demand of us, we are puppets while others pull the strings. But when we internalize the motives of others, which could enrich our personality and life—and as we do so, modify them in line with our life experience and genetic endowment, that is, make them ego-syntonic—then we are no longer operated by others, and become autonomous. In order to be able to do this, the demands coming from the environment must not be so contradictory or ego-alien that they cannot be internalized without a split in the personality, or other destructive consequences. They must also be sufficiently unified so that we don't have to try to internalize contradictory demands. In the family setting, internalization of mother and father are among the child's most important emotional experiences. If the parents are at cross-purposes, since we have to internalize the impact of both of them, we may not be able at all to integrate these contradictory elements within ourselves.

In addition to being neither ego-alien or contradictory, for something to be internalized it must be comprehensible; because what is incomprehensible is not internalized, at least not without damage to ourselves. If something is unintelligible, it can only be internalized by external or inner pressure to do so. Typically, the parents force the child to behave in certain ways; external pressure is exercised on him to make these ways his own. Since parents hold all the power to satisfy or to frustrate the child's needs, their emotional impact is very great; therefore, there is also inner pressure to please them, to secure their permanent good will by internalizing their values. If these values are consistent, they are much more easily comprehended than if there are inner contradictions among them. If the values are moral and consistent, and the child can understand why they are desirable, or at least feel they are, this contributes to the development of the child's moral sense and to his feelings of satisfaction that he is a good person. If the values are contradictory or incomprehensible to the child, but the outer and inner pressures are sufficiently powerful, the values will still be internalized, but personal difficulties will sooner or later ensue.

To illustrate this, consider the value of competition *versus* mutual help. For a long time, man had to compete to survive, so the first was obviously a value by which one had to live, and the second a distant ideal for which to strive. Today, in many middle-class white families survival seems assured, but the child is expected to defeat his competitors in school—if not also on the playing field—while at the same time it is impressed upon him that mutual help should be the guiding value of his life. Such contradictions make values incomprehensible; because of parental pressure they are nevertheless internalized. The result is a person who feels equally compelled by his internalized values to win in competition yet not to compete, because to do so means defeating somebody else whom one should, if not love, at least support. As a result, he is so torn that he can no longer act in ways which make him feel good about himself. This may go so far that some feel unable to cope and withdraw from a world which no longer makes sense to them. If the child had internalized only one of the two contradictory values he could cope well without internal conflicts, because each value alone is comprehensible; it is only in combination that they are not.

For these reasons any mental institution must be an integrated whole as opposed to a random assembly of parts. Only an integrated environment can serve as an image that fosters internalizing the need for, and desirability of, inner integration.

This is why some of the significant improvements which have been made in the operation of psychiatric hospitals, desirable as they are in breaking the empty tedium of the patient's life, fail to solve the problem of effective treatment. When psychotherapy remains an essentially alien element in the life of the patient because it is so different from what goes on during the whole rest of his time, it loses much of its effectiveness in promoting inner integration. (Matters are radically different when a patient, living his own life in society, sees a psychoanalyst in daily sessions. The experience is then entirely removed from the rest of his life—not a part of an institutional existence.) Working within its framework the therapist cannot help becoming part of the institution in the mind of the patient. He feels that he is spending nearly all of his days as if "in cold storage," waiting for his psychotherapeutic sessions, which are but a short time spent constructively. In all good psychiatric institutions, recreational and occupational therapy are added to relieve the monotony, which they do; they even offer some of the necessary challenges to higher coping. But these also remain isolated aspects of the patient's life. Since these therapies are not an integrated part of institutional life but seem to be independent experiences, they tend to operate against integration. For an integrative milieu an inner pattern of great cohesion is necessary, one which must permeate all the patient's experiences in the institution. To form an organic whole, all activities (especially therapies) must organize themselves around the structure of the hospital. But, imaginative and enjoyable as the experiences with recreational or occupational therapy may be in themselves, I have rarely seen this happen.

Paranoia and Depression

Differing delusional contents are characteristic of the two most widespread types of functional psychosis: paranoia and depression. In paranoia, forces that control the person from the inside have become externalized, because they are so ego-alien and overpowering that they can no longer be contained internally and integrated with the other aspects of the personality. These forces or demands so enslave the individual that the only way he can avoid being torn apart by them is to project them onto the outside. Persecution from outside oneself, incredibly painful as it is, originally seems less destructive to the so disturbed person than to be torn apart inside, with a total collapse of all aspects of the personality.

This is why some persons suffering from paranoia are able to function in certain areas of their lives which remain isolated from other aspects of their personality. Without the outward projection of inner persecutory forces they may not even be able to retain this minimal ability to cope. The trouble here is that while the projection was an effort at assuring at least the inner functioning of the personality, these persecutory forces, now located on the outside, become impervious to all efforts at integrating them. The person loses all power to influence them, and in insidious cases these forces can exercise total control over him. These figures, forces, or "influencing machines" dominate everything the person does, thinks, or feels.

In depression, a feeling of utter powerlessness and unworthiness comes from the person's not being able to live in accordance with his exaggerated values, nor to satisfy his most urgent desires, including the need to feel loved and respected by others, or to be able to love others.

This short enumeration is by no means a catalogue of the thoughts and feelings which are characteristic of severe functional disturbances. At least two more aspects of such disorders must be mentioned here. First, inability to cope, thought disorders, and defensive efforts to cover these up are accompanied by anxiety, and a total collapse may be imminent—which one is either incapable of protecting oneself against, or must at all times attempt to ward off by the most complicated defensive maneuvers (50, 51). Second, the inability to cope is projected mainly onto one's own body, which is then seen as the source of one's worthlessness and all other troubles. The consequence is the conviction that all sorts of things are wrong with one's body: that it is utterly disgusting; that it is apt to fall apart, or that it already has; that some organ is rotting away; that extreme medical measures are absolutely necessary (though one does not believe in their effectiveness); that some part of the body has become separated, has stopped functioning, or must be exorcised (13).

Among the most frequent reasons for legal commitment to a mental hospital is that the person has become a danger to himself or others. If he is apt to hurt himself or others, it is due to one or the other of the phenomena just described. In his bodily attacks on others he acts on his conviction that they wish to do him in, or the delusion that they have complete power over his life. Destroying them becomes the only device such a person can think of to protect himself, or to break their stranglehold over him. When attacking himself, the person doesn't wish to harm himself. On the contrary, it is the same desire that prompts him to commit acts of violence against others—to improve his condition; for example, by getting rid of that part of himself which he believes causes him all the trouble. In trying to kill himself, he attempts to destroy that which resides inside him and makes life so unbearable.

One must not discount the service the mental institution renders to an inmate by safeguarding him against hurting himself or others, and by protecting him in many other ways. Nor do I deny the value of simplifying and imposing routine on the patient's life, which makes him feel that he may be able to cope. However, most psychiatric hospitals are too concerned with the wishes of the public or the patient's relatives and the staff's anxieties to do as good a job as is desirable. They don't protect the patient against the possible consequences of his violent tendencies with sufficient gentleness, regard for his feelings, and, most of all, for his self-respect; nor do they protect him adequately against the continued onslaught of feelings which members of his family subject him to.

In the presence of such personality disorders, one would expect a psychiatric hospital to be designed and to operate in line with the task of freeing the patient of all impediments to his mental health. In actuality, many of its efforts have to be devoted to combatting some of the bad consequences of incarceration. To use only the most obvious example: so-called maximum security arrangements prevent the patient from harming himself or others. But locking him up in an isolation cell, depriving him of much of his clothing, and putting him under restraint, which interferes with his ability to move, are obvious demonstrations to him that he is indeed in the power of others who can do with him as they wish. These are measures which, while they protect, also destroy. They protect the body, but further destroy the limited autonomy the person possessed before having been made a patient.

In designing a building, a factory, for example, one must have at least three main purposes in mind: to manufacture the product in the most efficient manner; to prevent dangers which may be inherent in the process of production; and to create conditions which facilitate this production, be it by machine or by human beings. Thus it will not do to plan ways of production that entail the risk of explosion, which would destroy the factory. Nor can the designer overlook conditions that might lead to the exhaustion of those who work on the production line, so that their efficiency is seriously curtailed.

Proceeding on the basis of this oversimplified analogy, one might say that most of the planning for the psychiatric hospital goes into avoiding catastrophe: seeing that the patient does not hurt himself or others, keeping him alive by feeding and housing him, and preventing him from making a nuisance of himself in society; and some of the planning goes into making working conditions bearable for the staff. Very little thinking seems to have gone into planning the various steps involved in producing what should be the factory's reason for existence: a useful finished product—namely, the mental health of the patient. This requires an analysis of what is involved in that process, and an understanding of which experiences facilitate making one of these steps without impeding another. Finally, as in the factory where many parts have to be fitted together to produce the final product, it would have to be determined how to make it all coalesce.

I have used the analogy of the factory because when one considers how much analysis, planning, and experimentation has gone into designing factories for manufacturing, and creating the necessary equipment for them, it is astonishing what comparatively little effort has gone into designing for mental health. The reason for lack of more thoughtful design is an obvious one: it is so much easier to break down a production process into its single steps—to realize how the steps have to follow each other, either build on each other or interfere with each other—than it is to grasp what is involved in creating mental health. As long as we concentrate all our thoughts on the breakdown of mental health and the repair job needed, instead of on those conditions which create mental health, advances will remain slow and small. To go back to the factory analogy, we proceed as if the productive process itself could be created out of an understanding of the repairing process after the product has broken down. Most of our thinking on mental health derives from experience with mental patients who have lost it.

The trouble is that planning for mental health and analyzing what it consists of is an incredibly complex problem. At this moment, for example, we are at a loss to know what form of physical setting for home or school would best promote mental health; the evidence seems convincing that those we presently use are unsuitable. It may well be that the demands made of home and school in this respect are so overwhelmingly complex, that the problem of how to design buildings to house them will be solved only after we have become able to design the mental hospital in accordance with what would best suit the tasks for which it exists. (Maybe what happened in psychoanalysis is applicable here. It was the study of neurotics and hysterics that permitted Freud to arrive at conclusions about normal development, to discover principles at work in it which could not be fathomed before he set out to understand what psychiatric patients needed to regain normalcy.) Perhaps an understanding of how a psychiatric hospital should be designed to serve its peculiar purpose of restoring mental health can help us design schools and habitats for families which will be much more suitable for promoting mental health than those that are presently in use.

Developing Autonomy, Abandoning Delusions

If, as in paranoia, the outer and inner life of the person is experienced as being controlled by forces beyond himself, the most serious efforts of the psychiatric hospital must be directed toward convincing him that this is not so. Creating situations which, because of their elements and setting, make it virtually impossible for him to maintain his belief that some outside evil force is controlling him, can make a difference. Only then does it become possible for him to realize that he invented the forces that persecute him, and that he alone invested them with power to do so. For this to occur, all that happens to him and around him must be open to his inspection. If decisions about his life are made somewhere in an office or staff meeting, without his knowing why and how, there will be no chance to convince him that he is not a powerless pawn, used and possibly sacrificed in the subtle game someone else is playing. If he is observed through one-way screens, tested to find out what goes on in his mind, all this feeds paranoia. What would be needed to extinguish the paranoia is the absence of any further events in reality which could be interpreted as manipulation by others, so that the environment no longer provides new fuel.

For quite some time the patient may interpret these efforts as the most refined method to fool him into believing he is moving of his own volition, while somebody else pulls the now more cleverly hidden strings. But if his entire life proceeds within an institution where the staff can know what is going on, which event produced what other one, it does eventually become possible to show even the most paranoid patient that happenings which he is convinced were due to inscrutable powers are in reality his own creations. A sufficient number of such experiences will have salutary effects in demonstrating, first, that these persecutory powers are less omnipresent than he previously believed; and second, that much of what was attributed to them was the patient's own doing.

Because his entire life now proceeds in the psychiatric institution, the patient who is depressed by his feelings of utter worthlessness must be exposed only to persons who deeply believe in his worthwhileness. Again, what they *say* will not be trusted; the depressed patient will view statements that he is a good person as another demonstration that people simply don't wish to bother with him and his agonies, because they know he is not worthwhile. They tell him that he is a fine individual because they're not interested enough in him to take *his* views of himself seriously. On the other hand, his continuing experience that the staff expends a great deal of effort and emotional energy on him will eventually be effective. What is needed is a positive acceptance of the great troubles he is creating; this will eventually persuade him, because even a mental patient knows that only people who think him worthwhile can possibly do so much for him. And he is right. Only a staff who are convinced of his importance as the person he is can accept all the hard work and emotional bruises which he inflicts. But their efforts are endangered to the extent that the patient is subjected to opposite experiences; that is, to having contact with other people who expect him not to "wallow in his misery" but to pull himself together. This attitude may be reasonable enough in the outside world, but will only undo the efforts of the staff. Hence the patient must be protected against exposure to such harshness until his self-esteem is sufficiently developed to be able to withstand it.

This extremely compressed discussion may suggest why it is only through living in the right kind of psychiatric institution that paranoia and depression can slowly be disintegrated. Only in the right kind of institution will experiences which are suitable to achieving this be permitted to occur, while experiences that might tend to support the patient's delusions or low self-esteem are as far as humanly possible prevented from happening.

The simplified and easily comprehensible reality of the psychiatric hospital should restore to the patient the conviction that even he can manage in the world he now lives in. As the staff invests his body with positive emotions through persistent examples of respect and care for it, the patient will come to view it as worthy of emotional investment. While complete autonomy must be the goal of the institution, those experiences which would be detrimental to it have to be restricted. The art of institutional care is to deny autonomy only for experiences that are clearly destructive to the patient, and to safeguard and encourage it for all others.

There is no direct access to autonomy. The approach to it is through self-esteem and a feeling of the worthwhileness of life. These are prime ingredients in mental health; true autonomy is their consequence and man's greatest achievement. Hence, from the moment a mental patient begins the process of entering a mental hospital, all efforts should be directed toward convincing him that it is designed so that he can gain autonomy. This includes the opportunity and ability to satisfy his own needs in interactions with others who respect him as a unique individual. The hope is that on the basis of prolonged exposure to such experiences he will recognize that he is indeed a worthwhile person who has a significant place in life, and importance for others. Once he can take pride in this, he will also be able to respect others as individuals in their own right and interact freely with them as one autonomous being to another; that is, without any need for mutual adjustments which run counter to any participant's self-respect.

While such is the hope for the patient's recovery, it must never be imposed as a demand. This is the crucial error of the existing psychiatric institutions, and one which defeats their purpose. Present mental institutions fail because patients are forced into a pattern—always supposedly for their own good—or demands are made on them which are alien to their personalities. Both things are destructive to autonomy; nobody is going to become an autonomous person by someone else's willing it. The desire and the ability to live an orderly life become part of one's personality only when this has been internalized by being exposed to an orderly life situation which is much more attractive than all countervailing tendencies. But even all the advantages of a well-organized existence in and by themselves are not sufficient for internalization; they have to be mediated through a personal relationship with somebody whom one loves and admires. The wish to become more like this cherished person, and to gain his affection more securely by living in accordance with his values, underlies the process of identification, and with it internalization of behavior and values. Something imposed by somebody who is not loved or deeply respected is simply not internalized, or if it is, it is against such resistance that as soon as the pressure is relieved, the negative reaction takes over. If the inner as well as the outer life of the mental patient is chaotic, subjecting him to an external order—routines—may afford relief; but as long as order remains something imposed by others, it will not lead to internalization.

The development of a style of life centered on mutually satisfying interactions with others—of appropriate inner attitudes and convictions—based on each person's autonomy, must be facilitated by the physical and human design of the institution. But this too can never be imposed. While some regimen may be unavoidable as an intermediary step to inner and outer freedom (as illustrated by the locking up of the jump rope described in the chapter which follows), a psychiatric institution is bound to be ineffective if it relies on enforcement as its basis for operating. It's not that the traditional mental hospital has been unaware of this; it is simply stuck in the enforcing and never quite manages to take those further steps toward freedom. Neither freedom, nor autonomy, nor self-esteem, nor a positive outlook on life or oneself, nor friendship, not to mention love, can be forced on a person. But the capacity for their development can indeed be facilitated, as good parents must facilitate the emerging of these traits in the infant, if he is to grow into a mentally healthy, personally and socially successful individual.

Hiring a staff for such a task and expecting them to achieve it because it is their job or profession will also never do. The human conditions which the staff has to create for the patients must be in some way similar to those which comprise good parenthood. The mother must positively accept and obey the infant's imperious cry for food. If she does, then there comes the time when the security that food will always be pleasantly and abundantly forthcoming when demanded becomes so well established that the command for food is replaced by desire for a pleasant interaction around eating. The person who feeds and the other who is being fed engage in an encounter in which the two are very unequally involved, but which is equally important to each. Ample and reliable satisfaction has changed the wish to dominate into a desire for personal relations.

The child's fear that his needs will not be satisfied, and the extreme lengths to which he may go out of his desire to secure them, can warp his personality and make him hate both himself and the world. It thus becomes a function of any psychiatric institution to be as completely need-satisfying as is realistically possible. The existing institutions fail the patient in this way because even the ones which do try to gratify the patient's needs, do so on the basis of the administration's definition of what these needs are. If the desire is for candies or meat, good healthy food of a different kind will indeed nurture the body but will not satisfy these emotional needs of the patient—which demand that his body should get what he wants. If all the needs which can possibly be gratified are met in line with what the patient considers satisfying, his anxiety about privation will lessen, and his sometimes psychotic defenses against it will become unnecessary. Again, those desires of the patient's which clearly endanger him cannot be satisfied. (It will not do to allow him to climb on a roof; but then again it is not necessary to bar the windows to prevent this.) Concern for the physical well-being of a patient all too often replaces sensitivity to his emotional needs, and camouflages either miserliness or the staff's acting out its own anxieties on the patient.

For example, there have been many times when I have encountered the rationalization that some food would lead to dangerous weight problems, so its availability was restricted. This was done even though the patient was not yet overweight, or long before his weight had reached dangerous proportions. If a patient were suffering from heart trouble or diabetes, this would change the requirements—but even psychotics can be quite aware of these exceptions. They can also differentiate between limitations enforced only for their well-being and those imposed out of the preconceived notions of what the staff feels is good for the patient. As the infant feeling abundantly fed—because feeding him is enjoyed by those who take care of him—will soon stop overeating, so will the mental patient who is driven to overeat because of anxiety, although it may take time for such care to alleviate the insecurity that underlies overeating.

The infant who feels assured that all of his needs will be well taken care of may eventually think that he is providing himself with what he is receiving (witness that his crying brought about his being fed—something no infant can feel whose parents want him to recognize that it all comes from them). Abundant satisfaction of the patient's desires eventually leads him, not to the infantile belief that he provides it all for himself, but rather toward healthy confidence in his ability to do so. As a result he will stop being overly concerned about this issue. Once we feel assured of ample supplies of satisfaction, we are no longer as concerned with its sources.

The significance of food as a source for gaining a feeling of basic security, and as a vehicle for forming personal relations, has been widely recognized; so much so that I hesitate to discuss it here, however briefly. But the shortcomings of our psychiatric institutions in this respect are striking. The degrading subterfuges patients have to employ to secure miserable tokens of what should be guaranteed to them are so prevalent that I could not help returning to what is essentially an inexhaustible topic. Abundance of food is only a first requirement for gaining security, and obviously food that is not experienced as enjoyable cannot offer it. Self-regulation, the cornerstone of autonomy, can only be a consequence of the availability of such needs as food. But autonomy requires even more—namely, the ability to choose for oneself not only how much, but what is wanted, and what isn't and the conditions under which it is received.

One of the psychiatric hospital's greatest services to the patient is facilitating his coping by routinizing much of his life. This will continue to be a reassuring and potentially strengthening experience for him to the degree that easily met challenges are provided, and help is given to master them. Instead of being something that remains inflexible, routine should be the most flexible arrangement of all. The psychiatric hospital is aware of this, and tries to solve the problem by, for example, moving a patient from a closed ward to an open one. This only means that he is subjected to a different set of routines, which entails leaving behind those human associations (with the exception of a few such as his therapist) which may have helped him reach a higher level of achieving. Essentially, the problem with these arrangements so far as coping is concerned is that while greater ability to manage leads to more "privileges," it doesn't really change the power relations. If the ability to cope is to be a step toward autonomy, it should not mean being "permitted" to do more, but actually to have more power over one's own life. As the patient's ability to engage in a wider variety of activities increases, all too often this actually means he has to ask for permission to do something (such as leave the ward or the institution's confinements) more frequently. Then he has to worry that his more frequent requests may be denied. Thus what should be a step toward greater autonomy is experienced as being even more dependent on the good will of others.

The most difficult form of behavior the staff must deal with is the incontinence and assaultiveness of the patients. Since the patients feel their bodies are worthless, it can become quite destructive when the staff express disgust on finding the patients soiling themselves. Even if open expressions of revulsion are frowned upon, the patients perceive the inner reactions of the staff all too well. But it is not enough to accept the patient's wish not to want to use the toilet to eliminate. Considering the low opinion he has of his body and its functioning, and his conviction that it is in extreme danger of being further harmed, the design of a psychiatric hospital must include arrangements which convince the patient how important and acceptable his body is, in all of its functions. It won't do much good to respect the patient's possessions, if his prime possession—his body— is not accorded even higher respect. This is most easily conveyed by the bathroom arrangements. More than the furnishing of many other rooms such as therapists' offices, ward parlors, or workshops, the equipping and decoration of bathrooms is of prime importance to convey to the patient that the institution respects his body and one of its most basic functions. Eventually the patient may be able to model his feelings for the body's worthwhileness, and on this basis his self-respect, in the image which is conveyed.

Volumes have been written about the importance of the ways in which children are taught cleanliness; how severe and permanent the impact is of bad experiences around toilet training; how many delusions of persecution center around it and are its consequences; how much of what then happens determines how persons later feel about their bodies and themselves. It would seem all the more reason to pay attention to how bathroom and toilet facilities ought to be designed and therapeutically used in a psychiatric hospital. But these facilities, the experiences had there, and the associations built around them are utterly neglected, both in practice and in literature about psychiatric hospitals. For example, an authoritative publication which in most other respects points the way toward much better mental hospital design states that "buildings which meet the psycho-social needs of our patients will go some way to prevent the chance of degradation, reduce disculturation and encourage resocialization." But when it comes to the place where things so often went wrong around one of the most basic socializing experiences of man, his education to cleanliness, of some 130 tightly printed pages less than a dozen lines are devoted to this feature of mental hospitals. The only recommendation is: "*Baths and toilets:* Space for these facilities should be the same as would be provided in schools, military establishments, etc." (52). Compare this with the average home. This guideline for mental hospital construction (an official publication of the American Psychiatric Association) devotes some thirty-four sketches and eighty-five photographs to illustrating a wide variety of design features. Not a single one deals with bathrooms and toilet facilities in any other way but as an insignificant detail of larger floor plans illustrating ward layouts.

The assaultive patient presents special problems to the staff. He is overwhelmed by the need to beat down or destroy, so that he may be safe. Hence his real, underlying need is safety. He imagines his physical or moral existence is in mortal danger—witness the many acts of violence which are committed by "normal" persons in defense of their honor. When one feels that his honor is respected rather than threatened, one experiences no need for violent defense. Therefore, what the violent patient requires is not a chance to satisfy his desire to act aggressively. It is a serious mistake to believe that this is so. If the therapist is sympathetic to the extent of telling a patient his violence is justified, it only convinces the person that even his therapist sees no other way for him to deal with the explosive pressures which induce him to attack. It is much more curative to make the patient feel that since there is no longer any *present* reason to hurt himself or others, everybody around him is convinced that he, being a decent person, will not do so. If nothing in the environment contradicts this, it is a convincing message.

Unfortunately, mental patients are surrounded by conditions and exposed to messages which tell them that the environment in which they live expects—and hence fears—that they may act destructively. If these conditions and messages were not present, we wouldn't need to feel so anxious about their—and our—safety. Schizophrenics are extremely sensitive to how we feel about them. If, for example, we fear that they may use a baseball bat to bash somebody's head in, this will so infuriate them that they may try to do exactly that. This, in turn, is taken as a demonstration of how dangerous they are, and that they must never be entrusted with having a bat. Now, it may not be very smart ever to hand a patient such an instrument unless he is taking part in a well-supervised game, but it is courting danger to let him have a bat if one is worried that he may use it to attack.

Children—and mental patients, who in this respect are much like them—behave in line with our inner expectations about them. If we expect a child to lie to us, or to steal, more likely than not he will do so. If we are convinced that he tells the truth and is honest, he may still occasionally lie or take something, but he will do so with such a bad conscience that he will do it in a most moderate way, give himself away, or in other ways soon try to correct himself. The same dynamic is at work in the mental patient. He, like the child, is so insecure about himself and about what he might do, that he looks for cues which will tell him what is expected of him.

Parallel observations may be made of animals. It is well known how ready a dog is to attack a person who is afraid of it, while the same dog may playfully approach an equally unknown person who thinks what a nice, friendly animal it is. This suggests that the more any sentient being is inclined to react on the basis of its instincts, the more responsive it is to our feelings about what it may do. Because their instinctive reactions are so much less overlaid with other modes of responding, children and mental patients respond much more to our inner feelings, to what goes on in our unconscious, than do healthy mature adults. Thus, if a mental patient sees us shrink away in anxiety, or feels offended by our repugnance at his behavior, however positive our conscious remarks may be, an attack may occur.

It's not the therapeutic task of mental institutions to be organized on the assumption that violence won't occur. This would be as foolish as is the parent who is convinced that his child would never lie. Instead, the therapeutic task is to hold the patient in such high esteem that the expectation is that he will always act like a decent human being. The knowledge that lapses may occur mustn't change this conviction, but it has to come from one's inner attitude and not from the realization that it will reduce attacks. Few dogs and no mental patients are fooled by a pretense of nonchalance when one is really afraid of what they may do.

When violence does occur, the therapeutic task is not to concentrate on preventing the damage the person may do, not even on what made him wish to act destructively. (The latter has its important place in therapy, but only later, after the patient is no longer in a state of agitated anxiety and hence his aggressiveness has subsided.) The immediate concern has to be with a human being's despair about himself, and with nothing else. The way to reach a person in such an emergency is by showing him that the deep empathic understanding that exists between him and those who take care of him has not been broken, but is still at work. This can be conveyed only through an appeal that is simultaneously directed to his deep unconscious and to his ego. The violent episode is brought about by these two levels of the patient's mind having lost contact with each other. Reaching both at the same time through the same appeal re-establishes the contact and the patient is no longer uncontrollably overwhelmed by the powers of his unconscious. This works instantaneously. When a contact is re-established, the person who is again in positive communication with the world no longer feels hopeless and hence does not wish to destroy.

A boy thought of himself as a machine; that he was run by motors. For months, in order to be able to move at all, he had to carry some motor with him wherever he went, otherwise his life, no longer powered by this machine, would immediately cease. Eventually he trusted another person to carry this motor for him, which permitted him greater freedom of movement. One day during this time he attacked some persons nearby. For their sake he had to be stopped.

His fury vented itself against his female counselor (attendant). She accepted his violent kicking, biting and scratching positively, well aware of how desperate he was. Nevertheless, his actions against his caretaker scared him sufficiently so that he turned his violence against himself and dashed into a busy street in front of oncoming cars. Running after him or shouting that he should stop seemed hopeless, even dangerous, because, feeling persecuted, he might have been even more likely to rush into a car. Almost automatically the counselor lifted the motor up and held it high for him to see, calling out, "Here is your motor." This worked and the boy, pacified, returned at once to his counselor (13).

This principle applies equally well when the violence is directed against another person. A patient felt cornered, lost all contact, became violent, and sank her teeth deeply into a staff member's arm. He called out with great concern, "Watch out, you're going to hurt your teeth!"—at which the girl not only instantly let go, but was back in contact. The staff member had intuitively understood that not only oral aggressiveness motivated her, but even more, oral anxiety. The girl was aware of the aggressiveness as she attacked, but not of the anxiety. When she became aware that both her aggressiveness and her anxiety were at work, she gained control over herself. Of course there was pain in the cry of the staff member, but the involvement with the patient was deep enough so that at the moment of crisis, awareness of the terrible predicament of the patient instantaneously won out over the counselor's concern with his own. This cannot be planned, but it is the natural result of a commitment to the patient, a commitment which becomes temporarily heightened in an emergency.

The attendant who restrains a violent patient is also concerned that the patient should not get hurt, but the concern comes from the outside, so to speak—is "alien"—and hence tends to aggravate the violent feelings. Any physical restraint, whether by straitjacket or the injection of drugs, is experienced by the patient as concern for others, not for him. Though he might understand later that it was done for his protection, at the time he is restrained he is convinced that it is done not *for*, but *against* him. This is what makes it such a destructive experience: even in the moment of his greatest anguish the concern is not for him. If it were, the restraint would not be necessary.

Attendants fool themselves into believing that if they restrain a patient their only motive is the patient's benefit. It may very well turn out that their restraint was indeed for the patient's benefit, but what the attendants feel as they are doing it is anxiety about what the patient might do to others or himself, and annoyance that the act of restraining seems to have become necessary. The patient feels only the anger, resentment, anxiety of those who restrain him, and their annoyance.

When the patient becomes destructive, concern for him will not be effective unless it has already existed for some time. In cases where this devotion is evident, it works so well that such scenes of violence are usually forestalled. Suicidal or assaultive tendencies subside as soon as the patient gets close to a person who is deeply concerned with his well-being, who has the inner conviction that the patient is basically a good person and becomes violent only out of despair, and who is therefore not afraid of what the patient might do. The worker thus concentrates on the ways to help the patient out of his misery, rather than on preventing his violent actions. With this inner attitude, we have found that it isn't necessary to use physical restraint.

In such places as the Orthogenic School this kind of staff attention and devotion to the patient and his needs extends over the daily, and nightly, round of all his activities. Unfortunately, in most psychiatric hospitals, people so seriously committed to helping the patient in his distress are only temporarily available to him. When he gets inundated by feelings of aggressiveness, usually there is nobody around who, through his deep empathy and concern, can assuage the patient's violence—thus, physical restraint or restraint through drugs becomes necessary.

Findings from other cultures confirm that these restraints are not needed if one person is continuously involved in a truly caring function with the patient. In Japan's private mental hospitals a female attendant, called *tsukisoi*, is with a patient at all times; during the day she takes care of all his physical and emotional needs, at night she sleeps beside him. As one observer puts it: "The constant presence of the *tsukisoi* and other personnel in the vicinity of the patient is the Japanese substitute for a heavy reliance on such security measures as steel screens, locked doors, and so forth" (25). Although in a radically different culture, the means these attendants relied on for quieting a destructive patient were similar to the ones used by the Orthogenic School. Since the schizophrenic person acts out of the same motives and has the same needs, regardless of his cultural background, this is hardly surprising. Caudill describes how a *tsukisoi* helped a patient come out of a suicidal phase. He had demanded a knife to kill himself, to which she said, "I am afraid you will be scared and frightened of blood if it comes out of a cut you have made in your body. All at once you will be afraid of killing yourself." And the patient, replying, "Do you think so?", no longer wished to do away with himself (25). Understanding the underlying anxiety, the *tsukisoi* addressed herself to it and not to the overtly expressed wish to do away with oneself. Her worry about how painful it would be to the patient was sufficient to restore his belief that some good things still existed in this world.

Simply to gratify a patient's delusional expectations will not help, but can only hurt him. A patient believed himself to be Louis XIV. As his family was extremely wealthy they bought an estate for him, decorated the manor house like a chateau, and staffed it with people who treated him as if he were a king. Yet it did nothing to help him regain his sanity. His deepest longing was not to be the almighty king, but to be safe from the dangers he feared, so that he would not need kingly power. The delusion of being king resulted from lack of respect for himself as a human being. Catering to his insanity did not increase his self-respect, it further damaged it. But building on whatever remnants of sanity remained might have helped him.

Luigi Pirandello, who had the finest understanding of various mental states, including schizophrenia, showed in one of his plays, *Enrico IV*, how destructive it is for a person to have his life arranged to fit his delusions. This makes him lose whatever little grip on reality he might have retained. Somehow, it is better to know one is crazy, and to be treated accordingly by reality, than not to know that one is demented in the eyes of others. If others act as if one's delusions are reality, insanity becomes too attractive to be given up. It prevents escape from a world of delusions.

Long before this play begins, a man—while dressed up as Emperor Henry IV—falls from a horse that has been maddened by thorns surreptitiously put under the saddle. He suffers a concussion and temporary insanity, which is characterized by the delusion of being the emperor. It is clear that among those responsible for the accident were some who for personal reasons wanted him out of circulation, and later they cater to his delusion by creating a setting in which he is encouraged to re-enact the life of the emperor. Among the unconscious purposes of the delusion, the play suggests the hero found his encounter with reality too difficult to handle and so set up a protective situation.

As the play opens, the delusions have worn off years ago. The hero would like to re-enter the normal world but because the setting of his delusional world is so seductive, he feels entrapped. Maintaining the delusional world for the hero has finally become tiresome for those who created it. They decide to shake him out of it. They do it in such a way that the hero knows his supposed friends have kept him entrapped in a mesh of delusions, for selfish reasons, rather than for his benefit, as he had assumed. He now sees that he has been induced to live in a world of insanity. He has been cheated out of a life of reality, which is the birthright of every person, and of course, he is in a great rage. At the end of the play he kills the person who, he feels, has gained the most from keeping him in a world of delusions.

After having committed the murder, there is no longer any way for him to go out into the world; he can only return to his madness and remain there (91).

Pirandello correctly observes that his hero, like all insane people, only partially believes in his delusions, and for only limited times. Much as they may wish to believe they do it out of consideration for him, those who cater to a person's delusions, consciously or unconsciously, engage in such deception only because deep down they do not want him to get well.

Life is often as strange as fiction. I have known many cases in which close relatives create a delusional existence for a person, ostensibly to make things easier for him. Unconsciously, though, they want him to remain a captive of his delusions; as much and as loudly as they complain about the hardships this entails, they want him to remain dependent on them. When the person comes to realize—as, at some level and to whatever degree, he cannot help doing—that what has supposedly been done for him has actually been done against him, it becomes that much harder for him to shed his delusions. Like Pirandello's hero, he comes to feel that he will be unable to regain his sanity as long as those close to him exist and continue to help perpetuate his condition. Only rarely, however, will he try to do away with *them*; much more frequently such *folies à deux, à trois*, or more, culminate in the sufferer's attempting suicide.*

The schizophrenic person doesn't need his delusions to be taken as reality. But it is necessary to understand just what it is that his delusions tell us about him, and his relation to reality, including where, how, and why his grip on reality abated, leaving his ego and his rational mind subservient to his id, his irrational anxieties, and fantasies.

In Pirandello's play, those who created the fictional world didn't want him to understand what made him escape from reality into de-

---

* I am here extending somewhat the application of the term *folie à deux* (*à trois*, etc.), which customarily refers to a delusion *shared* by two (three, etc.) persons. It seems equally appropriate, however, as a description for the sort of situation referred to here: that of collusion between a deluded and an (at least consciously) undeluded person in perpetuating the former's illness; and I have used the term in this sense at various points in the text.

lusion. Rather than face themselves and him, and look at the reasons which made him retire into his world, they catered to his sickness and thus prolonged it. It is very different when one explores the causes of this retiring: over a period of time, such understanding can help the patient regain a rational understanding of what it was that made him lose his mind as the only available way of coping with what appeared to be a totally unmanageable situation.

This is why the naïve therapist who tells the patient he has all the reason in the world for wanting to attack others, to get even for what was done to him, aggravates the situation rather than remedies it. He keeps the person caught within his insanity as the relatives of the delusional Henry IV did. It is beside the point to tell him that he no longer needs delusions or assaultive behavior to relieve his emotional pressures or to regain self-respect. To free the patient of his delusions or assaultive behavior, he must be given access to an existence which is radically different from the one that provoked his need to escape into a fantasy world. Contrary to his anxiety, he needs to find that life is now quite manageable through his own inner resources and the help the institution provides. We should be reminded that no animal attacks except to satisfy a want, such as food or dominance, or because it feels cornered. The same is true for man, though his needs are more than instinctual, so he can feel entrapped not only by physical enemies but also by symbolic, psychological, and moral dangers. Therefore the institution must be organized in such a way that the patient can learn, almost immediately, that his requirements will be met long before he feels a need to resort to assaultive behavior. Everything must be arranged so that he will never feel cornered.

For the rehabilitation of the mental patient half-measures will not do. This has been proven by the history of our psychiatric hospitals.

4 | Ambience: The Structure of Life

The institutional setting dominates the style of life that is possible within it. For instance, the standard of the furnishings available to psychiatric patients, in even the best institutions, is even lower than that of space, when compared with the minimum level a middle-class family would find acceptable. The most euphemistic statement about them I could find in the literature calls them "spartan" (114). Not much progress has been made since the time all a patient could call his own was a bed, a night-stand, and a chair.

Usually a group of patients—often many more than a dozen—have one loungelike common room available. These day rooms are typically furnished with some easy chairs arranged along the walls. There are card tables; sometimes such items as Ping-pong tables (although more often than not it is the staff who uses them, rather than the patients); and the ubiquitous TV. The TV is a very mixed blessing. It usually imposes more than it entertains since there are fights about which channel should be selected, and the decision is often made by the attendant on the basis of what he wants to watch. Disappointments, even lasting enmities, can result if a favorite program has to yield to somebody else's preference; and if one doesn't want to listen to the TV's noise, there is no escape from it. The lounge is supposed to serve as a living room, and even in a family sharing a room requires a certain adjustment of each person's desires to the comforts of others. But the members of a family, whether they realize it or not, have a great deal in common in background, outlook, and how things are done, which makes the sharing of a room possible. And if things become unpleasant, one can always retire to one's room, go outdoors, or busy oneself elsewhere.

The patients cannot do any of those things, unless they return to their bedroom from which they tried to escape into the lounge.

They have to share the lounge with people with whom they have nothing in common, except that the administration has decided they are to live in the same ward. Personal styles of life differ from patient to patient, and none is in accordance with that of the lounge. These rooms give the impression of a poorly and indifferently furnished waiting room, with anonymous chairs, nondescript tables, pictures selected to meet a common taste which is nobody's, and the old outworn magazines. The room has an air of empty waiting. It is made worse because those who use it know there is no end in sight.

That the patients are sensitive to this ambience may be seen from the remarks of a thirty-seven-year-old patient who at the time of this interview had spent nineteen months in a state mental hospital. When asked: "What do most of the patients do in these places?", she answered: "Waste time; that's the biggest thing on our hands. It's just a matter of wasting time." When pressed to say what they actually do, she replied: "Watch television or just sit there. Some of them just sit there, and you wonder how they can sit there for five, six, seven hours, just looking into space and not doing anything" (21).

Another obvious example of the ways in which the features of most mental hospitals condition the existence of patients and staff: If all the inmates of a populous institution—and for this their number need not be in the hundreds—have to be fed at the same time, by one central kitchen in one large dining hall, ways must be found to get them all there on time without creating chaos on the way. The simplest method to achieve this is to have them march in a regimented file. Even if there is no insistence that they do so, the arrangement of time and place of meals more or less forces it on staff and patients. "If at mealtime an attendant comes to the door and shouts 'Dinner' and sixty men get up and shuffle silently to the dining room," as is typical in mental hospitals, they might as well be regimented to do so (30).

If the noise in the dining room is not to reach upsetting levels—which would indeed be bad for both patients and staff—voices must be kept low, again irrespective of whether this is enforced by rules or made unavoidable by the situation. But to keep their voices low is not a simple thing for most mental patients; and then there are others who have a hard time talking at all in the presence of inhibiting influences such as the number of people present and the vastness of the room. Crowding many people into one large room makes for an explosive situation. Every teacher knows this, since most school riots break out in the school cafeteria. Thus behavior in large dining halls has always had to be regimented to some degree, and this applies to mental hospital eating facilities as well.

Even if the food is well prepared, mass cooking has its price. It is usually tasteless—which is particularly detrimental if patients are lacking in appetite because of their depression. Those who tend to overeat out of anxiety, or for other psychological reasons, will eat even more if the situation is not attractive enough to divert their attention from food to human company. Mass feedings interfere with individual choice in the fare, so what the patient eats is again regimented, even in a cafeteria-style arrangement. Regimentation of *what* one may eat thus compounds the regimentations of *when* and *where* one may eat.

It seems impossible to give a large dining room a homey feeling. This explains why those who have a choice—the staff—prefer to eat in relative seclusion, be it in a separate dining room, or a separate eating area. Even in the very rare hospitals where they eat the same food in the same room with the patients, the top hierarchy typically sit at a separate table by themselves. Some lower staff members, such as attendants and nurses, may occasionally take their meals with the patients; but the depressing feeling that the patients are shunned wretches is not entirely done away with. So the existence of separate dining facilities for the staff is another building feature that dominates the style of life likely to exist within it.

How the table is set, how comfortable the chair on which one sits, the attractiveness of the china, all symbolize the spirit with which one is received at this table, how welcome one is at this meal, whether one is considered important, whether it is going to be an enjoyable occasion. Little wonder that the psychiatric patient cannot enjoy his meal when the setting for it is unattractively "institutional."

There is also a vast difference between eating from a tray on which one has brought the food from a counter, all courses at the same time, to the table, and being served at the table one course at a time. The first method does not invite tarrying over one's meal, the second does; being pleasantly served gives one the feeling that one is important and well taken care of. The cafeteria style of eating, even when the food is prepared with attention to its quality, creates the impression that nobody personally cares very much about the meals. Even though the administration may seem concerned in general that all patients should be well fed, who can derive any satisfaction from being the recipient of a general concern, particularly on matters which are as close to us as the food we eat? We have all known times when even a particular kind of food we were not crazy about became very acceptable because some person known to us as an individual cared very much that we should enjoy it; and we know that what objectively may be excellent food can become rather tasteless when it is not spiced by personal attention.

Large institutional dining arrangements permit little else but cafeteria-style eating (and it is pretty much the same when the tray is brought to the patient in the ward or his room by an indifferent attendant). Lining up at the counter, having to pick up one's silverware instead of finding it nicely laid out at the table, all this and much more gives a patient the feeling of being a nondescript number in a series of people. The staff may be concerned that he should eat well, or that he likes his food; but such concern is only expressed in words, rather than by the institution's deeds. Therapists may try very hard to make the patient become a self-respecting, self-regulating person, but institutional practices such as these operate in the opposite direction for most of the day.

This situation exists even though we know that our primary attitudes to the world were originally formed on the basis of our earliest experiences, and that those we had when being nursed are among the most important ones. An ancient German saying tells that love comes from, or goes through, the stomach: *"Die Liebe geht durch den Magen"*). If we want to honor a person, we invite him to dinner; "breaking bread" together seals a friendship. How and what we serve him tells a person how much we care for him—or how little. As infants we first related to another human being as our mother nursed us. And food we eat pleasantly together remains the great socializer all through life. Knowing this, should we not expect that eating with others would be a most important situation for attempting to undo the pernicious consequences of the past, and to resocialize the mental patient?

According to psychoanalytic theory, psychosis represents—or is due to—a fixation or regression to the earliest stages of functioning, particularly to the oral level. (The same regression is typical also of senile patients, who form such a large segment of the population of mental hospitals; even more reason to try to counteract it through emotionally rewarding, that is, reconstructive oral experiences.) Since this is so, eating—particularly the main meals—and eating in company, or being fed by others, are experiences to which a therapeutic institution, and every therapist within it, ought to devote the most careful attention. Eating meals is a situation where old traumas could be counteracted by corrective emotional experiences in the very setting where they originally occurred. Since orality is the stage in human development to which the patient (emotionally speaking) has returned, it is therefore the locus from which his personality ought to be rebuilt.

Eating, sleeping, care of the body, and social interactions are the essential life activities. To these we must add personal relations, work, and thoughts, as well as kinesthetic and esthetic experiences. The emptiness of thought which the day room and all other hospital routines encourage has already been mentioned; and the buildings and furnishings are esthetically depressing. In regard to kinesthetic experiences, many have remarked on the dragging, shuffling gait in which mental patients move about, which visibly bespeaks lack of body tonus. While the presently existing mental institutions don't prevent kinesthetic experiences, they don't foster them either. Although most mental hospitals are located in nonurban environments, the lack of provisions and arrangements for hikes through the country, or swimming in lakes or pools, is pitiful. Even where tennis courts or ball fields are available, they are more often used by the staff than by the patients, like the Ping-pong tables mentioned earlier. It is often difficult to motivate mental patients to engage in any of these beneficial activities, but it can be done if the staff really wants to expend the requisite effort in planning, so that the activities become enjoyable to the patients.

The chance for meaningful work is largely absent, except for the highly scheduled opportunities offered by occupational therapy. The rest of the available work is stultifyingly routine. Outside mental stimulation—with the exception of the rare introspective hours spent in individual therapy—is denied, and the mind is permitted to lie fallow, with the result that thought moves mainly along depressive, delusional, angry, anxious, or compulsive lines.

Eating is the experience out of which our image of the world, and of our importance in it, grows. Early experiences around bodily care are the source of our feelings about our body—whether it is a good thing to be enjoyed, or a bad thing to be neglected; whether we derive pleasure from it or give pleasure; whether it creates anxiety in us, or arouses disgust in others. The way we were held, cleaned, and bathed as infants defines how we later feel about our body, and with it how we feel about ourselves. It also shapes our later kinesthetic experiences.

From our earliest experiences, it is customary in our culture that the bathroom is the place for bodily care. Its organization and equipment reveal what those responsible for it think about us in this connection. How much time we spend there and of what kind will reflect our attitudes about the body, both ours and others. Knowing the importance of good physical care of the patient, and Freud's thinking on the importance of the so-called oceanic feelings, as well as the deep emotional meaning of the fact that before birth we all lived surrounded by the liquid element, one of our finest psychiatric hospitals instituted the policy that all patients should receive a daily bath. As a therapeutic idea, this was certainly correct. But the number of bathrooms, which had to be used for other purposes as well, was insufficient to accommodate all of the patients who had to be bathed, so they were rushed through their baths. Rather than providing the intended emotional satisfaction, which would have increased the patients' well-being, it became a major source of aggravation to both patients and staff (114). And this is only an account of the physical aspects of the daily bath. It doesn't even include an analysis of the human elements—the only therapeutic ones.

The mother who believes that her infant's daily bath is for his benefit but rushes him through it, worrying about all of the other "more important" things she has to do; who feels obligated to bathe him when she doesn't really want to, will harm her infant. The same is even more true for the psychiatric patient. To derive real benefit from his daily bath, the patient should be able to utterly relax in it, enjoy it, worry about nothing, and luxuriate in how well he is taken care of by his devoted attendant who keeps him company. Rushed through by an impatient person, the bath which should have been an emotional boon becomes a physical and psychological insult.

Unfortunately, the bathroom is often also the locus of so-called hydrotherapy, including wetpacks, which is a restraining and punitive experience. This cannot help reflecting on the meaning of all other experiences in this room. Since its purpose is to get the patient "clean," it also has the connotation that essentially he has a "dirty" body. This is the exact opposite of the care which makes us enjoy our body and gives us the feeling that it's something to be proud of.

Clothes are important from an early age—what's next to our body reflects our feelings about it; what we wear on it adds to or detracts from our feeling that our body is worthwhile. Fortunately, most mental hospitals have finally done away with the abominable hospital gowns that patients used to wear. But while the use of personal clothing is much less degrading, patients still have to rely on others for access to them. Our personal possessions are experienced as extensions of our body, and they are all regulated by others in the mental hospital.

Not only is the patient crowded into far too little space, but the same is true for his possessions. There are many areas in addition to living space which we take for granted, and which we need; for example, closet space. The psychiatric patient is given about a fourth of the amount of closet area a middle-class person considers necessary. To make matters worse, the patient does not have free access to his closet, but must rely on the staff to open it, another source of much irritation for both staff and patient.

To use a psychological term of questionable scientific validity (13) but one which evokes an appropriate image, the psychotic person has typically "regressed" to much earlier stages of development; in many ways he functions like a young child. It is not just lack of organization, but insecurity which induces the child to want to surround himself with as many of his possessions as possible. This not only personalizes his living space but buttresses his still weak personality; it gives him a feeling of well-being and security. The child has a strong desire to be surrounded by his things, to feel that he can see and touch them at any moment. What he cannot see is simply no longer there for him; and what he cannot touch is not really his own. This is equally true for many mental patients. Their need for such reassurance is increased by the fact that they are forced to live away from home in an unfamiliar setting. Under such conditions we all have a greater need to be in close contact with something that is familiar, in order to have the feeling that we "remain in touch" despite physical distance.

Every mental patient has his measure of paranoia which makes him worry about his belongings and what others intend to do with them. Like the primitive man, he believes that those who are in possession of something that is ours have also gained power over us, and that they can use it to inflict harm on us. Thus the patient has probably a greater need than the young child to keep his possessions within easy reach. They will, he feels, create a wall of security around him, a boundary against an inimical world.

In the psychiatric hospital, things are further complicated by the insistence on cleanliness and order which comes from the tradition of the hospital as a place serving the physically ill. Clothes and other belongings get dirty when they are heaped on the floor or crowded haphazardly in a closet. So there ensues a sometimes silent and sometimes quite vocal and angry battle between the staff, who don't want the patient to have too many possessions creating chaos in the small areas available, and the patient, who feels that he would be better off if he could have more of his things available to him. As soon as anybody touches his possessions, the psychiatric patient, like the child, fears the damage that may be done to them and thus to him. If others put his possessions away or arrange them as they think it should be done, his anxiety increases. If his things are locked up, which is commonly done, it creates suspicion. If the patient had not been paranoid before, his confinement in a psychiatric hospital, and particularly the procedures over his possessions, may arouse and give substance to such paranoia.

Mutual aggravation and distrust are created when someone thinks we are wrong and we're convinced we are right. If we have to be dependent on those whom we distrust, it becomes detrimental to our self-respect, and in the mental patient, self-respect has already been badly damaged. Thus conditions imposed by the hospital structure are pernicious to the hospital's avowed purposes, and poison the relationship between staff and patient.

Even if the staff thinks these lock-and-key arrangements are the correct ones, they cannot like them. If an attendant is responsible for a number of patients, despite the best of intentions, he can't always drop what he's going to do and fetch something one patient requires. But he knows inside that the patient has a right to get his things which have been put away. This creates a conflict—the staff member knows he should accede to the patient's request, but he also knows that the situation forces him to deny it. It takes more awareness from the average attendant or nurse not to become annoyed at the person who is the cause of this conflict. But the staff member cannot blame it all on the hospital administration, which would be a way out of the conflict with the patient. He knows only too well what would happen if the patients in a populous ward were to get hold of all their possessions at the same time; how many arguments he would have to settle, how much policing he would have to do. Once more it is the way the building is constructed, with its inadequacy of space and its organization, that poisons the relations between staff and patient, yet these should be the means of the patient's cure.

This may be illustrated by the remarks made by a former psychiatric patient about the humiliation which comes from having to beg and being made to wait for the necessities of life, such as: a piece of wearing apparel, clean linen, toilet articles, a light for a cigarette. One of his most bitter complaints is that the nurses constantly brush him aside with an "I'll give it to you in a minute, dear," and go off, leaving him without the supplies he needs while he has to watch the nurses gossip with their friends (71). What the patient doesn't recognize, and cannot be expected to comprehend, is that the nurse is reacting to the emotions the patient's demands arouse in her. What appears to be a callous attitude to the patient's request is an unconscious effort on the part of the nurse to protect an endangered self-respect. In terms of her training, she is ready to meet the needs which come with or from physical sickness. This is her professional task and competence; that which gives her standing in her own eyes, and those of the world. But having to run and fetch all kinds of things all day long at the patients' request makes her feel reduced to the status of a menial servant. When being a servant is no longer viewed by society as an honorable occupation, this is particularly damaging to a person's self-respect. To demonstrate to herself that despite outward appearances, she has in fact not been reduced to such lowly station, she keeps the patient waiting as no servant could. Thus with the patients' possessions not freely accessible to them—in itself damaging to their self-esteem—the organization of the mental hospital forces the staff to behave in ways that further degrade the patients.

There are, of course, special situations where permitting a person to have free access to certain objects can be severely damaging to him, and where preventing him in a judicious and respectful way from getting hold of them may be therapeutic in itself. These are objects which, for delusional reasons, or because of past experiences with them, are threatening to the patient. What these may be is practically impossible to assess a priori; only the most careful observation of the patient's behavior can provide the necessary clues. Essentially, they are things which tempt a particular person to inflict damage on himself or others; for example, an object which he is convinced was deliberately left within his reach only because someone else—one of the staff, a member of his family, an enemy—wishes him to hurt himself or others with it. Practically any object, even the most innocuous one, can be invested with the most destructive potential and meaning from reasons which reside in the person's unconscious. A knife or sharp scissors may be perfectly safe with a given patient, but a pair of bookends may become part of a master plan to use them to hurt another patient. When the toilet water he had requested was given to a patient in a glass bottle, he was convinced this was done only so that he would break it and cut his wrists with a splinter. Another patient felt that any object that could be broken into sharp or pointed pieces was permitted to remain in the possession of another patient, accessible to both of them, only because the staff wanted her to shatter it and destroy her eyes with its pieces, at one time as part of a punishment for what she had seen and wanted to see, and at other times because the staff did not want her to be able to observe their nefarious doings.

There is no end to the destructive meanings psychotics can invest in objects. Given their paranoid fears and their conviction that the world wishes to do away with them (or that they deserve nothing else), practically anything that can be ingested becomes something for their self-destruction. If we offer candies, we do so because the sweets are poisoned. Thumbtacks and nails which are used to hang pictures are put there in the hope that the patient will pull them out and swallow them and die from a perforated stomach or intestines. Not just any pill, but even those they request or which are prescribed to cure a physical illness they know they have, are given to them so as to do away with them, or to control their mind. A jar of paint was only ostensibly given to a patient for painting; the staff really wanted him to swallow it and die.

This delusional meaning that can be given to any object, and the destructive use the paranoid person finds for it, is part of the justification for possessions being taken away from patients and kept locked up. There is some truth in the assertion that their things are locked up for their own good; it permits rationalizing psychiatric hospital practices, and justifies resistance to reform. Considering all the close observations and ever-changing decisions which would have to be made regarding safety, it is obviously much simpler to lock everything up.

It is important to convince the patient that his possessions will not be taken away from him, but will be kept inviolate; and that for his security and because of our concern for it, certain objects will be available to him only if and when it is absolutely safe. At the Orthogenic School, we solved this problem by putting certain objects temporarily under lock, but only in a place where the patient could inspect his possessions at any time and verify that they were still there. These locked closets were built into the rooms so that the patients could observe at all times whether anything was taken out of the closet. This can work in the way intended only if the staff is ready to open these closets for inspection whenever a patient requests it, and if the closet is so located that this can be easily done without inconvenience.

Without giving up their paranoid delusions, it is surprising how often paranoid patients can soon feel comfortable with objects they previously viewed as destructive, once they have observed both the respect with which their possessions are treated, and the staff's determination to prevent any destructive use of them. A girl who was convinced that we wanted her to hang herself with her jump rope asked many times a day for several days to see it where it was locked up, to make sure it was still there, and that nobody else was using it. During this period she also asked to jump rope many times a day. Each time she was given the rope, and when she stopped using it, it was immediately locked away. While using the rope for jumping, she would frequently try for a moment to wind it around her neck. After a few days, she had convinced herself that we were not angry with her for putting it around her neck, or for her testing our desire for her safety—that our main concern was her desperation. Observing that we were always there to take it away immediately without recrimination whenever she did test us, she said: "Now I know you don't want me to hang myself, and that's just a jump rope for jumping." From then on, the girl became convinced that the rope was locked up not for our convenience, or to punish her for the use she made of it, but only for her security. The rope, which had been extremely dangerous before, became a safe toy to be enjoyed. For a while, each time she used the jump rope she reminded us and herself, "It's just a rope to jump with," until all anxiety vanished and was replaced by the pleasure which comes with true mastery. In the process, those who had seemed to be her enemies—who had wanted her to hang herself—had now become people who could be trustworthy, at least on occasion, and who could help her gain mastery over haunting anxieties.

Afterwards, occasionally the girl would hand us the rope, saying, "You had better lock it up for a while," and later telling us, "I think I can keep my jump rope again." Locking up the rope under such conditions turned out to be therapeutic all by itself, as no other alternative could have been. She had to be able to convince herself that when she wanted to use it safely she could have possession of the jump rope; and that when it tempted her to hurt herself, it would be securely locked up. Moreover, locking things up and fetching them many times under such circumstances makes the attendant a person engaged in an important therapeutic task; this enhances his self-respect, and does away with any need to keep the patient waiting to prove one has not become a servant. This is a small example of how an architectural feature can make a mental institution more curative; not only by affording new opportunities for positive emotional experiences, but by offering the staff a chance to act therapeutically where they could not otherwise have done so.

In the case cited here, it should be noted that the respect with which the jump rope was treated—because an object with which we think of killing ourselves is not anything to be taken lightly—was as important as the respect with which the girl's need was dealt. In other situations it may be more therapeutic to destroy the dangerous object, to punish it for what the patient considers its murderous intentions. But this cannot be done casually, because the patient would not be convinced that we take him and his needs seriously enough. Under such circumstances any object may be destroyed only after much deliberation about whether this should be done and how, and if the patient should watch or participate in the procedure. To cast out such an object unceremoniously would be as ineffective as if the proverbial scapegoat were simply to have been thrown out on a garbage heap. The scapegoat could fulfill its function of cleansing the Jewish people only because it was appropriately exorcised, was treated ceremoniously and with great respect. The belief that the goat carried all this evil made it a most significant animal. Schizophrenics have invested deep meaning in many objects, including those which threaten them. Because the object is invested with vital—or rather, mortal—significance by the patient, we must treat it with great consideration so that he can believe that we respect both him and that which is important to him.

While having one's possessions locked up is damaging to one's self-respect, the battles which result are even more detrimental. Essentially the patient has two ways of dealing with the situation: he can fight for his rights, or he can give up and passively submit to the hospital routine, becoming an obedient patient. If he chooses to fight, which might seem more healthy, he is repeatedly defeated by not getting his way when he feels so strongly he is in the right. Continual defeat is destructive to one's feeling of self-worth. Many patients simply give in—to save themselves the energy that is wasted in a hopeless battle, and to gain those advantages which accrue to the "good" patient. They beg for what is their human right, and then reluctantly accept refusal. But in doing so they accept the staff's will over their own. They give up willing what they desire, and eventually give up desire itself.

Not to desire means not desiring to get well. The patient accepts somebody else's command, not only of his belongings but even over his wishes. This defeat does not originate in the staff's actual refusal, but in the power to refuse. To submit oneself to the command of others is most destructive to self-respect, much more so than not having access to one's things. The institution creates the perennial patient by having the patient give up desiring, by having the control of others imposed on him, and having him submit to it.

I am not suggesting that the locked closet, or insufficient closet space, does all that by itself. It is only one rather obvious example of how the building, and the spatial arrangements it imposes, goes against the putative purpose it was erected for. The most basic and crucial aspects of life—those which decide how we feel about ourselves and the world—when highly regimented, are made impersonal and unpleasant by the structure of the typical psychiatric hospital. Of course, some of life—especially work—in the outside world is regimented too. But this is bearable to us, because eating, sleeping, social interactions, kinesthesis and esthetics give us the freedom to arrange our life as we want—none of which is true for the psychiatric hospital patient. Since all that is available to him is the staff and the other patients, he has no freedom to choose his personal relations, or the surroundings where he may interact.

What is needed is a radically different way of thinking about how a mental hospital should be built, furnished, staffed, and operated, so that the life of the inmates would no longer need to be partly rigidly controlled and mostly left to chance.

Evolution and Change

In the chapters to follow I shall draw on what was learned from operating the Orthogenic School. Since this institution is not a dream of the future, but has been very much in existence for over a quarter of a century, it may serve as an example of what a mental institution ought to be like. What is described here is the result of experience; of years spent exploring how variations of features affected patients and staff, and experimenting to find out what is most suitable for the purposes of this particular psychiatric institution. What is said here is meant as an image to be emulated, not as a blueprint to follow slavishly. On the contrary, nothing is more stultifying for staff and patients than a static institution. Thus everything said and implied refers only to the Orthogenic School at one particular moment in its history: where it was when I left it.

If the mental institution is to symbolize a place where patients and staff become somebody different—where they can free themselves of the shackles of their sickness—then it has to be in the process of evolving at all times. Whether it is the use of rooms or furnishings, the planning of everyday life or celebration of special events, only that which still proves its merit should be retained, and even this may have to be adjusted to the changes-in-becoming. Rooms, for example, have to be rearranged to suit the present uses and users. If patients cannot rearrange a room and have something new provided in line with their changing interests and needs, how can they believe that the institution is serious about its commitment to the belief that things can change? But if it is shown that inanimate objects can serve new and better purposes, then the patient can take hope that change for the better is also possible for human beings in this place.

Freud remarked repeatedly that great artists and poets have always known what psychoanalysis tries to unearth through painstaking work—that nothing can be said about the workings of the human mind that has not long before been revealed as the essence of human nature. In regard to the principles which should inform the operation of a mental institution, various sayings of Goethe come to mind. First, from the last scene of *Faust*: The old Faust, unable to grasp what is going on, fools himself into believing that a state of near-perfection has been reached. Since he believes that things are so good as they are, he wishes that everything would remain unchanged (*Zum Augenblicke duerft ich sagen—Verweile doch, du bist so schoen*). He can believe this only because he is blind, and hence does not see the work of destruction which actually goes on around him. At the moment he believes that no change is needed, he dies: the wish for unchanging permanency is the death of life.

Of what it means to be truly alive, Goethe said:

> And till thine this deep behest:
> Die to win thy being!
> Art thou but a dreary guest
> Upon earth unseeing.*

(*Und so lang du das nicht hast,/Dieses Stirb und Werde,/Bist du nur ein trueber Gast/Auf der dunkeln Erde.*) Anybody who wishes to feel and be alive must be able to relinquish the old, to re-create himself. It has always impressed me how Goethe painted the picture of deep depression as the fate of those who remain static, who do not see life as a continuous process of becoming. Patients suffering from other types of mental disturbance than depression also need that continuous process of becoming. The institution and the staff, through the process of re-creating themselves, provide an image for the patients to follow, and by doing so give them the courage to believe that re-creation is possible, even for them.

This image of the old dying and the new coming into being should not be misunderstood as a mere thoughtless discarding; Goethe warned that whatever we inherit is not useful to us and is not really our own, if we do not through our own efforts succeed in making it so. (*Was du ererbt von deinen Vaetern hast—Erwirb es, um es zu besitzen*). Whether it is the furniture the patient is provided with, the routines of the day he is expected to accept, or the traditions about how a patient's birthday is celebrated—none of these or anything else will meaningfully ameliorate his disturbance, unless the patient makes them his own in his unique and personal way. As he

---

* Translated by Ludwig Lewisohn.

does so, he of course changes them to some degree. Thus with each patient's getting better, with each staff member's becoming more of a therapist—that is, with each of them becoming more fully a person— the institution also changes, all the time, often imperceptibly, but also often quite visibly.

II | *At the Orthogenic School*

5 | Needed: An Integrative Model

There are no good models detailing the ways in which mental hospitals should be built to serve modern ideas of institutional treatment. There are those who suggest a return to a family setting, or family-like situation, since at present psychiatric hospitals prevent the realization of these ideas. This is exactly the type of arrangement which was used earlier to cope with various social ills including insanity, but was given up as unsuitable for gaining the desired goal of rehabilitation.

More recently, similar plans are being proposed for housing mental patients or former mental patients in small group homes—the so-called halfway house, something between a family and an institution. Lately this model is also being widely used for the rehabilitation of addicts. There are a range of institutional alternatives to be considered—from a centrifugal design, such as the cottage type, to a highly centripetal one, such as the Orthogenic School—including other models such as the group home and the extended family. First let us consider the cottage system, so attractive to the eye of the beholder when compared to the huge prison-like structure of the old-fashioned institution.

The cottage-type institution, frequently used for children, tries to duplicate the character of a family setting. So-called cottage parents take care of what is considered a desirable, or at least manageable, number of children in a separate unit, the cottage. Several cottages, from three to twenty or more depending on the size of the population, form an institution, along with one or more central buildings which house the administration, staff offices, and school. The better ones among these institutions have spacious grounds which permit the single cottages to be separated from all others by lawns and gardens. Ideally, a cottage should not serve as a home for more children than could be found in a large family—six to eight—though most cottages house considerably more children. It is hoped that by copying family life as much as possible, children will fare best (45). There is little doubt that in the best of these institutions children are much better off than they were in the old-fashioned orphanage, or in the children's wards of mental hospitals.

More and more it has been recognized that not being able to live with his family is a considerable emotional insult to the child, no matter why it is necessary. It is felt, and for good reasons, that a child without parents is in as much need of therapeutic help—though his disturbance is usually much less severe, and more likely to be reversible—as the child who cannot live with his family because of the severity of his emotional disturbance. But when reshaping the old type of orphanage to the new cottage-system institution, too much attention was given to duplicating the externals of family living, and not enough thought to the family's essential internal workings. To begin with, if there are eight children in a family, they usually cover an age range of some twelve to fifteen years; while in most of these cottages the age span is likely to be a mere three or four years. With a wide age range, the cottage could not operate as a unit because the interests of the inhabitants would be too various and the styles of living too different. In a family, a wide range is possible because the children are all blood-related, have the same parents, and from birth have lived according to the same patterns set by these parents. But in the cottage system, youngsters who have shared nothing in common are thrown together.

The inhabitants of a cottage are expected to live a kind of white lie. They are supposed to form emotional ties of a child-parent nature to the cottage parents who, as authority figures and as providers, are much less than parents are assumed to be—so that the child receives double-bind messages as to what the cottage parents are all about. Even if the cottage parents live in the cottage, which is unusual, they are employees and not parents and of course safeguard their privacy within the cottage. But a "parent" whom one must not disturb during his off-duty hours is a false pretense, and is emotionally less acceptable than a caretaker who does not pretend to act as a parent. The children are well aware that the people who have real authority over them are the relatively distant and often seemingly inscrutable figures in the main building, which takes on something of the character of a Kafkaesque castle.

The greatest merit of the nuclear family is that it contains so few members, all living in close proximity, each member exercising significant influence on the others. Since the cottage patient has very little access to the main people in power, he has a feeling of power-lessness; the debilitating lack of influence on the powers-that-be inter-feres with his ability to become a self-regulating person. This same distance makes it difficult for the people who hold final responsibility to be fully aware of what goes on at all times in the cottages, therefore their decisions cannot be fully educated by such knowledge.

Wards Versus Cottages

Although adult mental hospitals are organized on the ward sys-tem, the patients' activities are split up over many locations and hos-pital floors, which makes the system similar to the cottage one. The cottage system has the advantage of a smaller and more human dimension, and because of the relative seclusion of the cottages it serves more autonomous living. While the distances between build-ings in the cottage system are greater, the walk back and forth is usually more pleasant because it takes one out of doors through gardened areas. There are, of course, differences between the two systems: the cottage system is frequently used for younger patients, and the ward system is used for most adults. In hospital wards, nurses and attendants rather than cottage parents are in charge of the minutiae of the patients' lives. But as a result of this, the lives of adult psychiatric patients are controlled and regulated to a degree that would normally be appropriate only for children. They have no access to their belongings. They depend on others for decisions on when, where, and whether they may go someplace, and what they may do there; their bed times, meal times, and all other details are under the control of others. Given the essential similarities, it makes little difference whether these others are called cottage parents, counselors, or nurses and attendants.

The more human dimensions of the basic unit of the cottage system, combined with the realization that most adult psychiatric hos-pital wards are much too populous, has led toward reducing the size of psychiatric hospital wards. Modern thinking also goes in the direction of giving each ward some measure of independence and some responsibility for the organization of its life, much of which is already true for the cottage system. Since the trend is universally going in this direction (as seen from official statements, such as that of the World Health Organization [2]), we should learn from the short-comings of the cottage system used by children's institutions, so that these mistakes are not repeated when adult mental hospitals are reorganized into smaller units.

. . .

Physical distance impedes communication; psychologically it is experienced as remoteness. Easy flow of communication should be the prime requirement in a therapeutic institution. In many cottage-system institutions those who have final responsibility for the well-being of a patient hardly know him by sight, they don't receive immediate reports on even very unusual events, and therefore they cannot help the staff in dealing with problems—at least not immediately. After a few hours or more usually days, when matters are hashed over in a staff meeting, and all of the emotional fervor has gone out of the experience, what was a deeply felt issue has become reduced to an intellectual problem. Thus an impasse in living is turned into a problem of therapeutic management, of psychiatric understanding. It is certainly necessary to understand mental patients, but what they need much more is a therapist relating to them in a live experience. The understanding should come from the immediacy of the experience rather than from later reflection. Because of the importance of direct contact between staff, patients, and the decision-makers, and because the patient needs to feel that he knows how the system he lives under works, a compact institution is preferable to the pleasant spacious lawns separating the cottages from the main buildings.

It is characteristic of the psychiatric patient to feel that he cannot comprehend or influence what goes on within and around him; therefore the institution's workings must be comprehensible for him to feel well taken care of, rather than imprisoned. Repeated direct daily access to those who hold the ultimate power is the best method for counteracting the feeling that one is powerless to influence one's fate.

It is not only the patient who feels that he is unable to understand why decisions are made in certain ways, or how he can influence the powers that rule his life. Most of the staff who deal directly with the patient are subject to similar feelings. Practically everybody who has studied psychiatric hospitals has stressed the discontent with its organization. When nurses and attendants are interviewed, they are uniformly deeply dissatisfied with the organizational structure of the hospital (64). Typically it is a system that has been described as "multiple subordination," which leads to a confusing overlapping and a multiplication of contradictory orders (57). A psychiatric hospital organized in this way is unable to provide that therapeutic clarity which the staff requires to help the patients, and the patient needs to reintegrate himself. According to a study by Jules Henry: "By dividing the personnel and thus facilitating the development of all those emotional problems consequent on a divided world, such an *external* system simply reproduces the *internal* system of the schizophrenic and, in no small part, the internal system of many others suffering from mental illness." (64)

After Henry had compared that system to the simple structure of the Orthogenic School, he noted how detrimental the former was to the mental patient. Though he had studied other psychiatric facilities before, it was only after he had become familiar with the direct and comprehensible way this psychiatric institution was organized that he could fully understand what is so wrong with the system under which most mental hospitals operate (see Chapter 17). He likened the School to a "small republic or a large family, depending on the point of view." It is the only system which does not externally reproduce the inner split which exists in the mind of the psychiatric patient. At the same time, it is so simple and well integrated that it can be easily comprehended and serve as an image for personality integration.

The good family is the best matrix for the development of a mentally healthy personality. This may explain why a children's institution can be a suitable illustration of what is wrong with the organization of most psychiatric hospitals, regardless of the age group of its population. With the exception of very rare special situations, such as the Israeli kibbutz system, mankind has not found any other arrangement but the family to secure personality growth. The important factor is not the biological parentage, as again the kibbutz and similar systems have made amply clear (15, 110, 111), but a setting which is of clear and simple organization like the family. Therefore an institution which attempts to develop a better-integrated personality should consider exactly which features of family living form the best setting for the growth of an integrated personality in the first place.

The Central Person(s)

Just as the parents have to be readily accessible to the child, the main figures of an institution must always be accessible to the patients. And as what happens within a family should be intelligible to the child, what goes on within the institution, in various buildings and their separate rooms, should be comprehensible to the patients. But above all, the patients ought to know and understand how the director operates. If the director is a distant figure, it will not work.

Because the Orthogenic School consists of a group of small

interconnected buildings, occupying less than about a third of a city block (the remaining area of the block is outdoor recreation space), I found it possible to meet each of the patients—sometimes in a large group, more often in small groups or individually—on the average four or five times a day. Thus any patient had at least that many opportunities to tell me directly, without need for any intermediary, what was on his mind, what had gone wrong, what he wanted me or somebody else to do for him. I visited with them every day, including weekends and holidays (with the exception of a month's vacation once a year and unavoidable short absences, when I attended scientific meetings), and in addition they frequently came to speak to me in my office. Consequently, I came to know each of the forty—and later fifty—children and young adults as individuals and they came to know me and what I was like, what I believed in, and why and how I functioned.

It wasn't just that I learned to understand the patients; they did as good a job in understanding me. It was often amusing to observe how they thought they got the better of me or other staff members by being able to predict what our actions would be. Unless they could come to do that, they could not develop that confidence in their ability to predict correctly which promotes ego strength and self-respect. The more one is able to predict, the more one is master of one's fate—provided the events are not destructive. Any occurrence that takes place without our being able roughly to expect it threatens our confidence in ourselves. Any event that somewhat conforms to our anticipations strengthens our belief that we are able to plan correctly for the future. Correct prediction also proves to psychiatric patients that despite the chaos in their inner life, there is a world outside where matters proceed in a reliable, and hence predictable form. Unless everybody can influence those who head the system, and unless the mode of operation is readily understandable and foreseeable, any system is felt as oppressive for staff or patients. The system is acceptable to one's self-respect only if it is dependable, predictable, and works reliably to one's advantage.

It's not sufficient for the patient to be able to complain to the director and thus secure the remedies he desires, or ask for explanations which make the operation of the institution intelligible and hence predictable to him. Those in charge of the institution must take the initiative in explaining why things are done in certain ways, in inviting criticisms and suggestions for making things better; and not once in a while, but as a continuous process of evaluating all that goes on. It is not even enough if the director frequently asks the patients about what they feel is wrong, or what could be done better. In doing so the director still exercises his administrative functions, and though the patient can influence the operation of the institution, it still dominates him (though he gets an inkling that it is there to serve him). There is a time for work and a time for play. It's a most important experience for the patients when the director sits down to play with them, something he enjoys as much as they do, not in the seclusion of his office as part of "therapy" but where their lives go on. Whether it is a game of chess or cards, Scrabble or Monopoly or pool or tennis, since the director—without deliberately trying to do so —loses as often as he wins in such games, it makes some of his decisions more acceptable, without oppressiveness. To some patients it is very important that they can beat the director fair and square, and they work hard at developing the requisite skills to do so—a training which brings them closer to respecting the rules of the game, and with it, the demands of reality. Within the limitations of time, even as little as one game every week or two is sufficient to make the impression; not only does the top person enjoy playing with the patients, but from time to time they can win out over him.

Mentioning a complaint while one is playing a game with the director, or while watching him play with another person, is much easier for some than replying to a direct question or button-holing him on his daily rounds. As a matter of fact, because of the casualness of the situation during such games, positive things are also said—about staff members, of something that has gone on—comments which otherwise might not have been made. Telling the "boss" what one likes about the institution has the quality of polishing the apple; but when he is in the process of being beaten in a game, one can do so without losing self-respect.

Meeting with patients as they return from an outing and asking them how they enjoyed it is much easier if their way back to their quarters leads them past the director's office—in which case such encounters are natural. Coming to the ward to ask such questions, on the other hand, gives it the character of an inquiry rather than of a friendly exchange. This is all possible only if the institution is compact, and no physical distance separates the top hierarchy of the institution from the patients or the rest of the staff.

By encountering the patients several times a day in their various activities, one also meets the staff at the same time in their different endeavors as they work with the patients. In this way one gets to know the staff not only as persons but also in their interactions with the patients, which one can observe during all aspects of their daily round of activities: how and what the patients eat, what they study, whether and what they read, how they fix up the place where they live; what and how they play, and how they rest; how they use the bathroom, how they go to bed, and how they sleep. Each day the last of these visits was at night, when the patients were either in the process of falling asleep, fighting sleep, or were already asleep. If the director often comes to visit with them where they are, it becomes much easier for them to visit with him, when they feel the desire for it. This only involved walking down one flight of stairs, and at the most crossing a hundred feet of corridor—which gave them the feeling that they were at all times in close contact with those who could affect their lives.

If there is no "main" building set off from the rest, and all activities go on in the same building where the patients live, this adds to the comprehensibility, and facilitates all interactions between staff and the patients. Having daily had the experience of some staff member bursting into my office or grabbing me as I walked by, of seeing him exhausted, desperate, or overjoyed by something that just that moment had happened between him and a patient, or between patients, I knew what everybody gained from such an exchange. But if the staff member had had to walk a few hundred yards from one building to another, through rain, snow, or scorching heat, he would not have come; or if he had, much of the emotional immediacy would have been lost (not to mention that he would have had to leave the patient for too long a time). The value of such immediate communication, and the opportunity to make on-the-spot decisions about both the meaning of an event and what action may follow from it, outweigh whatever the disadvantages of a congregate institution may be.

While this is based on a psychiatric institution serving children, adolescents, and young adults, I believe the same principles apply to all mental institutions, though some details have to be adjusted to the differences in age and the nature of the symptoms. Many of our patients suffered from the severest of all functional psychiatric disturbances; and at times, like all very confused, anxious, or angry people, all of them were extremely difficult to take care of. Therefore I believe that our experience is transferable to all mental institutions.

It must be emphasized that this system will work only if the institution is small, both in number of patients and in staff. Any additional person such as an observer or researcher makes communication, particularly of emotions, just a little bit more hazardous; and the knowledge that one is being observed interferes with spontaneity. While on the surface the addition of staff members bringing special skills to the work of an institution seems desirable, even one more person can make the system more complex and cumbersome, and less comprehensible to the patient. Ideally, the relations between staff members should be as clear to the patients, as consistent and definite, as those between two parents should appear to their children. It's not only children but staff who can feel lost in a maze of power relations and get caught in the complexities of the communication system, because of all the distortions that stem from one person relaying a message to another after a period of time. The smaller the institution, the fewer the dissensions and dissonances.

Country Versus City Environment

Today, when we all suffer from the effects of pollution, there is little argument that country air is healthier than that in our big cities. But I don't believe that this is the reason most mental institutions are still located somewhere in the countryside. The symbolic meaning of environments "out in the sticks" is not lost on the mental patient. It tells him that those who put him there did so because "Out of sight is out of mind." Though, in many of these rural institutions, the farm where some patients work is the best-run, best-equipped part of the hospital, nevertheless I firmly disbelieve that living in close proximity to cows and pigs has much therapeutic value. Such locations completely discount the merit of easy access to much-needed highly specialized skills, which are in short supply even in large urban centers. Equally neglected is the need for ready availability of a trained staff, and their desire not to be isolated from varied social contacts outside the institution, from sources of learning and culture, and from the many other experiences they need as relaxation after the demanding work with mental patients. Drained emotional energy must be replenished if staff members are to continue successfully to meet the challenges of their work.

Even if the institution has a lovely setting, wide open spaces and spreading hills are a tease if the patient cannot freely walk at will in the countryside. Prettily landscaped grounds impress the visitor and relieve the mind of those who relegate the patient to the place; but they do not deceive the psychotic person. He knows exactly what is put there for "show" and what is for his use. He recognizes the deceit only too well if the nicely kept lawns are not for him to play, rest, or sleep on; if the flowers are not there for him to pick, and if he were to take them to his ward there would be no vase to put them in. These show that those who come and go at will are considered more important than he, who has no choice but to stay.

Fortunately there has been a tendency lately to locate mental health services where the patients live. The catchment system tries to bring these services right into the communities where they are needed. But this system has rarely been extended to the services required by mental patients in need of prolonged hospitalization. It is detrimental to mental health for a patient to become disoriented, as we all do when suddenly projected into a strange environment. It is important for his feeling of mastery that he is at least able to manage his physical surroundings. Since the vast majority of people now live in urban and suburban settings, these are the situations in which the patient has been accustomed to live, and more important, to which he will return. This is another reason why an urban or semi-urban location is preferable. It not only attracts and revitalizes a better qualified staff, but also keeps the patient from feeling shut off from the only way of life he knows and understands.

Given the proper precautions, there is no reason to restrict even the most disturbed person to the institution at all times; on the contrary, such rigid confinement often adds to the disturbance. With the exception of short periods when the patient's fear of the outer world is so great that only the walls of the hospital can offer security, even a disoriented, delusional patient can manage some daily excursion into the wider world, as long as the company of a staff member makes him feel safe from the dangers which drove him "out of his mind." The patients feel some contact with an outside, "real" world, they get some practice coping, and preparing themselves for a fully autonomous life. A city environment offers better opportunities for continuing one's education, or for finding some suitable employment for the patient when he is ready for it.

Access to specific facilities depends on the population it serves. Being part of a great university, the patients of the Orthogenic School experienced the valuable feeling of belonging to an educational enterprise, and both patients and staff were offered a chance to participate in many cultural and educational activities. The more a setting permits both staff and patients to live in a community which best serves their needs and stimulates personal and professional growth, the more advantageous it will be. Nearby recreational, educational, and cultural facilities can greatly enrich the daily program and life of a mental patient. Most of all, daily walks in populated neighborhoods, with visits to stores and libraries, prevent the feeling of having been ostracized, put away, or of having to hide oneself.

For a large segment of the population, clothes have become a favored way to express individuality, which is all the more reason why patients should be able to select those they want to buy and wear (provided they do not use them as a way to further degrade themselves, as some patients will want to do). In a society where the ability to buy things for oneself is an indication of self-reliance (something that enhances self-respect), it is important that patients can do so freely. Sufficient funds should be available to the patient so that he can buy entirely new sets of clothing whenever he feels the need for this expression. Quite often a patient becomes determined to buy some outlandish piece of clothing. Agreeing that he certainly can buy it, providing the money, and helping him make his selections by visiting several stores, has often proved all that was necessary for the patient to decide that he really does not want to walk around attracting so much attention with his clothes. Experimentation in the store, and the demonstration that the institution will not interfere with his freedom of choice, is usually sufficient. But we have also found that some patients need to buy something outrageous, to convince themselves that they are indeed in charge of what pertains to their bodies. Once they had done so, the particular piece of clothing sometimes hung unused in their closet for a long time, until they finally disposed of it. Far from being a waste of money, if such experiences shorten the patient's stay by only a few days, they are dirt cheap compared to the expense of maintaining a patient in a mental hospital.

Whether we like it or not, ours is a consumption-oriented society. But since mental patients are excluded from production for most of the time they must live in an institution, it becomes more important that they keep in touch or regain contact with at least the consumer aspects of life. The significant principle here is that whatever the main features of a society may be, the more of these features that remain part of the patient's life, the better off he is; and the sooner he may be able to add others to the repertoire of what he can cope with. The more he excludes himself from these features of society, or the more his disturbance necessitates his dropping out of it, the more important it is that he retain those areas he is still able to manage at least to some degree.

The foregoing is only one example of an essential mistake made in the treatment of mental patients—a mistake which accounts for the prevalence of failures in institutional therapy. The institution thinks and acts therapeutically only in a few limited areas, such as individual psychotherapy sessions. In many other areas, it concentrates on facilitating staff work and the routines of administration, in ways which partly support therapy (the physical well-being of the patient, his protection against dangers) and partly undercut it (through imposing too much routine on the patient's life, and procedures which run counter to his self-respect)—with negative aspects outweighing the positive ones. Even worse, in its general planning and thinking, the institution fails to consider what might build up the patient's self-respect and personality. It approaches the patient on the basis of values which, while legitimate in society, are contrary to the handling needed for restoring a person to being a functioning member of that society. The institution must free itself of some of the dominant values of society, such as economic efficiency, or the "polite" denial of true feelings—which in many respects are open to question anyway. Many therapeutic failures are the consequence of the institution's applying, except in a few limited areas, the entire set of society's values to the patient's routinized, protected, semi-autonomous life, without considering how the patient experiences these values, within his distorted vision.

In an urban location, a judicious selection of society's features can be included so the patient can be exposed to these manageable experiences, while being protected from those that would overpower and further debilitate him.

Again, it must be re-emphasized that the institution cannot be too large, because then it would dominate the surroundings, rather than being a part of them. The World Health Organization has suggested that the best capacity for a mental hospital ward would be about thirty-two patients (2), which is similar to the number who may form a large extended family. In my opinion, the only problem with this recommendation is that it doesn't limit the entire institution to the size necessary to serve about this number of patients.

What good is a large institution that supposedly serves many, however economically, if it fails to help them? If we had the right type of mental health programs and psychiatric institutions, there would be no need to have so many hospitalized. Besides, small institutions which are well run have very little overhead when compared to large ones, even if calculated per capita. Finally, the breakdown in communication and torpidity of the large, complex hierarchy, so typical of large institutions, is one of the main causes of the inefficiencies which are obvious to every observer.

6 | The Eye of the Beholder: Architecture and Locale

The questions a prospective patient asks during the pre-admission visits—what he worries about, what he indicates doesn't interest him —reveal much about him and his disturbance, and, given his concerns, they permit us to offer him the reassuring experiences which count most. Here again, patients have learned to distrust what they are told. Therefore nothing we could say would be convincing if it were not in line with what the patient *sees*, and which obviously could not be arranged just to fool him into a false security. The rooms which he visits could be furnished just for this purpose. But even the mentally deranged person usually knows that the building itself—the walls, porticoes, and walkways—are permanent structures which cannot be momentarily prettied just to give him a good impression.

Because the outer appearance of an institution tells so much without words, it is very important. I am not at all certain that our admissions procedures would work if the prospective patient had not already formed an impression of us when seeing the building and some of the rooms. These impressions rarely reach the patient's conscious thoughts; they remain on a more effective subliminal level.

"Stone walls do not a prison make, nor iron bars a cage," we are told, but nonetheless they clearly bespeak the intentions of those who build such edifices and put others into them. And while a rare and extraordinary person with great effort may be able to transcend the conditions of his environment, for most of us, it is the environment which conditions the kind of life that unfolds within it. This is especially true for the psychiatric patient. Locked doors and barred windows don't provide the setting where a soul is likely to become able to free itself of its shackles. The vast majority of our mental institutions are castle keeps that imprison the soul rather than homes where a badly torn mind can be so tenderly cared for that it learns to live comfortably within its body, and with itself. Body comfort can go a long way toward making the soul comfortable.

Mental patients are far more affected by their first emotional experience on seeing the institution than by any rational judgment. The outer appearance of most institutions bespeaks little hope that the patient will find his way back out of the jungle of his mind. Once inside, the way his room is furnished or usually hardly furnished; the way his movement and the use of other rooms is regulated; the appearance of the corridors he must pass through—all these tell the patient he must now subordinate his needs to the institution's convenience. Henceforth he has no say in the arrangements of his life or the place where he is to live. Things ought to be precisely the other way around, so that he might regain a feeling of competency and personal worth.

Through an early experience I learned how a mental hospital reflects whom it is built for, and who is important in it. On my first visit to an old state hospital, famous for its pioneering work in moral treatment, I walked through a forbidding gate to enter an oppressive compound with heavy stone walls that looked like an eighteenth-century fortress. After a tour of barren, overcrowded wards where all a patient could call his own was a bed and a chair (and even these he could only use at certain set hours), I was entertained at dinner in the palatial apartment of the director, with a dining room and living room the size and furnishings of which reminded me of European castles. This and other experiences taught me how well the architectural arrangements and furnishings of a mental institution express who is important, and who gets the right and wrong end of the stick within.

If I hadn't learned this lesson earlier, the patients would have taught it to me during my first weeks at the Orthogenic School. Changing a number of the School's features and practices took some time; one of the first new arrangements was to unlock all doors, except those to the offices, because the patients' records were kept there. The patients had difficulty adjusting to these changes since they had been kept in bounds for a long time by rigid controls, which the staff had imposed on them. Naturally they overreacted. The many changes made in short order led to various temporary disruptions, which I considered a fair price to pay for improving so quickly the ethos of an institution.

Though I did not like the large, impressive director's office with its huge imposing desk, I felt that moving the office could wait. But I was wrong here. I learned the hard way that to the patients it symbolized the institution's spirit. With the director's office went a closet in which cookies and sweets of all kinds were stored. My predecessor had kept it carefully locked, although it was located behind his big armchair and accessible only to him. From there he would dole out the goodies as he saw fit. I unlocked it, but because of its location it was not readily accessible to everyone at all times. One morning when I walked into my office, I found a huge meat cleaver on my desk. A note was attached: "This time it's on your desk, next time it'll be in your head."

In the rash—and ambivalent—excitement about all the changes going on, a staff member, trying to go along with new principles he did not yet fully believe in and which therefore could not implement correctly, had taken a group of adolescent boys to fix a fancy meal for themselves in the kitchen late at night. I had suggested that he do so, despite his objection that it would never work out without something untoward happening. I had wanted to prove that one *can* trust mental patients if one is trying to make life more pleasant for them. However, I had failed to wait long enough for this staff member to understand emotionally, as well as intellectually, what was involved in the new spirit. I pushed him to do things for which he was not yet really prepared.

If I had known then what I learned from this and similar incidents, I would have explored at length why the staff member believed something would go wrong—what and how. But I was in a hurry to improve things for the patients, and also to gain their good will, without which the improvements would not work. I had not yet understood that unless certain underlying attitudes in the staff were changed, even vast improvements in the institution's program would achieve little. So instead of working with the staff member on his inner attitudes, I tried the short-cut of having experience teach him. When he objected, I simply replied: "Why don't you try to find out for yourself?" As I learned to my chagrin, this invitation prompted him to try methods which would prove him right, and me wrong. (Later, when similar things happened, I referred the staff to the story of *The Good Soldier Schweik*, in which the Czech private executes all the orders of his Austrian officers to the letter but in such a way that things turn out all wrong, making fools of the officers [61]. The novel illustrates how easy it is to pervert the intentions of others into the opposite effect, if one is deeply opposed to them.)

While the patients and this staff member were cooking and eating the meal, everything went fine, and everyone had a good time, as anticipated. But as the night got later and the boys were taking their time cleaning up, fooling around in doing so, the staff member's ambivalence got the upper hand. Suddenly switching his tone, he roughly ordered them to hurry up, get busy, and get everything in

order, and leave the kitchen in five minutes. He switched from participant into jailer, watching the clock instead of joining in and observing
the activity around him. One boy reacted to this total change in
attitude by returning to his old deviousness and hostility, and hiding
a meat cleaver under his jacket, took it with him back to the
dormitory. The staff member, in a hurry to get the "experiment" over
with, failed to notice anything unusual.

The boys didn't use the cleaver to break down the locked door to
my office, but to pry open a skylight which led into it. Once inside,
they carefully unhinged the door to the candy closet and left it lying
on the floor. The message was clear: "You are reforming this institution all wrong; dangerous instruments such as the cleaver should
not be accessible to us—but cookies and candy should." When I saw
this, the goodies were moved at once from the closet to a place that
was accessible at all times to everybody. Then the staff members were
advised on how to behave with patients in locations where potentially
dangerous objects were within reach.

A few days after the closet incident the same group of adolescent
boys broke out of their second-story dormitory, where the bars had
just been removed from the windows. They decided to climb down
from a window instead of walking out of the now unlocked doors—
because walking out would not be breaking out of a jail, as they explained later. They purposely made a lot of noise so that we would
catch them "in the act," as we did. I begged them to wait a moment
until we had time to carry some mattresses out and put them on the
ground in front of the window, so that they would not get hurt if they
fell while climbing down. They watched with amused interest until
we had piled the third mattress on top of two others, then they
changed their minds, and came down to help us carry the mattresses
back indoors. Our manifest concern for their safety had instantly
changed the "jail" into a relatively desirable home.

The two incidents were closely connected. The same staff member and some of the same boys were involved in both. The first time
the boys had acted when neither the worker nor I was around. This
time, while they acted fairly late at night again, they did so while the
staff member was still with them and they knew I was around. They
wanted to find out whether he would again let them do something
destructive by misusing the act of giving them greater freedom, while
making sure that I was around, so that somebody would protect them
against themselves in case he again neglectfully gave them scope to
hurt themselves or others.

In both cases the issue was safety. No matter how much they
were frightened of their own behavior, this time the staff member

worked doubly hard to make things secure for them, using what he had been able to learn from the last experience. The day after the cleaver incident, when he began to understand that he had provoked what had happened, the staff member had apologized to them for his negligence. This had provisionally restored him to their good graces, since he was one of the few holdovers from the previous régime who sincerely tried to adapt to the new ways. But the patients knew that words come easier than deeds, so they tested out whether the apology had really reflected a change in attitude. The second incident showed them that we stuck to the new policy of not bossing them around unless we felt it necessary, but that we would make it safe for them to do what they wanted. This was permitted only when we were sure that there was no danger involved.

The two events taught different but equally important lessons. It was not enough that the sweets were freely and equitably distributed. To help restore their self-esteem the patients needed to have free access to the candy rather than having to depend on another person for it. Removing the bars from the windows did not change a prison into a home, nor did an acceptance of their wish to leave. But, at the moment when they defied the institution, our concern for their safety made it become a home.

Since mental patients feel totally devalued, we can help them regain their sanity only if they can feel from the beginning that the mental hospital is a place that is entirely there for them, that they are all-important, and that here the very best is not too good for them. Then it will be possible to silence the overpowering voice within them, which tells them that they are no good at all.

The foremost guiding concept in building and furnishing the mental institution is that it should be designed truly to serve the needs of the *patients*—not to satisfy an irrational anxiety that the staff and the world-at-large must be protected against the patients. The desire to spend as little money as possible on these patients is equally irrational and detrimental. Our experience has shown that the nicer and more attractive the surroundings we create for the patients, the less deliberate or careless destruction takes place. On the contrary, the patients soon take pride in taking good care of things entirely on their own (without any suggestion that they do so, as this would only interfere with their spontaneous desire to keep what they themselves enjoy in good order).

.   .   .

First Impressions

Like other Germanic cities, Vienna used to have its "Fool's Tower," the forbidding prison-like structure where the insane were locked up. The more intractable ones were chained to the walls, which spectacle served as pastime for the solid citizens on Sunday afternoons. Under the humanitarian impact of the Enlightenment, around 1800, Vienna's Fool's Tower was abolished, and replaced by an asylum not dissimilar to those erected in the United States during the last century, many of which are still in use. It was an institution based on the conviction that only a strictly regimented life could offer the "moral treatment" which would cure insanity.

By 1900, based on an uninterrupted tradition of research and innovation dating back to the 1700's, Vienna's medical school was one of the most famous in the world. In 1902, precisely the time psychoanalysis had its beginning in Vienna (though the city paid no attention to it), the government of Lower Austria (of which Vienna was the capital, as well as of the entire Austro-Hungarian Empire) decided that this asylum was no longer a fit place for mental patients—that it should be replaced by a different type of institution, which would serve its patients better. Not only was this an unusual decision, but the world-famous Austrian architect Otto Wagner was commissioned to design the new institution. Wagner (127) was Austria's greatest architect at the time and one of the fathers both of the art nouveau style and of modern architecture in general (together with his American contemporary, Sullivan). It was Wagner's desire, as much as the decision of the government, that this institution should not be hidden, but be erected at a dominant location in the city of Vienna, where it could be seen from far away. To avoid any harmful connotation such as "Fool's Tower," it was decided this mental hospital should be known simply as an institution for the cure and care of patients, to which would be added the name of its location. Thus its official name was Lower Austrian State Institution for Care and Cure at the Steinhof (*Die Nieder-Oester-reichische Landes Heil und Pflege Anstalt am Steinhof*). From the time of its opening, it became a center of psychiatric research and teaching.

The overall plan for the entire institution was Wagner's. Unfortunately, he was responsible for the design and erection only of the central building, which dominates the institution and may rightly be called its "crowning" feature. This was a church which could be seen from afar—particularly its striking golden cupola, which reflected the sun and immediately became a Viennese landmark. The church's interior, and many features of the exterior, were designed and executed by the foremost avant-garde Viennese artists, who had just formed their own movement, the Secession. The church's stained-glass windows, for example, were the work of the painter Kolo Moser. Beyond doubt, this church was the greatest achievement of the art nouveau style in Central Europe. (Although nearly seventy years have passed, to my knowledge there is no other mental institution which the most famous architect of his day was asked to design.)

The patients knew that this building, one of the most beautiful and impressive in the city, was there only for them. The building which housed the administration was clearly less impressive and of secondary importance. (It is also not lost on the patients of our mental institutions that almost always the most impressive edifice is not for their use, but houses the administration, the director, and the top hierarchy of the staff.) In a deeply religious country such as Austria was then, it meant a great deal that the patients had a much more beautiful, impressive church for their use than nearly all the other citizens. It meant even more because in this church, the most important building of the institution, they were all equals—according to Catholic tradition the lowliest patient counted as much as the director himself.

The psychiatric methods applied in the Steinhof institution, and the new treatment methods being developed by Freud, were worlds apart in those days. But perhaps it was the same new spirit of enlightened humanity toward mental patients which gave Vienna's institution for the insane a dome of gold, and inspired Freud at the same time and place to devote himself to the treatment of the "neurotic" and the "insane." This deep interest led him to find that the two have more in common than differences with the "normal" person—that the mental patient and the rest of us are much more alike than anybody had ever thought.

The importance a building has in creating the spirit within it should not be underestimated.

If patients are to be introduced into a mental hospital as it should be done, in a way that starts them on the road to recovery as soon as possible, care must be taken that the patient has ample chance to look the building over before he enters it. Even if his anxiety does not permit this, the sincere suggestion that he might do so can be sufficient to set the stage for what is to follow: namely, the attempt to restore his mental health, based on his own evaluation of situations and not on that of others. Such a suggestion cannot be a standard "procedure" without empathy for what it all may mean to each particular patient.

In a small institution everyone knows the approximate time a prospective patient will arrive, and the staff are prepared for it. I have often formed the most important ideas about how to approach a patient by watching him on his arrival, through the window of my office, which was located close to the entrance: observing what he scans, how he reacts to what he sees, how he pretends not to look at anything, or in all directions except toward the institution; from the interactions between him and those who bring him, whether they give him a chance to look things over, and do so themselves; how he walks up the few steps leading to the door or tries to avoid doing so; how he rushes or is rushed into the building. I could gain clues from all this about how to relieve the patient's anxiety, or even how to gain his confidence. These initial observations are far superior for getting a "feel" for the patient than can be gained from studying the often voluminous records. Although the records may be full of significant material, they don't refer to the particular anxieties and interactions of the moment.

For psychotics of all ages, every experience becomes a symbol of intention and attitude, which matters far more to them than the experience's rational purpose and meaning. To us, one color is more pleasing, cheerful, or depressing than another; to the psychotic, one color (or form) means good will, another means evil. Since the walls in most mental institutions are painted white or gray, that is, a non-color, the patient sees that these are lifeless places to be. This happens although it costs no more to paint or maintain walls in cheerful colors.

How should the patient see the institution? It shouldn't be too small, so that it seems confining, nor should it be so large that it appears overpowering. It should fit unobtrusively and harmoniously into the neighborhood but without any loss in individuality. It should have a character of its own, but not so much that a patient will feel conspicuous as he goes in or out. It should be sturdy and substantial enough to protect us, without seeming restrictive; a comfortable home that fits for living as a comfortable old shoe fits for walking. Hopefully it will bespeak some grace in living, reassure any sense of insecurity without domination, and make a positive appeal to our esthetic feelings. It should convey unity, but it should contain well-articulated individual features. It should show us an open face and convince us that within it, individual man is the measure of all things. It must suggest dignity and self-respect, since this is what the mental patient needs most. If such dignity appears to be time-tested, this is to the good, but a new building will do, if it conveys these feelings. In short, the building should invite us in. If this seems a lot to ask of a building, we must remember that bringing mental patients back to health is a very difficult undertaking.

When planning a mental institution one must realize that mental patients can see one object as safe, and another as personifying persecution or despair. Irrespective of how the rest of us view the object, everything becomes a symbol (106, 107). Most of the patient's mental energy goes into ruminating on the hidden meaning of each color, each object, and its placement; what it tells him about the institution's intentions and his future. Everything has its private meanings and secret messages which he tries to decipher. If we want to reach the psychotic, we must resort to the symbol first of all, long before we can count on reaching him through rational thought. This is even more true for emotionally disturbed children. Even the normal child will gauge our intentions not so much by what we say, not even by what is implied in the gift we bring him, but from the way we spontaneously treat his teddy bear. He will also estimate our feelings from the ways in which we decorate his room and, most important, whether he can keep his room the way *he* wants it; whether he can have the walls painted in the color he chooses, or if he can paint them himself and put up whatever he likes on them.

The more disturbed a person is, the less he believes what we say and the more suspicious he is of what we do. From their own past experiences with double-bind messages, these patients know better than to trust what we say. Since the patient knows that he himself lies to dissemble his true feelings, he is even more convinced that he can't really trust what anyone else says. He is a little more ready to believe what we do and how we approach him. But most of all he believes what he can experience himself: with his own eyes, by touching, and, especially, by doing.

Recognizing these facts, mental institutions should not rely on conveying meaning only through rational arrangements. They should also know that every detail of building, action, and attitudes is a carrier of symbolic meaning. If every room is furnished alike, the patient will know right away that we don't respect his individuality, but that we want to fit him into a common mold. Therefore the ways in which an institution is built and furnished—down to the last detail of its light fixtures and chinaware—must convince the patient that this is a place where he is truly welcome. It must convey to him that everything has been made ready for an esteemed guest in the hope that he will deign to stay for a long time. When he can feel that he is respected as a unique individual, he can afford to let down his defenses.

Fairy tales, as much as any consciously literary production, reflect primordial human anxieties and hopes. A recurrent theme is that of being pushed out of an unfriendly, if not outrightly destructive, home, as were Hansel and Gretel, for example. Fear of losing one's home, abandonment, what has been labeled "separation anxiety" in psychiatric literature, is one basic, "existential" anxiety; fear of damage to one's body, including death, is the other. Fairy tales often end with assurance about both: after meeting and overcoming the dangers involved in encountering the world—symbolized by dragons and witches and the like—the reward is a safe and fitting home, and a long, happy life. Here is a reflection of how bodily safety, a happy life, and a good home all go together in the unconscious of mankind; one without the others can hardly be imagined. A good home in our unconscious symbolizes a good life; a good life cannot be imagined without a good home.

The body is the abode or home of our soul; since it did not sufficiently protect his psyche, this residence has failed the mental patient. Our "home" is what should give security and structure to our life; tangibly it houses our body, and symbolically our soul. If the mind falls apart, the "home" has failed in both of its protective functions—it has provided neither emotional comfort nor symbolic security. If for no other reason than its incredibly important symbolic meaning, the patient should see the mental institution as a good home which will shelter his soul and his body, permitting both to abide in a place of security.

Now it could be argued that since some real home has failed many a mental patient, the institution should not look like or pretend to be a home, since this once proved so disappointing. Indeed, the institution must be very different from the home the patient had to leave for his sanity, and maybe also for the safety of his body. But in all who have had unhappy homes there is the hope that eventually they will find a good one; the institution should have the potential to become the patient's new and better home.

In a building that looks like an institution the mental patient, feeling "at home" nowhere and with nobody, not even in his own body, will not gain what he needs most: the feeling of finally having found a true home. But he may feel he has a chance to find this in what looks like a potentially good one to him. A spanking new building is not likely to convey this feeling; it gives the impression of not having lived long enough to understand all the troubles of life. An older building, giving a lived-in impression, seems to have gone through and survived a lot. This is why it is preferable to adapt a suitable old building for the purposes of a mental institution. When this isn't feasible, all effort should go toward giving a new building a lived-in feeling. The place he is about to enter should convey to the patient that here is a place not only for him, but also for all that ails him, his old troubles and anxieties. It is counter-therapeutic to tell a person that in the institution all that he fears will no longer threaten him. The fact is that a person's anxieties are very much intrinsic to him. Though the psychological difficulties that crush him are what make his life miserable, they are nonetheless an essential part of his existence. To promise that he will be freed of them means that we really don't seriously consider that which is oppressive to him and hence we don't take him very seriously. He also fears that something is to be taken away, and then he does not know what will be left, if anything. To give up the bad may leave us with nothing, unreasonable as this sounds when viewed rationally.

However, our unconscious is anything but rational. In the unconscious, the bad can be let go of only after the good has filled the space; then there will be left no hollow emptiness. Therapy with the mental patient should thus concentrate on making good experiences available to him—which eventually will counteract the residues of the traumatic past and thus reduce the impact of the bad on his present life.

Boundaries

The schizophrenic is uncertain about the boundaries of his body. He is confused about what pertains to his self. The earliest precursor of the ego is the so-called body-self. Only as the mind matures and comprehends what goes on inside and outside of us, do the two become separated in our experience into our body and our self. But so closely do the self and the body remain related in the unconscious that nobody who is truly secure about his body can "lose his mind." What *it* can do comes to be experienced as what *I* can do. If I feel there is nothing I can do about my life, I also feel that my body is badly deficient. Though many schizophrenics have prefectly good bodies, because their self has disintegrated they are convinced that their body has also fallen apart.

A typical manifestation of this is the hallucinatory voices which are heard as if coming from the outside, though they are the person's own thoughts. Much of what goes on inside the mind or body is experienced as residing outside it by the schizophrenic. On the other hand, he also begins to feel that because he wishes them, he causes things which are quite independent of him. Somebody stumbles and falls, and the patient is convinced that he pushed the person down, though he was yards away. He wishes for something and he is therefore convinced it happened, or will soon occur. His body will at one moment expand to contain things and events that are outside it, and at the next moment shrink to near-nothingness. As his body has no definite, ascertainable, permanent form, objects also change in size and appearance, depending on how he experiences them at the moment.

Since his body (thus his self) has no definite boundaries, things on the outside become terribly important (106). The study of people whose personality development is most severely arrested, such as autistic individuals, has made it apparent that since they feel their self has no permanency, for them not to get entirely lost in a quagmire, objects have to remain unchanged; they must always remain in the same place, in the same position (73). These objects must provide some order, since the patient finds none in himself. When the patient begins to try to establish a more definite, circumscribed self through therapeutic help, he will create definite boundaries on the outside—so that the self has some definite limit and won't inexorably spill out or be helplessly invaded. Limits on the outside have to contain the self until it takes on definite and permanent shape and there no longer exists a question as to what is happening inside the body and what outside it (13). If the building has to serve as a temporary substitute boundary for a self that has not yet achieved its own boundaries, it is important that it should appear worthy of this task.

Normal persons in crisis situations provide examples of this intimate connection between feelings about the body and the self, and how these influence each other. In adolescence, the body which seemed so reliable and permanent in shape suddenly begins to "burst at the seams." It undergoes rapid change, and develops new functions for which the person is unprepared. This uncertainty is accompanied by deep feelings of insecurity about the self. The adolescent in crisis, today as in times past, makes it amply clear that he feels two opposite ways: he feels unable to exercise control, controlled and pushed around by others; and he also feels that he can run the world much better than anybody else. At one moment he is convinced that he can do practically everything (the self spills over), and at the next that he is helpless and can do next to nothing (the self has shrunk into insignificance). No longer truly at home in his body, he cannot feel at home in the world. Rapid alterations in the feelings about the body, and about the self, are so inextricably interwoven that it would be difficult to be sure what causes what, if the crisis in the adolescent's self was not so clearly preceded by changes of his body in form and function.

Without being conscious of it, schizophrenics and other less severely disturbed persons feel the need for safe boundaries. To reduce their confusion and give form to their formlessness, they require noticeable structure and with it security. The institution is thus immediately evaluated by the prospective patient as to its dangers and suitability in this respect of substitute boundaries. As one student of the psychotic's break with reality put it: "Letting the ego flow into objects is an exquisite schizophrenic mechanism which always causes great pain to the ego, which thus feels deprived of its identity and responds with anxiety to a state of extreme impoverishment" (33). Thus the building (and later all of the furnishings, the daily round of life, the staff, in short, all of his existence within the institution) must seem doubly trustworthy so he can let his ego flow into it. This will be ego-supportive rather than destructive, as he can incorporate and identify with its significant aspects and build up his personal identity. This needs to happen because the tragedy of the schizophrenic is that his life circumstances forced him to spill out his ego energies into a world which devastated him, while his efforts at incorporating significant figures were utterly destructive to him. Thus what he wants to know about every aspect of the institution is not just what it may mean to him, but also how he can relate to it, and how each relates to the others. He worries: Will this place provide greater safety, or again disintegrate me? Will it help create order out of my confusion, or only disorganize me more? Will it hold me safely together when I am about to fall to pieces, or will it force me into a mold? Is this building attractive and reassuring enough to become the shell which will protect me as I discover and ascertain my self-boundaries, and do this without overpowering me? Deep down the patient knows that this place will have to serve as a chrysalis for him if, after a period of dormancy and inner development, he is to emerge a full person.

7 | The Silent Message: The Unicorn and The Phoenix

For more than forty years a part of the Orthogenic School has been housed in a building that looks like a spacious Georgian home. It had previously housed a Universalist minister, his family, and a small seminary of the church; thus in a way, it had been the home of an extended family all along. When in about 1930 it became the home of the Orthogenic School, the *genius loci* did not change: it continued to be both the home of an extended family (although a much enlarged one) and a place dedicated to serving humanitarian ends.

When we began our work at the School in 1944, we didn't have the freedom to create an entirely new home for it. But as we began to reshape it after our convictions, we found that reorganization, when compared to an entirely new creation, conveyed an important message to patients and staff: in regaining mental health—that is, in restructuring human personality—one never begins from scratch. We must rebuild, reorganize, use for new and better purposes, unify, and integrate the pieces which happen to have accumulated—whether we are dealing with buildings or an individual's personality.

Originally, when the Universalist Church had moved to another location in 1930, the University of Chicago acquired three buildings: the church proper, the Sunday school, and recreation facilities directly connected with it; the large minister's home which also served as a dormitory for ten students of the seminary; and a third building which had housed the seminary's library and classrooms. At this time the university assigned the minister's home and two classrooms of the former seminary to the Orthogenic School. In 1944, the library building, a vast basement under the church proper, and the church building's gymnasium all became available for the Orthogenic School. In 1950, a rebuilding of the entire complex began and a new dormitory wing, larger than the old dormitory building, was added. In the sixties, a new building was erected to serve as an adolescents' unit and the church itself with seven more rooms also became part of the Orthogenic School. The entire School was then again radically remodeled.

In 1950 when we first became ready to add a new building, we planned it in terms of what already existed, since that is exactly what we have to do in our work with patients. We carefully assess what is already there and should be retained as it is; what requires only minor modifications; what needs to be more radically changed; and what can be added without doing harm to the original. This principle of slow organic growth has guided all our later expansions, each of which we tried to fit carefully into the old so that through the new, both old and new would function better together.

Symbolizing the place where life unfolds and emotions are shaped, the original homelike edifice, remains the most important part of our building complex. The church itself, acquired much later, is still used as a place of assembly, but no longer for worship. It was rebuilt to serve as an auditorium: a place for dances, for showing movies, for special celebrations, and for all kinds of social activities. The planners and architects originally suggested tearing down the old church, because it was cheaper to replace it than to rebuild it to serve new purposes. To us, it seemed fitting to preserve the church structure and appearance, as it seemed to symbolize how new tasks grow out of old ones. Between these two older buildings—one looking like a home, the other like a church—we placed the adolescent unit which, though modern, has romanesque, cloister-like features. These are meant to symbolize protection from the stresses of the world, and also contemplation, learning, inner growth. The erection of this building permitted us to place a ceramic mural by Jordi Bonet on its façade, which conveys how the School conceives its task to everybody who approaches it (Plate 1). The three buildings, while clearly distinct from one another, are tied together as all aspects of life should be.

The reasons why we wanted the old church preserved and put to new uses reflect our prime obligation. The saving of souls, which used to be the task of the church, has to a large extent become that of the mental institution; and this will be even more true in the future. But far differently from in the church, our patient must learn to become master of his fate, to direct his own life. His salvation will have to be sought in the here and now, not in a life after death. He must learn to take care of self and others; not to believe in supernatural powers or rely on outside sources to give direction and meaning to his life. And he will have to live the good life because he wants to, not because a god demands it.

Thus only some of the church's connotations will remain with the mental institution: those of contemplation, of a quest for the self, and of learning to live with others. The mental institution must provide interim protection from the turmoil and violence of the world, and convince the patient he is not only well cared for, but respected and appreciated. Then he will slowly begin to believe that he not only can manage his own fate but also be his brother's keeper.

It was our intent partially to re-create the image of the cloistered life which offers a respite—for reflection, for finding oneself, for the company of those engaged in the same search. Considering the educational bent of our work, we cannot overlook that for many centuries learning and the monastic life were identical. In the work of psychotherapy, our own beginnings and archaic past must never be denied; we must accept and rework these until their strength can empower us to deal with the present and the future. The old has to be revitalized, and given new meaning. Thus the symbolic signifi-cance of an architectural heritage from the past—especially one that symbolized security from the struggles of the world and concentration on the mind—is not denied, but becomes the bearer of new mean-ing.

Psychotherapy is a period of transition, and the stay in a mental institution should be a transitional period where one moves from a stage of disorganization to one of higher development. This makes all aspects of transition very important; so a mental institution should pay particular attention to places of transition such as corridors and stairhalls. Unfortunately, as far as design and decoration go, these places are usually even more neglected than other portions of the buildings.

The fact that contemplation is enhanced by a sheltered, lei-surely, horizontal moving about was appreciated in ancient Greece, where the philosophers walked in the stoa, a colonnade well decorated with images. We planned the arrangement of corridors at the Orthogenic School with this in mind, trying to make them places of both movement and repose. One cloistered corridor with twelve romanesque arches which lead from one building to another serves this purpose. Given Chicago's climate, the arches are closed by stained-glass windows, diaphanous but so substantial that over the years only one got cracked and none broken, though we never made or needed to make any effort to protect them. Beauty which is for one's personal use is its own protection, even for potentially violent mental patients. These windows give a soft, soothing atmosphere to the corridor; a light many-colored and restful. The setting invites fantasy and a thoughtful turning inward; while the strongly emphasized corridor element, symbol of passing onward, directs toward new vistas. This corridor conveys subliminally to most visitors, as well as to patients and staff, the feeling we were after: the restful, sheltering aspects of the institution for periods of emotional gestation; and also the invitation to move on and out when the right time comes.

There are three additional center arches in this corridor which lead onto a semicircular porch, a covered play area, and another structure supported by arches. The porch opens onto a garden area and further into a large playground. The dominant features of this porch are a circular sunken pool and a circular sunken sandbox, inviting sand and water play. But we intended further symbolic meanings, and experience suggests that patients respond to these also: besides an invitation to play, the pool and the sandbox also symbolize two bodily apertures and their functions which so preoccupy children and mental patients—the one filled with water suggests ideas of urination; the other filled with sand those of defecation. Certainly the children use the circles consistently for grappling with their difficulties in these two problem areas.

While we had these connotations in mind when we arranged for the circular pool and sandbox, knowing that all architecture is viewed both as an extension of the body and as representative of it or its parts, we were surprised how many children found another symbolic meaning in the circles that we had not thought of: they see nourishing breasts in them. This had not occurred to us because we had been too rational, despite all our commitment to and experience with the patients' symbolic use of objects and features of design. Since the two circles were sunken rather than protruding, it did not occur to us to think of them as breasts. But to the children, whatever gives them vital nutriments—whether food or emotional meaning—becomes associated to and representative of the nourishing aspects of the mother. Since the children got so much from these two circular features, they became symbols of the breast. This goes to show that users will find deeper symbolic meaning than even conscious planning allows.

Like any work of art, the more artistic architectural forms are, the more they can be endowed with multiple symbolic meaning. Since therapists are not artists, we have to entice artists to create what serves best our purposes. While we can tell the artist what we feel is required, only he can give it artistic body. The most recent additions to the institution—including the adolescent unit, the remodeling of the church, the cloister-like corridor, the fountain, and much else—we owe to Ike Colburn, who gave beauty and architectural body to our, and his, ideas. The stained-glass windows, as well as the tiled and colored brick stairhalls to be discussed next, were created by Harold Haydon, as a result of many years of collaboration and conversations about what has meaning to our patients. While based on our ideas, essentially they are the realizations of his creative genius.

Even before the addition of new buildings, other artists helped make the interiors of the original building more attractive while at the same time conveying symbolic meaning in artistic form. In each case the work was preceded by discussions about what would be meaningful to those who lived and worked in these buildings, what symbolic connotations we hoped the artist's creation would convey. During the designing stage, we tried to assess what specific messages various features were likely to have for the patients. It was information which normally was alien to the artists, but they all felt it was a fascinating challenge to their creativity. We attempted to stimulate their inventiveness, while scrupulously trying not to exercise any control over their artistic imagination. The results were usually effective beyond our original expectations.

Since the beginning of human history, art has embodied and conveyed symbolic meaning. Thus an institution that wishes to make an impact on mind and emotions, and also desires to directly reach their deepest layers, will make use of art. It will respect the patient's art, which expresses what goes on within him; and will use great art because it offers an opportunity to understand symbolic meanings which speak directly to our unconscious and tell us about a host of things, far beyond the specific content of the object. This is why the symbol can be much more effective in conveying global impressions which we would otherwise extract slowly, by assessing many objects separately and combining these evaluations to gain a total feeling. Even when we tried to assess this, we wouldn't trust our impressions.

Stage designers know this very well. If we have to study the various objects making up the play's scenery to form an impression, we will not get "the feeling," the atmosphere of the play. A good stage designer must be able to create this atmosphere the moment the curtain rises; when it is well done, it immediately gets across to the audience, as attested to by spontaneous applause. In the same way, the various features of the School add up to more than a collection, and succeed in giving the impression of an integrated whole where the separate details neither match each other perfectly nor were meant to. If everything were to fit perfectly together, there would be no room for individual selections, idiosyncratic preferences, or for the institution to continue to transform itself with time. Perfection would make not only the mental patient but others uncomfortable; it is beautiful to behold, but impossible to live with day in and day out. Perfection is timeless; and to accomplish it is beyond average man's reach; hence it is not suitable as a matrix for the vagaries of everyday life, or for changing preferences as one's view of oneself and the world evolves. When it is said that the features add up to give more of an impression than each would by itself, this is to say that they don't clash with each other; each fits with all others. While in its own way each is meant to give a reassuring and encouraging message, each does so in a quite different manner.

We planned to avoid uniformity; our intent was to increase the patients' feeling of being accepted; to add to the impression that here is a place of hope and of ample satisfaction through a variety of paths. We wanted the message to the patient to be that while everyone will be helped in becoming able to have a good life, this will be given to each in an individual way. What the good life will consist of will also be entirely different for each of them.

Therefore, the design accumulated over the years, and both patients and staff had a hand in it. Someone would see something which he thought we should have. We would then discuss whether we really wanted it, what it might mean, and where we could put it. If somebody was excited about getting it, this seemed a good omen that others would find it equally important. Sometimes a group of staff members, occasionally with patients, went on an excursion to look for something particular to enhance a special event—such as the new arrangement of a dormitory, or to create a better spirit for Christmas when everybody seemed exhausted by preparations for it. But more often by chance we would spy something that would make the School more attractive. We would get it and find a place to put it, not worrying about how it would add up or fit in.

Most mental institutions recognize the value of the patient's expressing his inner concerns symbolically through engaging in what is called occupational or art therapy. But if the patients draw, paint, and sculpt and then must keep their productions in a special room, this removes art from their everyday life. It is as important for the patient to have his creation close to him—perhaps to decorate his room with, making his living quarters more an expression of his personality—as it is for some parts of the institution to be decorated by patients (if they want to do so). But these creations are only potential messages from the patient to others; he also has to receive such communications if he is to be lifted out of a solipsistic into an interactional experience. Therefore, in addition to the art provided by the stained-glass windows and murals in common places, we encourage the patients to select from a wide variety the reproductions of masterpieces which they want to look at frequently, and then these are hung in their rooms.

Whenever some part of the building was remodeled or added, whenever common rooms were redecorated or refurnished, all the patients were consulted. In their own rooms, they can have the final choice of wall colors, patterns for drapes and bedspreads, and some pieces of furniture such as tables and chairs, lighting fixtures, and so forth. We submit three different selections (samples of colors, materials, pieces of furniture) to the patients, all of which the staff like and find appropriate. The patients choose the one they like best; if none pleases them, some new possibilities are submitted to them. Since we offer only a limited number of choices, the patients do not feel overwhelmed by the task of making a wise decision. Although the selections we offer are all different, we submit only those which we ourselves like, so we are pleased by whatever the patients choose. Therefore, whatever changes are made give pleasure to everybody, at least all those who do not suffer extremes of depression or negativism. But even they might gain from being invited to participate in the selection. Since several areas of the instituiton are refurbished every year, but never all of them at one time, we have the feeling of a microcosmos in slow but continuous evolvement, and of improvements in which each patient significantly participates.

Beauty is important in the cure of sick minds because of its impact. But art is not only to be admired, it must be made truly one's own. A piece of sculpture must be touched and climbed on, so that it can convey its meaning not only through the mind and the eye, but with the immediacy of touch and kinesthetic experiences where body speaks directly to body. The patients' favorite sculpture is a twice-lifesize reclining female figure, placed in the garden area (Plate 6). It offers the patients a chance to deal with feelings about the mother, and hence with his or her earliest experiences. Since we provide such a figure and give it prominence, it is symbolically stated that we welcome dealing freely with these often conflict-laden emotions.

At first the individual may be too afraid even to approach this female figure. Then he may mistreat it—stepping on it, kicking it— until one day, he may begin to enjoy curling up in its arms, lying on its belly, and finally being tender with it by petting it, washing it, and rubbing it down. The frequency and intensity with which the patients would scrub this figure was as much a surprise to us as their experiencing the pool and sandbox as breasts. When planning and creating the female figure, we had thought of love and hate for mother figures. Though we were well aware of the importance bathing has for the infant, and how this can be either a pleasant or a destructive experience, it had not occurred to us that this figure would be used to retaliate for experiences involving being bathed and cleaned.

The patients gave the figure a neutral name, "The Lady," probably because on a "Lady" they could discharge violence as easily as tender care; while if it had been called "Mother," the same freedom might not have been possible for them. Being a stone figure, she invites abuse and she can take it, as even the best flesh-and-blood mother cannot. It was fascinating to watch how some children changed, over a long time, from violent scrubbing attacks to giving it good and gentle care; to observe the change in a child as he progressed from stepping and jumping on the figure's breasts, to resting his head contentedly on them. This mother never got tired, never struck out if a child's fury vented itself against her or if he soiled on her. Of course, if he is to learn the nature of true two-way human relations the child also needs a responsive mother, one who would recoil from a blow. But initially and for some time, a stone mother can be a useful safety valve that allows for tentative deeds without panic.

Partly because of its size, this figure became an important socializing agent, which was completely unexpected. It became the locus and maybe even the source of important interpersonal experiences. Children who had been isolates all of their lives began to play with others for the first time, as they crawled all over the figure. It had never occurred to us that the naked maternal body could be such an invitation to relate to others; we had been too removed from primitive life. We had only seen that behavior before in infant animals crawling over their mother's body. We were aware that socialization—relating with others—has its origin in the infant's relation to his mother as he nestles against and into, and nurses from, her body. The children's behavior showed that experiences with others may be much more directly rooted in tactile and kinesthetic experiences with the mother's body than is generally assumed.

We searched for other works of art, until we happened to find those that met our needs—such as pieces of antique furniture which, in combination with modern pieces, helped to symbolize the desired fusion of the tried old and the stimulating new.

It took many years to find a sculpture which would symbolize the kind of human relations we wish to form with the patients. A sister group (by the sculptor Joachim Karsch) in which the younger sister is being cared for by an older one expresses our ideas about this

(Plate 5). It is quite different from the passive, receptive, placid, great (since twice-lifesize) mother figure. The sisters sculpture symbolizes that while we are all children of Cain, if we are to enjoy the good life we must each transcend this heritage. Thus, if he is to get well, every patient will have to transcend the anger which ruled him in the past. He must learn to perceive in other people not only the stranger he always saw there but also the fellow man who will help him out of his desperate isolation, toward closeness with others. The patients immediately understand this symbolic meaning of the sisters, although for a long time they doubt that we can really be our brother's keepers.

This sculpture is placed within a fountain which forms the heart of a little quadrangle. Here water plays a central role, as is typical of cloisters. The continuous flow of this quietly playing fountain, the music of its rising and falling, remind us not only of what should be (the easy flow of human life) but also of the origin of all life in the liquid element. Those familiar with Freud's writings know of his remarks about the "oceanic" feeling he traced back to the earliest phases of ego feeling—to our most basic experiences, and our first encounters with life. Many people gain relief from loneliness and distress, and feel at peace, when they behold and listen to the sound of moving water. So water, a symbol of the origin of all life, from which the chain of evolution extends, stands at the very center of the Orthogenic School. The presence of water as a nurturing element in a restful courtyard inviting meditation, and the play of a fountain over a work of art suggesting that we are each other's keepers, seems an appropriate symbolic statement.

The symbolic effects of horizontal movement, as in corridors, are of great importance; but no more so than those of vertical movement—up and down, as in stairways. In the School, for example, there is a transitory stairway from the dormitories down to the dining room. Such up-and-down movement is even more important psychologically than horizontal movement, because of the delight in reaching higher vistas; and of the fear of falling, or of being dropped. The latter are among the most ancient anxieties, as evidenced by the infant's need to be held firmly lest he drop to the floor. Falling was an ever-present danger for our ancestors the primates; the infant had to cling to his mother's fur or risk falling from the tree and being lost, injured, or killed. I don't know if this ancient fear is still working in our dreams and unconscious. But most people have dreamed of flying or of dropping down, particularly down stairs. These anxieties are still very active in many psychotic individuals, those who have lost their secure footing in life. It is thus imperative to make stairways safe but also to decorate them with images which convey the right feeling.

In selecting the appropriate imagery, we were guided by the fact that stairs and stairways, in addition to their obvious purposes, have deep symbolic meaning. In Christian imagery, the stair appears as an ascent to Heaven, or a descent to Hell. So deeply ingrained are the meanings we attach to up-and-down directions that it is almost impossible to think of a descent to Heaven, or an ascent to Hell. This is even more reason to make sure that our patients don't find walking downstairs unpleasant; for we must help them descend safely into their past and into the chaos of their unconscious, before they can rise to the tasks of present living. Thus symbolic use of stairways is another vehicle for suggesting the nature and purpose of the patients' stay at the institution.

It was around this stairway problem that we first began our happy collaboration with Professor Harold Haydon in 1956. Being stuck with a stairway we didn't really like, we tried to improve matters first by changing the plain large window to multi-colored glass bricks. (The great success of this small innovation with patients and staff led years later to the much more ambitious stained-glass windows of the corridor.) While this helped, it didn't improve the stairhall enough. Finally we got the idea of tile walls which, since easily washed, would also eliminate the dirt that seemed to collect particularly fast on these unattractive stairwalls. Professor Haydon had created beautiful mosaics and murals for churches and synagogues. Once we had decided on tile walls, it seemed appropriate to ask him to help us with our problem. The results went far beyond our original hopes. As we pondered and discussed with him why we wanted this figure rather than that included in the mural, one story depicted over another, we learned more about the symbolic content of the murals than we had guessed possible. When we then complained to him of the drabness of the risers, he suggested painting them in colors of the rainbow. After we had done this, we couldn't understand how we or anybody else could have lived with drab and uniformly colored stairs.

This was the first experience to teach us that even the most competent craftsman, without our providing the psychological guidance, cannot design a unique setting for mental patients which also suggests a symbolic meaning. The stairhall, which had been an unsightly part of the building, was changed into one of its most attractive features. It taught us not to be afraid of possibly drab places, but to see them as challenges to our imagination and turn them into something of special attractiveness and meaning. Since then several similar areas have been transformed into places of unexpected charm, sometimes adding more to the institution than the deliberately planned features. It was important to the patients to observe the almost "miraculous" evolution from depressive dullness to vital and meaningful sources of pleasure. During his stay at an institution if a patient cannot watch—or even better, participate in—such a transfiguration, he misses an experience that can greatly help him to believe that a similar transformation can take place in his life.

Clearly, one of the themes to decorate our main stairway in the ceramic tile mural—each tile hand-painted by the artist before firing—had to be that of ascent and descent. The movement was not toward Heaven or Hell, but toward an enrichment of life in either direction. So the images of this stairhall convey the merit of exploring both the highest and the lowest expanses of the world—and by implication of the mind (exploring both the rational-scientific and the emotional realms). The highest reaches of our planet are represented by the sky and the stars; the lowest by the depths of the sea. Between the two resides human life, both real and symbolic—the images reflecting both mythology and reality as each enhances the other. Once more the message's connotation is that the gap between one's irrational feelings about things and their rational order can be bridged.

At the very top of the stairhall one sees children exploring beyond the earth through telescopes; and then imaginatively, the original vortex out of which the sun and planets were formed, the beginning of our world. At the bottom of the stairwell is the deep sea with its animal life, where all life began on our planet. Here too is an example of scientific exploration, in the form of a bathosphere. If one wishes to extract one of the many levels of significance: at the bottom, the watery element in which the chain of life begins; and at the top, primordial chaos. In between the two is the place where orderly life can unfold.

At least one other level of symbolic meaning exists here: at the very top of the stairhall children are shown exploring the heavenly bodies, particularly shooting stars. To the infant, the heavenly bodies represent the nurturing mother—mother nature, if you like. This relates to why the galaxy is called the Milky Way and why, in ancient imagery, both the Milky Way and comets' tails represent the milk streaming out of some goddess's breast. Our children know little mythology and astronomy; but they are enshrouded by magical thinking, so that these ideas reach their unconscious in direct and immediate ways. Also it is important to them that we want them to behold symbols which tell that even the heavenly bodies welcome them, and that we encourage exploration of these bodies' secrets.

At the bottom of the stairway, children are seen investigating the lowest depths of the sea: the dark and moist netherworld. These murals tell that exploring in all directions is safe at this institution, and that we welcome it; that here children are invited to enter and examine both their personal heaven and their darkest depths. Neither the highest reaches of experience nor the lowest are to be neglected. The richness of our world, our life, and our personality cannot unfold until we are equally familiar with both reaches—free from the persecution of an over-strict superego, or the projection into utter chaos by a lawless id.

There are many stations in between these two extremes in the mural. There is an emphasis on historical experience, true and imagined, implied in the images, as there must be in all psychoanalytic therapy—what the past means for the present, and how the present can be understood in terms of the past. There are the images of boyhood and of our American past, as evoked by Tom Sawyer and Huck Finn sailing down the Mississippi on their raft, the myths of Johnny Appleseed, Paul Bunyan and his Blue Ox, Casey Jones, and John Henry (Plate 4). But there are also renderings of true historical events such as the Puritans at Plymouth, the movement to the West, the American Indian and his buffaloes. All these have their place in the mythology of our country and in our personal fantasy life. At the very bottom of the sea, there is a pirates' treasure chest. The message intended is that if we fathom the furthest reaches, go down to what is most deeply buried and lift its secrets, we will find a fund of wealth—of which we were robbed so long ago that we no longer know of what it consisted, or how much we lost by letting it sink down out of sight.

The mythical and protective meaning of animals that marks the origins of civilization, and also early childhood experience, is the message on another stairway. Like the ancient Babylonians and Assyrians who found security in the images of powerful animals, which protected and enhanced their entrances and great halls, our patients find messages of enjoyment and security in this stairway decorated with animals made of colored brick. Some of these animals symbolically represent the child's hidden instinctual desires, and others his protectors; animals which invite thoughts of instinctual freedom, such as monkeys playing in the trees, and animals who are strong protectors, such as lions. But there is also the warning image of the ostrich which helplessly buries its head.

In the most prominent places of this stairhall are placed two mythical animals: the unicorn, which willingly relinquishes its phallic power when encountering true love; and the phoenix, the bird that rebears itself out of its own ashes, thereby of its own free will shedding its former existence to gain a new and better one.

Sensory Perceiving: Look, Smell, Feel

Schizophrenics often trust the information they receive from their immediate receptors—touch, smell, and kinesthetic sensations—much more than that derived from the distant receptors—sight and hearing—on which the rest of us predominantly rely. Most buildings have a quite distinct smell; its character is very important for the patient's feeling either dejected or exhilarated.

Unfortunately, most psychiatric hospitals smell "bad" to the patient, and to everybody who enters them. If the odor is not outrightly offensive, there is a "stale" scent, even if the institution is air-conditioned. If an institution smells "clean," as some of the better do, it is a "cold" smell, when it should be a "good" and refreshingly clean one. The existing smell can't be covered up by injecting "good" odors, for example, by spraying with fragrant substances; the patient will see this tactic as just another deceit of the institution. Such camouflage methods do not succeed, because the fragrance is not genuine; it is out of kilter with the *genius loci*. The resulting combination of underlying "bad" and superimposed "good" odors fight each other, and end up as an experience of dishonesty. The antiseptically clean stench characteristic of many institutions is even worse; it is less human than other smells, because its specific content is the battle being waged against germs. Many apprehend this antiseptic odor as ominous, which can be a worse experience than an "honest" bad smell.

When I came to the Orthogenic School, its old façade was still charming and rather well preserved. But even before entering one got a foreboding feeling which became overwhelming when one opened the front door and was hit by the oppressively nauseating smell. Inexperienced as I was, I thought a vigorous attack of washing, scrubbing, and painting would do. It turned out that exorcising the evil smell was a most formidable task; it had taken over the institution and settled into all cracks, nooks, and crannies. When washing walls and floors, repainting walls and woodwork didn't help, the next step was throwing out curtains, bedspreads, blankets, and rugs, disposing of furniture. Then came other drastic measures. Each step helped reduce the offensive smell, but finally I realized that my well-intentioned approach had been short-sighted. I had vigorously attacked the externals, but that wouldn't do where essentials were at work. While these radical measures at last gave us clean air, they did not give the right "smell." This could and did come only from the right operation of the institution, which took longer to achieve.

After a time, the Orthogenic School finally achieved a "warm" and "friendly" odor. It required continuous washing, cleaning, and redecorating as a basis, so that the good smell would not be overpowered by one of dustiness. It contained some whiffs from the kitchen, some from the outdoors, since there was now continuous coming and going, but the most important odors come from the persons who live in a house. We became convinced that a reassuring odor emanates from bodies that feel well within themselves. Perhaps we learned it through empathy, or psychic osmosis from the patients, but after a few years all senior staff members, when walking into the institution or one of the rooms, like Hamlet, could "smell" a rat if something was amiss. The place didn't smell "right," and on the basis of this observation it was often possible to find out what had gone wrong. Words and appearances can lie; but we can trust what "feels" and "smells" right.

I am sure that temperature sensations make a significant contribution to the phenomena just described, but I was not able to analyze their specific impact. There is reason when we describe a person as "warm" or "cold," and I have known mental patients not only say of a person, "He makes me shiver," but actually begin to do so when he appears on the scene. As for temperature, a mental institution should feel neither warm, nor cold, nor hot, but comfortably "right." Achieving this was relatively easy with modern air conditioning and temperature controls; infinitely easier than making the institution smell right. While the importance of sensations and experiences derived from proximity receptors can hardly be overestimated for mental patients, we have not even begun to explore how this can best be made use of therapeutically.

Quite a bit more is known about the importance of kinesthetic experiences for feeling comfortable and secure, and how disoriented we become if our kinesthetic sensations are unpleasant or upsetting, even if they are exciting. We can experience this on roller coasters, for example, and every mother knows her baby becomes upset when it is not comfortably carried, because the hold is either too loose or too tight. It is of the utmost importance to feel well supported and securely balanced. These feelings are strongly conveyed by buildings, as some seem to weigh us down, while others soar. The column brought to us by ancient Greece is the architectural feature which seems to convey best a feeling of well-balanced security, more so than columns and pilasters used by other cultures, because the Greeks made the necessary corrections to counteract optical illusions. While individuals differ greatly in their responses, columns invite me to rest and remain, while a row of arches tends to make me feel like moving along with it. Hopefully, giving such matters more thought in the future will lead to our replacing the fortress-cum-prison-style institutions, not with what is now considered good hospital design, but with one based on a deeper understanding of what conveys feelings of safety, stability, and emotional comfort.

Considerable awareness already exists in regard to the sense of touch. Designers know how different textures and materials make different appeals to our tactile sensations, even if we react to them only through sight. Children and mental patients, who are much less ready to trust distant receptors than normal adults, need to run their fingers over the material to "get the touch" of it. This makes a great difference to how they feel about it. Tactile sensations are particularly important to the person who has "lost touch," and who needs to be able to "get in touch" again. The buildings and furnishings of a mental institution should speak to this sense, and do so in reassuring ways. The more architectural features invite touch, and give an impression of security, the more readily the building can be accepted as a safe home.

A banister, for example, that feels good to the touch, that permits a firm but at the same time comfortable grip, will not only help us up the steps but it gives us a feeling of safety in doing so. On the outside of a building, if steps run along its entire front, this may look fine to the person interested only in the superficial appearance. If there are many steps, they give the edifice an imposing appearance but do not lead into the structure. They confuse the location of the entrance, while the mental patient needs clear direction. A few steps with the right type of banister, both of which clearly lead to the entrance, conveys a better feeling of direction. Giving a slight upward movement—always more reassuring than one leading down—the steps and banister may be experienced as an invitation to enter. If we add a small columned porch to this, we have described the entrance to the Orthogenic School, which serves the purpose of giving a desirable first impression. I am sure there are many other ways to achieve the same result; nothing would be more deadly than if one example were to be slavishly repeated. But this is a possible way to solve the problem of making the institution inviting and reassuring when entered.

Our choices in these decorations were the consequence of personal taste, experiences, and convictions about the silent messages we wished to convey. Entirely different features of design could serve these purposes as well or better. What matters is the intention with which something is done; the serious thought which goes into the selection; the wish to please; and arranging things to make a strong positive appeal while transmitting pertinent meaning.

Mental patients believe that their difficulties reside outside themselves, and not within their psyche. Providing them with the best possible surroundings to live in—however different the specific forms and details may be—bespeaks of the care which has been taken to give them the best possible physical and human environment. Thus it becomes more difficult for them to maintain that it is not themselves, but other persons, who create their biggest problems. The more pleasing, life-enhancing, need-satisfying, understanding, and supportive their environment is, the harder it is for them to avoid recognizing that their main difficulties reside within themselves—a realization which is a significant factor in inducing people to engage in therapy to restructure their personality.

8 | The Silent Message: Situational Symbolism

In addition to making the institution pleasant and appealing and trying to convey the institution's intentions through symbols, decorative features also have a very practical value. Every mental patient is not only anxious, but confused; nothing seems to hold together. Therefore it is very important that he should not feel lost in the institution. He will not believe it possible to find his way in life there if he cannot find his way around the buildings. We all orient ourselves by landmarks that have some meaning for us; we all tend to get lost if one feature of a building or landscape looks like all the others to us. Thus distinctive decorations, which make an impression and are easily remembered, permit even the most disoriented patient to find his way around. If the entrance to his room is where the lion is, he will not take the wrong turn by mistaking the door by the giraffe.

From the very beginning, efforts must be made to show the patient around, explaining where everything is, and how he may find his way most easily. At the Orthogenic School, once the patient is settled somewhat in his room, not later than a few hours after his admission, he is shown around the entire institution. The first time he may remember only a few landmarks. But the fact that he has been shown his way around is not overlooked by him. This is part of the School's effort to make the patient feel at home; to show him that he can understand how this place all hangs together. To comprehend this, a few tours of the entire institution are just the beginning. The patient must feel free to explore every last nook and cranny at his leisure; he must be helped to understand what these various places are used for. At first he will be accompanied in his wanderings around the institution, but later he can go around on his own. There are areas we prefer the patients to stay out of—although they are encouraged to explore these places at least once, for example, the offices where the records are kept, to know what they are for and what goes on in them.

The institution has to have a unity which is more than the aggregation of its parts. This way the patient can grasp the School in its entirety. To convey the image of an integrated existence, it must be compact enough to be easily understandable. It should not be too big, because in vastness the patient feels even more insignificant; though small size alone does not guarantee comprehensibility. This comes with an intelligible organization apparent not only to the minds of the senior staff, but to everyone connected with the institution—patient or attendant, janitor, cook, or secretary. Everyone, but most of all the patient, must understand the purposes—all serving him—of the various parts, why they exist, why they are located at certain places, and how they all fit together. This is especially significant because different places unpredictably attain special meanings for patients. For one, the food storage closet near the kitchen became one of the mainstays of his security; for another, it was a certain place atop the jungle gym or a window seat on top of a radiator.

The patients must not only have ready access to all places, they must get a feeling of what the institution is all about; that it is their institution. The working together of its various parts must be an example of inner integration, and its advantages. Free movement in and out of all rooms is characteristic of a family home. To preserve this image, the institution has to function as a large family where everyone has his respected and important place in the arrangements of daily life. But the image will not be the nuclear family, with all the intensity and difficulties of emotional ties, or the horror of their absence. It will be the image of the extended family, where the members relate intimately with some of the others but not all; where each has his appropriate place and all manage to cooperate and help each other, without getting in each other's way.

Ready access is symbolized as much by open doors as unavailability is by locks. The worst feeling any physical environment could give one is that of being cooped up—not to mention being locked in. Mental patients know that locked doors prove the staff's fear of them, whatever other explanation may be offered. The argument that locked doors and barred windows are to protect patients from hurting themselves is fallacious. This danger exists only if they are left alone or are put in a setting, both physical and human, that is lacking in empathy for their needs.

The suicidal person is more adversely affected than any other by impersonal restraints on his actions. They only tell him more forcefully that life isn't worth living. He needs to live under conditions which convince him that life is worthwhile even for him; and that he matters a great deal to those who take care of him. He needs maximum human care to counteract his feelings of isolation; not barred and barren rooms, but the most attractive surroundings to reverse his mood of depression and desperation.

If there is a "maximum security" room in the institution, there is a great temptation to utilize this means of making things "safe." The unacceptable thought that one locks the patient into such barren rooms not to prevent him from doing harm but to punish him for the aggravation he causes is rationalized away. Strenuous efforts are made to keep up the claim that such rooms are for the patient's benefit, by calling these spaces "isolation rooms" or places where he "can get hold of himself." Given the obstreperous behavior of mental patients, if there is any kind of room in which a person can be locked, it will be used to make life easier for the staff. It must be acknowledged that staff work in psychiatric hospitals is difficult, upsetting, and demanding; the temptation to ease it is great. Yet there is one overriding reason why such means of escape from patients and their demands should not be available to the staff in a psychiatric institution. Cold packs, "isolation rooms," and the like make it unnecessary for the staff to counteract suicidal or homicidal tendencies by means of human intervention—the only means which eventually lead to permanent improvement. Even if patients are only rarely locked up with their anger, despair, and misery, the threat that they might be is ubiquitous and damaging. Thus the very institution where all efforts should be bent toward reducing the patient's anxiety is using threats which increase it. The "maximum security" rooms have a symbolic meaning which casts its shadow over all of the patient's life.

I have stressed the symbolic meaning of structures, arrangements, and objects; but before any of them become symbols, they are first of all real things: a barred window, a locked door, a thick set of keys. Therefore, one of the first steps in redesigning the School was to change all locks so that it was no longer possible to lock anyone into a room or into the institution. Since outside doors need locks to prevent strangers from entering the institution, new locks were constructed to keep people from entering, but never from leaving. Even a wide open institution has certain places or things that need to be locked up. But one and the same key can open outside doors, staff offices, files, the locked closets in the dormitories, and any other places that may need to be secured. So the second change was to eliminate all the different keys and gear all locks to a single key that could easily and unobtrusively be put into a pocket. The implied message to the patients is: "We don't want you to feel locked up, and this is why we refrain from openly displaying keys."

When I came to the Orthogenic School each staff member carried a key ring heavy with keys that opened a variety of doors, files, cabinets, and whatnot. As a matter of fact, the importance of a staff member could easily be gauged by the number of keys on his ring, and it was a visible rise in status when he was given a new one. To arrange the changeover to a single key was a simple matter; but the staff members requested that a certain area be set aside as accessible only to some, through a special key. Usually a very good reason was given, but the wish to believe that "only a few selected people should have access to this area, because it is more important than others," was always behind it. Occasionally over the years the issue of keys would pop up under one guise or another, with most convincing rationalizations: one of the open-everything keys had got lost; something had disappeared and was probably stolen; patients and staff members should not be tempted to take things not their own. One time the purse of a secretary was stolen, another time that of a cook—weren't they entitled to lock their things up? Each of these requests was revealing in some way, because it was connected with status positions: some should get a new key, others not. This held so true that I came to the conclusion that wherever there is a variety of keys, there will be complex status hierarchies; and conversely, that there is no way of eliminating such hierarchies unless the variety of keys is done away with.

Of course, we were also obligated to see that staff members didn't suffer hardships because of this change. When things do disappear or get stolen, the injured party must receive full compensation. To counter criticism of what may seem like largesse but is only in fairness required, a careful record was kept of how expensive this compensation turned out to be. All damages, which were freely compensated, amounted to less than 0.0005 per cent of the institution's budget—considerably less than the cost of one change of locks. This sum even included monies paid to the staff members to take care of damages inflicted on their clothing, and so on, by patients. Since all things that could be locked had a common key which many people had in their possession, staff members were warned to be extra careful, so that probably fewer thefts occurred than if there had been many different keys.

Eventually, the staff stopped caring that there was only one key to everything. While one and the same key came to open all doors or cabinets of the institution equipped with locks, there was actually an exception. Each staff member's private living room has, of course, a key of its own—since it will not do for others to gain entrance to someone's room without invitation. For the patients, the absence of loaded key rings did away with their being reminded of that which was not open to them.

In addition to being symbols of who has access to something, keys have the real purpose of locking in or locking out. Since keys usually open doors set in walls, a line of Robert Frost's comes to mind:

> Something there is that doesn't love a wall,
> That wants it down.

Until very recently in history, it was walls—real or symbolic—that made us secure. No citizen was any stronger or safer than the walls of his city; a breach in the wall spelled destruction or worse. Even Frost recognizes that despite change, some walls have their place, so he qualifies reasonably:

> Before I built a wall I'd ask to know
> What I was walling in or walling out . . .

As he enters the institution, the mental patient is so desperate that he either wants the safety of being wholly walled in, or else he wants all the walls torn down, however unsafe that leaves him. So an important first lesson is that walls and locked doors at the Orthogenic School are neither all one thing nor the other. The patient must learn that some walls are there to protect what is inside, and what the walls are giving protection against. The patient cannot take this on trust, so he is encouraged to test these things out repeatedly on his own, in a variety of situations and times.

Unfortunately, the problem of a suicidal or homicidal patient is usually stated so as to permit no way out other than the use of locked wards. For example, in discussing milieu therapy, Schwartz writes:

> Some patients may resent being treated as prisoners, on the other hand some patients may want the protection afforded by a locked door. Although an unlocked door may

*indicate the institution's trust and respect for the patient, it
may also place a responsibility on him he cannot handle. It
might, for example, give him an opportunity for escape or
suicide that he has to take because he misinterprets the opportunity as a wish on the part of the personnel that he do
these things; or he may see it as a rejection of him by the institution (105).*

That study, like nearly all similar arguments, concludes that
locked wards cannot be dispensed with; very rarely do such reports
state that it is the patient's privilege to commit suicide; that no one
has the right to prevent it forcefully, except for trying to talk him
out of it. But in such discussions the crucial question is begged:
Why place an unmanageable responsibility on the patient, or give
him the chance to misinterpret the intentions of the institution?
Misunderstandings are possible only where ambiguities remain, where
things have not been made clear. There are ways to assure, beyond all
doubt, that one wishes the patient not to hurt himself—more effective
ways than locking him up. Witness the fact that mental hospitals,
despite locked wards and so-called maximum security measures, fail
to prevent suicides altogether. Suicides do happen in psychiatric institutions, and it is questionable whether closed wards materially reduce their numbers.

At the Orthogenic School we have worked in an entirely open
institution for many years with numerous suicidal patients who had
a history of several serious attempts. Not only did no suicides occur,
but there were not any attempts at the School. Physical attacks on
the staff did occasionally take place, but though some were quite
painful, none had any permanent consequences. While part of this
had to do with the fact that the School didn't resemble a prison, it
was primarily because the patient never doubted our intentions, and
because we went to any length to prevent a suicidal attempt by inter-
posing ourselves between the intention and the act. We were there
to see that nothing untoward could happen, and so no unmanageable
responsibility was placed on the patient. Whether an institution can
afford never to lock a patient in depends on its ability to ensure that
he knows how terribly important his well-being—which is much more
than mere safety—is to everyone there. For example, this sometimes
requires sitting with a patient all night; accepting his attacks if need
be; making sure he knows that in an emergency his welfare is important above all. Being subjected to this experience seems to make
suicide almost psychologically impossible.

It is not maximum security measures but our importance to

others that keeps us going on living in our most desperate moments. Or rather, knowing how important one is to others who have come to play a significant role in our life *is* maximum security. Many suicidal attempts, including (no doubt) some that succeed, have no other motive than trying to find out whether one is really important to some other person. If one already knows this, there is no need to try to find out.

Another reason given to justify locked wards is that the patient needs to be confined so he will not escape and behave in destructive or self-destructive ways outside the hospital. But "escape" makes no sense if the staff is ready to "run away" with the patient, to make his escapade more pleasant and secure. It was the patients' certainty that we would either be able to convince them not to "escape," or would go with them, that led some to go to extraordinary lengths to plan and prepare an escape, although our doors were always unlocked. But their knowledge of our concern was also the reason they took the initiative to return. This was summed up by one of our runaway boys when he said: "I never knew you cared so much." This is also the reason why, as an ex-patient who had run away innumerable times, he came back to visit more often and regularly than any of our other former patients.

A wide open mental institution does not necessarily foster escape; the patient is held by the psychological bond of the feeling of his importance to the staff. He is much more securely tied by this to the institution, whether he knows it and no matter how he may try to deny it, than any physical bond. We do not tell the patients this, but they learn it through our efforts.

When coming to the School, every patient is told that the locks on the doors are so constructed that no one can enter the institution against our will, but that nobody can be locked in. This is demonstrated to him by inviting him to try it out. We want him to fully understand that here he will decide whether he wishes to stay in or go out, but that he is safe from intrusion. All this, however, remains a set of mechanical facts to him until he meets the spirit behind it head on.

Once patients realize that doors will always open for egress, other features of the institution that appear (and are) confining, such as fences, become protective in the intended sense. Suddenly safety screens—put only on upper story windows—are no longer seen as barring them, but as protecting them from falling out, or from the temptation to throw themselves out. With these, a patient can sit freely on windowsills, looking out and enjoying himself there. High places, which frighten many, suddenly become safe to a patient just by his living at the institution. To achieve such meaning, safety screens must obviously be to protect the person, not to protect the window from being broken. To protect the window would be taken to mean we expect the patient to break it, and this would provoke him to do so. Therefore the screen must be placed normally, on the outside where it will protect both from insects and from the danger of falling. In addition, the screen, like the doors, protects from the ever-present fear of kidnappers, robbers, or relatives suddenly appearing.

One more example may illustrate how even the most commonplace physical features can become carriers of deep meaning. There are innumerable ways in which patients try to find out whether the institution is operated for the staff's convenience or for their own well-being. An important test of the staff's good intentions comes when patients feel free to use institutional safety devices to protect themselves from being deceived by the institution.

One near-mute autistic girl lost trust in her safety with us because one of her counselors was about to stop working at the institution—which meant desertion to her. So this girl pulled a fire alarm, which quickly brought the fire department inside the School. Perhaps she hoped the firehose would quench the flames of anger which threatened to consume her, and thus the fire image motivated her. But it is more likely that, angry about the desertion, she wanted to get even by doing something destructive to us. Yet since she had also learned to believe that by and large our intentions were positive, her action was a compromise between her anger and her trust. To vent her anger, she used one of the institution's features which she had learned could give extra safety in emergencies. She was experiencing an emergency, so she took appropriate action. Everything depended on whether her expression of anger was really safe and was accepted positively.

This brings up the importance of the institution's establishing the right understanding and spirit of cooperation with agents of the surrounding world, if in its totality it is to create a therapeutic setting. The local police, the fire department, and the people of the neighborhood must all be made familiar with the institution's way of approaching problems the patients present. Our experience showed that neither the fire chief nor his men minded getting occasional false alarms from the institution. They understood that it was important to our children to be able to test safety in the face of felt danger. The firemen didn't mind coming when called, realizing that while there was no fire to be extinguished, they had indeed contributed to the feeling of safety and were glad that they could do so.

While creating such willing and understanding cooperation takes some doing, such as explaining what the institution is all about and why it proceeds as it does, in fact we found it quite easy to achieve—in one of the largest cities of the world, not usually known for the neighborly cooperation of its citizens. We didn't expect the fire department or the police, or any other public or private organization, simply to serve us because it is their duty. On the contrary, we convinced them of their importance to us as partners in a common enterprise.

The girl's power to control the huge fire trucks helped, as did the friendly attitude of the fire chief; but what counted in the long run was how the School reacted to her distress signal. Since we had appreciated the message in her action, this nonspeaking child thereafter let us know when she felt anxious or angry by looking at the fire alarm. She would remember then how her burning anxiety had been positively met, and we would recall how great her distress had been. She no longer had to pull the alarm; just looking at it was enough to bring the remedy she needed.

Thus even the most regressed and isolated patient can use the institution's appurtenances ingeniously, autonomously, to his advantage; and in line with the institution's therapeutic purposes. Moreover, the fire alarm, used in line with the patient's inner needs, made the institution's work so much easier. To insist that it be used only as originally intended would have set back the therapeutic work seriously. The girl would have lost the very belief the institution is designed to create: that it exists, and the staff is there, only for her.

A symbolic message which lies—to which the reality does not conform—is worse than no message at all. The mental patient, much more than the rest of us, has been tricked by symbols. Words are symbols and we often find that the patient feels that these symbols, words, have been used to confuse him about what people really thought and felt. His parents may have told him when he was a child that they loved him, when at the same time he felt that they wished him out of the way. His feeling was real to him; the words which stood for feelings lied. But wanting to believe what he was told, he tried to believe the symbol—only to be endlessly disappointed until he no longer could trust others, nor even himself. Thus his ability to ascertain what is true and what is a lie is undermined, and he becomes unable to manage reality.

If this is so, why use symbols? Because, as said before, the mental patient particularly reads symbolic meaning into things he encounters. But when he tends to find one kind of symbolic meaning, a threatening one, in almost everything, the best we can do is to try to make reading negative meaning into things as difficult as possible, and encourage positive interpretation of the symbol. Since positive symbols raise the hope of the patient, it becomes even more important that he not be disillusioned by the reality behind them. He has so often been disappointed in this respect that he is afraid to explore and test reality. Too often it has been found destructive.

The girl who pulled the fire alarm was not testing reality. If she had wanted to find out whether and how it worked, she would have done so long before. This would have been as much in contact with reality as a normal youngster who takes things apart to find out how they work. But this girl was not at all in contact with reality; only with her fantasies. When she pulled the alarm she had begun to trust that the symbolic messages (or more accurately, vague impressions) at the School might be giving her correct information about our intentions in placing objects at her disposal. When she pulled the lever, she was testing whether she could trust the *symbolic meaning* inherent in the object. She did it to find out whether the pledge of safety implied in the fire alarm was correctly received by her; or whether once again she had been carried away by wishful thinking into believing symbolic messages that had no substance to them. What counted heavily was that the symbol of safety had not fooled her. This is why when in distress later she would glance at the symbol of safety for her; it provided her with much more security than the fact of a fire alarm itself. Since we had understood her message and acted positively on it, a look at the alarm always restored her faith in our intentions.

9 | Living Room and Lebensraum: Spatial Messages

When we meet a patient (or potential staff member, or a patient's relatives) for the first time at the School, it is done in a room which permits us to interact with him at a distance. This way, we neither expect nor impose intimacy; if the person desires, it readily allows a "keeping one's distance." This "living room" facilitates maintaining relations comfortably on a distant level, but it is equally possible here for people to come closer to each other. It does not invite intimacy between persons, although it does invite intimacy between one person and some of the furnishings.

In this room, the first that any visitor enters, there are several unusual pieces of furniture (Plate 3). There is an antique carved wood throne. Next to this is an antique rocking crib—antique because the modern ones are neither as sturdily constructed nor as comfortable. This seventeenth-century crib is so big and so solid it can easily hold and rock a six-year-old; even teen-agers have managed to curl up in it. Implicitly the crib tells how important we think the infant's first experiences are and continue to be even later on in life. Next, there is a huge, elaborately built and furnished Victorian doll house; no modern large doll house is as well built. Moreover, this old doll house gives the feeling that several generations of children have played with it, as indeed they have. The doll house shows that it has had a long history as we all have, young though we may be—and this adds to its appeal. There is a seahorse from an old merry-go-round, on which a child can ride; some antique toys on the mantel of the fireplace; and a wall hanging depicting a fairy tale.

It is not only children who enjoy these furnishings, who sit on the throne, or busy themselves with the doll house. Since the room is there for both adults and children, there are furnishings which are clearly for everybody, such as one or two open bowls full of candy on small tables for people to help themselves from. There is comfortable modern furniture—a sofa, and several easy chairs of various sizes to relax in—and on the walls there are pictures and shelves full of books. This room is also the place where patients will meet later with visitors.

The way in which the room is equipped states that the child's needs and pleasure are as important as the adult's; and the two types of furnishings and their usage do not clash, but actually enhance each other. This is not lost on either children or adults. The symbolic meaning of some of the pieces shows also that reality and fantasy do not need to fight each other, that each has a rightful place in our lives. (If the same spirit were to permeate not only the living rooms but the lives of more families, perhaps there would be fewer patients for us to take care of.) Thus a special type of living, one that adult and child can enjoy together, is presaged by the way this room is appointed. It is another of the silent messages to which the mentally ill person (though he may be reluctant to admit it) responds much more readily than normal adults, who don't permit themselves to experience consciously the spontaneous reactions of their unconscious. The room indicates that a combination of the child's reality and the adult's is not only possible but more pleasant and constructive for both. The shelves of professional books show that the problems of the mental patient are studied very seriously here by all staff members, and that the patient may do the same himself whenever he so desires. If the psychiatric library contains knowledge which is withheld from patients, read only by specialists, then the presence of these books would be a sham and soon recognized as such by staff and patients.

The elaborately carved throne was used as the university president's chair in the old chapel. We rescued it and had it restored to practical use. To the staff, it symbolizes the possibility of things being returned to new and better life. The new patient is not aware of this history and meaning; but since we are, it carries our feeling that what others have neglected is especially deserving of our efforts as well as our enjoyment in such undertakings.

To the patient it will have different meaning. The megalomanic person who believes himself an emperor and the child who plays at being a king or a queen are both involved in the same thing: an effort to deny one's own feelings of insignificance. In fantasy they magnify their importance, because they are so convinced that they are worthless. To enjoy this role the child requires that we agree to the importance of his fantasy, by our telling him in some fashion that he is indeed like a mighty ruler. To be able to rid himself of the delusions that set him apart from the world, the mental patient needs to be convinced that far from being of no account, he is of great importance to some people; then, eventually, he can feel worthy himself. To do this we have to construct a reality which makes it much easier for him to succeed in than the one where he feels degraded and miserable. A first step in this direction is to show that his delusions are important to us. The furnishings of this room can begin to convey the message.

The throne, the cradle, the doll house, and the seahorse—while all real objects—give credence to the importance of delusions: megalomanic ones; the narcissistic ones which belong to the earliest period of human development; and those in which segments of reality are combined into fantastic creations. (What we call a seahorse is really an imaginary creation, an animal half horse, half sea serpent.)

Freud remarked that the psychotic must painfully invest large amounts of vital energy in the work needed to keep reality from intruding upon his delusional world (41). Eissler tells how for the psychotic panic may be replaced by relative peace if he experiences his therapist's consideration of his delusions as having some validity (33). If somebody else is ready to share the psychotic's world picture, he can spare himself part of the energy needed to protect against reality, and thus he is relieved of some of his pain. These furnishings suggest the possibility that here the patient may find people who are willing to arrange a room and to provide furnishings which encourage some play with delusional ideas because they deem them worth considering. This is limited, though, because the rest of the room is arranged and furnished in accordance with everyday reality. The psychotic is unable to achieve this comfortable relationship between fantasy and reality and hence has given up efforts to do so; the result is that just as he fails to grant importance to external reality, so others refuse to concede validity to his internal reality.

Thus the implicit message this room conveys to the patient is that although this institution is well anchored, functioning safely and securely in the real world, it nevertheless does not deny the psychological validity of delusions for those who need them; such delusions are given their place in the order of things. Further, it believes that the inner reality of wish-fulfilling fantasies can be—and here is—used to enrich the external reality of the common world.

In therapeutic work with psychotics, the distinction between psychological pertinency and objective reality is important, and so is the task of relating the two to each other. Neglecting this has led to serious confusions, as evidenced in some of the writings of Laing and his followers (80, 81). Too frequently it is assumed that the psychotic's delusions have no validity at all. To counteract this error, it has been claimed by some that these delusions reflect or even constitute a higher reality; that they presage superior states of consciousness yet to come. Inner experiences are indeed real enough; but they can yield information about external reality only to the degree that they have been harmonized with it. Psychotherapy with the psychotic must be firmly based on the knowledge that while his delusions are pertinent for his internal reality, they also tell solely about his inner mental process and correspond to external reality only in vague and distorted ways. As a matter of fact, an important part of therapeutic work deals with those aspects of the patient's external past world which have psychologically validated his inner distortions of reality.

The living room wasn't deliberately furnished in this way to fulfill all these intentions. We did it because, having tried a variety of ways to equip and arrange the room, at last it felt "right" to us, and we liked it. We wanted it to express our therapeutic convictions, as well as our human concern for the feelings of a patient just arriving at the School, and we wanted it to be in accord with both. As with so much else in our work—from the way we arranged the building and its details, to how we treat the patient—we started out on the basis of our theoretical convictions of what we thought might feel good to him, and did in fact feel good to us. Afterwards, if it did indeed appeal to the patients, we tried to understand how and why; if not, on this basis we changed things around. So it took quite a few years before this or any other room of the School finally felt completely "right," at least for the time being. When it ceased to feel right, it was time to replan it.

Not unexpectedly, since the way we use a room, feel about it, or relate to it is the consequence of our personality, this room turned out to be a good projective test. On first coming to the institution, none of the mentally sick children ever touched the doll house. A family home, representative of their own family, evoked emotions that were too difficult. Since they had not previously had a throne to sit on, a seahorse to ride, or a crib like this one to crawl into, these seemed less contaminated by their past experiences; these objects were more readily, though tentatively, explored. Practically all "normal" children are spontaneously attracted to the doll house, though older boys prefer the throne. Most "normal" people inquire about the latter, probably because they don't expect to find this type of furniture here.

Physical settings, like words, can also lie. That is why psychotics have to "case the joint" in attempts to form their own opinions. To offer them a chance to do so undistracted by us, we let them have some time by themselves in this room; thus inviting them to meet the institution first on their own, before meeting us. When we do enter the room, our manner is warm but reserved, suggesting that we prefer the visitor to take the initiative; and we let him cue us as to the distance he wishes to maintain for the moment. It would be forward to join a relative stranger without being specifically invited to do so, when, for example, he is leafing through a book, sitting on the throne, or riding the merry-go-round horse, to say nothing of being curled up in the crib.

From our work with psychotic patients we learned how important it is to assess correctly what is the right physical and emotional distance to keep from them. This depends most importantly on the degree and nature of their anxiety about and their desire for and fear of physical closeness. They may feel we are too distant to be "in touch" with them, or too close for comfort. They need to feel that we can keep the "right distance" and stay "in our place," though at one time this can be quite close, at another quite far away.

In the earlier discussion of assaultive and suicidal patients, it was mentioned that everything depends on whether the institution is able to restore sufficient security to them so that they no longer need to act explosively or destructively. The best way to do this is through personal relations, and the worst is through restraints. In these relations, much depends on beginning the interacting at the right distance from them, in order to give them security without being threatening or overpowering. Empathy with the patient almost automatically dictates what is the best physical distance.

Since the destructive patient is overwhelmed by negative feelings, and knows his own inner violence, he expects others either to flee from him or to attack him. If others keep too far away, he interprets this as fear of his violence and it outrages him to be viewed as so out of control. It leaves him isolated when he needs help, and this also angers him. The difficulty in approaching him at this moment is that it is likely to be interpreted as an intended attack or effort to restrain him. Much as the patient may wish to control himself, when others try to control him he feels it is an assault. I have often been able to quiet such a patient by asking others to stand back and leave him alone, as a first step in assuring him that no attack is intended. But this leaves him isolated with his destructiveness. Then, by asking him to please come closer to me so that we can talk things over more comfortably, I convey that I am neither afraid of him nor consider his explosiveness as devastating, so I don't need to keep my distance from him. But most of all, I put him in control of his actions. Many a violent patient who threatened, "You'd better stay away from me," had no difficulty in accepting the invitation to shorten the distance between us. The implication that he is well able to be in charge of what he does is reassuring. If he should then move in my direction, everything depends not only on the inflection or tone of voice in which he is asked: "Come, tell me what is the matter," but also on it being said at just the right distance as he is approaching. In other cases an attack can be avoided by the simple device of sitting down, thus showing that one neither intends nor expects any violence. This must not be done too far away from the patient; one must appear not distant but smaller, with the patient superior in looming above one; followed at the right moment by an invitation for him to sit down, too, so that we can look at things together and find out what can be done about the situation. Being in control of himself and not carried away by his anxiety, annoyance, or anger, the therapist creates an aura, an atmosphere which facilitates the patient's gaining control of himself.

The importance of distance should be obvious, and not just when dealing with potentially violent individuals. Anyone who has dealt with people must have learned that different emotional situations require different physical space for optimal interaction. But it took zoologists studying animals to clarify what is involved in this problem.

Hediger was the first to observe and discuss the importance of what he named "personal distance" and "critical distance" in animals (62, 63). "Personal distance" refers to that amount of space between itself and another which the animal selects as comfortable; in human beings this will change according to the situation and other variables, as in the first meeting between staff member and patient in the living room. There are two "critical" distances. First, if the animal is approached beyond a certain critical distance, it is driven to immediate flight. If it is approached still more closely, at the second critical distance flight changes suddenly to attack. The personal and the critical distances vary widely from species to species, but they are the same for all members of a species. This behavior rule is so exact that, for example, with many different big cats Hediger could measure within centimeters the same distance for the critical reaction of flight, and for attack. An attack of this kind never has the character of a calculated offensive—except when the great cats are hungry. It is always of a defensive emergency nature (63). The same absence of calculation is true for mental patients, and it would be well if society, and those who deal with them directly, were aware of this and kept it in mind.

Hediger also describes how trainers use this distance factor to teach animals to perform. By approaching the animal, they get it to withdraw toward the rear of the cage or ring in the circus. They don't have to do this with their bodies; pushing a chair or whip closer to the animal is enough. Then by approaching even closer, as they reach the second critical distance, they force the animal to change from withdrawal to defensive attack. If, for example, a stool is placed between them, the animal will move forward onto it, at which moment the trainer, through sudden withdrawal of himself or of the whip, increases the distance. No longer within the critical distance for flight or attack, the animal "stops in its tracks" and remains standing or seated on the stool.

It would be convenient if things were as definite and consistent in man. According to how he feels about the person he is encountering, the human being may wish to keep him at a certain distance; he may step back if approached abruptly, or even feel provoked if the other comes "too close for comfort." There is, of course, great diversity in this respect on the part of individuals and among groups, variations which are typical for different social classes. Even wider divergences can be found among different cultures. Hall discusses the disparity in this respect between North Americans, the British, Germans, Japanese, and Arabs (58). Much also depends on the mood of the moment, the nature of relations to the other person, and innumerable other factors. Within these limitations, Hall suggests that in addition to the two distances (personal and critical) which Hediger established as characteristic for animals, the study of human distances requires more detailed subdivisions. It is to the great detriment of our therapeutic work that these findings have been neglected; they could be most useful in regulating the distance between people so that human interactions could become more effective—particularly those between the mental patient and the people who wish to establish and maintain optimal contact with him. These patients are much more sensitive to the inherent message of distances than normal persons. The correct use of such knowledge could make the difference between helping a potentially violent patient to get hold of himself, or his feeling pushed to destructive acting out.

A huge man when being approached in a threatening way is less apt to turn and run than a small one. The trouble with man is that with him such reactions have much more to do with how big he feels, rather than how tall or heavy he actually is. Nevertheless, if we wish to succeed in our work with mental patients, we have to learn how to approach them and how to keep our distance. For each one we need to know—having learned from experience with him and with others, further relying on our spontaneous feeling for the situation—whether to stand still and only extend our hand, or to move in his direction; whether to move fast or slow, but never too fast or too slow, because either shows our anxiety; too fast is interpreted as an attack, and too slow as shying away. We have to regulate our distance because in this way we can help the patient feel in control of the situation, and with it of himself.

According to Hall, man in society functions on the basis of four distances in addition to the critical ones. He calls these the intimate, the personal, the social, and the public. Man is so much subtler than other animals that for each of these four distances we must differentiate between a close and a far phase. Also, because of his complexity, his being subject to much wider variations in his feelings for other people (depending on the vagaries of his life history and social and emotional development), his ability to function in some of these phases is poorly developed, to the point that he cannot handle them. Some people are unable to perform in the large space required by public gatherings; they are uncomfortable and become unable to express themselves well if the distance from the people they address becomes too great. The incapacity to function within intimate distance, as is characteristic of psychiatric patients, is more serious. If they were able to manage intimate relations, which all unfold within this distance, they would not be isolates but comfortable social beings, well rooted in a common humanity.

Starting with the greatest distance, the *far phase of public distance*, Hall estimates that persons in it are separated from each other by 25 or more feet. With people so remote from each other, the subtle shadings of meaning that can be conveyed by the normal voice are lost. It is a distance unsuitable for reaching others in any personalized way, with the exception of those short emotional messages which a scream conveys. Hence we interact with patients over such distance only in an emergency, when a shouted "Watch out," "Stop it," or "Wait, I'm coming," may demonstrate our concern even over such space.

Before we know another person, particularly when he may be afraid of what we are up to, the *close phase of public distance*—roughly 12 or more feet—may be reassuring to him in the sense that it prevents us from imposing our physical presence. If he should feel threatened, it is enough space for him to take evasive or defensive action easily. He can readily get in and out of contact, as he wishes. When there are no external noises, it is a span over which the normal voice can easily be understood, even when we speak fairly softly, for we are almost automatically more careful about how we enunciate; words are more deliberately chosen, sentences have a more formal ring.

The comparatively large size of the living room at the Orthogenic School—some 18 by 26 feet—permits keeping one's distance from a new patient, who may be occupying himself with the throne, the crib, the rocking horse, or whatever. This space permits one to stay in contact with the patient while giving him plenty of room to do what he wishes. Paying attention to what he is doing without interfering or imposing oneself, trying to understand what he is telling us through his actions, and patiently waiting until he is ready to include us in some fashion—conveys our respect to him, and also tells him that we respect what he is doing. In precisely this way, one can eventually establish contact much more successfully than by any direct action.

Of course, this is nothing but what common politeness and tact require. Nonetheless, I have rarely seen such regard exhibited in psychiatric institutions outside the therapeutic sessions. Particularly on first meeting the patient, most institutions seem pressed to do something for or to him. They show little respect for him and what *he* is doing—demonstrating right from the start that the staff do not feel that as a unique individual he is worthy of their time. For example, plying him with questions, or subjecting him to a testing program on arrival, is asking the patient to do something for the institution, before the institution has done anything for him. There are many ways of intruding and imposing, and not giving the patient sufficient "elbow room" is one of them. Providing the right amount of space suitable for him, and according to the way he defines the situation, is showing respect for him and sensitivity to his needs.

The arrangement of chairs in the "living room" is such that the patient or visitor can readily indicate what distance he needs to be comfortable. Two easy chairs are placed on each side of the fireplace, separated by about 12 feet. A few pieces, such as a rocking chair, are placed quite distant from all the others. But two other chairs are quite close to each other, separated only by a small table; and there are some foot stools that can easily be moved anywhere, according to whatever the situation suggests.

We soon learned that nobody likes to be imposed on immediately when meeting another person, particularly one who is viewed as possibly becoming important. This is why, at first, we give people who are still strangers plenty of room, and remain separated by the closer phase of public distance, where the space is enough to see the person easily, even when he is standing, and permits one to form an impression of the other "as a whole." Upon meeting a person, we all feel the need to "size him up," which we can do only if we can observe him in his entirety. If we have to look him up and down to gain an impression of what he is like, this is impolite and intrusive, if not outrightly aggressive. A distance of at least 7 feet is required to see all of a person, and 10 to 12 feet if he is to have space to move about and give us a chance to observe him in movement, which is a significant aspect for gaining a better understanding of what kind of person he is. To be able to walk and not bump into a wall or "maneuver himself into a corner," the room must be longer than 15 feet, at least in one dimension. This is all easily possible in our living room. And unlike an office, which belongs to the people working there and which cramps one's style and restricts one's freedom, the room and its furniture are obviously there for the visitor. This gives him greater freedom to use them as he sees fit; the furniture is spaced far enough apart for him to move about freely.

Standing and keeping one's distance for a short time also permits the other person to take you in, for it is a two-way process, before he proceeds to study details of mien and manner. After he has had a chance to do so at his leisure, and before the atmosphere becomes still and uncomfortable, a first big decision has to be made: how far from the stranger to sit down—whether it is preferable to continue "keeping one's distance," or to reduce it to the *far phase of social distance*, which in our culture is from 7 to 10 feet. This is typically the distance which separates people who sit on opposite sides of a desk.

While most business is transacted at that distance, it is nevertheless too close for comfort when one of the parties is not sure whether he can trust the other. It is a distance at which we no longer feel free to stand up if we want to, or to increase the space between us if the topic under discussion causes discomfiture. In a bigger room we can increase and decrease the distance between us at will when we feel we are getting "hot under the collar." If things become tense and we cannot do this, we begin to feel trapped; the person on the other side of the desk seems to keep us captive at an unsuitable distance. Respect for the autonomy and the feelings of the other person requires that we meet him first in a room where the furniture does not give us a decided advantage over him; and where he is free to sit down or get up without awkwardness, or to seat himself farther away to remain comfortable as the conversation—or silent interaction, as the case may be—changes.

I mentioned earlier that the living room is also the place where patients later meet with those who come to visit them; and there are several reasons why we selected it for this purpose. First, it is the place where the patients originally separated from all those others. So at least as far as the room is concerned, they take up where they left off, which suggests continuity in their relations. Second, when close relatives such as parents and children see each other again after a lapse of time, it seems natural, at least to some, to embrace as they meet. But as soon as this is done, they want to take each other in; assessing how they each may have changed, and in what direction. To do this they must be able to step back and take a good look at each other, which again requires considerable unobstructed space. Given the complexity of emotions that exist between a mental patient and his closest relatives, some very much wish or need to keep a distance from the other. The size of the room and the various distances between the easy chairs allow the patient to sit down as far away or close to his visitors as he desires.

When given the freedom and a chance to do so, mental patients use the opportunities the room and its furniture offer them cleverly. On meeting his parents, for example, a child will climb up on the merry-go-round horse; "high on horseback," he feels equal to a parent who might otherwise dominate him. Others achieve the same results more explicitly by sitting on the throne which, like any throne, is quite distant from where anybody else can sit down. As the inner security of the patient increases, he dares to openly show his defiance. Long before he can afford to challenge the other in that way, he may react to the encounter by moving himself into the farthest corner, turning his back to one and all; or shrinking away in some other fashion. Once he has learned not only to manage but to feel comfortable in the intimate sphere, then if he feels like it, he will sit down close to his visitor, side by side with him on the couch, which is there precisely to permit such closeness. Occasionally, a relative will try to force a patient into greater closeness than the patient feels is right or comfortable. Most patients, however, are clever enough to find ways to protect themselves, either with some piece of furniture such as the doll house or by claiming they have to go and fetch something from their room, only to return and sit down away from the closeness that had been imposed on them.

The living room permits the new patient, the resident, or the visitor to control what distance he wishes to retain.

Nothing is more displeasing to the mental patient than for the staff to give him a "hearty welcome." It is intended to make him feel comfortable and at ease, but overpowers him because it doesn't permit him to decide whether or not he wishes such emotional contact then. Moreover, the feelings expressed mean nothing to him personally, since he is not yet known, and the scene convinces him that he is being "glad-handed" in a general way, like all other new arrivals. Like any other serialization and regimentation of mental patients, it reflects their being processed by the institution without due regard for their uniqueness as persons. Some of this anxiety can be counteracted if the institution's director is the person who meets a patient first. I made it my business to be the first representative of the institution who met the patients as people. Somebody else, usually the institution's secretary, would open the door for them, help them out of their coats, show them into the living room, ask them whether they wanted or needed anything, such as a cup of coffee, and invite them to make themselves comfortable, adding that the director would be with them shortly.

I felt it important not to relegate this crucial first encounter to anybody else. The newcomer should be able to form his own opinion of what the "boss" is like immediately, since he is expected to represent the institution's anima more than anyone else. The director's actions should make it obvious to the newcomer that the institution exists only for the patient.

Since most of our patients were young enough to be brought by adults (usually their parents), this posed some problems. (However, the same problems occur with adult patients, who are usually accompanied when they arrive at a mental institution.) It takes considerable skill and tact to prevent these others from taking the center of attention away from the patient without offending their sensitivities, since this is also a most difficult encounter for them. But it is of the greatest importance that the patient knows the institution is here to serve *him*, rather than the desires or convenience of those who bring him and obviously want to place him here. Most persons who accompany a patient understand when they are told that he should have an opportunity to speak or not speak for himself, without anyone doing it for him. Often, though, appropriate gestures convey such meaning even more effectively, such as asking them to remain seated while oneself turning away from them to the patient. Those accompanying the patient are, of course, also entitled to form their opinion of the institution based on their meetings with the director. But there are other times and situations for the director to converse with them.

Since they had been told by the secretary, they knew who I was when I entered the room and we met for the first tentative interaction. The optimum distance to maintain between each other at any time is not too difficult to gauge, because the moves in space from "keeping one's distance" to "getting down to business" are typical, though the verbal content during this maneuver differs radically with each person. Some newcomers move fast, others very slowly; some wish to keep the initiative, others to be enticed; but in any case the task is to help them move, out of their own free will, from the public into the social distance and to interaction. When this point was reached, I would invite the patient to continue getting acquainted in my office.

For the patient to come with me to the office I sometimes had to reduce the space between us to that of "personal distance," even intimacy. For example, there were those patients, particularly mute ones, who could not activate themselves to move out of the chair, or whatever position they had assumed, but who were willing to come with me if I held out my hand for them to take hold of, or to reject. If I kept my hand tentatively extended long enough, without any pressure to grasp it, after a while—occasionally a long while to convince themselves that I would not rush them—they would take hold of it and come with me. In no case was my hand rejected, but sometimes, sensing that they were not ready for any "getting to know me," I knew better than to try. The first meeting would then be conducted entirely in the living room. On the second meeting, they were always willing to come into my office; the fact that I had not insisted on it the first time gave them sufficient security to risk it the second time. (It is easier for the patient's relatives to make this move, but even they feel much more comfortable if they have a chance to look me over in the less demanding public distance before moving within the social space.)

Once in the director's office, which is about 10 by 15 feet, the space necessary for the remoter "public" encounter no longer exists. The size barely allows for the farther reaches of "social distance"— from 7 to about 10 feet between people—but for all practical purposes it suggests the closeness of the "personal" or the close phase of the "social distance," (a distance of about 3–6 feet). In this space one can no longer see the entire body of the other person, another reason why one should not meet anybody—least of all a patient— for the first time sitting behind one's desk. The desk hides part of one's body, and usually obstructs the view of part of the body of the other person. It is a distance for the meeting of minds, but it is not close enough for the meeting of bodies, which belongs in the intimate sphere (the remoter intimate distance is about 1½ feet), a distance where one is literally "in touch" with the other. When so close, one can not only see but smell the other person, even feel his body heat.

Obviously no room precludes moving into this "intimate" distance, and the smaller the room the more inviting it is for this possibility. But the appropriate distance can be clearly indicated by the furnishings and room arrangements. Sitting down behind the desk after inviting the visitor to take some other chair signals that this is not a place for intimacy. Even the chairs, placed close to each other, keep those sitting in them at least 3 feet apart—that is, out of "touching" distance. By choosing which of the several conveniently placed chairs to sit in, the visitor could remain at least 6 feet away or place himself much closer, within 3 feet. Both are good distances for freer interactions after the ice has been broken. Two persons keeping within this space can comfortably discuss personal matters without becoming intrusive. The farther distance of about 6 feet encourages conversing even about quite personal matters in an objective way; it permits talking about very important issues without fully committing oneself to the other person. This is an interval to which most in our society are well accustomed, since it is the distance which people keep who are used to working closely and comfortably with each other.

This is also the distance where, as noted above, one can see only part of the other person's body; but this part can be seen well and in detail. It is close enough to observe the lines of the face, the movements of the lips, the sparkle—or its absence—in the eye; all of which reveal so much about how the person is feeling about what he is saying or not saying.

Artists know all this; a full-length painting of a person gives us his "public" appearance: how he is dressed or simply how he holds his body. This has to be rendered at least some 10 to 12 feet away. The story is entirely different when, as in a portrait, the artist wishes to tell about "the inner man" conveying more than his outer appearance. The best distance for studying a portrait—that is, how far away the face should seem—is from 4 to 8 feet. As one artist put it:

> *Four to eight feet is the portrait distance . . . here, at the normal distance of social intimacy and easy conversation, the sitter's soul begins to appear. . . . Nearer than three feet, within touching distance, the soul is far too much in evidence for any sort of disinterested observation . . . the sitter's personality is too strong. The influence of the model on the painter is too powerful, too disturbing to the artist's necessary detachment* (56).

One could wish that those to whom the fate of mental patients is entrusted would study them with the attention of the artist and learn how to "liberate" the patient's soul, what the right distance is for reaching his body, for touching his mind, and for permitting him to be himself and interact autonomously with others.

10 | *Dormitories: Group Living and "Territoriality"*

None of the institution's rooms can compare in importance with the one in which the patient will live. Unless the promises implied by the external and internal appearance of the institution, the symbolic messages it tried to convey, and the experiences the patient had when visiting are all fully borne out by the room provided for him, the promises will only turn out to be a bigger cheat than the other lies he has come to expect of life. The best appointed public rooms, the most careful apportioning of space for specific human interactions, the most marvelously equipped treatment rooms, the sensitivity of the therapist to the patient's needs—all will be perceived as a beguiling sham if even greater care does not extend to the place where most of his life goes on and which is to be the center of his existence. Reintegration of the patient's personality requires that his life attain a clearly defined center; a core to which he can refer all his other experiences either directly or by implication, so that they coalesce, rather than confuse or tear him further apart. To facilitate this, his most important experiences at the institution should occur right where he lives, in the place which more than any other is his own. If the institution sees that this is the case, then it both carries the symbolic message that he should gain a center to his life and facilitates his doing so. He is most secure where he feels truly at home, and better able to work through whatever he experiences there.

In most psychiatric institutions, however, the places thought to be most important for the patient's integration are definitely not his. The therapist's treatment room or the occupational worker's shop, for example, are his for temporary use only. Though every psychoanalyst knows that the patient will not get well as long as he tries to use what goes on during his analytic hour to replace living his own life, this situation still prevails in psychiatric institutions. Conscientious analysts stop treating a patient who does not stop seeing his treatment hour as the essence of his life, because for therapy to be effective, what he gains in it must be applied to the true center of his life. A mental patient who has no center to his life must be helped by all possible means to create one for himself, and the best place to do this is in one which is most his own. To encourage this, the institution has to emphasize the importance of the patient's own place, because it is his and nobody else's. If for economic reasons skimping is thought necessary, it should take place anywhere else except the patient's living quarters.

As obvious as it may seem, such thinking does not appear to have penetrated the practice of mental institutions. Even when serious efforts are made to improve things, they usually start everywhere else but the patients' quarters. One example given in a study promoting the reformation of mental hospitals tells how

> *a significant contribution toward improving the physical appearance was made by the medical director, who felt the importance of setting an example to others. He ordered the complete redecoration of his office and that of his secretary, at his own expense. . . . The change served as a dramatic example to the rest of the personnel that he was seriously interested in developing the physical as well as the interpersonal aspects of a warm homelike environment* (54).

It is admirable to spend his own money on redecorating part of the mental hospital, but wouldn't it have been more impressive to staff and patients if this director had improved some of the patients' living areas? Obviously he could have afforded to redecorate only a small part of these spaces; but wouldn't that have shown much greater concern for the patients, and acknowledged what the hospital was there for? It is open to speculation to what degree he did it for himself, since we also learn that before redecoration "his office had been shabby indeed." Though it may have had beneficial consequences, it still reflects an ancient and still quite prevalent attitude by which the director's quarters receive the prime attention, with things proceeding from there. I am convinced that improvements should move in the opposite direction: the patients' quarters must be improved first and foremost.

Age and sex make some difference in room arrangements, because each group is best served by that which is most advantageous for it. But the differences are only in detail; there is no difference in the principles which must underlie the thinking and planning for the patient's daily life, and what facilities ought to be offered to him. Originally, the Orthogenic School population consisted of grade-school children, but with time we increased the scope of our efforts, first to the age range from five to eighteen, and during the last fifteen years of which I write, up to age twenty-five. At first we thought such widening would require a differently organized plant. To our surprise, we soon learned from experience that this was true only to a very small degree. While I cannot speak from personal knowledge about older adults and the old-age group, my feeling is that the organizational differences they would require would be smaller than is generally assumed.

For example, we expected that older adolescents would feel more comfortable in single or double rooms than in dormitories; so we tried single and double rooms, and found them far from satisfactory. It turned out to be too easy a solution for the patient to withdraw to his private room. Many crises in human relationships were thus prevented from surfacing, but with the result that they were solved only after much delay or not at all. Easier night rest was not even guaranteed by such sleeping arrangements, because many felt fearful when alone at night. The greatest drawback was the unavoidable neglect of one or another patient, since there is never sufficient staff to provide each patient with his own *tsukisoi*. If a staff member was with one patient in his room, he was literally out of touch with and—potentially more dangerous—out of earshot of all the others.

Naturally, while not wishing to give up any of the benefits to be derived from group living, the patients wanted all the advantages of a single room. Within a year it became obvious that those placed in single or double rooms had made considerably less progress toward being able to cope with life, to relate to others, and to take advantage of what the institution had to offer, than those who had continued to live in small groups. It was a clear sign of the patients' knowing what was best for them when some requested to live in a group. Others invited a third person to join them in a double room and thus, on their own, formed a small group. They were not unaware of the advantages of living in a single or double room; but since the group protected their privacy within it as much as possible, and since they never felt shut off from the world in the group as they did in their private rooms, they realized how much they had gained from group living. The result was that most of those living in single or double rooms spent nearly all of their waking hours, when not otherwise occupied, in the common living room and went to their room only to go to bed. At night they felt somewhat cheated before they fell asleep, because the staff member taking care of them could only be in one room at a time; thus they felt less well protected when asleep.

Therefore, when we planned the new living quarters for the adolescents, we arranged for some five or six patients to form one group, living in single or double rooms (Plate 11), opening directly into a larger central living room. In this way we hoped to retain all the therapeutic and human values of group living, while still providing for greater privacy. (I need not elaborate on the great value of group living when it is arranged to serve the needs of the patients and be therapeutic in all aspects, since it is amply discussed in the vast literature on group work [7, 93, 94].) To our dismay, however, we realized that despite our efforts not to lose any of the benefits of group living, something very important got lost. This occurred even though the patients soon spent very little time in their own rooms. There were many disadvantages to double rooms. When two patients room together, each is more dependent on, and at the mercy of, one other person—so that either is over-vulnerable if things get sticky between the two of them. For example, one may want to unload what is on his mind and the other may not want to be bothered; or one may invite a third person at an unwelcome time for the other. If the second occupant then walks out, he offends the other two persons; if the occupant and his visitor wish to have privacy with each other, this places the second occupant in the position of the unwelcome intruder in his very own place.

For the staff member, the patient's single or double room never feels like one where he lives *with* the patient. It is undesirable for the staff member to feel like a visitor in a room where events of great emotional import should take place, for he cannot extend himself emotionally as readily and deeply in a room that is not also his. Not having a room in common weakens the bond between staff member and patient. So, in regard to the intimacy of patients with each other, little was gained with these new arrangements. This was not a clear disadvantage because patients don't always profit from such intimacy with one another, but often may suffer from its consequences. Much was lost, however. The quality of intimacy between staff member and patient suffered—that relationship which is the most effective emotional constellation for helping the patient get well. This became so apparent that, as I write, the plan is either to change the rooms into, or to make them more like, dormitories for six persons.

A single room always implies that one has to rely on one's own resources; that there is nobody who wishes to share one's life intimately. This must also have been the experience of others studying the merits of mental patients living in small wards *versus* private rooms, since the World Health Organization's report on psychiatric services recommends small dormitories for six to eight patients as the best solution (2). Others have arrived at the same conclusion we have, that

> *Eight appears to be the largest group in which it is possible for one person to be sensitive to each member's interactions and to fully observe the tone and temper of the remainder of the group. When there are more than eight people, some are likely to go "out of field." However, groups can also be too small. If there are only three or four people, there is danger of intense affects developing among them, along with unnecessary vulnerability to loss and overuse of one set of relationships at the expense of others requiring different ego organization. (30)*

I believe this is true for all ages. But if patients live in groups (or wards, to employ the designation commonly used in psychiatric hospitals), the number living in one ward has to be small, and rooms must be readily available to them where they can have some temporary privacy if they want it. If they choose to withdraw, we have found that they are even more in need of a staff member with them, since they tend to withdraw only if something is seriously bothering them. While either solution, small wards or private or semi-private rooms, has its advantages and liabilities, as long as each patient cannot be provided with a staff member for the entire time he is awake, the small group seems preferable.

It is of prime importance to determine the optimum size for group living. Four is too few for constructive group living, while eight is probably the maximum. In our experience, groups of six or seven were most successful. Interestingly enough, through human history this seems to have been the average size of the nuclear family, at least when it comprised grandparents and unmarried adult family members (82).

The physical space a group or ward this size requires must be properly gauged. Because of the overcrowding in most mental hospitals, and the tendency toward ever bigger homes in our middle classes, one might easily think: the more space, the better. This is by no means true. As stated earlier, psychiatric patients are not given sufficient living space, and by and large there seems little danger that they will be given too much of it. But if they were, this would also be undesirable; while the intention is to develop the patient's autonomy, too much of a good thing often has the opposite effect. Just as one can easily get lost in a welter of planned activities, one can get lost in too much space. Weighed down by his feelings of insignificance, the mental patient particularly is at a disadvantage in a too-large room, which makes him feel even smaller. As so often in life, the right middle ground between extremes is best suited to develop our true humanity.

Unfortunately there are no good studies available yet on the ideal living space for one person in the United States. Data have been published for French working groups, but it is entirely possible that there may be differences from culture to culture on the best spatial allocation per person. In France, too, the original assumption was that the greater the expanse a person had at his command, the more comfortable he would be. But the findings contradicted this easy belief; not surprising when we stop to think about it. If children grow up in a setting which surrounds them at all times with public or social space, as adults they may suffer and even fail in those experiences which require personal or intimate spacing; they may feel "out of touch" with things or themselves. Children who grow up under conditions which allow only for the closer phase of personal distance may always feel imposed on by others; as if they do not have enough room to be themselves.

When the French investigators tried to understand the consequences of crowding on the basis of how many persons lived in a dwelling unit, nothing significant emerged. But when the question asked was how many square meters were available to each person living in an apartment, they found that where each member of a family had less than 10 to 12 square yards available, the indices of social, personal, and even physical pathology doubled. This was according to expectation; but it also emerged that when each person had *more* than 16 square yards at his disposal, it increased his pathology, though not as sharply (27). Perhaps there is more to territoriality in man than we are yet ready to accept. Animals rarely stake out a larger area for themselves than they need; but like man, they are adversely affected if their normal territorial space becomes reduced in size. We all know that man suffers badly from having too little territory; but we are not equally aware that too much of it also seems to be detrimental.

Long before these studies appeared, however, our experience at the Orthogenic School had taught us the same. Being Americans and of good will, we also had started out with the assumption: the more room the better. When we began our work at the School, children had been crowded up to twelve in one ward; this was an abomination. So we radically reduced the population of each dormitory; but soon the children appeared to "rattle around," to get lost in space. Before, they had "stepped on each other's toes"; now, they seemed at all times "out of touch," "beyond reach" for the staff member who tried to maintain continuous contact with them. Experience forced us to realize that the patients seemed to thrive best, and our work to proceed most successfully, when the dormitory was of a size that allocated roughly 14 to 16 square yards to each person for his private use. (This figure does not include the space available to him in various public places, such as lounges, the dining room, the shops, classrooms [Plate 12], various meeting rooms, etc.) Therefore, in our experience, there is an optimum space or territory within which human beings seem to live most comfortably, and as the French study suggested, it is a rather narrow range lying between no less than 10–12 square yards and not much more than 16 square yards.

This amount of living space seems optimal for Western man. In other cultures things are different. Hall remarks how closely Arabs crowd together in a bazaar, for example, where they push and jostle each other without discomfort; but as for the rooms in their houses, the more spacious the better. (It should be mentioned that in addition to the dormitory area, there are many other rooms available to the patients of the Orthogenic School.)

In our middle-class sleeping arrangements, we may have gone too far by giving each person his own room. Caudill and Weinstein, in discussing Japanese sleeping customs, mention that

> A person in Japan can expect to co-sleep in a two-genera-
> tion group, first as a child and later as a parent and grand-
> parent; to sleep alone is considered somewhat pitiful be-
> cause a person would, therefore, be lonely. These patterns
> of sleeping are not a function of "overcrowding" in the
> Japanese home, but rather a matter of choice. (26)

Perhaps more than an occasional "pajama party" is needed to combat middle-class children's feelings of isolation; their enjoyment of these and instances like camp life where they sleep together in tents and otherwise crowded living quarters, which some adolescents prefer, suggests that communal sleeping meets a strongly felt need.

But even within a group operating fairly well, each person needs his own territory, a clearly designated private space, just as any group living requires an area which commonly belongs to all members of the group. Again empirically we found that this "private" area, the patient's very own "elbow room," has to be from at least 6 to 8 square yards, thus comprising not quite half of the space needed for each person to live comfortably without feeling either too crowded or lost in it. So although our patients live in dormitories, each one has a private area, into which nobody is permitted to intrude except by invitation. When an individual retires into this private area, everybody else in the dormitory is then beyond both the intimate and the personal distance. Privacy, as far as distance is concerned, can thus be assured even in ward arrangements, provided the staff is respectful of it. It is a sign of great confidence when a patient invites a staff member, not to mention another patient, to join him in his private realm, and even asks him to sit on the bed. Nobody, of course, is permitted to take this liberty without permission.

Usually this space is bordered by the patient's bed and his dresser and comprises the area between them. Most patients like to mark the area out further by a small rug; others, more fearful, have to create more specific boundaries around it. For example, many children set up their stuffed animals in a line to delimit their private area, so the animals can protect them against intruders. One adolescent girl, to whom shoes had a very special meaning, required a line of them around her private domain to feel secure within it. It is interesting to watch how each person goes about in his own way to protect his territory, and how none begins to feel "at home" and secure at the institution until he has done so. For some it may take quite a while to believe that this area is really his very private world. Then he begins to stake out his territory in some physical way as described above, and after this he will finally feel as much at home as his pathology permits. He may then protect this territory as fiercely as animals protect theirs. Of course, how the rooms are arranged and furnished has its influence. Here something similar to the findings on territoriality in animals may be at work. For animals trees, fences, streams, and so on, change the amount of territory they require to feel comfortable and secure. The furniture arrangements made for and by the patients serve parallel purposes.

Often human beings, as well as animals, can feel free of such territorial anxiety only after they have made the boundaries secure. Some of Hediger's stories about animals elucidate most directly what is involved in this. A tiger, brought to the zoo in Zurich to be mated, stayed in a corner of the cage totally uninterested in life until

> two and a half months after his arrival, the tiger made his
> "proprietary tour" of his cage, the periphery of which he
> "marked" with squirts of urine, in the same way in which a

tiger in liberty "marks" the limits of his individual territory.
The next day there was a remarkable change in the animal,
he felt at home, and his attitude toward the tigress under-
went a change and so, as a result, some months afterwards
she brought into this world a new little tiger (62).

While most of our patients used different means to stake out their
territory, none felt "at home" in the institution until he had come
to feel safe when eliminating; human beings seem to have this much
in common with their animal ancestors. Thus, besides making the
area around his bed his own, he still feels a stranger until he has
also made the toilet, and the room where it is located, into a friendly
and familiar place. (How the institution can help this process through
its physical arrangements is discussed in the following chapter.)

For human beings, the best way to secure their territory seems
to center around their beds. Strangely enough, it is not sleeping in the
bed which achieves this, but sitting on it; chairs may be used by
anybody, but only the individual "owns" his bed to sit on. Repeatedly
we found that once patients were secure in possession of their private
space and especially of their bed, they preferred to sit there and take
the world in from this particularly safe location. It was from their
bed that often they dared to speak up, saying things they would have
been afraid to utter when not symbolically surrounded by the safety
zone of their territory, and the security which their bed gave them.
This is another reason why we found single rooms less satisfactory,
because how can the activities of the world be taken in or influenced,
when one is sitting on a bed all alone in a private room?

Of course, it takes some doing to make his bed take on all these
important security-giving meanings for the patient, and this requires
help from the institution. Simply buying a fancy bed and assigning
it to a patient for his use will not have these results. Nor does it depend on how the bed is constructed or decorated, though this is also
important. Furniture can attain special significance for patients only
to the degree that it is invested with such meaning by the staff.
Beautiful furniture can be as cold as ice; it does not make up for
human warmth.

We didn't provide each patient with new furniture; if he remained at the institution long enough, eventually he would have his
say in making suggestions for new furniture. But even then his opportunity to choose was restricted, because the furniture had to fit in
with that of the rest of the dormitory. As described, the patients
living in or using one room selected the colors the walls were painted,

and the design of curtains, bedspreads, and so on. We felt unable to give them equal freedom when selecting the furniture, although we did not rely on what was available in the stores. Instead, we designed different furniture for each room in collaboration with an artist, whose task was to translate our ideas into something that was comfortable, sturdy enough to take hard wear, attractive looking, and still conveyed the messages we intended. The furniture had to reveal the care we had taken selecting it not through showiness, but by suggesting our feeling of trying to communicate emotionally to the patient.

For all this to be possible, the furniture had to be custom made. Occasionally we could find appropriate pieces of furniture on the market, but never beds, chests of drawers, or dressers. Even when we could find a chair or couch in a store, we could use only the very best designs, because nothing else would still look good after even a short time. The specially designed furniture, which required considerable craftsmanship, was quite expensive but economical in the long run. Given the heavy use made of it, and the abuse to which it unavoidably was sometimes subjected, we had to have it built much more substantially than anything in the stores, which further added to the expense. Even the best and most sturdy pieces bought in stores did not remain truly serviceable for more than four or five years, and began to look shabby after a year or two. Furniture specially designed and constructed to our specifications easily lasted twice this time and even longer. To a considerable degree this was due to the care with which patients treat things they like, and the staff things they have helped to plan.

To quote only one observer: "Patients rarely destroy things which they feel keenly are for their own benefit, or which they thoroughly enjoy" (54). So we always found that the best—not in terms of somebody else's views, but those of the patients and staff—turned out to be the most economical. (It should not be necessary to add, after all that has been said, that we did not protect the furniture; it was expected that a piece got a hard knock once in a while. Since the piece was well made, it could easily be repaired; some parts, such as the padded part of head and foot boards, or the cane weaving of other pieces, had to be regularly replaced every couple of years or so. This was expected and the furniture was constructed so that it could readily be done.)

Unless the staff feels that these furnishings are the most comfortable and attractive available, they won't invest the furniture with positive feelings, and then the patient cannot either. If the maintenance staff does not see them as something special, which they want to take good care of, this will also subtly affect the patient's feelings. While some may wonder how the cleaning staff, for example, manage not to be resentful of the patients having so much better equipment than they can provide for themselves and their families, the answer is that a person who becomes involved with mental patients soon realizes how desperately unhappy they are; and one is simply not jealous of those who live in such hell. But to feel this, one must have some empathy with them. To bring this empathy about on the part of everybody working at an institution is one of the main tasks of those responsible for its operation.

When we began to re-equip the School, we provided each patient with a special metal chest about a yard long and half a yard wide, so that he would have a place to store his important possessions; he could lock them up if he wanted to or even carry the whole thing around with him. The patients liked this idea and called the boxes "toychests"; they became the repository of an incredible variety of objects of great personal significance. Protective of the contents, the patients tried to keep their chests as close to them as possible. Soon they felt they were too small, so we got chests twice the size; but this made them unwieldy and too heavy when crammed full, as they always tended to be. To be sure of the chests' safety, particularly at night, many felt secure only if they slept on them. Again we took the cue, and from then on we had every bed constructed so that there were two drawers under it where the patients could keep what they wanted to have closest to them. Sleeping on top of these possessions they felt surer about them than if they were kept any other place. This is the reason why a patient's chest of drawers is placed so close to his bed that he can reach it from there. The shelves where some of his possessions are stored, and his closet where he keeps his clothes, are also located so that they can be easily surveyed from his bed, or any other place in his dormitory. In this way, at any time of day or night when he is "at home," he doesn't need to worry about whether his belongings are safe.

If our home is our castle, our bed is the place where we should feel most secure in it. Sometimes I regretted that limitations of space did not permit us to offer the patients beds which are "as big as a house," as some medieval bedsteads were. But the same idea can be hinted at through design. Comfort has to come first, but comfort alone is not enough. The patient's furniture must also be in accord with the symbolic messages discussed, or else belie them, since his private space is where the patient will be most at home. I have not given much thought to the ways in which beds should be designed for adult patients, but even our late adolescents in their twenties were delighted to find a bed waiting for them that, because of its design and decorations, suggested it was ready to receive a mighty warrior after his day's trials and tribulations.

Thus the beds in one room where adolescent boys live have huge backboards which arch in a Gothic style, decorated at head and foot with a coat of arms and a heraldic animal made out of metal, which are repeated on each drawer of the chest that belongs with this bed (Plate 10). Each bed is a different color, and the coat of arms and heraldic animal differs for each. A different theme prevails in each dormitory; in one for teen-aged boys, beds are designed for discoverers, decorated with antique maps at the foot, and old prints of sailing vessels on the headboard. We cannot chart the voyages of exploration into the furthest reaches of the patients' minds or even their dreams, which they will have to undertake to get well—but we can indicate that we know this exploration will be necessary, and that we will make it safe for them. So each bed has a lighthouse at the side, to suggest protection if and when dangerous areas are entered. Even quite grown-up girls like beds with head and foot boards softly padded with material, decorated with floral or Pennsylvania Dutch design (Plates 7 and 8). The beds of younger girls are more like beds for little princesses in a fairy tale. Since none of the patients has ever had a bed or dresser like these, since the furniture of each dormitory is unique, and since the care with which it was constructed is obvious, the major message comes across that we tried our very best to please— even if the particular piece of furniture does not entirely meet with the inner desires of a particular person. If by chance it does not, then we hope that the way he may add touches of his own, which we always encourage, will compensate.

When designing the furniture, even with the greatest ingenuity it is obviously impossible to know the fantasies which are most important to an unknown patient. Here we can only draw on the experience of the past and on the current experience. But as long as the invitation to indulge in a specific fantasy is a genuine declaration, then it really doesn't matter what the fantasy is. That is what counts; the patient will take it from there. As a matter of fact, we got the idea of building beds as a knightly abode from a boy who went around for years fully armored—so we fixed him up with a knight's bed. Once the boy had slept in the bed, he was able to join the rest of us in the everyday world. Many of the other teen-age boys were so attracted by this that we provided similar beds for them too, much to their pleasure.

Any defensive system is like an armor, designed to protect. But while it protects, it inhibits all freedom of movement. A psychological armoring prevents freedom of thought and feelings; but it provides some small measure of safety in encapsulating the individual.

The boy with the armor had been run over by a car when he was three, at the height of his Oedipal conflicts. There were just enough details surrounding this accident to convince him, when delusionally elaborated, that his mother, or possibly both parents, wanted him out of the way and thus they permitted the accident to happen, maybe even arranged it. In the first idea there was a small element of psychological truth; in the latter, only in that sufficient care had not been exercised to forestall an accident which could have been avoided with special attention. For a long time the boy's leg was kept in a heavy cast, inhibiting his movements.

If he had been in the cast prior to the accident, he reasoned, he could not have moved out into the street and been run over; thus armor protects. The cast also permitted healing; another indication of how life-protecting it is. To be safe against what he believed were the evil intentions of his parents—and by extension of the family, the entire world—he put his whole body into a heavy, and heavily constricting, armor. When he arrived, he behaved as though encased in stiff, heavy armor so that he could move his joints only in the most rigid and minimal way. He could not bend his knees, or turn his feet, although he was physically quite strong. The armoring extended to his mind, so that he performed on a feeble-minded level and therefore was considered to be brain-damaged and feeble-minded. But after many years of treatment, he turned out to be very bright.

For the first few years with us he could not move physically, intellectually, or emotionally. Under the impact of the positive emotions by which he was now surrounded, he began to unfreeze just a bit emotionally; but he became afraid that his limbs might also begin to move. With our encouragement, this was the point at which he constructed the most ingenious pieces of armor out of cardboard and other materials. (Interestingly but not surprisingly, wearing them he could move with considerably greater freedom than otherwise, though still only stiffly.) Protected by this armor, he could be induced to move his limbs within it, that is, as much as the armor permitted. But by doing so he learned, much to his surprise, that he could indeed move, where before he had been convinced he could not. With this small movement of his body, he began to move intellectually; but only by studying all about knights, their times and lives. He accumulated an amazing amount of the most detailed and accurate information on the history and myths of knights, which went far beyond what most historians know, unless they specialize in that period. Eventually, the boy needed to feel armored only when he was asleep and unable to watch out for the dangers of the world.

The point of telling this boy's story is to show how in this case, as in many others, the restriction of his delusional system to the bed, and with it symbolically to sleep and dreams, was an important step which freed his daytime active life from being enslaved by it. It also illustrates how the symbolic meaning of architecture and furnishings can play a vital role in curing a schizophrenic.

Another boy made his bed into a most elaborate machine, which made it possible for him to breathe and which powered his digestive tract. One patient turned his very own area into Sherwood Forest, another into Mouse Town, and again another into a different planet. One created an Arabic empire; there on his praying rug turned toward Mecca, he said his daily prayers. He didn't do this because he was a Moslem. On the contrary, it was because he was Jewish, but felt unable to do battle against his overpowering family. He hoped the Arabs might win out over them so that he, too, might have a chance to be victorious. An adolescent girl who could manage to avoid total breakdown only by identifying with Juliet turned her area symbolically into fair Verona.

The reason we encouraged the use of the bed and the immediate area around it for fantasy elaboration was not because we wished to encourage living in a delusional dream world; I have warned many times against the dangers of fostering this. But there is one place for dreaming, and one for living in reality, and the bed is the place for the first. We slowly tried to direct the world of dreams to the bed, making it distinct from fantasy, which should be freely available to us whenever we wish to engage in it. But during our waking hours we should be in control and able to direct our fantasies or stop them at will; one has no such conscious control over dreams and delusions. The farther away the patient moved from his bed area, the more he could enter common reality. To have a private dream world is the privilege of us all, and recent dream studies have given scientific backing to Freud's conviction that without dreams our life is sorely depleted (60, 77). But dreams should be concentrated around our sleeping hours, which we spend in bed.

11 | Dining Room and Bathroom: Trauma and Treatment

Many schizophrenics are very confused, literally, about which end of their body is up; which end of the digestive tract serves what function. Physiologic functions, intake and elimination, are often inextricably interwoven in their minds. Since the importance of eating and everything connected with it has been repeatedly stressed, only a few additional remarks on the importance of eating arrangements are needed.

The infant's first experience with life is being supportedly held, just as a person's first experience after admission at the Orthogenic School is settling into his bed and life space. Within the context of this first experience in life—and at the School—feeding takes place. The nature of these first experiences foretells future security or distress. One of the foremost messages that the patient receives about the intentions of the institution is whether he will not only be well fed, but fed with loving care. This message is not only symbolic but also real. To provide food only at set mealtimes in the dining room is not the best way. But if tasty food is always available, then eating main meals at prearranged times—which feeding a fairly large number requires—will be acceptable, because if one does not feel like eating then or eating much, he doesn't lose out. Therefore at all times, and in all places of the School, we had food readily available to be eaten in relative privacy whenever anybody, staff or patient, felt like it. A box filled with cookies and candies stood within everybody's reach in all rooms, those used by patients, staff, or visitors. In addition, various snacks—sandwiches, fruit, milk, juices, etc.—were brought to the patients three times a day between regular meals: at mid-morning, mid-afternoon, and nighttime, and more often when it seemed appropriate. In case they didn't like these or if they got hungry for something else, there was a kitchenette with supplies for preparing other foods adjacent to each dormitory. Thus when the time came for the three regular meals, the patients didn't need to be hungry and didn't have to eat what was offered; nor was there any reason for them to fear that if they did not fill up during the meal, they might have to go hungry later on.

At first the tables in the dining room were rectangular, one for each dormitory group and one for the staff who at the time were not working with the patients. But we soon learned that these tables were not suitable for our purposes. Conversation flowed freely only between those who sat at the small end of the rectangle and those next to them, sitting at its sides. The reason was that those three persons were not only close to each other, but could face each other without having to turn their necks in a somewhat strained way, as people who sit side by side have to do when conversing. While the staff member sitting with the patients may have put an arm around the shoulders of the one sitting at his side, he was still more likely to talk with another who sat across the table from him, since they faced each other. (This observation was later confirmed by a study which showed that persons sitting across a corner conversed twice as much with each other as compared with those sitting side by side [108].) So we replaced the rectangular tables with circular ones, which resulted in a much wider variety of interactions among those sitting at one table.

Our table tops were of polished rosewood, so we used tablecloths only on special occasions such as a patient's birthday or holidays, since the patients seemed to feel more comfortable without such formality (though they liked it occasionally). Before anyone entered the dining room, the tables were set carefully for exactly the number who would eat at each one. Although each setting included a knife, nothing untoward ever happened. Occasionally an angry or upset patient dropped a plate or threw some silverware, but never at another person, and never a knife, though spoons and much less often forks were tossed. It seems that the trust implied in the constant provision of knives restrained even the most out-of-control patient. Sometimes it was necessary to remove a knife temporarily, in the same way that we made inaccessible the jump rope referred to earlier. But this was done only after a patient had shown that at this moment during the meal the temptation to use the knife destructively was too great. Since the patients knew that as soon as they said they were ready for it, the knife would be returned, there was never any objection when it was removed; and again as with the jump rope, a patient would sometimes spontaneously hand over a knife or on rare occasions a fork to a staff member for him to put it out of reach temporarily.

Some of the food that was cold, such as bread and butter, a salad, and so forth, would be waiting on the table. All warm food was served to the tables by maids only after a group was seated. Seconds, thirds, and more when desired, were served by them as requested. Each course and the plates and cutlery for it were removed before the next one was served. At the table the food was served to the patients individually by the staff member who ate with them.

When food was spilled on the floor or a plate or glass was thrown down, naturally it was immediately cleaned up, usually by the staff member eating with the patient rather than by a maid. The act of hostility was not directed against the maids, nor did the frustration which may have caused the behavior originate with them; much more likely it originated with the staff member himself, possibly because of a person in the patient's past he represented at the moment. Therefore, only by accepting the task of cleaning up in good spirit could the situation be improved between them. It is difficult to maintain one's rage against a person who, with a positive attitude, cleans up the mess one has made. Moreover, the dropping of a plateful of food on the floor is, as much as any verbal statement, an expression of feelings; of how perturbed one is at the moment and how unable to control oneself. A patient is not likely to believe a therapist who, while encouraging him to tell him what brought on this drastic expression, lets someone else bear the brunt of it. Telling the patient that one is not annoyed with him for giving vent to pressures he feels unable to contain is much more believable when it has been preceded by an action that demonstrates that the staff member's true inner feelings are positive.

If plates and glasses are made of unbreakable material such as plastic, it implies an expectation that the patient may smash them; a tacit message that so annoys him whether or not he is consciously aware of it that he feels tempted to throw them around, since this is what the institution obviously expects. It is not fragility but quality, as in nice china and glasses, that conveys the idea that the person who arranged the tableware not only wanted to make eating a pleasant occasion, but also didn't expect nice things to be deliberately destroyed. If the patients are given things to use which they think are nice, they are protective of them (that is, within the limits they are able to impose upon themselves). These limits are always more effective, often more stringent, than those any other person could impose even if he wanted to.

It is also helpful for the patients to have a hand in selecting the menu; suggestions for the menu were regularly solicited and carried out. When replacement of china became necessary or desirable, the patients chose what they liked best from several patterns of china or glasses, or tried out which types of chair felt most comfortable to sit on when eating. This made them protective of these things, even though overpowering emotions still could momentarily sweep away all such concerns. Because they came to the institution after the choice had been made, there were always a number of patients who had not participated in the selection of the dishes from which they ate. But given the several years most patients require for getting well, usually a considerable majority had participated in some of the choices; and their protective intent and critical inner attitude to deliberate break-age was a much more effective brake on impulsive acting out than any-thing a staff member could muster.

As with drapes or bedspreads, an assembly of all patients and staff was presented with three different designs of plates, glasses, or silverware, and invited to try them out and tell us whether they liked them well enough to choose one of them. If they did, they would take a vote and the preferred pattern was bought. If they didn't like any, three new patterns were submitted to them. If they liked only one of the designs, and nobody liked either of the other two, two more were added to make it a real choice. Since we made the initial choice of what we submitted to the patients and didn't include anything we thought uncomfortable, unsuitable, ungainly, or unattractive, there was no reservation on the part of the staff regarding what the patients picked. It was amazing how after a period of vacillation, the patients always came up with a very good selection. For example, I once presented a set of dinnerware that some of the staff and I were quite taken with. But the patients pointed out that the plates were too flat, and eating from them would require special care not to spill food on the table, and who wanted to be bothered with that while eating? They were absolutely right, and I thanked them for preventing us from making a stupid choice. What we ended up with was never what producers call institutional patterns or qualities. Those either sug-gested that the users might not take good care of them because of their sturdiness, or were so bland in appearance that they ended up not really pleasing anybody.

Of course, this only works if these objects are not guarded or anxiously watched. The only correct attitude is one that says: "You should have the best, and what is the most pleasing to you. Since it is here strictly for you, we know that whatever way you use or misuse it is due to important needs of yours that must be accepted by us. Also, whatever you do carries an important message about you and your feelings that we are here to consider and respect; and these are in-credibly more important than the most valuable object."

This, of course, is a statement of theory and has to be applied with common sense. We don't use precious antique plates to eat from, nor anything ostentatious. But if a nice plate costs some $4, as compared to a serviceable one priced at $1, since patients and staff are much more careful of the nice one the difference in the cost of breakage makes no significant difference in the budget. (Given quantity buying directly from the factory, as is customary for institutions, for what we considered very nice tableware we spent in 1970: dinner plate $3.10, cup and saucer $3.50, and colored water glasses, engraved with the seal of the university as staff and patients decided they preferred, $2.80. If bought at stores in small numbers, the price of each item would have been considerably greater, of course.)

One could correctly object that many adults, and most children, don't care how they eat; as a matter of fact, some enjoy eating very casually, even messily. Nothing that has been said should give the impression that because we offered them pleasant surroundings and tableware they were expected to eat "nicely." Demanding something in return for what was given would have destroyed its value. While sometimes we all enjoy eating casually, maybe even more so than eating in formal settings, the fact remains that we all want others to be concerned about our enjoyment of meals. One frequent source of discord between mothers and children is the mother's feeling: "I extended so much care preparing this food for you, now you show me your appreciation by the way you eat it"; but the value of the food to the child comes from the mother having shown her care by the attention with which she prepared it, while he is given the freedom to do with it as he desires. Otherwise it is tit for tat, and nobody gains pleasure from it. Since we neither required nor expected anything from the patients as compensation for our efforts to make their meals nice, this made the experience all the more constructive for them.

Erikson has shown how our perspective on life depends largely on whether our early experiences have instilled a "basic trust" in us or, on the contrary, deep and lasting distrust. He stresses the importance of experiences around being fed for development of this "basic trust" (35). The determining factor is whether the infant feels that he can depend on his parents' intentions and have confidence that he will be reliably well taken care of. Nobody who has experienced this basic trust will ever need a mental institution, unless as a result of an organic impairment of his central nervous system. Even if the latter happens, much will depend on the degree to which trust can be established in spite of it. But given the early stage of development he speaks of, unfortunately Erikson does not equally stress that trust is a reciprocal process. If a parent is not convinced that his child is a good, lovable one, the child will not be able to develop trust in the parent.

At the beginning of his hospital career, the mental patient cannot really trust anybody. The most one may hope for is that during
his introduction to the institution his experiences will have evoked
some fleeting feeling that the people there might turn out to be trustworthy. Though he may have an inkling of such hope, he still cannot
believe in it. This is even more reason why the institution, on its part,
must try to get the process of trusting started as soon as possible. For
example, nice plates imply a trust in the patient, just as unbreakable
material bespeaks distrust. And the tableware signifies trust in the
circumstance where trust should have had its origin: the eating situation. This trust is not violated if a patient breaks a few dishes because
he cannot control himself; who can criticize him for doing something
he cannot help? The smashing of some plates because of unmanageable pressure, including the wish to make a point, is "damage" only if
it is not used constructively. To oppose this happening signifies opposition to the patient's expressing and satisfying a need. If the event is
accepted the way it should be, as a signal of great anger or distress to
which one must respond sensitively and with understanding, then a
good deal can be gained by an incident involving breakage.

The breakage at the Orthogenic School is much smaller than in
any restaurant feeding the same number of persons. Despite excellent
care on the part of those working in the dining room and kitchen, unavoidable breakage by them far exceeded the damage patients did
out of anger or frustration, or by chance. Given the salaries psychiatrists command, a few treatment hours cost as much or more. Many
individual therapy sessions may be needed to deal with a patient's
feelings that the institution is more concerned with preventing damage than with the emotional conflicts raging inside him when he goes
on a rampage. If his parents were quite able and willing to spend
large amounts on nonvital things, while denying the child some
simple pleasures because they were "too expensive," months or even
years of treatment may be required to undo the resulting damage to
an individual.

I have known cases where, as a matter of unavoidable necessity,
a mental institution readily accepted psychiatric treatment hours
costing thousands of dollars to help convince a patient that he and his
feelings are more important, and more valuable, than was suggested
by what his closest relations refused to spend on him. In such a case
the patient's low evaluation of himself was based on how little the
important people in his life were willing to extend themselves to and
for him. We found that true acceptance of what was erroneously
viewed by others as "wanton" destruction, amounting to a few dollars

of damage, proved to the patient that now he was accepted as a person, that his feelings were more important than what he was supposed to do or not do. This was more effective than months of psychiatric therapy sessions. Yet, as I've stressed repeatedly, none of this will be effective if used as a clever device. It will not work unless the inner conviction of the staff is: "Who cares about these dishes, they are replaceable; your feelings are what count, because it is as easy to buy some new chinaware as it is difficult to heal emotional wounds."

Many times when I served as a consultant to therapeutic agencies I was asked to help them prevent expenditures which totaled over an entire year less than what they were happy to pay me as a fee; not to mention what it cost them to have some thirty or more highly paid staff members attend the meeting. In other words, the institution or agency was quite ready to expend several hundred dollars to find ways to prevent "damage" of a tenth of that amount. And these damages were, to begin with, clearly the consequence of not dealing correctly with the patients' needs.

A Jewish tradition comes to mind in connection with the deliberate breaking of dishes. At a wedding it is customary deliberately to break a very nice, expensive goblet or a china plate. Psychoanalysts have suggested that this is symbolic anticipation, acted out, of what will soon take place: a most valuable possession, the hymen, will be broken. The Talmudic explanation is that it should be a reminder of the destruction of the Temple in Jerusalem; that even on the happiest occasion one should never forget this sorrow. I believe it also symbolizes something much simpler, though possibly even more important. The breaking of a valuable dish symbolizes that things will occasionally go wrong in a marriage, that one must be prepared for it, and that the success of the marriage depends on the partners' ability to accept broken dishes as preferable to hurt feelings. It also very definitely symbolizes that one must be ready to sacrifice something very valuable in order to pacify or exorcise evil spirits.

How simple it would be if as soon as a patient enters the institution we could invite him to break something valuable so that he will know of the institution's readiness to accept the bad as well as the good in him. But that would not work. The patient would interpret it as the staff's viewing him as a savage, and while hating them for such an opinion, he would oblige. The damage would be great, and only harm would be done.

The acceptance of breakage as a valid expression of genuine feelings will work only in the right situation, and when the time is ripe. It took some patients up to two years to trust us enough to destroy something in order to find out whether we would respond to their testing the way they hoped, or the way they feared. We can't try to hurry them with the attitude: "Go ahead, you'll find out we are all right," without infringing on their autonomy and losing much that way. As Freud so often pointed out, in psychoanalytic treatment a correct interpretation is unimportant unless it is made at exactly the right moment, in the right context, in the right spirit. And the right time is when the patient is ready for it, not before, and preferably not much later.

The Bathroom

It is common knowledge that too rigid an education concerning cleanliness can damage one's personality. It is utterly destructive if the parents experience a child's body, and its products, as disgusting. Nevertheless, most bathrooms and particularly those in institutions are equipped in a way that shows concern only for the cleanliness of the place. Where they should convey an atmosphere of relaxed comfort, they suggest distaste for elimination. It amazes me how even many psychoanalysts, whose patients spend uncounted hours and very large sums of money decrying their alienation from their own body and its functions, who suffer from how dirty they feel their body and its excreta are, provide only impersonal, "hygienic" toilets for their patients, like those typically found in the office buildings where they practice. How can a patient believe deep down in his bowels that the analyst means it when he tells him he should accept and enjoy his bodily functions, when if the patient needs a toilet, the analyst's is as cold and uninviting as was his mother's toilet training? As long as psychoanalysts ignore these issues, how can we expect our psychiatric institutions to be any better?

Man does not secure the boundaries of his territory by means of depositing his excreta along its frontiers, as dogs and cats do, and as the tiger did in the zoo as described earlier. But many patients really began to feel at home only after they had managed to eliminate in ways which were germane to their inner desires, giving elimination a very personal touch rather than simply in the conventional way in which they had been trained.

It is a well-known fact of psychoanalysis that the patient must not only recount his traumatic experiences, but in order to master them once and for all must emotionally re-experience them with a very different outcome. He can do this in therapy because he is protected by the presence and help of the therapist. The patient's intellectual understanding of what had happened will achieve little in re-structuring his personality; it may even be a powerful defense against the emotional experience which alone can be corrective. Months of effort at recovering such experiences in the treatment room may ac-complish considerably less than the patient's having a parallel ex-perience in reality—surrounded by entirely different physical and human conditions, and thus having a different outcome. Our spend-ing hours, when appropriate, cradling the patient or merely holding his hand while he is sitting on the toilet, carries more conviction than any readiness to listen to or talk about his feelings, problems, anxieties. For example, a staff member's stepping into the toilet bowl and in-viting a brilliant, hippie-type schizophrenic to flush her down (which the patient experimented with by repeated flushings) was both a turning point in their relationship, and a change in the patient's view of the world from uniformly persecuting to perhaps genuinely re-warding. The patient, who had never dared to sit on or to flush the toilet, after this event began to use it normally.

We can testify from many examples that the corrective emo-tional experience is even more effective when it occurs in exactly the same situation as the one where the trauma was inflicted. There is a great difference between the patient's telling a dream or a fantasy of a serpent emerging from the toilet bowl and attacking him while he is sitting on it, and re-experiencing this anxiety as he eliminates into the toilet. But this time he is secured against being overwhelmed by anxiety by his therapist's presence and help; together both can once and for all exorcise this ancient serpent, making it dwell only in the primordial past, never again to emerge into the present.

We were so completely convinced of the role which the bath-room experience played in milieu therapy that we felt compelled to rearrange things immediately to make the bathrooms attractive and have them become an integral part of the patients' home ground, rather than being something separated or hidden away. The buildings we inherited had bathrooms which were typically institutional and could only be reached from the corridors. All of the dormitories and bathrooms had to be reconstructed to make them more attractive and to permit easy access back and forth between the living area and the bathroom.

As body and mind, id and ego, should function in unison rather than in isolation from each other, one not knowing what the other is all about, so the area devoted mainly to the social life and the area serving the body should also form a larger unity—a symbol of the integration of the functions of a truly unified person, which the patient in his own good time can emulate.

A patient who is relaxing in the tub, for example, can hear what is going on in his living room through the open door and does not feel isolated from the social life of his dormitory when he concentrates on the care and needs of his body. When a staff member moves freely from the patients' living area to spending time with someone who is using the toilet or taking a bath, he impressively testifies, through his actions and without needing to say so, that what happens in the bathroom is by no means something separated from all other life activities. This is very important because the basic split in the personality is between mind and body. It is from this split that all the others derive. This split comes much earlier in development than the split between conscious and unconscious, id and ego, ego and superego; wishful desires and threatened punishment; or even between good and evil. The primordial myth of our culture teaches that when this separation occurred, we were expelled from Eden where unity reigned.

It is very significant if a living area is deliberately designed as an integral unit. Still, if a staff member feels that what goes on in one location and what goes on in another are separated from each other, no design will undo this effect. If the staff's attitude is: Now that you, the patient, are taking a nice long, relaxing bath, we will drop what we are doing, concentrate lovingly only on the body, and forget about everything else—it fails to undo the separation between body and mind, even if this convinces the patient that the staff member is really devoted to the care of the patient's body. It gives the body its due, and is a very valuable experience, but it doesn't heal the split in the personality. Yet despite our best efforts, this was the impression patients had until the bathroom was not only designed but used as an integral aspect of the entire life that was going on. In order to be accepted as part of the totality of life, the bathroom had to be part of the living space architecturally and symbolically; it also had to be so attractively equipped and decorated that being in it—as opposed to merely using it—was enjoyable in itself (Plate 9). As with other rooms, all depended on the staff's attitude to the bathroom and what it stood for.

To serve a therapeutic purpose well, bathrooms and toilets must not only be comfortable and attractive for the patient, signifying respect for his body in all of its functions; the bathrooms must also be comfortable and pleasing to the staff. For a staff member to wish to spend time with a patient who is using the toilet or taking a bath, the room must be conveniently set up and give the staff member space to feel at ease. If he cannot sit and even stretch out comfortably, how then can the patient acquire a relaxed attitude toward his own body?

For example, it helps to have a variety of toys to play with in the bathtub. It might be thought that this applies only to children. But the regressive nature of the mental patient's personality is too easily overlooked if the prevalent attitude is the sooner he acts his age the better. After the patient has had those emotional experiences he originally missed out on, and whose lack led to his regressed state of mind in the first place, he can genuinely act his age. Some of our twenty-year-olds gained more from playing with toys in the tub or even in the toilet than certain younger patients, just because their toilet experiences had been more severe and crippling.

The typical institutional bathroom can be dreadfully austere and unwelcoming. One device for getting away from the coldness of white or uniformly colored tiles is to use colorfully painted Delft or Spanish tiles. Walls thus decorated and floors of mosaic glass, for example, are easily washed and avoid the deathly antiseptic appearance of the traditional institutional bathroom. And as the patients adorn walls, fixtures, and toilet stalls as they like, with pictures or whatever, they make the place all their own. Having spoken at length about locks, I should add that toilet stalls without lockable doors symbolize a lack or loss of autonomy in our culture, since one then has no chance of privacy with his body and its function. If the patient has company in the stall then, he does so because he has invited it, or at the least, accepted it.

What if a patient locks himself in and commits suicide? This question was often asked. If the institution operates in such a manner that suicide is a real possibility and not just an idea played with to explore what lies behind it, the suicidal patient will find his opportunities to carry it out. Still, the question remains whether giving him the chance to lock himself into the toilet might not be construed as a wish to keep away from him, which is exactly the notion that can lead to suicidal attempts. But there are ways in which the institution can make clear that it is aware of this danger and wants to be able to reach the patient immediately in any emergency; all that is needed is a little planning. Thus we have lockable doors hung in such a way that a normally agile person could crawl under them or climb over them without much difficulty. As a matter of fact, over the years it happened repeatedly that a patient would lock himself in and then call for company or help, or just make some noise suggesting distress, only to make sure that a staff member was willing to crawl under or over the door to reach him—which then led to a happy reunion. Of course, if the toilet stall is constructed so that the staff member has trouble joining the patient there and helping him with his anxieties, it implies the staff's wish to avoid getting involved with the patient around one of his body's most important functions.

An incident, not connected with the School, helped me understand the importance some psychiatric patients invest in the atmosphere of their bathroom. A young woman asked to make my acquaintance when I happened to lecture in a distant city. It turned out that she had been a patient in a famous psychiatric hospital for many years, had been cured, and was now living successfully on her own. It seemed very important to her that I should drop in and visit her in her apartment. What she told me about herself—the origins of her sickness, the psychological ordeals she had had to go through to find herself—was fascinating enough to make me agree to do so, particularly since it seemed obvious that she had something important in mind. Her apartment was furnished with taste, but nothing out of the ordinary. After a while she asked me to look at her bathroom. She had decorated it herself. On the walls she had painted truly beautiful frescoes which created a fairy-tale jungle world, probably because animals live there in instinctual freedom. But what she was most insistent for me to see was how she had dealt with the toilet. The wall behind it, the toilet seat, and every detail was decorated to make it a perfect royal throne. A crown was painted as if hovering at just the right height, so that it seemed to fit the head of the person sitting on the toilet. It turned out that this was what she had wanted me to see. She wanted to see my reaction—I guess to find out whether I thought she was still "crazy" to want to eliminate under such circumstances. I congratulated her on the ingenious way in which she provided herself with what she needed.

I couldn't help being reminded by this of a ditty we sang as children, when one of us used the toilet. It expressed the spontaneous feelings of children when their elimination is no longer controlled by others, and went about as follows: *Sir* (first name of the child) *de Cohn—Sits on this throne—From his behind comes a big tone.* (My English translation fails to do justice to the impressive emotional impact and rhyming quality of the original German.) These rhymes tell of the need to regain the power over one's own elimination which one loses as an infant when the rulers of the world (one's parents) take control. It is not that eliminating should be experienced as a royal pleasure; but if eliminating has been traumatic, if there are feelings that one has been deprived of one's autonomy, then being restored to true self-control, as far as this function is concerned, one has again become one's own ruler. We never decorated our toilets as thrones, though some of our patients—interestingly enough, usually those who according to age were fully grown—came pretty close to doing so. But we did try to make this room emotionally important.

The following brief description of a case at the School may serve as an illustration of the symbolic importance of bathrooms.

An anorexic psychotic late-adolescent girl suffered from a severe washing compulsion. She literally spent all day taking showers and scrubbing herself so that her skin was all raw. She stuffed large amounts of toilet paper and facial tissue in the toilet. For weeks, before and after the patient eliminated, her counselor would clean out the stuffed toilets. After the patient watched this for a time she began to see that her counselor wasn't repelled by her body or the task of cleaning out the bowls, and she began to feel that her counselor wasn't disgusted by her body. The patient then began to inundate not only the bathroom but the dormitory living room, too, with her real and symbolic excreta, using an average of twelve boxes of tissue—2400 sheets torn into small pieces—a day to achieve her purpose.

Her symptoms were highly overdetermined; they had a great deal to do with excessive parental pressure to be perfect and to achieve sooner and better than anybody else, particularly academically. She had been the top student in grammar and high school for years. The symptoms' meaning was roughly as follows: To assert her independence—which she did not dare to do in reality—she wanted both to hold onto her stools and to smear them on those who had persecuted her with their demands, as if to scream at them: "Here, have it all, all that you force out of me and force me to do for you!" But this made her feel all dirty, as if contaminating everything she touched. Consciously she could not accept this wish; so she denied it by burying her stools under incredibly heavy layers of "clean" stuff. By not permitting her excreta to be disposed of, she asserted herself; by covering them up neatly and cleanly, she obeyed parental demands which by now had become a part of her.

The heavy layers of paper put into the toilet bowl before she eliminated prevented her excreta from being flushed down the toilet, so they were preserved. Other, even heavier layers of clean tissue covered them. Still, even covering her excreta with clean paper contaminated her permanently and created a danger to herself and others. Her only protection against this was to take showers continuously, heavily soaping and scrubbing herself. She was forced to live her days and nights in the bathroom. She began to relate to her counselor when the counselor freed her of some of the dangerous "dirty" work by stuffing the toilet bowl for her with tissues, and after the patient had eliminated on this, by covering it up with equally heavy layers. The patient then felt less contaminated and she began to take fewer showers; her skin became less raw, and she began to feel just a bit more comfortable. This proved two things to her: that we wanted to be of help to her *on her terms*, and that we could do so. Her counselor could not encourage her to smear her stools over us. This would have been too threatening to the patient, too directly regressive. But when the patient covered her with facial tissue, which by now represented feces, the counselor could respond positively.

As we encouraged her to spread these tissues, we implicitly told her that we wanted her to live with us; that we accepted her symptom in both its meanings. There was no demand that she should flush the toilets—as a matter of fact, this would only have clogged them up more seriously. If she stuffed up one, she could use another one. There were enough toilets available at the institution so that nobody suffered hardship except our janitors—and if they didn't succeed, we called on the engineers—who unclogged one toilet after the other. If it were to be done in her presence, she would have felt we were against her, so we accomplished this without her observing it. Because her counselor not only provided all the needed material to be shredded by the patient, but expressed pleasure at being of such real service—carefully collecting the tissue and disposing of it at night to make space for the new production of the following day—for the first time the patient responded in a positive way to another human being.

Here the bathroom expanded for her to the entire world; to this patient it was the whole world, since all her time was taken up with dirtying herself (eliminating, and the time-consuming rituals around it) and cleaning herself (her compulsion to take practically continuous showers). Permitting such extension of the bathroom into the living quarters is one way to create a unity of living, which greatly helps in establishing a unity of personality.

In cases like this, the institution's use of symbolic expressions of intent creates a framework, which facilitates the patients' expressing themselves symbolically. This framework makes it easier for the staff to accept and deal constructively with the most primitive behavior. If this were acted out directly rather than symbolically, it would be degrading to the patient and too difficult for the staff to handle.

Of course, symbols won't be effective if reality refutes them. For example, helping a child in the bathroom or on the toilet with his elimination, and then withdrawing in disgust when he wets his bed or his clothes, will be experienced by him as a sham. Therefore if the patient has wet his sheets and his counselor waits for the maids to change them, rather than doing it himself, the message is doubly disappointing to the patient.

Some patients' anxiety prevents their using the toilet altogether. There were those who temporarily refused to use or even enter the bathroom at all, and they eliminated only in the living quarters. Then we provided garbage cans for this purpose. One patient, whose I.Q. was that of a genius, became persuaded that we accepted his brilliance (as had been the case in his past), but also his body, since it was not only permitted to function, but welcomed in the living room. Up to then he had functioned only as a mind; now he could permit himself to have a body. Previously he had been convinced that his body was detestable and belonged in the sewer; that he could exist and be accepted only as a brain. When his living place—which had only permitted his mind to function—accorded his body and its functions equal importance, he could begin to integrate the two. It eventually became possible for him to give up the idea that using the toilet and bathroom normally meant that his body was utterly disgusting and that his mind would be hopelessly contaminated. When this started to change, the split in his personality began to heal.

The same considerations apply to various sexual behaviors, such as masturbation. If his counselor responds with a feeling of inner embarrassment or disgust when the patient openly masturbates—during a bath, for instance—it will be useless to tell the youngster that masturbation is a normal, acceptable way to deal with sexual pressures.

While this is often difficult for the beginner, those staff members who want to help the patients with anxieties centering around their bodies soon learn how to convey the right messages to the patient.

12 | *The I of the Beholder: Pre-Admission Visits*

One of the most thoughtful and enlightened mental hospital administrators of today, who has introduced many important improvements in his institution, makes the critical point that "The newly admitted patient is *desocialized*—and one of the prime objects of the mental hospital must be to repair this breach in social relationships" (90). But even he doesn't suggest how this should be put into practice. There are no analyses in the literature or elsewhere of how the patient's introduction to the hospital should be arranged to prevent desocialization, nor is there any description of how it is actually being done.

It is not enough to concentrate on the negative. At the beginning of his experience with the hospital, the patient needs humanization, not mere avoidance of desocialization. In a discussion of the theoretical and practical aspects of how humanization can be promoted, the most important principle must be kept in mind: recovery from insanity is dependent on the patient's conviction that he or she is an autonomous human being, one who has an important place in the particular segment of the world and society in which his life is unfolding at the moment. Therefore when a patient comes to a mental hospital, all efforts ought to be geared toward convincing him that this is a small world where his self-respect is of prime concern to everybody, and that the institution is organized and equipped to further this goal. It must also be an institution which he can comprehend; one that is not overpowering or confusing, but simple and, no matter what he thinks, manageable for him.

It is very important not only that the prospective patient be given a chance to find out for himself what the institution is all about, but also that the institution does everything in its power to facilitate the investigation. Thus the institution may not even accept a patient without his having had a pre-admission visit. At the Ortho-genic School, we found one pre-admission visit inadequate, because having had time to "digest" what happened on the first visit, many prospective patients reacted differently the second or third time. As they gain trust that we may understand and respect their view of things, their pretense that nothing is wrong with them disinte-grates. (Sometimes the emergency is so great that we cannot extend the "getting acquainted period" over the four or five days which we found worked best, but speeding up the introductory process is undesirable, though occasionally unavoidable.)

The task is to show the patient that the institution wishes him to form his own opinion about it. This must be done without pushing him, trying to influence what he needs to know, or present-ing the mental hospital as something better than it is. Right from the start the patient should recognize the institution's philosophy, which expects him to act only on the basis of his own judgment, not on what somebody else wishes him to think; and that the patient's view of things and his consequent decisions are of great concern to the staff—though they will not necessarily agree or act on them as he wants. Respect for the prospective patient's autonomy is shown by letting him decide what and how much he wishes to investigate and what he feels he needs to know as opposed to what the staff may think he ought to know before reaching a decision. Attempting to show the patient "everything" would only overpower him through the mass of impressions.

In all psychiatric institutions, the patient is psychologically examined when entering. I believe it much more important that he be encouraged to examine the institution. The patient does in fact form his own judgments immediately. He is far too anxious for an attitude of wait-and-see. If a relaxed state of mind were available to him, he wouldn't need hospitalization. Unless the institution facili-tates and encourages his investigation, he has to rely on vague im-pressions and will feel he can study things only surreptitiously. Since he will do so anyway, it makes a difference whether the official at-titude he is first exposed to is that he is an *object* being studied for the institution's purposes, or a *subject* who has every right to scruti-nize the institution and the staff carefully and critically. If the in-stitution and the staff are to be evaluated by him, as he knows he is by them, then it's clear from the beginning that patients and staff alike are never just objects, but subjects in each interaction.

Further, a psychiatric patient should be able to expect the hospital to do everything to relieve his anxiety and not add to it—as being examined does (everybody has some fear of examinations).

Telling a person not to be anxious and explaining about the examination will only show good intent to relieve the anxiety; unfortunately such statements fail to provide relief, and relief—given the patient's state of mind—would count much more heavily than good intentions. These explanatory efforts also show that the staff has little realization of what truly relieves anxiety. The message to the patient in the examination is that the institution is so anxious about him that it must find out what he is all about, before he has a chance to find out what it is all about.

When the patient is assured that all this investigation is done for his benefit, he cannot believe it. If he could truly trust it, again there would be no reason why he should be considered for placement in a psychiatric institution. The statement that he is examined so that the staff "will be better able to help him" implicitly asks him to accept the procedures of "big brother." On the other hand, an invitation to question it all might give him a first inkling that maybe here, in some respects, he has as many rights as "they" do. In this situation, if his wish to examine and form an opinion is given as much weight as "their" desire to do so, then he might see that his needs could even be given precedence. From the start, the one-sided examination in essence gives him the feeling that the institution is a place where "they" are doing things, and little activity is expected of him in important matters concerning him. Facilitating the patient's "doing things" should be one of the main tasks of the institution, even if the doing might consist in doing nothing. But expecting him to do things he doesn't want to do is never helpful. Doing things for him (the staff, of course, considers examining him as doing something for him) is justified only if he wants it. But even if one tries to get the patient's assent for the examination, the institution's viewpoint differs from the way the patient sees it. The examination is a central aspect of the introduction of the patient to the mental hospital, because it creates the frame of reference into which he will fit all later experience there.

Before we even see a patient at the School, we know quite a bit about him, since it is on the basis of this information that we pre-select patients for possible acceptance. We have studied whatever records are available; his history, the accounts of previous examinations and treatment attempts. This isn't quite as one-sided an advantage as it may seem—we publish reports on our work, so the prospective patient has a chance to form an opinion about us through reading, if he should be able to comprehend it. As a matter of fact, over the years there have been quite a few self-referrals just on the basis of people having read books describing the Orthogenic

School. Even if a candidate has read extensively about our institution, we warn him not to trust the impressions he received because these might be misleading. Instead, he should base his evaluation on his impressions during his visits with us, just as we (without necessarily telling him so, though we do occasionally in answer to spoken or unspoken questions) don't base our final decisions on the material studied before meeting the patient. All too often the live person is very different from what we had expected from his reports. On the other hand, we rarely erred in our initial evaluation of a patient during the days of visiting and our casual interactions with him.

This can be summed up by noting that everybody is afraid of having his mind read or made up by others; everybody wants to have control over his own mind. The delusion that others can control his mind is common to the mental patient. He is convinced that the purpose of a psychiatric examination is to enable the institution to read his mind more effectively. Even more reason that the psychological examination should be postponed until the person believes that to some degree the intentions of the institution are benevolent. A person forms opinions which he can trust only through his observations and then only if he can go about his observation in the way he thinks best. Repeatedly we experienced how, if we didn't pry into the patient's mind and instead showed our concern with more mundane matters, his ominous expectation of the institution was dissipated, to be replaced by a more optimistic and realistic one. For example, a patient who had previously been in psychoanalysis said, "I thought you are supposed to be interested in my dreams." He was relieved when he was told it was more important to us to think how the big and small matters of life could be arranged best for his convenience. From the moment the patient meets the institution, it should show the greatest respect for his autonomy. One of the simple ways to give patients this feeling was to ask them what would be the most convenient day and time for them to enter the institution, and arrange matters according to their desires. Many times this or similar experiences convinced the prospective patient to enter the institution.

For example, a teen-age anorexic girl was brought to the Orthogenic School by her parents in a state of extreme emaciation; at the moment her dehydration posed the most severe threat to her life. She knew of the plan to enter her into the Orthogenic School as a patient, and she resisted the idea. Meeting her on her arrival, I invited her to investigate whatever interested her about the strange place in which she found herself, and to make whatever inquiries she wished. Convinced that her fate was decided anyway, she didn't want to do anything. This was quite in line with her state of utter exhaustion. When I told her that she didn't have to come to the institution unless she herself wanted to, she didn't believe me for a minute. She was much too weak to want to stay or leave.

So I had to take the initiative. I told her that since her life was in danger, she would have to do something about making a decision. If she would drink a glass of some liquid, she could leave the room and the institution if she wished, but she had to stay right here with me until she had done so. Despite her great weakness, her remaining energy went into carefully observing me and her surroundings. I concentrated my thinking on her, of which she was aware, though I refrained from intruding into her thoughts with the exception of a very few remarks. I repeated the invitation to ask whatever questions about the institution or me she was interested in having me answer.

Given her dangerously weakened condition, I told her I had to insist that she could not leave the room without drinking at least one glass of liquid. Since she didn't react to this or to the question of what liquid she would prefer, I decided that milk would do best, though I knew that she drank, if at all, only liquids without any nutritional content. After a while I had a glass of milk brought in, and told her that as soon as she drank it she could leave, but not before. Again I stressed how much it would please me if she would drink it, while assuring her that I would not force it down her throat. So we sat quietly, but nevertheless involved with each other, for a very long time. She later told me that she was convinced that sooner or later I would lose patience and either try to force her to drink, or tell her that since she would not, she had to become a patient at the institution. Finally she asked whether, if she drank the glass of milk, she could leave. I answered that I had already told her that this was so twice, and I could not see that a third time would add anything. If she did not believe me before, further repetition would just be boring.

However, because of her question I knew that she was considering whether to drink the milk, but without help she could not overcome her resistance to drinking. I held the glass for her and when a near-imperceptible movement suggested to me that it might help if I fed her, I held the glass to her mouth. At that she drank it down in one long draft and asked, "Can I go now?" to which I answered: "Of course." I opened the door which, like all our doors, was not locked. Having not believed me until the moment I opened the door, she then got up, walked out of the room, and out of the

Part of the School facade, showing the mural by Jordi Bonet

This mural is composed of four sections which interpenetrate each other, to present the central ideas of life, and the difficulties man experiences in his search for self-realization. In the first part the beginning of life is symbolized by a pregnant woman whose belly, in black and white, encompasses the equality of all races of the world.

The eternal unknowns of life and the many wrong starts we all make, as well as the one path which leads to the true center of our being, are symbolized in the second part by the labyrinth with its many dead ends. Loving care permits us to find meaning in life and uplifts us; this is suggested by the various breastlike structures which together represent a bird in flight.

All labor, all battle with the problems of life, center on the struggle of finding oneself. This is expressed in the third section by the arrows which suggest contemplation and introspection, and direct us toward the rectangle which is the symbol of a spirit that, though it had lost itself, nevertheless is able to find itself again and in the process surpasses its old self, and finally frees itself through self-transformation.

This rebirth of the spirit is the theme of the last part, where the earth appears at the bottom as a half-circle. The wavy lines which enter it suggest that nothing is ever lost, and that all things can be transformed. From there arrows rise to meet the three birds which project themselves into the sky, symbolic of the victory of the spirit over the matter that has constrained it.

2 First view of the School's interior

The "Living Room," where the newcomer gains his initial impressions of the School; the place where the outside world and that of the institution meet each other

4

One of the scenes depicted in the stairhall, showing American Indian life, and the legendary railroad laborer John Henry

5

Interior court with fountain and figures of "the sisters"

"The Lady"

6

View of one girls' dormitory

Detail of this dormitory, showing part of one patient's private area

9

Bathroom

Detail of a boys' dormitory, showing part of one patient's private area

12

A classroom

One staff member's living-bedroom

13

institution. As I said good-bye to her at the outer door, I suggested that she think it over and decide whether or not she would like to come to live with us. I told her that if her decision was negative, there was no need to inform me; but I would like it very much if her decision was positive. At that she asked me, "If I came here, how would you get me to eat?", indicating how seriously she considered this possibility. I replied, "Ah, that's our secret—to find out you would have to come here." The next morning she told her parents she was ready to enter the institution, and she did so the afternoon of that day.

Her decision (besides the desperate straits she found herself in—wanting to live, while being forced by an inner compulsion to do away with herself by not eating) was based on a vague feeling of trust derived from a combination of many experiences. I had obviously wanted her to drink the milk but did not physically force it as she had feared, being familiar with tube feeding. By allowing her sufficient time I had convinced her that I would not lose my patience and hurry her about drinking or coming to the institution. Then, while she still doubted that her observations were correct, when I allowed her to walk out, she was convinced that I meant what I had said, and that I had not said it to trick her.

As my account shows, I didn't entirely respect her autonomy, since I had told her that I would sit with her until she drank one glass of liquid. And I would have done so even if it had taken all that afternoon, evening, and night. I didn't think about what I would do if we had to sit together until the next morning, because I was convinced it would not take so long. Though I didn't tell her this, she must have felt my determination when she decided to drink. In some way my behavior conveyed to her that the only infringement I would make on her autonomy was where her life or well-being was at stake—not where my convenience was concerned, such as ending our visit after a certain lapse of time. My implied regard for her autonomy in all other respects, including the paramount issue of her becoming our patient, induced her to decide that this might be a place where she could get the help she needed to become a person in her own right.

It was a rare exception where our fear for the patient's survival forced us to dispense with the more typical getting-acquainted arrangements, which usually consist of daily visits lasting a few hours, over a period of four or five days. (During the visits the prospective patient continues to live wherever he used to, or in a hotel—with attendants if necessary—when coming from out of town.) This is a sufficient amount of time for the patient to form an opinion. We usually don't require that much time to arrive at our own evaluation. In matters of admission our autonomy must also be a grave concern, because in restoring the patient to his autonomy, we cannot begin by taking ours lightly. During the first visit we make it clear that these visits are intended for us to get to know each other. On the basis of what has transpired during the time we have spent together, we hope that at the end the patient is able to decide whether he wants to come to the institution. We, too, have to decide whether, given his personality and problems, and our personalities, we will want to live and work with him; and whether our experience and skills will permit us to be of real use to him.

In our first conversation with the prospective patient, regardless of whether he is willing or able to talk, we ask him why he thinks he is visiting with us. If he gives one, usually the answer is that somebody else—his relatives or a psychiatrist—thought that he needed the institution and told him it was the best place for him. We reply that such a far-reaching decision about whether to enter a mental institution cannot be made on the basis of other people's opinions. We ask the patient to state his own views about it, adding that we have received information about him (if we hid this, we would be starting our relation with a tacit lie, by withholding pertinent facts from him). We ask him whether he thinks we should arrive at decisions about him on the basis of what other people say, or whether it would not be better to be guided by what he himself has to tell us. Typically, he answers that these other people know better than he does. If we accepted this surrender, he would take it as reason to believe that his paranoid anxieties were fully justified; we would be agreeing that others should be in charge of his destiny. Therefore, we stress that no expert can know us better, or know more about us, than we ourselves do. If the patient insists, the staff member adds that we would never believe that somebody else has a deeper understanding about what is good for us than we do. Since we're certain about this for ourselves, we believe the same is true for him. We try to make him see that basically in all of our deeper concerns we are alike.

If we stated this categorically, the patient would view it as another trick to lull him. But when we put it in terms of how *we* feel about something, he can compare this with how he feels about the same issue, and arrive at his own conclusions about whether we feel similarly on the big issues or whether we are at cross-purposes. We emphasize as much as possible that we, too, have to make a big decision; that it will be influenced by what he has to say about it all.

We ask what circumstances of life reduced him to the predicament of having to consider entering a mental institution, and whose fault he thinks it was. By this time, nearly all patients have given up the pretense that others know best. Some can now admit that they cannot go on any longer the way things are; others insist that someone else—the person who brought them, for example—is the one who should be institutionalized.

The way the conversation develops from here naturally depends on the patient's answers to our questions. But in this first meeting we try to convince him that we believe having to come to a mental institution is among the worst things that can happen to any person. Seeking help is a severe trauma to the patient, a terrible blow to his self-esteem. To depict it as anything else would be patently lying; and in such a crucial situation nothing is worse than pretense. When first coming to a psychiatric institution, since the patient is scared and bewildered, and either totally exhausted or extremely angry (though he may hide it all behind a feigned indifference), the staff may try to ease his mind by presenting his coming to the institution as a boon for him. When he is convinced that the world is out of step and that it had better hurry up and fall in with him, trying to describe the advantages he will derive from the institution merely convinces the patient all the more that here, as everywhere else, people see the world only in the way they wish to, without any appreciation for how he views it. But since the very first experiences set the stage for all that is to come later on, it is most important that from the beginning he should be received with a therapeutic attitude; that the staff member pays the greatest attention to trying to understand, respect, and act on the basis of how the patient experiences things. Telling the patient that coming to a mental institution is among the most unfortunate things that can happen to a person shows him that whatever our actions may be, we are not unaware of his own feelings. But whatever his feelings about it may be, we also let him know that we would very much like him to come to the institution, and that we would like to live with and be of help to him.

To accept his view that he doesn't need the institution would be to initiate a *folie à deux* with him. But by agreeing with him about the validity of his feelings, and demonstrating that we can appreciate and comprehend them, while at the same time reserving the right to take actions which we feel may be beneficial for him in the long run without forcing our views on him, we reach a viewpoint which contains some of the most important elements of all psychotherapeutic interactions: that of understanding and appreciating the patient's views as the logical consequence of how he experiences the world, and using these views as the starting point of our common understanding.

There is no point trying to convince the new or prospective patient that his stay at the institution will enable him in time to live more successfully in society. Psychiatric patients needing hospitalization are incapable of being future-directed. This is the difference between one who can be treated as an outpatient, through psychoanalysis, and one who needs hospital care. To undergo psychoanalysis means to be future-oriented: one works on, when necessary even controls one's behavior, difficult as this may be, where there is the hope or belief that things can get better. If the mental patient were able to do any of this, he could be treated as an outpatient.

Many verbal patients set traps by asking whether they can and will be helped. Answering in the affirmative, hoping to set their minds at rest, is only falling into the trap. Such a reply confirms the patient's worst anxiety: that everybody is out to force him to do what he is convinced is detrimental to him. If he were not sure that his behavior is the only possible way, given his situation, he would behave differently. Therefore our response to the "trap" question is to wonder why he thinks he is in need of help. When we ask this with the knowledge that the patient is convinced that *not he* but all the others are wrong, he will reveal that he wants the institution to straighten out those who cannot see he is in his right mind.

To the patient's disappointment, we cannot promise to do this. But we explain that since we are unable and unwilling to do so, he may wish to enter the institution to possibly find some peace and be rid of these people. We can promise him some quiet to be himself, without being pestered by others to act or be the way he cannot. And he will believe this if we have not taken sides against him, by joining all the others in their conviction that it is he who is "out of tune" and must be made to "shape up."

This can lead to the impasse of the patient's asking us why *we* think he ought to come to the institution. The only legitimate reply is to state that we believe he needs to find out who and what he wishes to be, without being pushed by others in some direction.

The only claim I would make in these first encounters is that living at the Orthogenic School might be a bit, maybe even considerably, better than living at some other mental institutions. If during later experiences the patient observes that I had drawn too gloomy a picture by exaggerating the hardships and neglecting the positive aspects, this will be all to the good. But if by bad luck, despite our best efforts, a patient should feel things are as bad as I had described—something that actually never happened—at least I had not tried to lie about it. That is always something in an institution's favor.

We are equally direct with the relatives who bring a patient to us. Since we work with young people, in most cases it is their parents. We empathize with their sadness that such a step has become necessary. We agree that given the condition of the patient, placement seems unavoidable, and while hopefully it will provide relief for the rest of the family, it is a terrible thing for them. We make no promises but that we will try to do our best. We stress that given the seriousness of disturbances which require residential treatment, we can tell them no more than what the percentage of full recovery in similar cases has been in the past. There is no way to predict how this particular patient will eventually turn out. We don't get involved in speculating on what may have caused it to happen nor in explanations of what we shall do for the patient. This should be his private affair, and what we will do depends on what we think best at any moment. We make no promises about visits or any other matters; it must be quite clear that they have to trust us.

As we get to know the patient, we try also to get to know his parents; so each parent is interviewed in depth by only one staff member, usually a psychiatric social worker, a different one for each. These interviews easily require four or more sessions, each of about two hours' duration. This gives us a chance to gain a "feel" for the setting in which the patient has lived; and unavoidably the parent forms an opinion of the institution from the way he is interviewed and from the details in which we show interest. If we accept the patient, we try to convince the parents that they must be satisfied with the thought that they have done the very best for him, and that nothing is to be gained by feeling guilty about placing him in an institution, or about what they may have contributed to his difficulties. While guilt may show their concern and morality as human beings, it serves no good purpose; it helps neither the patient nor themselves. What is most constructive for all is that they now try to reconstruct their own lives, which must have suffered severely from the impact of having a mental patient living with them. The better life is for them, the better this is for the patient.

We don't suggest that parents seek treatment for themselves, partly because often they have been exposed to it, and partly because if they wished to secure it, exposure to the institution would by then be sufficient for them to ask advice and help. If they do ask, we try to direct them to the proper person. If the patient decides not to come, or we don't accept him, we suggest (when asked) what next steps might be best.

As a result of their desire to make things easier for the patient and reduce his anxieties, beginners in this work tell him how he will be well taken care of at the institution at all times. Although their conscious wish is to reduce the patient's anxieties, this fails to do so because, despite his insanity, the patient knows that this is an empty promise. He recognizes that if a person makes promises which cannot be kept, it is done out of trying to assuage unconscious anxiety. By telling the patient that we will be available to him at all times, that we will always take good care of him, that all of his wishes will be met, we pledge ourselves to services which obviously go beyond anybody's capacity. Such promises may be motivated by a beginner's unrealizable ideals. But the patient interprets them as either meaning that the staff wishes to cater to him because they are afraid of him or that they are outright liars, who wish to fool him into feeling false security, contrary to reality—and so he cannot trust them or anyone else. Experienced staff members stress the benign reality which the institution can and does provide.

We are convinced of the institution's devotion within humanly possible bounds to the well-being of the patient. Therefore, the staff can truthfully inform the patient that while they will try to make themselves available as much as possible, there will be times when they cannot be available; but some other staff member will then take their place. Further, while the staff cannot promise to be always at a patient's beck and call, we will try the best we can, and in an emergency the patient would always be immediately taken care of. By openly admitting the staff's and the institution's limitations, statements like this carry the ring of truth.

If the staff are convinced that they are doing their best for the patients, at considerable physical and emotional expense to themselves, they feel no need to advertise their good services in advance. This is because they feel sure that eventually the patient will find out more effectively for himself. The staff know that actions speak much more impressively than words, and that initially, rather than showing off their wares, the important action is to show concern for the patient's feelings and questions. This is another reason why we refrain from immediately showing the prospective patient the entire institution, but wait until the day he comes to stay, which is usually the day after his last visit. During his visits he sees only a small part of the institution, and we do this to protect the privacy of the patients. The prospective patient is thus shown that his privacy would be likewise protected. In the first encounters we concentrate on having the future patient form an opinion of us, as he has already done about the institution. The experienced staff have learned that if we are accepted at all, it should not be on the basis of what we tell, but of who we are; that is, the spirit in which we proffer ourselves and our services to him.

During the several days of visiting, the prospective patient becomes acquainted with a number of staff members; thus he has a chance to find out what they are like, *who* they are, before there is any need to find out what they can do. He meets them one at a time, preferably not more than three each day, so he will not feel overwhelmed by staff nor subjected to excess scrutiny. We make it clear to him which of the staff members he is introduced to will be the ones most directly concerned with him. This could affect his decision about whether to come. The two whom we have preplanned to work most intensively with the patient spend, if possible, some time alone with him each day. During these visits we invite him to study them, but also the rest of us, to make up his mind, and also to ask whatever questions he has. And we volunteer some information which we think might be particularly useful to him.

Though the purpose of these visits is for us eventually to get some impression of each other, by the second visit nearly all patients begin trying to find out what we do. The issue the patient selects as a test of our inner intentions often reflects his main area of concern. For example, it may be a problem around eating; or soiling himself and us. People who work in mental hospitals know that they are supposed to accept a patient's soiling himself; but their inner reaction is clearly revealed by the way in which they respond if the patient soils them. It is as if the patient has studied Freud and knows that attitudes about the world are derived from those centering around one's body; and that what we feel about our bodies is a reflection of what others felt about it in the past. Since we also know this, we can convince the patient of our intentions by showing our concern for his body. This is how we won the confidence of a potential genius (I.Q. just below 180), and thereby convinced him that he needed to come to the institution: After listening to his erudite explications of the origin and workings of the universe, we interjected that these are the heavenly bodies, but that we, after all, have our earthly bodies—and that sometimes we explore the heavenly ones because we are afraid to find out about the earthly ones. We added that the earthly body and its workings were the concern of the Orthogenic School.

At the very end of these getting-acquainted days, we ask the patient whether he wishes to come to the institution, now that we have done our best to explain what this will entail for him and for us. Though he may have declared his wish to come earlier, we ask him again, to make sure he has not changed his mind. Even mute patients have their own ways of informing us whether they wish to enter an institution. For example, when asked whether they prefer to stay or to leave, some simply remain sitting—or resist leaving in some other way. On several occasions I have had such experiences with mute patients. When I had asked them this question and given them considerable time to reflect and react, after ten minutes or so of silence, I said that since they didn't respond I could only conclude that they wished to leave. Opening the door of my office, I suggested they do so. One patient got up and carefully closed the door; two others slammed it shut with a big bang—in all three instances the patient then sat down with a satisfied expression. One mute patient had sat rigidly through all the visits, as if "at attention," despite all our efforts to make him relax. When we asked him whether he wanted to live with us or return home, he suddenly relaxed, and, stretching out on a couch, pretended to fall asleep.

Others demonstrated their desires even more vividly. A mute autistic twelve-year-old who had remained silent throughout a variety of interactions began to scream wildly when told to return to her parents, who were waiting for her; and when the door was opened, she ran away from them rather than toward them. These and similar behaviors are also used by patients who can talk. They might turn toward the interior area of the institution or walk up a flight of stairs leading away from the place where they came in. All these methods indicate that they wish to live with us without having to commit themselves verbally.

As mentioned earlier, somewhere during our conversations we try to make it clear that our acceptance of a patient is also a decision of great import to us—though not quite as life-changing as for him— because with his arrival much of our life will be altered. His presence as a patient has far-reaching consequences for us, and additional obligations; hence it is not something we can decide on lightly. It is amazing how reassuring it is for most patients to realize that their coming to the institution is also a difficult decision for us. This somehow seems to bridge the gap between us, and makes the patient feel more important, less like the manipulated object.

In a quarter of a century, only two prospective patients decided not to come, and on those occasions the staff agreed that it was better for all that they had not come. There were more occasions— though not numerous—when we felt that a particular patient was not suitable for us to accept. There were quite a few who almost immediately decided that they wished to stay; then we could agree only if the circumstances were unusual enough to warrant it, since we feel that both the patient and the staff have too much at stake to risk rash decisions.

From what has been said already, it should be obvious that we did not accept any court or other involuntary commitments. I don't believe our methods would work if a person was forced to submit to hospitalization.

Of course, patients who decide to come may sometimes regret it later; on rare occasions they may run away. When things get difficult, as they sometimes must, it is natural that some will seek an easy way out to stop it all. If a patient runs away, we do whatever we can to have him return; even having the police return him. On his arrival we welcome him back. After the immediate pressure which motivated his leaving is removed, after he has seen that there were no recriminations but only a positive welcome on his return, and after we have had a chance to talk things over, the patient realizes that if things get too rough he can leave again without any unpleasant consequences other than his and our concern about it. With this needed reassurance, without exception the runaways decide to stay. One older adolescent boy, convinced that if we knew his intentions we would be able to dissuade him, for weeks had planned the most elaborate arrangements to run away in the early morning hours. That same night around midnight, he called asking whether we would take him back. My answer was that only if he really wanted to return would we be glad to have him back. He did return, and remained for another two years until his treatment came to a successful end.

I have discussed these intake procedures in some detail because in most psychiatric institutions the acceptance decision is a one-sided one, made by the institution without the patient's participation. Unless the patient knows what his future life will probably be like, is encouraged to think it over carefully, and has a chance to get to know those who will be most directly involved in working with him, his decision is made in ignorance and despair. If the patient's decision to enter an institution is not made mainly by him, his autonomy is not from the very beginning being given the necessary respect.

13 | Receiving the Newcomer: A Social Transition

The Orthogenic School, encouraged over the years by its successes, proceeded to concentrate on increasingly severe disturbances, including autistic children, adolescent drug addicts, and suicidal cases. These required treatment of longer duration, and, given the limited patient population, departures and consequent new arrivals became less frequent. There were rarely more than six arrivals a year, and sometimes fewer. A new arrival was a big event, particularly since the staff most concerned with each dormitory group did not have to cope with more than a couple of new patients a year. Since they knew they would be living and working with the patient for a long time to come, it was of the greatest importance to them who he might be, and how their relations with him were likely to develop.

The director made the preselection of persons who were to be considered as possible candidates for the opening. He did this while keeping the main purposes of the institution in mind: to do research in those areas where there was little knowledge about certain psychiatric disturbances; to advance the training in this field; and finally, to consider the existing group at the institution, both patients and staff—their personalities, their particular talents, their liabilities. But even before this tentative choice was made, the staff were able to exercise their autonomy. They would inform the director what kind of person they thought would best fit in with the present group. If there were several possible candidates, as there usually were, the staff's preference affected the decision of who should get top priority, and the time when he should visit—the latter depending on when the staff thought they and the group were ready to receive him.

The need for the services of the Orthogenic School was at all times so great that it seemed pointless to keep a waiting list implying that a place would definitely become available. Applications were considered and processed only if there was a likelihood of an opening in the near future, and most importantly, if the nature of the applicant's disturbance seemed not to seriously interfere with the needs of the patients already under our care.

The patients knew that an empty place would be filled soon. Some had a hard time dealing with the uncertainty about whom they would have to contend with. Others needed time to undergo some period of grieving for a departed friend and new readjustment to each other as a group, before they were ready to accept a new member. The pressure to fill an opening was great, and while the desire to serve those who needed our help was an added pressure, sometimes an opening might not be filled for months. But as soon as the staff felt that they and the patients were prepared for it, a candidate was invited to visit with us, and after a few days of getting acquainted it could then be decided whether we were ready to undertake the common work.

Before the patient's first visit, background material on him was studied by at least three of the staff members who would work most directly with him: two counselors of the group, his prospective main teacher, and also the social workers who would be talking with his parents or other relatives. All other staff members were free to familiarize themselves with the available information too; there was, after all, no certainty that the group placement we had in mind would turn out to be best, and eventually the patient might have to be moved to a group under the care of other staff members. All who were involved had to feel they could be of help to the new patient and enjoy this sufficiently to compensate for the great investment in time, energy, and emotion they would have to make in enabling him to develop a functioning personality.

Since the entire staff always got together on each weekday for one scheduled meeting, as well as talking things over informally at least twice every day including Saturdays and Sundays, there was ample opportunity to exchange views on the visitor's personality, his difficulties, what our chances seemed to be for helping him, and what our reactions on meeting him had been.

At the scheduled staff meeting, those who had spent time with him told first what they had objectively observed; then what they thought it revealed about him; and finally how they felt about the prospect of his coming to the institution and their having to take care of him. Usually by the third day, but sometimes only on the fourth or fifth, we were ready to reach a decision; we knew it would be unfair to keep him in uncertainty about it any longer. When the time for decision came, we as a staff would have spent four hours or more talking about how we felt about the newcomer, how we evaluated him, and ourselves in relation to him. In addition, those who would work with him had devoted many hours alone and with each other discussing whether they wanted to work with him and if so, how they would go about it; how the group was likely to react to him and how they would help the other patients with the problems of assimilating a new person.

We felt strongly that we were all very much together in the enterprise of the institution; we knew that once we decided to accept a patient, we would all have made a very strong commitment (those who would work most directly with him even more so than the rest, including the director). Therefore, at the time of decision, those who would be most involved were the first to state whether they preferred this person to any of the other possibilities, so that we could understand their motivations and why they felt this way. After their statements, everybody was free to speak his wishes, fears, hopes, and hesitations, and it was the director's task to see that many did. The decision was influenced by such matters as whether we could expect cooperation or difficulties, and what kind, from those who wished to place him; how much longer the staff members most directly concerned planned to continue working at the institution; and anything else that seemed pertinent to the prospective patient and his coming to the institution.

There were always a few of the staff who refrained from stating views, either because they felt they had none, or because they would be only peripherally concerned with this patient and wanted the decision to be made by those who would have to carry the heavier burden of work with him. In order not to influence junior staff members who had not yet become fully convinced that the more openly they stated their opinion, the more respected they and it would be, I expressed my views only after everybody else had stated his. If I felt that the person would be ill served by the institution or that his coming would be a severe and lasting detriment to the patients already with us, or that his disturbance was of a nature that could be treated as well somewhere else, I freely said so. I had no compunction in exercising influence when I was convinced we should *not* accept him, stating my reasons in detail. Only on three or four occasions during the twenty-seven years of my tenure did I overrule a few staff members who wanted a patient to be accepted.

On the other hand, I carefully avoided influencing the staff to accept a patient. To accept him had to be their autonomous decision, especially for those who would have the main responsibility for his treatment. But before the matter came to decision, I tried to the best of my ability to state in detail whatever difficulties I fore-saw. I did this for much the same reason as when not giving the visitor too positive a picture of the School. If things did not turn out as badly as I warned they might, everybody would be happy; but if they did, at least we had gone into it with our eyes wide open. Unless those who would have to work directly with the patient were unhesitatingly in favor of his coming, and unless all other staff members agreed or had no opinion, the patient was not accepted. To use an appropriate analogy: unless those who adopt a child are sure that they want to adopt this particular child at this unique moment in their lives, the adoption will never work out; nor will it if other members of the family are opposed to it. In much the same way, those who will be responsible for the patient will literally have to adopt him or he will not recover, a failure with possible catastrophic consequences for him, and for the staff as well, damaging to their self-esteem and future security as therapists.

As with any other adoption, those who are about to adopt a mental patient have to prepare themselves for it: not just for the challenge and the anticipated satisfaction but, given the nature of the illness, also for the severe hardships which will certainly ensue. Throughout the years, each newcomer has been received with a welcoming party. Thus part of the preparation for his coming was planning for the party. This involved the selection of presents he and the other patients would receive and deciding what kind of party would be most appropriate for all concerned—particularly for the new patient, for whom all this would be the most difficult. This was the first time those who would work most intimately with him not only had to think about him, but actually do something: buy the presents, select the food, and do whatever else goes into the making of a party. Most important of all was choosing the special gift he would find waiting for him on his bed to welcome him.

Given the age of our patients, it was often felt by his future counselors that a stuffed animal would be appropriate, though what they had gleaned from being with him during his visits might suggest other possibilities. They had to project themselves into what the patient's feelings, hopes, and anxieties might be on his arrival in order to decide, for example, whether a ferocious animal of great power, such as a lion or tiger, or a cuddly stuffed animal like a teddy bear or kitten, would be more suitable to convey the message they intended. Should it be a horse, or something more exotic? A baby doll, or a grown-up one? Maybe a blanket which could serve as the proverbial "security blanket"? Or perhaps a fancily carved box to which only he would have the key? Maybe the box should have a welcoming poem in it, written by those who would be taking care of him? A book of poems, provided they were the right ones to carry the message? Or would it be wrong to let someone else speak for us? We knew it would make a great deal of difference whether we succeeded in selecting something that would exactly convey the message we had in mind, so only after considerable thought would his counselors go to select and buy the right object. They tried to experience within themselves what receiving this particular gift would mean to them if they were in the patient's position, and they let this influence their selection. As they gave intense thought and much time to the present, they became ever more deeply committed to the patient, and this had to communicate itself to him if they wanted the enterprise to succeed. What they selected had to mean a great deal to them; otherwise, how could it mean as much to the patient?

A person who cannot thoroughly enjoy buying a gift for somebody who plays an important role in his life, or is about to do so, had better give up working intimately with people. But since the staff universally liked being able to do this, there was also some very personal pleasure in arranging all these details for the new arrival, an important emotional experience which can and did shed a glow over the gift. If they had not had the freedom to select what they thought appropriate, if somebody else were to have the say about it, then from the very beginning the care of the patient would not be their own personal project, but a task to be met as defined by others.

There were many other preparations to be made for the new arrival. As soon as a patient had departed, those who were left behind had to decide whether they wanted to rearrange their dormitory. This could not be left entirely to them, since there were always some who wanted change for change's sake, hoping that moving themselves and their furniture to different places might solve their problems. So knowledge of what motivated any desires for reordering of a room had to influence staff decisions. The decision was also influenced by the staff's knowledge of who the newcomer would be, and who would be most suitable as his neighbors. If any proposed new arrangement seemed reasonable, it was preferable to provide the patients with the experience of having a hand in deciding matters.

How important all this could be was brought to my attention when a former patient reminded me of an incident by then nearly twenty years past. He had been in a group where a newcomer was expected the following day. As I was visiting the dormitory, I looked over the bed and the space around it which would be the new patient's area, to make sure all was ready. An empty hook was still on the wall over his bed, where the previous patient had hung a picture. I asked the counselor what he thought the newcomer would make of this hook from which nothing was hanging; what would he think was our reason for leaving it there? What if—in line with his fear that we did not want him, or wanted to do him in—he should decide it was left there as an invitation to hang himself? How would he feel if, in what was to be his very own place in this new world, he had to contend with the remnants of some unknown person who had preceded him?

In discussing why he hadn't removed the hook, the counselor realized that he had difficulties in accepting that the patient who had left was indeed gone. He had not been aware of how painful it was for him to lose the old patient, and to have a new person take his place. He had unconsciously wished that something be left of the presence of the person who had been so important and had so recently departed. The counselor had thought he was emotionally well prepared for the new arrival; now he realized he was not. As he talked about all this, he also recognized that the newcomer must not be burdened by the remnants of a past that was not his, that he had to be given a chance to have a truly new beginning.

This incident had been quite an experience for the former patient who reminded me of it. It had convinced him more than anything else that neither his coming nor his eventual leaving was a small matter to the institution. He had not believed up to then that we took one person's leaving and another's coming that seriously. As we arranged things so that the area around the new patient's bed should become entirely his own domain, the other patient finally began to accept what he had always doubted before: that his own area was really his, not just loaned to him begrudgingly. In such ways, each new arrival provided an opportunity for the other members of the group to work through what they had not as yet solved about their own coming and belonging.

It was always difficult but important to decide what to talk about in front of the patients, and what to discuss in privacy with a staff member. Naturally, much depended on how secure a staff member felt in his relationship to both director and patients; whether he welcomed such open discussion or felt threatened by it. The more secure a staff member, the more he preferred open discussion in front of the patients, feeling sure it would only add to their confidence in him, even if it turned out that he was in error. At least this would show he did not need to pretend to be without failings; and it would demonstrate that he did not try to have secrets about things which concerned the patients most directly. Patients formed many of their

opinions of us and of the institution by observing how we behaved toward other patients; being less involved themselves, they were better
able to see our actions for what they actually were. They also got a
much better understanding of the institution by seeing how staff
members handled disagreements among themselves. The patients
were usually delighted to discover that we didn't try to cover up for
each other, or pretend we were not in error when we were. For all
these reasons, whenever it could be done without hurting a staff
member unduly, things that pertained to the patients were openly
discussed in their presence. Of course, anything that was private to a
staff member or to a patient had to be kept confidential. It would not
do for staff members to discuss a patient's anxieties, their origin, and
how they could best be handled, in front of him or any others.

The patients, as well as staff, needed time to prepare themselves
for the event of a new patient's arrival. Usually a day or two beforehand, the director informed all patients, stressing the importance for
everyone involved with the life of the institution. This was further
emphasized by the fact that all the staff were present for the announcement. The patients were told a few facts about the person
they were to receive into their midst: his name, age, what time he
would arrive, and who of the staff would be most involved with him.
As always when any announcement of importance was made, the
patients were invited to react to it in whatever way they wished—
voice their misgivings, ask whatever they wanted to know, but with
one big reservation: we would not, of course, divulge confidential
information or reveal details about the newcomer that were solely
his privilege to make known about himself. The patients knew from
previous experiences that we would insist on their forming their own
opinions about the new person after they had got to know him. Still,
there were questions which could be answered, such as what part of
the country he came from (there were always some patients who
feared that some relative might move in on them, and this anxiety
could be alleviated). Others wanted to know whether he was mute,
and they could be told this since they would find it out anyway immediately on seeing him. Some were anxious about whether he was
much bigger than they were, and this information could also be
given.

Only patients who had not yet become imbued with the ethos
of the School—and at any one time there were always some—would
press for what might be called a diagnosis: What were his problems?
Why did he have to come to live in an institution? And so forth.
While we did not answer these questions, we acknowledged that
these were things they would naturally worry about. One way to

show the inappropriateness of speaking about such matters was to show them that what the staff might view as *their* problems could be very different from what *they* themselves thought they were; reminding them how offended they would feel if we spoke our views about them to others. If they still pressed on, as happened occasionally, we would remark how much better it is to make up one's own mind about another person; to decide what he is like, what's right and wrong with him, in line with one's own observations rather than on the basis of what someone else might say or think about him. Since every person, certainly including mental patients, knows very well how to behave toward another person—even if he chooses for his own reasons not to act on such insight, which is his privilege—it would be a presumptuous insult to suggest how he should think or feel about someone. It does remain our obligation, however, to protect the newcomer against anybody's acting toward him in an obnoxious way, since he has enough to contend with in meeting so many strangers. And although we maintained the right to criticize when necessary, even to actively interfere on the newcomer's behalf, we would not fail to recognize the validity of the feelings underlying old patients' wish to act toward him in unacceptable ways.

The patients' questions on how they should respond to this new person for his own sake were a bit more touchy. Some wondered whether it would be better if they kept their distance from him for a time. We suggested that they would have to be guided by their own feelings, both about what they surmised he might prefer, and by how they thought they would feel if they were in the newcomer's situation. After all, they had all been in the same position, and they could be guided by what had felt good to them then and what objectionable. In this way, as on all other suitable occasions, we tried to remind them how much we all have in common; however this new person might turn out, deep down he would not be too different from us.

We also stressed that since they had not met the newcomer, there was no way to predict what their own wishes might be: whether to keep to themselves, or to reach out to him. To decide beforehand how to behave damages our humanity, which requires that we do not act on the basis of preconceived notions, even the most laudable ones, if these are not supported by genuine feelings. Only after we know how we feel about the other person, and after we have seen how he reacts to us, are we able to decide how we will interact.

More often than not, these more personal problems were raised and discussed not at the assembly of the entire institution, but by the patients in their own small groups where talking was much easier, and with their own counselors whom they knew best. After the announcement had been made and the patients' general questions answered, the various groups would retire to their own abodes to give free rein to their reactions, the intensity of which depended on how closely their lives would be affected by the newcomer. On these occasions, not only the counselor who was working with the group about to receive the newcomer would talk with the patients about the important event, but the group's second counselor and other staff members, such as teachers who were involved with these patients, would also drop in, making themselves available. The presence of all these staff members was meant as an unspoken but effective reassurance that the patients would not become less important because of a new person, who would also make claims on the staff's time and interest.

An undercurrent of jealousy and resentment in this situation was a fact of life that had to be faced. In making the announcement at the general assembly of the entire institution, the director gave recognition that a new person might be viewed as an imposition on those who would have to live with him. We also said that while we regretted that our work sometimes inflicted hardships on them, such as being inconvenienced by the coming of a stranger when they had no say about it, this was unavoidable, since the institution was here to help all the patients it could. We reiterated that we did not expect them to be unresentful about it. But we hoped they would direct their resentment against those responsible for it—mainly the director, but also the rest of the staff—and not against the patient, whose coming was not his fault, and who would be much less able to deal with resentment than we. A question frequently asked at this point was, Why then did we do this to them? Our answer was that as strong as their understandable resentment might be and as much as we could accept it—even find it strange if they did not feel this way—this could not deflect us from our obligation to help as many patients as we were equipped to serve. Occasionally, someone who felt outraged was asked to consider what he thought the other patients' reactions might have been when his own coming was announced; this usually led to some quite sober thoughts.

All this and more was intensely ventilated in the dormitory groups, particularly the one the newcomer was to join. Hopes and anxieties were talked about, and when possible the latter were dealt with. After all, the patients knew from the experience of their own arrival that the staff members most concerned with the newcomer had by now got to know him. While the staff resisted the pressure to tell more about him, all efforts were concentrated on helping the patients with their anxieties, which didn't really originate with the new arrival but in their emotional makeup and past experiences.

Naturally, their greatest anxiety centered on the idea of desertion. How could those who worked most closely with them, who were so intimately involved in their lives, also become interested in a new person? How could they devote themselves to someone they hardly knew? This was difficult for the staff to handle, but an issue of great importance. Essentially the reply had to be that the reason the staff worked with mental patients was because they felt deep concern with helping them get well. At this moment it was true that their involvement was less with the new patient himself than with the help they might be able to give him. Even more true, as long as this involvement remained on such an objective level it would not do the new patient much good; but this was the starting point from which the staff members would soon proceed to get personally involved with him and in him as a person, rather than as somebody who needed help and whom one wished to help.

After the patients had talked themselves out, reminisced about their own coming and how they had been then, and how they were now, it was helpful for some practical arrangements to be worked at. If the dormitory had not been rearranged at the time the previous patient left, now was the time to do so; and even if this had already been done, now that they knew at least a little bit about the new person, last-minute changes could be considered. This permitted some doing on the part of the patients, which made them feel a bit less that things were all managed without their having any say. We tried to have them do things for themselves, rather than make things "nice" for the newcomer, which was our task and which it was hard enough for them to accept, even though we always did it in their absence. But there were still things for them to do. Some felt they had to put away their most valued possessions, so that they might not be harmed. Others used the occasion to reorganize their personal area to make it more their own, safer from the intruder, or in other ways made themselves psychologically ready for the coming insult.

One more detail pertains not to something done in preparation for the new arrival, but something which often happened soon after. A patient would become worried about whether his responses to the newcomer had been all right. He might ask a staff member: "Was what I did O.K. or was it wrong for me to do that?"—whether refuse to play a game, not answer what he considered a question about his private affairs, or the way he criticized the new patient's behavior. Exploring with the patient why he was in doubt usually provided a much more penetrating answer to his question than anything else we could have said. If it did not, we offered our opinion if we had one, such as what we might have done had we found ourselves in his situation, and why. But always with the proviso that while an alternative action might have felt better to us, it obviously hadn't to him, otherwise he would not have acted the way he did. Mostly we stressed what the patient really wanted most to hear confirmed from us, and what he already knew from his own experience: that each person is unique, and that if two people act differently in the same situation it doesn't make one response right and the other wrong; the variation flows naturally from the differences between the two people, or from one's relation to a particular other person.

The patient would then need reassurance to quench the fears which had motivated his question in the first place: Did we want or expect him to set aside his own interests to serve the needs of the newcomer? Or were we as involved with him and devoted to his interests as we had been before the new person entered our lives and demanded our attention? Here, and in many other situations, the patient was told that his help with another would be appreciated if it was genuine and hence constructive; that is, only if it was what he wanted to do on his own; but that it would be detrimental if he did it to please us, in order to receive praise for it, or for other reasons he thought he ought to have. We stressed strongly that he was here to help himself but not to help others, and to receive our support in the first undertaking, but not in the latter.

Thus, from their first meeting with this new person, what they needed was our questioning why they would *want* to be "nice" to him, since he would to some degree take the staff's time and energy away from them. For us to criticize their "being nice" unless it was clearly to their own benefit convinced them that their interests would not be sacrificed to the newcomer's. They were neither to do him favors nor to court favors from him; certainly not before they had developed an honest-to-goodness relationship with him.

And meanwhile the newcomer was to have a rite of passage of his own. The gift which had been so thoughtfully selected would be waiting on his bed. He would take possession of it just as he would of the bed itself; not as a present given to him by the institution, or the staff members who had selected it, but just as something that was there waiting to receive him, as we were. He would decide what he thought of it, and how he might wish to use it and us.

III | Creating the Therapeutic Milieu

14 | From Pilgrimage to Psychoanalytic Setting

Efforts to deal with inner difficulties must be as old as man himself. Modern preliterate societies have quite elaborate procedures for handling mental disturbances. Witch doctors occasionally achieve impressive "cures," and modern psychiatrists who studied their methods found some interesting parallels with those they themselves use (76). Horace warned that man changes only the sky, and not his soul, by traveling across the sea (*Caelum mutaris, non anima, per mare currens*), and that he felt compelled to make this point suggests that many must have tried, in his time, as before and ever since, to escape from themselves by journeying to the four corners of the world. Some may even have been helped by it.

There is little that psychoanalysis brought into a comprehensive system that had not been around for centuries in disconnected bits and pieces; though it made possible both a systematic understanding of heretofore only vaguely known aspects of man, and a therapy for mental disturbances. Change of the environment (with insufficient understanding of why the old one had created or aggravated the disturbance, or any specific comprehension of what the new one ought to consist of to provide relief or cure) was one of these pieces. While it was all pure chance, this change must have had some benefit —from the moment men began thinking about how a person might be helped to overcome feelings that oppressed him, it was recognized that one of the most effective ways was through a radical change in his environment. In addition, the mentally disturbed person's kin experienced temporary relief due to his absence. In the Middle Ages, when mortified by a feeling of sinfulness—or as we moderns might put it, by an inner conflict between id desires and superego strictures —some people sought and found relief by going on a pilgrimage. Even long before then, voyages to holy places were a well-established custom. Viewing the holy relic or even touching it did little by itself for the pilgrim; but it achieved a great deal because of the meaning it carried.

Pilgrimages seemed to work as a combination of escaping the customary setting and at the time experiencing a more rewarding and stimulating new one. There were innumerable holy places to be visited, and thousands of people were always engaged in such journeys. Leaving the accustomed environment with its demands and routines which had become tiring; escaping burdensome emotional involvements with those closest to one; forming stimulating new associations; concentrating on one's inner voices and feelings, as in religious contemplation—all this renewed the spirit and gave strength for returning with new vigor to meeting the tasks of living. When the spirit faltered again, there was always a new pilgrimage to go on.

A pilgrimage also afforded relief in reducing inner pressures. A superego which relentlessly castigated a person became appeased by living for a time according to the more stringent morality expected of those on pilgrimages. One could thus purge oneself of some sin of which one felt guilty. Other, similar ventures, such as the Crusades, relieved both id and superego pressures. The original motive was to satisfy superego demands, but the lure of the pleasures of the East also promised id satisfactions. Thus the efficacy of pilgrimage didn't come only from the new and different stimulation of a changed environment but also from a temporary rebalancing of the personality as the ego became relieved of superego and sometimes also id pressures, and could function better. (Not only were original pressures removed but, since acting in accordance with religious claims conforms with superego demands, the superego invested some of its libidinal energy in the ego. Little wonder that the pilgrim experienced an increase in well-being, his ego suddenly being so much stronger.)

There is another time-honored method of gaining a higher feeling of well-being through what, psychoanalytically speaking, could be described as the ego being invested with additional energy by offering id (or body) satisfactions in line with an ego—perhaps also superego—demand: that of restoring health. These were the balnearic cures which also required a change in environment, this time to serve the body, not the soul. But whether they are id or superego demands that are quieted along lines the ego considers correct, the result is the same: the ego becomes strengthened for the tasks of living in this world.

Only very recently in this country have balnearic cures become obsolete, replaced by more scientific methods such as chemotherapy.

Nevertheless, balnearic cures were and are effective, whether the disturbance is purely psychological or of a psychosomatic nature. Scientists here who make light of these sulfur, radiant, or thermal springs because their chemical ingredients cannot possibly remedy a disease, are forgetting that the distress often resides more in the patient's imagination than in his body. European physicians, being more pragmatic and ready to accept something that improves a patient's condition even when they have not the slightest idea how and why, continue to use balnearic cures with some very good results. The patient feels a subjective sense of well-being which more "scientific" regimens fail to provide when much of the trouble is not physical in the first place. "Taking the waters" can do a great deal for the psyche, because of the attention concentrated on the body, and as long as we cannot measure "well-being" or "relief from inner pressures" in any objective way, the case for the balnearic cure can be made only on a most subjective basis: the patient feels better.

Typically, the cure was taken not by the entire family but only by one member alone, who thus could escape the emotional onslaught of mate, children, or parents, and at the same time concentrate all his attention on himself and his body without concern for any other obligation. Once arrived at the spa, a person who all year long had begrudged moments of attention to his primitive bodily needs suddenly spent hours immersed in hot sulfur, salt, or radiant water, or in mudpacks—suggestive of reliving and working through in barely sublimated form ancient repressed wishes to play with and be enveloped by a hot liquid, or a soft and viscous substance. After this he comfortably showered, or was gently rubbed down or massaged. At the end of all these ministrations to his body a person may end up feeling (one is tempted to say) like a contented baby. As all of life began in a liquid element, and our own life began surrounded by the amniotic fluid, so the long bath in thermal water seems to both revive and relax us as it takes us back to vaguest memories of a state when we had not yet been separated out into an isolated existence.

Other cures at the spa may entail drinking purgative waters, which force the person to pay a great deal of attention and time to the eliminative processes; for years these may have been neglected because his toilet training had forced him to deny interest in them. But whatever the regimen of the spa, there are leisurely and delicious meals, usually accompanied by pleasant music; enjoyable, relaxed, and aimless walks in the woods, such as one has not taken since childhood; siestas; and long hours of sleep at night. For most of those who go to the spas, life there is the exact opposite of how they spend the rest of the year; and to some degree it is as undemanding and concentrated on the body as the life of an infant. Psychoanalytically speaking, it is "a regression in the service of the ego," since by providing the total person with id satisfactions it strengthens (not weakens) the ego for the tasks of living (79).

What makes the spa so attractive is that a psychological disturbance is viewed as a physical one; what is an impasse in meeting the world is ascribed to a malfunctioning of the body; we are allowed and made to believe that the difficulty is of the soma, and not of the psyche. During the cure, a basically Puritanic neglect of our "animal" nature is replaced by attention. Desire for such relief is still widespread, as illustrated by health farms and beauty spas. But the basic attitude is not altered. This is the crucial shortcoming of this type of therapy. It provides a transitory relief, restores neglected physiological and psychological functions by satisfying basic needs and reducing heavy demands, but it does not lead to an improvement of what produced the pathology in the first place; and so the "cure" has to be taken again.

While Freud was engaged in developing psychoanalysis, his experiences prompted him to invent a very special physical and human setting: the analytic situation. The seclusion during the analytic hour in the treatment room; the absence of all stimuli but those coming from the patient's introspection and the analyst's reflections on it; the supine position on the couch; the absence of any physical exertion; the assurance that nothing from the outside will be permitted to interrupt the concentration on psychic processes suggested that Freud felt psychoanalysis needed a unique setting. The general rule that the therapist should avoid any alteration in the arrangements of the place where treatment takes place, even in the waiting room, is part of the effort to keep the outside world from intruding on the very special milieu which is required for psychoanalysis.

The psychoanalytic environment is one that guarantees security, including the very important protection that what the patient says or does here will have no deleterious consequences in reality. If his allegations are false, nobody else will learn about them and he will not be taken to task for them; if his desires are unacceptable to society at large, are vicious or even criminal, expressing them will not lead to criticism; his threats will neither create anxiety nor evoke retaliation. The promise that whatever he says will remain secret between the two of them and that the therapist will refuse any contact with the patient's family, friends, or employers—unless the patient requests it, and even then many an analyst would refuse if there were not most compelling circumstances—adds to creating a situation that offers the maximum security possible. As soon as the patient has tested this particular setting and has convinced himself that here he is indeed secure, he can relinquish paying careful attention to potential dangers of the outside world, and can afford to let down his defenses. It may take years of testing before he fully believes in the security of the psychoanalytic situation since it runs counter to his anxieties and to his other experiences. To the degree that he does trust, he can relinquish the pathological defenses he had erected to protect himself against real and imagined dangers, and concentrate entirely on the inner workings of his mind.

This security is combined with the absence of any demands for age-appropriate or socially fitting behavior. The supine position, silence that is essentially broken only by the patient, and the attempt to suspend reasonable control of thought and to follow one's fantasies are all that is required and appropriate in this unique setting. This process induces the re-experiencing of early traumas, and makes it safe to do so. It is a setting that encourages reliving in fantasy what was too painful and threatening to master when it happened in reality. The experience can now be worked through in all of its ramifications, even though only in thought. Without this protection it still would be overwhelming. But what makes psychoanalysis efficacious is not the recalling of the past, not even the reliving it in imagination, nor the uncovering of the unconscious, though all these are facilitating conditions; it is the restructuring, the integration, of the personality. The psychoanalytic setting promotes this because there are no outside demands to deflect vital energy from this difficult psychological achievement.

All this is much more commonplace than it may seem. We all know that if we wish to concentrate on a very difficult task, we retire to a place where we will not be disturbed by anything extraneous to our undertaking. Nobody doubts that the success of biochemical research requires not only a specific laboratory setting but also a single-minded intentness on what is going on in an often incredibly small segment of external reality. A search into one's own soul demands a parallel absorption in the narrowly circumscribed phenomena of the mind, in a setting which is as carefully designed for its purposes as is the chemical laboratory for its very different type of investigation. Thus any human undertaking which presents serious difficulties demands a special environment and the exclusion of all distracting outside influences. Concentration on a very small segment of reality, artificially separated from the larger matrix in which it normally exists, is necessary for arriving at findings which have implications, or direct consequences, for large areas of experience.

The milieu to which the patient is subjected must be truly therapeutic to achieve a lasting solution to a severe impasse in living. It must be constructed on the basis of a clear understanding of what caused the psychological disturbance and what the particular emotional needs are that must be met.

Although he speaks only of children, Redl has stressed the importance of dealing with psychological problems as they arise, and in the situation in which they occur. The principles of what he calls the life-space interview apply equally for all ages. It is an important concept for understanding the difference between how psychoanalysis and the milieu therapy operate. He states:

> In contrast to interviewing in considerable detachment from the "here and now" of Johnny's life, like the psychoanalytic playtherapy interview, the life-space interview is closely built around the child's direct life experience in connection with the issues that become the interview focus. Most of the time, it is held by a person who is perceived by the child as part of his "natural habitat or life space," with some pretty clear role and power in his daily living, as contrasted to the therapist to whom he is sent for "long-range treatment."
>
> One of the great advantages of the life-space interview is the very flexibility in timing that it offers us. We don't have to hope that the child will remember from Friday noon until his therapy hour next Wednesday what was happening just now. Or having watched the event that led to a messy incident, we can quite carefully calculate how long it will take the youngster to cool off enough to be accessible to some reasonable communication with him, and we can move in on him at that very calculated time. (92)

For neurosis, hysteria, and various other character disorders, ambulatory psychotherapy or preferably psychoanalysis should be the preferred method of therapy. But it is not equally effective for some of the most deep-seated psychiatric disturbances; persons who suffer from these need hospitalization. Occasionally even severe disturbances end in spontaneous remissions, and it is the very harshness and cruelty of the mental hospital environment which can cause sudden remissions for a small number of patients. In this environment, their masochistic need to be punished most severely for their evil intentions, or for deeds they believe they have committed, gives them the feeling of atonement. (This phenomenon is akin to the effect of some pilgrimages, which imposed severe pains on the sinner so that he might expiate his sins.) While a patient may thus be enabled to return for a time to society—for example, by no longer feeling he has to destroy himself, or provoke others to do so—only the worst manifestations of his underlying disturbance are gone. The patient is not free of it, and is cheated out of his chance for a life that is not haunted by delusional guilt.

Unfortunately the psychiatric hospitals, without intending to do so, often merely satisfy masochistic needs instead of doing the only thing which could free the patient of them, and hence cure him: that is, permanently remove their cause. It is true that "punishment" can lead to temporary relief when the superego feels that for the moment the person has been sufficiently punished. But in actuality, punishment not only perpetuates but aggravates the disease. The procedures are considered curative because the patient "feels" less persecuted for a short time; whereas actually they convince him that his delusions are in accordance with reality, as demonstrated by the fact that such punishment is inflicted on him. He can explain the punishment to himself only by seeing it as verification that the hospital "knows" he deserves to be mistreated. Thus despite the relief which comes from the temporary quiescence of persecution by the superego, the whole process projects him only deeper into insanity.

Once, while visiting the psychiatric hospital at a distant university, I witnessed a rather dramatic example highlighting how the protection psychiatric hospitals afford can account for a remission of psychosis without effecting any cure. For all practical purposes, though not according to work classification, the person in charge of the hospital grounds was a long-time mental patient. He had been picked up years ago, totally disoriented and incoherent, in the capital city of the state. For reasons not clear, rather than being sent to the local state hospital, he ended up on the psychiatric ward of the university hospital. He was at first agitated, but soon quieted down and from then on fitted himself easily into the hospital routines, though he kept mostly to himself and his gardening. He had never regained an identity, and did not know his name, where he came from, or anything else about his pre-morbid past. He obviously had excellent knowledge of horticulture, though he did not know how he had obtained it. So every day, including Sundays and holidays, long after everybody else had quit working, he happily labored on the lawns and gardens, and over the years had vastly improved them. Yet he remained a mental patient; any suggestion that he should leave the hospital and get a paying job threw him into a severe state of anxiety and agitation. All efforts in this respect had been given up years ago. He worked under a foreman, but it was he who in his quiet way was responsible for most of the improvements, and for teaching the paid workers how to be good gardeners.

Shortly before my visit, a young resident took an interest in this nice old man whose quiet ways appealed to him. The resident started regular psychiatric sessions with the patient, encouraging him to tell his dreams. In the dreams certain unique geographical landmarks appeared which the resident recognized, since he happened to come from exactly the same out-of-the-way spot where the patient must have lived at some time. He made inquiries, and found that a short while prior to the patient's being picked up on the streets of the capital, a man of about his age had suddenly disappeared, leaving his farm, wife, and children. The resident tried to convince the patient that he had come from this area, but any inquiry or remarks about his past only elicited agitation.

So the resident arranged for a startling experience, which he hoped would produce a shock of recognition and restore the patient's memory. He brought the man's wife to the hospital for a confrontation. For a short while the patient remained calm, claiming he had never seen the woman before. As she insisted that she was his wife, begging him to return with her to his family, even threatening to take him there, he suddenly became violent, dangerously attacking her and the resident. It took several attendants to subdue him and he remained so violent that he had to be put under restraint. When I was told this story he had been under restraint for a couple of days, and the case was presented to me as a visiting consultant.

I was given permission to handle the situation in whatever way I wanted, and was promised that my suggestions would be executed. I asked the hospital's chief of psychiatry, the head of the ward, and the resident—all well known to the patient—to accompany me in visiting the patient in the maximum security room, where he was still in restraints. After I had explained my presence, I tried to converse with him about the flowers which I so admired, and said I had been told they were all due to him; but to no avail. Then I asked him whether he knew all the people who were with me, and what authority they wielded. This gained nothing but an angry reaction. I then asked them to guarantee to him, with all their authority, that he would never again have to meet anyone out of his past; would never again be in any way reminded of it or of his previous name; and that he would be permitted to live out the rest of his life peacefully in the hospital, taking care of its grounds. They all did so, and the chief psychiatrist spontaneously told the patient that he would not know how to keep the lawn and flowers so beautiful without the patient's help.

At that, the patient asked whether they really meant what they had promised; they all reassured him as convincingly as they could. I now asked whether he did not think it was time for him to return to his work, which was suffering from his absence, and he nodded. I requested that the restraints be taken off. This done, as he stretched himself he said, "I'd better go and look what a mess they've made of my flowers." A few years later, when I happened to encounter one of the hospital's psychiatrists, I was told that the man was still peacefully working at his flowers and gardens.

After the confrontation incident, the resident had to convince the patient's wife to accept these arrangements, which she did, realizing that the patient's violence was a real danger to her life. From information provided by her and other villagers the following story of the patient emerged. His father had died when he was a little boy and as a youth nothing he did could please his mother. Everything the boy did was wrong; she derided his masculinity and was convinced that he was a complete fool. The boy worked very hard, much too hard for his age; but nothing he did was ever enough, and all he earned for his arduous labor was criticism, derision, and further demands. When his mother abused him, he found peace by puttering with flowers. His mother arranged his marriage to a wife who treated him exactly as she had done.

Running away in a classic amnesiac fugue from the remote village he had never left before was this patient's first and only act of self-assertion. The hospital offered him not only protection from this unbearable persecution first by his mother and then by his wife, but also true appreciation of his very real contribution. It provided security and a respite from the onslaught of external demands that he had taken into his superego, and therefore permitted remission of his psychosis; but it did not cure it. At the time of the confrontation which threatened his defenses and threw him into a violent episode, he was in his fifties—a man not so much chronologically as psychologically old. Within the hospital he had been leading a protected and productive life. When he was faced with the possibility of being forced to leave and manage by himself in the outside world, he experienced a return of the engulfing hostility and fear which had driven him to "lose his past" by running away from it originally. It would have required considerable therapeutic effort for him to want to change. Without this wish, no psychotherapy could be effective, and even with it the course would have been long and uncertain, given his age and the limited mental resources at his disposal. So it seemed best to let well enough alone and devote the limited therapeutic resources of the hospital to more hopeful cases.

For a milieu to be truly therapeutic, it must protect the patient, until he is able to cope, against potentially devastating encounters with the figures of his past who contributed to his inability to deal with life. This is why at the Orthogenic School we did not permit relatives, friends, or any outsider to invade the patients' privacy. It would take a patient quite some time to believe that those who had before been such overwhelming or dangerous figures in his life had lost their power over him in reality, though they might continue to overwhelm him in his fantasy. New patients inquire most often and with great intensity about whether this is really so. Many experience great relief when they learn from other patients that our promise is valid, and that nobody but the institution's staff is permitted to enter the patients' quarters.

Occasionally, but only very rarely, we did permit visits by those whose interests we felt were legitimate. If such an intrusion was impending, we informed the patients beforehand of the reason why the visit was arranged, and who these people were. It was then up to each patient to decide whether or not he wished to expose himself. If not, it was arranged that he would not encounter any of the visitors; either by not permitting them into the rooms where those patients were who did not want to be seen, or by those patients going on a trip outside the institution during the time the visitors were there. But nobody whom a patient knew before he came to the School was permitted beyond the living room.

When visits with relatives were arranged, they took place in the living room described before. It was the only place within the institution where the outside world and that of the patients met. But even with such precaution, visits had to be handled carefully so that there was no threat to the patient's security, or his feelings of being protected against those who either had seriously interfered with his life or who too painfully reminded him of the person he used to be.

Had the hospital informed the amnesic gardener that his wife would be coming to visit with him, but for only a very short time, and that not she nor anyone nor anything else would be permitted to interfere with his remaining permanently at the hospital, his response to her might have been very different. Instead of being overwhelmed by the impact of the past, he might have been willing to take a glance at how she was now, secure that she could no longer wield any influence over his life. Certain that his life at the institution would continue undisturbed, he might have slowly over time been willing to consider not only how she but also how he had changed. Eventually he might have contemplated a return to an environment which was interpersonally now radically altered.

Patients need to make very certain that the therapeutic environment is indeed able to shield them against all threats coming from the outside, and from their past. For example, even if the possibility of a visit with relatives has been discussed with them, and although they themselves may have requested it, when the time for the visit arrives, some get cold feet. There are many ways in which they need to test whether they are really secure against these people who still control them in fantasy. On a few occasions awkward situations occurred when such testing took abusive form. This happened rarely, but when it did, we had to intervene and ask the relative to leave. That he could now effectively ward off those who before had held so much power over him was always sufficient warranty to the patient, and there was never any repetition of such an incident. Since we could not only explain why it had happened, but also from our experience could promise there would be no repetitions, the offended relative was able to accept and not be devastated by the occurrence.

On the next visit—several months later, to allow time to work with the patient and see why he felt compelled to act as he had—the worst that ever happened was that the patient silently turned his back on the visitor after a short time and ended the encounter by walking back to his dormitory. Even with this refusal there would never be any repetition; it was always sufficient when he had finally proved to himself that he was protected by the institution so that the visitor could not prevent his action, or make him suffer for it, and that there would be no other consequences. On later visits, the patient would interact more positively with the visitor, though often still guardedly (as described in Chapter 9). The patient was now sure enough of his security that he no longer needed to test it or defensively assert it. This experience leads the patient to realize how much things have changed, and once he has gained this security, limited home visits become not only possible but useful. They activate as yet unsolved psychological problems, and may provide incentives for working them through.

On the other hand, it is very dangerous to the patient if he gets the idea that the institution wants to be rid of him before he feels ready to go. Just because so much security is derived from the knowledge that he is safe within the institution, this safety cannot be lightly withdrawn without far-reaching consequences. If the institution succeeds in giving the patient the strength to feel he can now cope, he will leave even the most pleasant surroundings, as I have tried to make clear before. If he does not feel he can cope, even undesirable conditions are preferable to the danger of his being projected back into what he thinks caused his break with reality. Thus there are serious risks in forcing a patient to leave, when he wishes to remain in the mental hospital.

One example may stand for many. An older man, after shock and drug treatment, made an excellent adjustment to life in a psychiatric state hospital. He was quite resourceful in creating a small concession for himself, selling newspapers and various odds and ends to other patients. The hospital did everything to induce him to leave—that is, everything short of the restructuring of his personality, which would have made it possible for him to want to leave—but to no avail. Finally one day, despite his pleas, he was told he had to go. This was not because anybody wanted to be rid of him, but because there seemed no reason to have him occupying a space which was badly needed for other patients. He consented at last to go, and decided to walk on his own to the next village, to take a bus to his home town. On the short walk, he jumped from a bridge into a river and drowned. As in the case of the gardener, the mental hospital had been an environment which offered sufficient security for him to manage well within it; but it failed as a therapeutic milieu. It did not lead to that reintegration of personality that marks the difference between even the best custodial hospital care and a truly therapeutic institution.

The patient's symptoms, distressing as they may be to himself, and upsetting or even dangerous to his surroundings, are nevertheless his foremost achievement at the time. Since the symptoms are what society objects to, and since they make life difficult both for the patient and for those who attend to him, the efforts of the mental hospital are typically directed toward altering symptomatic behavior through drugs, or by conditioning through "behavior modification." Trying to make the patient relinquish the achievement which his symptoms are to him correctly convinces him that the institution wishes to shape him as it thinks best; not as he, in a strenuous and tortuous process of self-discovery, might wish to do.

While Kesey's bitter satire, *One Flew Over the Cuckoo's Nest* (74), grossly exaggerates the inhuman treatment of patients in public mental hospitals, there is some underlying truth in what he describes, including the sham which passes for individual or group psychotherapy, and the occasional misuse of shock treatment to make a patient malleable, supposedly in his own best interest. Even in the best of private psychiatric hospitals, an abyss separates the most imaginative and devoted psychoanalytic treatment of the patient during his sessions with his psychoanalyst from what goes on during the rest of the patient's existence there, as demonstrated in some fictional but nevertheless in a deeper sense true-to-life accounts (47, 53). A few treatment hours with one's therapist is not enough, and patients realize this. Anna Freud quoted a late adolescent schizophrenic girl who complained that psychoanalytic therapy failed to offer her what she needed. This patient said:

> *You analyze me all wrong. I know what you should do; you should be with me the whole day, because I am a completely different person when I am here with you, when I am in school, and when I am home with my foster family. How can you know me if you do not see me in all these places? There is not one of me, there are three.* (39)

She thus showed that she felt it necessary for her to live in an institution which would encompass all aspects of her life, and do so in line with psychoanalytic thinking. This combined with psychoanalysis would have helped her. But the psychoanalyst could not provide the patient with a living situation which would permit her to overcome the utter disorganization of her personality, an environment that in its entirety would be conducive to achieving such integration. What is needed, then, by a patient of this kind is an institution with a total therapeutic design based on what has been learned from psychoanalysis. The Orthogenic School tried to achieve this as, two decades before the beginning of the School's reorganization, Aichhorn did outside Vienna in a short-lived experiment with a total treatment design (1) and as later Redl (1947–8) did at Pioneer House in Detroit (95, 96).

Essentially, in the examples of the gardener and the old man who jumped from the bridge the patients were in the mental hospital for their own safety, or to protect others against their violence and the destructive consequences of their anger and anxiety—not for help in restructuring their personalities. Mental hospitals are scarcely organized for the latter, as we have seen. The therapeutic milieu should be so designed that it takes matters out of the realm of chance and, by submitting them to careful planning and scrutiny, effects a healthy integration of personality based on a permanent resolution of those conflicts, or whatever caused the disturbance in the first place.

15 | Experiments in Total Treatment Design

It is ancient wisdom that the health of the body and the mind are related; therefore the therapeutic milieu has to serve a unity of mind and body. Treating only one or the other, or both separately, will not heal the inner fragmentation of the schizophrenic whose mind and body are often at war with each other. Even if they were not, concentrating on one and neglecting the other will only further a split that needs to be healed.

The spa and the psychoanalytic settings were described in some detail to show that everything needed to create a total therapeutic milieu has been long available, but in pieces; nobody had put it together. Milieu therapy did not come into being, however, through combining the lessons of the spa and the pilgrimage with those of psychoanalysis. Treatment through a total therapeutic milieu in combination with psychoanalytic therapy as practiced by the Orthogenic School was derived from a background of psychoanalytic theory combined with a more or less chance experience, the experiment of having an autistic child live in my home (see Introduction).

When the University of Chicago, because of my experience with this autistic child—infantile autism having just then been named and described (73)—asked me to assume responsibility for the university's Orthogenic School, the institution had been in existence for several decades. If first served the study and education of feeble-minded and brain-damaged children. Later, it concentrated on spastic and epileptic children, and did pioneer work in establishing effective methods for their education. During the years just preceding 1944, the institution had been decreasingly successful in meeting its task as a research and training institute. A university-wide committee appointed to plan its future decided that it should concentrate on the most severe functional disturbances of childhood, such as the various forms of childhood schizophrenia, since these did not respond to treatment methods then available. I was asked to reform the Orthogenic School in line with its new tasks.

Surveying the situation and acting on what needed immediate attention, I also ruminated on my experience with the autistic child who had lived with us, a problem I had paid little attention to during the intervening years. In retrospect, it seemed obvious to me that what she had needed most for complete recovery was a setting specially designed to meet all the requirements of her treatment. It would have to encompass all aspects of her life, and be organized so that those caring for her would be able to share the burden by taking turns with others; despite long hours and extremely taxing demands, these workers could then still continue to have a life of their own. Although more than two people would be involved in parenting her, they would have to be in complete accord as to what was best for her, and in terms of their own personalities be able to set this into practice in the widest variety of situations.

All this could be possible only if consistent and deep commitments to a clearly understood common treatment philosophy transcended all individual differences. With the entrusting of each individual patient to several persons, they would all have to work together intimately as an extended family, each member living harmoniously with all the others, at least as far as the common enterprise was concerned.

From my experience I realized that in the ideal setting, those who parented the child—the psychoanalyst, the teacher, and all other staff members, including cooks and maids—would have to be completely integrated into the total life of the therapeutic community at all times. They would all have to be committed not only to the common philosophy in regard to therapy, but also to understanding each child and his specific needs of the moment. While the time they would have to spend with the patients would be more limited, and the obligations would be shared, they would have to live with the patients as intimately as we had lived with the autistic girl. The place for all this would have to be as compact and comfortable as a well-appointed home; but it would also have to be a setting encompassing facilities which no family home could provide, such as rooms for recreational and educational activities, and individual treatment rooms.

So far so good. But how to achieve it? The hierarchical attitude in hospitals, where the psychiatrist knew what was best for the patient, and also how things ought to be done, did not provide total treatment design. The psychoanalyst who had treated the little autistic girl had indeed more knowledge of child psychoanalysis, as we, the foster parents, had readily acknowledged. But in retrospect, I realized that although we had accepted it, we had not accepted it without resentment. Thinking about it all six years and a continent away, it became apparent that while we had readily given credence to the psychoanalyst's superior understanding of the child's unconscious, we had not as fully accepted her suggestions of what we should do for the child in our home. After all, it was our home; we had to live with this little girl not 50 minutes, but more like 23 hours, each day. (Interestingly enough, one of the most recent publications on residential treatment [123] has the title *The Other 23 Hours*, suggesting that even today many workers view the therapy hour and the rest of the patients' lives as separate entities rather than insisting they must be an integral whole if the child is to be able to attain wholeness of his personality.) We resented being told how to understand the child, even though we had no doubt that the psychoanalyst had gained deeper knowledge of the girl's unconscious mind from treating her. But hadn't we greater knowledge of what was involved in living with her all the other hours of her life, of how she reacted to the events of the day? So that being told, ever so politely, what needed to be done created a resentment which, I am now sure, was not lost on the child. What we could understand even less well, partly because we could not consciously acknowledge the irritation we were experiencing, was the psychoanalyst's reluctance—presumably in order not to aggravate us—to make many or forceful suggestions. And this, I submit, limited our therapeutic endeavors and effectiveness.

In other psychoanalytic institutions, for adult patients as well as for children, efforts had been made to put psychoanalytic insight into practice, and these had failed too. Recalling my pique at the psychoanalyst's thinking she knew what was best for the autistic child who had lived with us, my first thought was that this was the consequence of the existing hierarchies. Though the entire staff wished to work closely together, this hierarchy could not help arousing resentments, feelings of inferiority, and even anxiety about a staff member's particular position or therapeutic tasks in the scheme of the organization. So in the reorganized Orthogenic School there would be no such hierarchy: as far as the work with the patients was concerned, everybody would be equally important, and the common psychological understanding of the children's needs would form the basis of the institution's integration. While each staff member would possess his own special skills and knowledge, this must never confer any special prerogatives or interfere with the unity of the environment. The situation which best facilitates the psychotic's reintegration of his personality is one in which, whatever the complexities, vagaries, and many crises of his life, he can encounter them within a setting free of inner contradictions, one not pulling him in different or opposing directions. At the same time, the people he encounters must respect the importance of his pathological defenses and try to meet his needs, no matter how different they may seem from their own. The required institutional changes were the first steps made in the Orthogenic School reorganization.

The theory of staff equality may have been correct; but it did not work in practice. Within the course of a year of experimentation, with an almost entirely new staff deeply committed to the new philosophy of total treatment design, it became clear that this ideal of equality was an artificial way of achieving the goal. There were obvious differences among staff in the depth of understanding of a patient's needs and what might best be done about them. As soon as a patient came to the institution, some staff members made themselves much more important to him than did others; and often the patient, too, singled one or another out as most important to him. So each person, whether patient or staff member, created his own hierarchies irrespective of theory, and we had to respect these. The patient's own hierarchy had little to do with any special training a staff member possessed; but rather with what kind of person he was, and how deeply and sensitively he committed himself to a particular patient.

Soon it became apparent that neither utter equality in importance to the patient, nor shared philosophy in regard to treatment, nor common understanding of psychology and pathology— although these are all important ingredients—creates the integrated and total treatment design which by then was a cherished ideal we all embraced. As we worked together to make the ideal become reality, we saw that it was not so much the working together for the patient's benefit, although this was very important, as the *working out* of things together which allowed the integration we wanted. The sharing of hopes and anxieties, of successes and defeats, bound us together much more intimately in our undertaking than concentration on what it meant to the patient. This was a theoretical requirement, important though it remained as a guiding principle in all respects. What made it a common enterprise was what all of us poured into it; as we experienced it together, it made our work and even our life so much more meaningful to all of us.

As we realized this, the various things we did to achieve an integrated institution assumed a different order of importance. In staff conferences it became more important to understand why a particular staff member had been unable to achieve an insight on his own, than to have the psychoanalyst do it for him. We wanted to comprehend fully why one person handled a situation one way, while another handled it another way. By doing this, we learned about the various staff members' inner attitudes toward themselves, the patient, the philosophy of the setting, and the challenge the work presented. Who had been "right" or "wrong" in the first place assumed less importance than the understanding. What was exciting was understanding how and why the way a staff member handled a patient and his problems flowed from the member's personality and past experiences; and how the aftereffects of these could be mastered to his benefit, to the patient's benefit, and—most important in this context—to that of the total treatment design of the institution.

Understanding and overcoming the undesirable residues of their own past within the relationship to a patient permitted staff members a quite different, more immediate and intimate understanding of the patient's problem; and of themselves in the context of what they did with, and felt about, a patient. On the basis of the staff's struggling to understand themselves better *vis-à-vis* the patient and their own work, as well as the institution's work for him, staff consensus could be established on what was the right approach to help a patient. At the same time the integration of the staff fostered a truly therapeutic milieu. As we devoted ourselves to this task, its beneficial effects for the patients, for each of us, and for the total institution became ever more obvious. We realized we had started out with a too static, not sufficiently alive conception of what comprises an integrated institution.

It was not possible to integrate the design of the building, the planned activities of staff and patients in all their interactions, plus the other aspects of the operation of the institution, and expect them to remain integrated forever. On the contrary, the integration of the total institution had to be a vital process of forever becoming —an ideal always strenuously striven for, never to be fully achieved —because the being alive and the liveliness, and the resulting therapeutic effectiveness, came from the seriousness of the efforts at achieving this goal, never from having accomplished it. It turned out to be tremendously important that the patients—working toward the integration of their personalities—live in a setting continuously striving for its own integration. We tried to live and work by this image; and this spirit, which pervaded the institution and all of the life that unfolded within it—much more than the specifics of the setting, or of what we did for the patients—helped them to help themselves, and permitted us to help them do so. Although of course we certainly had to work on the specifics, too, most arduously, all day and much of the night, 365 days a year.

As we learned how to do this, it was as if blinders were being removed. It became completely obvious that if, in handling a difficult situation, their own problems were not accorded equal consideration, staff members could not approach and react to a patient's symptomatic behavior with sincere respect. How could they treat a patient with the greatest sensitivity to his emotional needs, if their own were not seriously taken into account?

I have often wished that every staff member who came to work with us had taken a balnearic cure somewhere; it would have taught him the difference between believing something with one's head, and experiencing it through one's body. It is not easy to pry into what a staff member's inner feeling is when he takes a bath; and there were those who at first never took baths but only showers. Observing how the staff member gave a patient his bath could be one starting point for opening up such conversation; another, even more innocuous, was inquiring what he thought the patient got out of his bath. Had it not been so serious in terms of our work, it would have been amusing to listen to a long account of how enjoyable and meaningful the time spent in the tub was for patients; how important to convey the feeling that the purpose was not to get them clean, but for them to relax and get simple bodily comfort—and then ask the staff member why he did not provide all that for himself? The answer was what one might expect: the staff member did not need it, he didn't have the time, or had more important things to do. So, if the value of this particular experience in the tub was on such a low rung on the ladder of his importance, how could he feel it stood so high for the patient? Unless, that is, he believed that the patient's and his own needs and sources of bodily enjoyment were radically different? Essentially, this was the limit of how far it was possible to pursue this issue with a staff member.

Quite a few staff members consequently tried to find out how a relaxed bath, similar to those given the patients, felt for themselves; and in doing so discovered something of the nature of their inhibitions against it, as well as what they liked about it. They all got a much better understanding of their own emotional response to the entire issue; they could no longer naïvely assume they could make it pleasant for the patient if they had strong reservations about doing it for themselves. As soon as the staff members were able to enjoy similar experiences of bathing to those they tried to give the patients, they were much more successful in expressing the feelings which made it truly a constructive experience for the patient. Everyone understood how many obstacles there were between just saying that the differences between us and the patients were not all that great, and truly believing it. Those few who never became quite able to relish lolling in the tub, at least recognized that by helping the patient to do so, they could vicariously enjoy it; and this was better than not enjoying it at all.

Discussing such matters will be acceptable and constructive rather than offensive to a staff member only after he is sure that his feelings and actions, even if they may seem a bit strange, will be treated with the greatest respect and consideration. Such discussion has to wait until this conviction is established. Since talking about these things is important for success in his work, these feelings of confidence in the purposes of the institution (not only for patients, but also for staff) have to be established as soon as possible. Thus, much of the director's and the senior staff's efforts must go into creating a spirit where such discussion becomes possible and fruitful.

There was one staff member who did indeed spend a great deal of time in the bathroom; feeling she had to take four, five, or more showers a day as she had since childhood, because she always felt so dirty. She did not believe that her feelings about her body being so dirty could possibly influence the patient's feelings when she gave him a bath; but they did. It is a reflection on how modern middle-class youngsters are brought up, possibly going back to their infant bathing experiences, that few staff members took showers or baths for any other conscious purpose but to get clean. In the case just cited, it was relatively easy to help the staff member comprehend how haunted she had been for years by the fear of her body's inacceptability. Her deep desire that none of her patients should have to suffer similar agonies was what saved the patient's enjoyment of the bath she gave him. Her importance to the patients, what she could do for them and help them do for themselves (including achieving a positive attitude to their bodies), and the respect of the staff for her and her work permitted her to change her feelings about her own body; she then became able to enjoy taking good care of it.

Having repeatedly experienced it oneself, or watched it happening to fellow staff members, one comes to believe that whatever one's background and attitudes are, if they can be understood, they can be turned from a liability (the feeling that one is dirty and has to take many showers) into an asset (determination that the patient shall not have to feel this way about his body). This is what gives staff members the courage to open up about secret thoughts or emotional difficulties. It makes one realize the world of differences between "You must do it *the right way*," and "You and the patient are so much better off if you do it the way which is *the only right way for you*; and if we search, we shall always find a way that is both *your way* and *the right one for the patient*."

It is possible to find this (unless a person is too disturbed, too intellectually limited, or too emotionally blocked; and such people should not work with psychiatric patients, so staff selection methods must protect patients against being exposed to persons with such liabilities), but it is not always easy. For some participants, one of the fascinations of staff meetings was to speculate on how it would be possible to turn what obviously was an impasse (such as the one described above) into a positive experience, leading to a constructive solution. I had not thought it was all that difficult. If it was possible for some people to extract positive value even from such terrible experiences as the holocaust, then it seemed not all that difficult to turn the liabilities of persons of very good will into assets, provided one did not expect perfection. For the staff to do the best they can for a patient, not just as a superficial statement of intent but as something they work hard and against difficulties to achieve, is all the patient needs to get well.

If the patient believes, and if the changes in the staff member's behavior show him, that the staff member has worked hard to understand and do things better, then the patient has the feeling that he is really important to the staff member and truly worthy of such efforts. When he feels he is not, it is an incentive for him to try to become so. The patient will become convinced that he has indeed achieved full humanity—at least in this one relationship—if he begins to realize that, directly or indirectly, because he is important to the staff member, the staff member can and does change himself and enjoy life more; for example, by gaining the ability to view his body more positively. Since the patient has inspired such an important development in the life of a staff member to whom he has become attached, it turns him from somebody who was only the passive recipient of services into one who also can give significantly. More than anything else, this provides the conviction of his own human dignity.

16 | Staff Organization and Unity

In *The Brothers Karamazov* Dostoevsky wrote: "True security is to be found in social solidarity rather than in isolated individual effort." To offer such true security to the patients, the staff must possess it; and while not every worker will be able to call a full measure of it his own, the staff's social solidarity around their work provides it for the patients, and for themselves.

It has been stressed that the reason all parts of a psychiatric institution have to hang together, spatially and symbolically, is to facilitate the patients' orienting themselves; so they can once again find their way around their world, and feel that this is the right world for them. Life within the institution must have unity, both external and internal, for the splits and contradictions in a patient's inner life to be healed and the dissonances between him and the world resolved. But this cohesion only provides the basis for the patient's security; the structural elements are human relations, which make us feel secure and heal the split in our inner world, as well as between ourselves and others.

The attitudes and feelings stemming from human relations can effectively counteract the patient's negative views of himself and the world, while even ideal physical arrangements or the best-planned program cannot. The most arduous efforts to integrate all of the patient's activities (and thus his life) will be ineffective if they are not based on, and reflective of, the staff's integration around the needs of the patient.

What do the staff bring to their work which makes this possible? What institutional organization permits this potentiality to become reality? These two questions cannot be separated. Neither the ability of the staff to develop the needed social solidarity nor the cohesiveness of the institution can exist in isolation, but only in simultaneous unity. What the work can mean to the worker personally is conditioned by the institution's functioning. It has to permit the actualization of his potential, just as it has to make the patient's potentialities available to him as his new reality. It is the structure of the therapeutic milieu which facilitates both. Some of the characteristics of the therapeutic milieu's organization can be highlighted by comparing it, not to the large state institutions which suffer from inadequate funding, poorly trained staff, and antiquated buildings, but to relatively small, well-staffed private psychiatric hospitals with adequate financial resources.

The literature on these psychiatric hospitals abounds with reports showing how lack of agreement among various departments or individuals even on crucial issues, along with the absence of spontaneous cooperation, has a most destructive impact on patients, who supposedly are unaware that such dissensions exist (116). In better institutions, serious efforts are made to keep disagreements away from the patients, who neither hear nor see them. But the patients sense them nevertheless, usually as soon as they occur, and often before the staff themselves have become aware of them. Patients react to subliminal signs; to changes in movement or tone of voice which remain imperceptible to the average person. This is because patients live in such mortal anxiety that anything pertaining to those who have power over them is keenly observed. The consequence of dissension among staff is a major concern to everybody seriously involved with psychiatric hospital operations. But discussions always stop short of the logical conclusion that psychiatric hospitals require an entirely different form of organization. While correctly assessing the causes of disagreements and the effect they have on patients, there are no statements of how new mental institutions should be set up. Caudill, in summing up a careful study of the problem, states:

> *One of the most discouraging obstacles to be found in psychiatric hospitals is the tremendous weight of apathy and inertia. One of the reasons for the failure of attempts at improvement is that they usually are constructed as additions to the content of the over-all program while carefully staying within the already existing form of the hospital.* (24)

It is always assumed that the operation of a psychiatric hospital requires its being divided into several departments. If so, it is inevitable that the life of the patient will be split into various compartments. A hierarchy—for example: director → ward chief → treating psychiatrist → resident → psychologist → social worker → occupational therapists → recreational therapists → head nurse → floor nurse → attendant → aide—is taken for granted. Added to these usually are managerial departments which influence all others, such as financial management and housekeeping, not to mention students and their supervisors, administrative and research departments, and so on. Most of these groups then have to contend with the hierarchies above and below them, as well as those within their own department. Both staff and patients suffer from the complexities of decisionmaking when several hierarchies, all motivated by best intentions of serving the patients, run into trouble with each other because they are either required or wish to proceed in their own way.

The complexity of such an organization is seen in the chart from Stanton and Schwartz (reproduced on page 225), which describes the operation of a relatively small private hospital, one of the best in the country, which is at least aware of the problems of such complexity (114). The larger the hospital, the more unwieldy the hierarchies become and the more cumbersome the operation.

Sporadic efforts are being made to correct some of these shortcomings, to reduce dissension and enhance cooperation. But there seems to be no recognition of what it does to the patient's own integration to live in a human environment which is lacking in integration: the institution expects him to become integrated although it cannot integrate itself. In regard to this problem too, no attention has been paid to the importance of symbolic messages, positive and negative, which originate from the institution.

The relative lack of deep personal involvement of worker with patient in even the better psychiatric hospitals, because of the split into departments, makes it impossible for the worker to feel deeply committed to his patient. Were the worker to experience the patient as truly his own, he would soon feel torn himself as he watches the patient being pulled in different directions by the various departments of the institution, by their professional convictions regarding what he needs, and also by their vested interests in their particular contributions. Only in rare instances do various departments actually fight over the patient on a specific issue. On the surface, most disagreements are usually soon settled amicably; but the battles are usually over matters of greater concern to the staff members involved than to the patients. The patient's situation may be likened to that of a child whose parents are not deeply involved in their living together, nor in the same central issues. By and large, such parents agree on the surface; but when they get really steamed up about

Formal Routes of Oral Communication
of Clinical Information

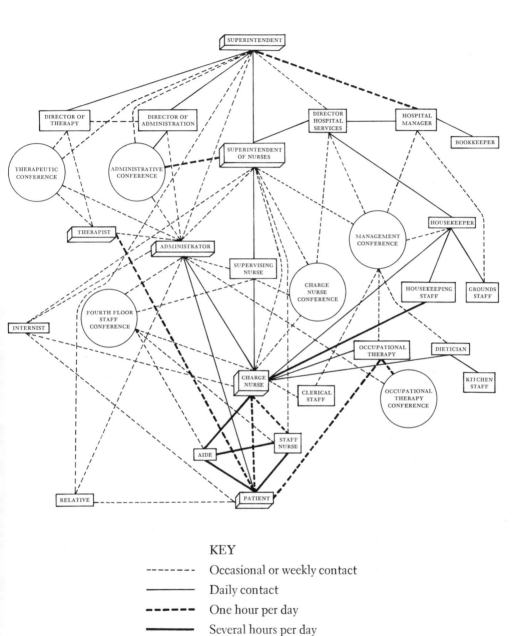

KEY

- - - - - - - Occasional or weekly contact

———— Daily contact

- - - - - One hour per day

———— Several hours per day

SOURCE: A. H. Stanton and M. S. Schwartz, *The Mental Hospital: A Study of Institutional Participation in Psychiatric Illness and Treatment* (New York: Basic Books, 1954), p. 40.

something important to them—their relations to each other, or to the child—disagreement becomes overt. Even if it doesn't, since they aren't in accord they cannot send the same unconscious messages to the child about what is important in life or what makes it meaningful. If a parent is truly emotionally involved in the child, he cannot help pulling him in his own direction; the surface agreement breaks down and the child becomes emotionally torn apart. If, on the other hand, the parents are not strongly committed to him, the child gets little from them of deep meaning.

Given the departmental structure of the psychiatric hospital, deep commitment to the patient as a person would necessarily bring a staff member into conflict with the vested interests of other departments, if not also with those of his own professional group. Each department concerns itself with specific features of the patient's sickness; or with those parts of his life it is responsible for. Its members are expected to devote themselves to these aspects, though mainly in a professional capacity which remains separated from other aspects of their personalities. In any endeavor, total personal commitment usually brings out the best in a person; yet devotion to a particular occupational or professional capacity unfortunately does not have the same desirable effect. "Professionalism" and spontaneity, including spontaneous empathy, do not mix easily, except in extraordinary persons. But a psychiatric institution cannot rely on securing only extraordinary people as staff members. For effective operation, it needs to be so conceived that it will bring out the best in fairly ordinary persons.

"Professionalism" is a protection against the worker's heart "going out" to the patient, against being carried away by his emotions. Busyness with routines is a defense against relating to patients (24). Workers in the mental health field are warned against getting personally involved. They are told that only a professional attitude is an effective safeguard against emotionalism which could be as detrimental to worker as to patient. It is true that persons working with psychiatric patients have been carried into a *folie à deux* with them, equally destructive to both; or to hold out promises of a commitment which later they are unable to live up to. Hopes aroused in the patient are then demolished with devastating impact on him. To tender the patient maximal help, the worker's commitment has to be at the same time both rational—that is, professional as based on the best knowledge and most consummate skill available—and emotional. But once the value of professionalism is firmly established, it tends to assert itself as the overweening concern. Of course, working with psychiatric patients is very taxing; so one's own professional group becomes a mutual protective society, which provides support to its members against the demands or criticism of all other professional groups—and against one's nagging conscience that one does not do enough for the patient. Thus, if social solidarity does not encompass the entire institution, the individual worker naturally wishes to rely on what professionalism offers in the way of support and security.

Once one has committed oneself to professionalism in general, it becomes self-perpetuating and self-reinforcing. While the professionalism of the members of one department encompasses an obligation to cooperate with all other professional groups for the benefit of the patient, it remains a cooperation rather than a coalescing of all services. Higher competence through the particular contribution one's own profession makes to the patient's improvement is sought—not higher personal integration through a commitment of one's total person to the patient's needs as a total human being.

While the psychiatric hospital wishes its staff to gain a higher degree of proficiency in their work and a deeper sense of professional identity, it feels it cannot expect more. The total therapeutic milieu, on the other hand, cherishes these goals but operates on the conviction that integration is indivisible. The degree of integration depends on how seriously those who work most intimately with the patient strive to integrate themselves. This should come from the worker's experiences of being part of the milieu, and of working with the patient. Only if these efforts are characteristic of all integral participants in the milieu will the patient's identification with his closest worker be eventually transcended to the next step of making the worker's goal of optimal integration his own. If the patient's final identification is not with the worker as a person but with the goal of optimal personal integration—which must be different for each individual—then he will be able genuinely to use what the worker and the milieu have to offer.

In the context of this discussion it may be instructive to look at the initiative and autonomy available to those working most directly with psychiatric patients in a small and rather expensive private psychiatric hospital, where the orientation is psychotherapeutic, and where the psychiatrist carrying final responsibility for its operation is a psychoanalyst. Caudill studied the issue of who exercised initiative in staff meetings, where most decisions were made (except for those made by the director himself). Besides the psychiatrists, only the heads of services participated in these all-important staff conferences—the supervisor of nurses; the two nurses, each of whom was in charge of one of the two wards; and the group workers in charge of general activities and occupational therapy. Those who did most of the direct work and probably all of the "dirty" work with the patients (floor nurses, attendants, aides) had no chance at all to participate directly, or to make themselves indirectly heard in these meetings; much less any opportunity to influence decisions. These workers with whom the patients spent most of their time, and who thus controlled most of the patients' lives, failed to influence any decisions and learned about them, if at all, at second hand. Not being part of the staff meetings, their opinions were not sought, nor was any information about the patients' activities elicited from them. In addition to this, they never received explanations of the underlying reasons for certain decisions. Caudill felt this reflected "the general consensus in the conferences about which role group 'knows most about the patient.' Even the head nurses who attended the meetings apparently felt they had 'little to contribute' or that 'it wouldn't be recognized anyway' if they reported on the behavior of patients on the ward" (24). There was not too much difference in this respect between the head nurses and the group workers.

Caudill's data show that the overwhelming majority of all interactions took place between the senior and junior psychiatric staffs. On the average two senior psychiatrists, five junior psychiatrists, three head nurses, and two group workers participated in these staff conferences. It seems natural that the senior psychiatrists were those who most frequently asked for information; 68 per cent of such requests originated with them. As for who answered and gave this information, it emerged that 43 per cent of the information and opinions came from the junior psychiatric staff. Almost the same amount came from the senior psychiatric staff, while the head nurses provided only 10 per cent and the group workers 13 per cent. The largest percentage of requests for suggestions came from the junior psychiatrists (57%), the smallest from the head nurses and group workers (each 15%), the rest originating with the senior staff. When it came to making suggestions about what to do, the senior psychiatrists provided most of the interactions (79%), the junior psychiatrists 14 per cent, the group workers and the head nurses only 4 per cent and 3 per cent, respectively. Considering the negligible contributions the nurses made in the decision-making process, one can imagine the way in which the supervising nurses transmitted these opinions and suggestions to the staff nurses, students, and aides, who had to deal with the patients all day long and during the night.

As long as the duties of a nurse or an aide consist of executing doctors' orders as in general hospitals, their nonparticipation in the decision-making process does not seriously interfere with their commitment to their work. But when they are expected to exercise initiative in treatment; when the nature of the patient's illness requires feeling for his importance as a person, not just as a body that needs attending to, then exclusion from a positive contribution to decision-making has devastating consequences for the workers' ability to commit themselves emotionally to the patient.

While psychiatric hospitals generally realize that patients' needs demand cohesion of the institution, even very good hospitals fail to recognize that, to function best in their own and the patients' interests, the staff needs the institution's cohesiveness every bit as much as the patients. I am convinced that the relative success of the Orthogenic School, even with extremely sick patients, is largely due to the conviction that what benefits the patients also benefits the staff, though obviously in different ways. The curative effect comes not from a staff member's professional training and affiliation, but from what he actually does with the patient.

Fant decries the idiocy of the notion that if a case worker does something with an individual patient, this is considered case work; if the psychiatrist does the same, it is psychotherapy; but if a nurse does it, it is nursing care. If a group worker devotes himself exactly the same way to a group of patients as does a psychiatrist, then in the first case it is group work, in the second, group psychotherapy; if the psychiatrist should also be a psychoanalyst, then it becomes group psychoanalysis; but if a nurse does it, it is still nursing care (36). As long as the definition of the patients' care comes from the worker's professional status and affiliation rather than from what he accomplishes, little wonder that coherence around the common enterprise of helping the patient is absent, replaced only by the false cohesiveness of each professional group.

Loyalty to one's group, assuring its coherence, thus requires of each member that he suppress some of his individuality for the sake of group cooperation. The main concern that dominates thinking in psychiatric hospital organization is: How can several different professional and quasi-professional groups of various training and background be made to function smoothly together? If organization were to be truly based on the healing task, it would become obvious that a hierarchy of various groups, each functioning primarily in line with its narrowly defined professional competence, is, to begin with, the wrong image to guide a psychiatric hospital's organization. It is particularly pernicious if the professional image of a group is not derived from what a psychiatric patient needs but from a very different occupational task. The nursing profession, for example, is committed to the care of the body of the physically ill person, not to that of the psyche of a physically well individual. If a psychiatric institution is to help its patients, each professional group must transcend what are commonly viewed as its professional tasks and roles. For example, the casual way in which a nurse feeds and washes the patient, or makes his bed, is only annoying or discomforting to the physically sick person. But such an impersonal approach makes the psychiatric patient sicker. It compounds his illness when he sees that attending to her routine duties, answering the phone or writing nurse's notes, take precedence in her scheme of values over attending to his psychological needs. Her feeling of disgust about something a patient does, and her impatience with his reaching out for her attention in his often clumsy, provocative or rejecting ways, has the worst possible effect on the patient. It may severely increase his feeling that nobody thinks him worth being well taken care of.

So the psychiatric hospital that wants to do a good job must ask something more of each professional group. The nurse or attendant has to add new psychotherapeutic tasks to the customary obligations of his professional group. This often entails giving up some of the old ways of doing things. A typical example is that doctors and nurses in many psychiatric hospitals no longer wear hospital gowns, but their own street clothes. This seems a good idea, yet by itself it can create more problems than it solves. The nurse can accept a patient's soiling or tearing what she wears much more readily when it is an easily washed white gown, in which she is little involved, rather than a pretty dress she likes very much. But what kind of message is it to the patient if those who attend to him wear only clothing they care little about?

I would guess that very few psychiatric institutions compensate all staff for whatever damage patients may do to their clothing. The result is that the staff are more protective of their own clothes than they are of the hospital's gowns. At the Orthogenic School, the policy of repaying staff for whatever damage a patient did was well established; yet in many cases it took special efforts to have staff members accept such compensation.

The psychological reason for this was again the organization of the School. The more a patient was a staff member's very personal project, the more the worker felt that it would somehow take away from the importance of what happened between the two of them if anybody else—even the institution to which he was so closely bound —were to pay for what the patient did to him. On the other hand, workers were always quite ready to accept compensation for damage done by some other than their very own patients. Though they didn't usually claim it, it seemed fair, since it did not interfere with a very personal involvement. As soon as a staff member's commitment to a patient became such that he no longer much cared for his clothes and what might happen to them—being mainly concerned with the incident's meaning to the patient and being fully ready to accept hardship within their relationship when necessary for the patient's well-being—damage to clothing hardly ever occurred, with the rare exception of chance mishaps.

To give up the uniform that signifies rank is quite important; calling everybody by his first name seems very democratic; but none of it means much as long as rank is maintained. The doctor is no less the one who gives orders, nor the nurse any more than a person who executes them, as long as her identification is with her professional group. So one aim of the organization is to get all of the groups—usually with the exception of the doctors—to give up some of their special prerogatives, to accept some additional tasks, so that they can work better together. Again as an objective idea this is unassailable, but a psychiatric institution ought to know more about human psychology. One's work does not become more attractive when it requires giving up some of one's prerogatives, and adding some different duties. The story is entirely different, however, and work becomes extraordinarily attractive, if it adds to one's personal dignity.

The nurse, for example, will not be able to feel herself—and hence be able to function—as a psychotherapist if when she does so she is not also accorded the prerogatives which normally accompany this status, such as making, or being in on making, psychotherapeutic decisions. What usually happens in psychiatric hospitals, unfortunately, is that at best she is taught only the language and other externals of psychotherapy, but not its essence, and the attendants are not even taught that. Since the nurse receives little or no help with what forms the essence of psychotherapy, she concentrates instead on trying to learn its theory, which is particularly gray when compared with the liveliness of good psychotherapeutic practice.

While it should not be this way, I have found that, at least in psychotherapeutic work, "understanding" is sterile if it is gained without regard to the problem of *why*, and particularly *how* it can be set into practice. Diagnosis without a treatment plan or course of action is mainly of academic interest. Unfortunately, most of staff teaching in psychiatric institutions is of this nature; though it calls itself clinical teaching, it is nonetheless entirely academic. It tries to promote understanding the patient's present problems on the basis of diagnosis, pathology, life history, and psychological theory; it teaches what tasks need to be done, as if knowing what is required makes doing it automatically possible. It's not that conscientious staff members don't try to do things that they are told may best benefit the patient. But if they do as they are instructed, their actions are derived from somebody else's (the psychiatrist's) understanding. Such actions do not flow from their highly individual way of comprehending psychological problems, nor from their equally unique way of relating to this patient.

It is a little like the psychiatrist, social worker, teacher, or whoever explaining to a parent that his child needs to be loved, and why, even telling him how to go about it—as if this would help. If the parent were able to love this child, he would have done so long ago, and known exactly how to do it. One of the more extravagant examples of this phenomenon is provided by what happened in the life of a patient of ours. Because of his severe disturbance, he was in treatment with a prominent psychiatrist who got nowhere with him (which eventually led to his living with us). The patient's mother was too disturbed to be of help, so the psychiatrist asked his father to spend time with his son, because there was nobody in his life who seemed to take any interest in him. The father asked how he could best do it. He was told that if he just would spend an hour a day with the boy, this would mean a great deal to him. The father, a most conscientious man in terms of the way he saw the world, asked what he should do with the boy during this time; the advice was just to play with him. He took the suggestion seriously, but since he was a very busy man, whose day was full of things he felt he had to do, the only way in which he saw he could implement the suggestion was to get up an hour earlier than usual, and have the boy do the same, so that both would play together for an hour before each one began the day. Understandably, by the third day both father and son thoroughly hated to lose an hour's sleep. The father was intelligent enough to give up by the end of the week, rather than have them spending an hour at each other's throat while ostensibly playing together for their mutual enjoyment.

Had the psychiatrist started by asking which of his various important obligations the father could forego to have some time with his son, and what he would like to do with him, the story would have unfolded entirely differently. He might have said that he could not spare the time during the week, and then the foolish enterprise could have never been undertaken. Given this father, probably he would have said that he would like best to take the boy along to the golf links. In and by itself, there would not have been much in it for the boy. But since playing golf was what the father enjoyed most, this pleasure might have given the boy the feeling that it was also his company which was giving such satisfaction to his father. If so, what turned into an experience which defeated both might have been one that did a little good.

Much of the teaching of nurses and attendants—that is, of those who, to use Noshpitz's (88) term, must "englobe" the patient, not like his psychotherapist for a few hours a week, but for many hours each day—is well meant and to the point, as was the advice given this father; but it is rendered without due regard to the feelings of the person to whom it is given. It hardly ever starts with the question of what the attendant or nurse would most enjoy doing with this particular patient and why. When therapeutic tasks are added to a nurse's duty, the question of which others of her jobs she might wish to be relieved of is hardly ever raised by her superiors, and she does not dare to ask such a question herself. She might at least expect that such relief would be volunteered by those in charge of making such arrangements. Since it is not, she stops making spontaneous suggestions which are based on her knowledge of the patient and of what she enjoys doing and is good at. Her contributions having elicited no more than praise, and not having led to any changes in her role or status, she cannot wax enthusiastic over what the psychiatrist suggests in the way of new tasks to be added to her regular ones. On the very rare occasions when I witnessed a nurse being relieved of some of her other obligations when a new therapeutic responsibility was added, it was never she who decided which were to be dropped. The decision was made by her superiors on the basis of what they thought she should drop. Since these were often activities she enjoyed, she soon learned better than to volunteer for additional work.

The most common procedure is that in response to an emergency or a question from a staff member, or on the basis of his observations during his psychotherapeutic session, the psychiatrist in charge explains from time to time what the patient needs, and why. This in turn implies a tacit obligation that anybody working with the patient, a nurse or an attendant, should do what is therapeutically required. Even if the reasons for this have been made quite clear, such rational understanding does not do away with emotional blocks. As a matter of fact, the negativism often increases when one feels one has to do something. The worker then goes about the task in a "determined" way, does it with his teeth clenched. And when, so to say, "his heart" is not in the doing but rather the not doing it, the patient derives no benefit from such effort.

If the worker should assert himself and reply that his regular duties, or his commitments to other patients, do not permit him to do what was suggested, he is already on the defensive; he feels that, given the needs of the patient, he should find some way to do it, nevertheless. It is around such issues of one's own guilt that loyalty to one's professional group proves its value. The other members of the group agree with the worker's opinion that the demand for such additional work is unjust. If a member of another professional group, for example, the psychiatrist, makes this suggestion, the group backs up the worker with an: "If he thinks it's needed, why doesn't one of them do it?" The implication is: "If they don't feel guilty for not doing what they say the patient needs, why should we?"

The cases I have known of a worker successfully doing things with a patient when the psychiatrist had recommended them resulted from the psychiatrist's having done an excellent job of teaching the worker to understand how and why it was important for the patient to have something done for him, not just in a particular way, but also by the particular person the worker is. Only the very best psychiatrists, or I should rather say, only those who are very secure within themselves, are able to say convincingly: "Only you, and nobody else, can do it in ways which are truly meaningful to the patient." The less secure person finds it difficult to admit that, though he has greater knowledge and prestige, in this particular situation he actually can do less than some other person. If, on the other hand, the staff relationships are characterized by social solidarity, of which the psychiatrist is an integral part, then giving the worker the appropriate recognition comes fairly easily. When this happens, a worker can usually make the psychiatrist's recommendation his own because he has personalized it in a most attractive way.

To keep from giving too favorably skewed a picture of the reality of even very good psychiatric institutions, it should be mentioned that in general the opportunity of the ward worker to be educated by the psychiatrist—that is, his participating in a staff or supervisory conference—is quite rare. In working with psychiatric patients therapeutically in a hospital setting (as opposed to maintaining hospital routines), the most demanding tasks fall on the attendants and nurses, who are in a position of inferior status to the psychiatrist. This is difficult to accept, and is bearable only if one is convinced that one is indeed inferior in knowledge and skill. In order to justify to himself not just the greater remuneration but the more convenient working arrangements and high prestige, the psychiatrist must not only believe in but demonstrate his superior abilities. He can easily do this by justifying himself through his superior knowledge of psychology and pathology, which is not simply come by. This is why he stresses it in his teaching, at the expense of those things nurses and attendants could do as well as he, if only they were helped in doing so. The complex hierarchy of psychiatric hospitals depends on the belief in the superior ability of the top hierarchy to know how to help patients, even where it does not directly apply; because that belief alone justifies the power structure, both to those on top and those below. But this prevents the staff from doing as well with the patients as the psychiatrist, even in those areas where they could. Thus an existing hierarchy defines what workers in various positions can do with and for the patients, rather than letting what they could do for the patients determine the hierarchy.

This should not be taken as suggesting that there is a Machiavellian plot, hatched by the administrators of psychiatric hospitals for their personal advantage. On the contrary, while nearly everybody is basically decent and well motivated, truly everybody is caught in the system. As long as the system is accepted, people will be hired as nurses, attendants, and aides who, in the vast majority, do not have the intellectual and personal requirements to learn direct psychotherapeutic work with psychiatric patients. It is not taught to them; or if taught, they fail to meet the requirements of the tasks. And this in turn justifies the system. This inertia of the system conditions what is possible in a psychiatric hospital, as much as do the buildings, furnishings, and regulations to which I have devoted so much space.

Power, unless carefully restrained, corrupts; the power of nurses and attendants over the psychiatric patient corrupts if they are permitted to exercise it. The same goes for the director, the psychiatrist, or whatever his title may be. Whoever is in charge of a psychiatric institution must make up his mind whether he sees his role as teacher of the staff, or one who gives orders. If the latter, the staff will expect to do as told, and both accept and resent it; and they in turn will control the lives of the patients, who will also both accept and resist. Thus the staff will find it impossible to become self-directing, and the patients will be unable to give up their negative resistance. Rather than being humble midwives (Freud's image of the psychoanalyst), staff members will be tempted to pretend they are the ones who can not only help bring the child into the world but decree what he is going to be like.

The many and various needs of the psychiatric patient necessitate the staff's performing a great number of tasks for him. If he is not to be further confused, these tasks require unity. So nearly all psychiatric institutions try to achieve unity by having all the staff members who perform one group of tasks do these as much as possible in the same way. Unfortunately, tasks done in such fashion do not create unity; the most likely consequence is uniformity; that is, different people performing similar tasks as if they were all the same person.

The rationale given for this is that one patient should not be singled out for preferential treatment; they all should be treated alike. Sometimes the impression received is that one of the main concerns of these psychiatric hospitals is jealousy, as if this were the most important emotion that needs to be taken account of. Jealousy is a powerful emotion and people do suffer very much from it, but the fear that one patient may receive more than another leads in practice to a situation where none of the patients gets very much. Jealousy is avoided at the expense of what the patient most needs to get well: the feeling that he is a person worthy of very special attention. The potential jealousy of some patients becomes a convenient excuse for the staff to do less than they could. Giving a lot to one patient not only arouses jealousy in the others but also arouses guilt in the staff about depriving other patients.

The patient sees through all this. He hates being treated as if he were a number; he resents it if a person does something for him the same way it is done for all others, as if *he* were not a different person from the other patients. He recognizes that such a staff member acts in line with what he considers his duties, rather than in accordance with the patient's personality. The patient dislikes it equally if several staff members all perform tasks in the same way, as if *they* were not different persons. He realizes that when they do so they are withholding themselves as persons. The patient is thus surrounded by images suggesting that having a unique personality is not what the institution cherishes; but he is told by these same staff members that he should have the courage to be his own man, develop his unique individuality. The more they say this, the more they appear as liars to him, since they deny in their own work what they preach.

Patients themselves sometimes contribute to the uniformity of treatment by objecting to the way one worker does something and telling him that another staff member does it differently. Just as the patient cannot see himself as an individual but views himself as a "thing," he wants to do the same with others. From my experience, the complaint: "You don't do it the way Jones does it," has a much deeper and more important purpose. The real, anxious query is: "Do you do it because it is an obligation which the institution forces you to meet, or are you doing it for me because you want to? Because if the latter is so, you couldn't possibly do it as Jones does it, since two different people cannot like a person exactly the same way." Thus we found that the answer: "I do it my way, because I am not only different from Jones, but I feel differently about you than he does," was so important that the patient had to test if it was true, by pestering for things to be done as Jones did them. Only when we resisted such pressure was he finally able to believe a task was done for him, and not because it was simply required. When he could finally trust that this was so, the outcome was an eventual: "I'm so glad you do it your way."

But if the institution is to help the patient get well, there must be some unity to all these different tasks that have to be performed for him. There are two radically different philosophies on how institutional unity can be created in a psychiatric hospital. According to one, this is accomplished by having the same tasks performed in as many similar ways as possible; the various tasks are entrusted to different professional groups, each of which executes them more or less uniformly with what they consider their "professional" knowledge and manner. In addition, the various groups and individuals are each asked to go a bit beyond their usual professional duties to accommodate themselves to the needs of the patients, and to work together to meet them, rather than at cross-purposes.

Clarity for the patient is expected to come from the fact that he will know what to expect from each professional group; unity, from the accommodation of these groups to each other and to the requirements of the institution, based on communication among them. Unfortunately, this communication, while a two-way process, is quite different in its nature depending on the direction in which it flows. Ideally, the lower echelons (aides, nurses) report on their work with the patients to those higher up; but in actuality, they do little of this. Those higher up, such as psychiatrists, do not report to the lower echelons on their work, or only in a most limited and general way. Their communications are ostensibly "recommendations," but in effect politely camouflaged orders to be executed. In upward-flowing communication, criticism is hardly ventured; in the downward flow, it is often the order of the day. Praise, also, in the better institutions frequently comes down from above; but it would be considered presumptuous coming up from below.

The status structure of the psychiatric hospital impedes communication and a true working together, despite all efforts to loosen professional rigidities, and to have all workers act therapeutically toward the patient. Status structure is most effectively maintained, not by enforced rules and regimentations, but by everybody "knowing" his place and keeping to it. Efforts to improve externals are useless as long as criticism, orders, and praise flow only one way, and everybody keeps to his place in the order of things. The patient knows that those in charge of him are of the lowest orders; and that, at the most, for only fifty minutes, a few times a week, is he worthy of the attention of the higher orders. His body care, so important for forming his view of himself, is entrusted entirely to the lower orders.

The other way to achieve unity is to do away with all status structure; to outlaw it from everything pertaining to the patient's psychotherapy, by entrusting all possible tasks to a very few and always the same persons. Each person goes about his work in his very own way, though always with an awareness of what the others are doing. To surround the patient with an atmosphere of unity, thus giving to his life as much unity as can be given, requires that those few who work with him serve him in all tasks. True professionalism in a psychiatric hospital comes not from the nature of the particular task and one's training for it, but from a staff member's own convictions about what best benefits the patient.

As far as the patient is concerned, unity comes from the person who takes care of him, through the unity of his personality, and the unique relation that exists between him and the patient. If such a staff member—as is the case at the Orthogenic School—devotes himself to several patients, then there is the variety within a unity which Kant considered the prime requirement for a true work of art. The variety comes from the differences in the relations. The same person relates somewhat differently to different persons but the unity which binds the variations together resides in the personality of the staff member. Using a musical analogy, milieu therapy could be likened to variations on a theme: the theme is the institution's philosophy and the social solidarity of the staff, as set into practice by individual persons; the variations are the differences in the relations of this person to a very few patients, depending on their personalities and current needs.

Though implemented in terms of their personalities and their relations to the patients, the unity that holds together what various workers do for and around the patient comes foremost from the milieu's philosophy, which is common to all the workers. It is based on these workers' common understanding of the patient and his needs and their working together to reach this understanding; an effort that binds them and their tasks much more closely together than does the understanding itself. At the Orthogenic School, the first time they struggle to achieve this for a particular patient is often when they select his welcoming gift. They truly begin to work together as each worker tries to make his co-workers understand why he thinks one gift more suitable than another. Compared with what goes on in them as they develop their social solidarity around this patient, the reaching of the final agreement on the gift is quite limited in impact; its selection is only the culmination of what has been achieved beforehand.

Obviously, if too many staff members flit in and out of a patient's life, even the unity derived from the fact that their actions are mostly of one piece would not be sufficient to prevent inner confusion. At the School, to counteract such dangers, we arrived, through trial and error, at the conclusion that while one person—the patient's main counselor—would have major responsibility for everything pertaining to a given patient's life, he would be helped by a second worker who, though less important to the patient, would nevertheless also be central to his life. These two were further complemented (given the age group we served) by one teacher. To these three, one of them considerably more important than the other two, was entrusted the entire well-being of the patient—distantly supported by the director and helped by a few others—in the hope that eventually he himself would entrust it to them. Only after the concentration of just three people helped him to bring some unity into his inner chaos were other staff members added to this group, such as a person who saw him in individual therapy. But as long as the patient was truly schizophrenic, individual sessions were also conducted by his main counselor, to bring as much unity to his life as possible.

Such working arrangements are so demanding, both of time and emotional resources, that the staff must rely on the reassurance and security which can be gained from social solidarity. Without such support, they will not be able to remain committed to the patient; to persevere steadfastly in their efforts to relate to him despite his rejection and even abuse of them. His obstinate refusal to relate to them can be overcome only by a commensurably greater determination on their part not to permit anything to interfere with their relating to him. This is one major difference between other human relationships and that of a therapist to a patient. Ordinarily, personal relationships are engaged in by the partners more or less simultaneously, though there will always be differences in intensity between them. In the therapeutic relation, the worker for a long time must genuinely relate to the patient without any expectation of reciprocity. If, as is usually the case, the patient refuses to relate, the worker has to continue to invest himself in the patient, keeping his interest in him going and growing. When eventually the patient makes tentative efforts at relating, even when he actually does relate, there will always be great inequalities between what the worker brings to the relationship and what the patient can contribute. The patient's contribution will remain minimal until he can reciprocate to a considerable degree. Once he can do this, he has gained a main attribute of mental health and, becoming able to form true relationships, he no longer needs a therapeutic one.

In matters of deep psychological importance the beginning contains in nuclear form what will later unfold. The relationship of the main counselor to his patient is to a considerable degree predicated by what happens on the first meeting. At the Orthogenic School, the worker who according to preplanning would work most closely with the patient was the first to meet him after the director. He had to make a go of it right away. (There were instances when the worker, after having met the patient, felt he did not want to work so intimately with him. The situation would then be immediately reviewed with the entire staff. On such an occasion usually another staff member would express a desire to take over the first one's place, in the pre-enrollment visits and ever after.)

Since the worker had planned to become this patient's mainstay for the time he remained with us, the newcomer was terribly important to him. He therefore invested himself deeply in the patient, as abusive, indifferent, or rejecting as he might be. Not only that, but the worker also knew he would be expected to give the first report on how he felt about the patient, what he observed, what he thought it all meant. He would have to explain why he thought the way he approached the patient was best, whether he tried to induce him to respond or respected his wish to remain in emotional isolation. He had to either hold his own when others stated their reactions and observations, or build their views into what he felt and thought about the patient. As this process continued, it gained in depth and intensity. When he was with the patient, and between times when he thought about the patient and about himself in relation to him, the worker would invest more and more emotional energy in him. As he did so, he related ever more deeply to the patient, as a person and as a therapist. He had to relate as a person because he knew he would be dealing with the patient not just in a narrowly prescribed treatment situation but in all the interactions of life; and not just those of normal living but also the demanding ones which milieu therapy requires.

If unity for the patient is to come from all important tasks being performed for him by only three persons, everything depends on their commitment to the therapeutic relation with the patient. For this relationship to be spontaneous—that is, the worker's own creative achievement—he must feel that nobody else has influenced him in establishing it. This does not preclude later feeding into it whatever he may learn from others to enrich it and make it more effective therapeutically for the patient, as well as more meaningful for himself. As soon as a true relationship between one of our workers and his patient had been established, the worker wanted to get whatever help he could to make it succeed, eager for every suggestion, although they were by no means always accepted or followed.

The most erudite discourse on a patient, his problems, and his therapy, or on psychoanalytic insights, while they might occasionally dazzle a worker, did little for him or his relation to the patient. Such expositions grated on the nerves of the best staff members. What they needed for their work was not brilliant insights in general, but something that was not too complex to use in the worker-patient relationship.

When famous specialists were invited to speak to the staff on issues of importance to them, they hardly ever addressed themselves to what the staff needed. Though some of them as psychoanalysts knew very well that with their patients they could not go too far or too fast, when invited to teach the staff, even when told by them what they needed or wanted to know, not being imbued with the social solidarity of the milieu, they uniformly went much too fast and too deep. In so doing they lost the worker. Concerned not with theory but with his work with his patients, the worker would become too preoccupied with thinking how he could apply some detail to follow the learned discourse. There were always a few staff members fascinated by theory; they enjoyed such presentations a great deal, even learned something of importance from them. But from such formal clinical presentations, little was gained that could be used directly by the worker; stimulating as the presentation might be, the effect on day-to-day work was small. Going over the same small amount of material again and again in the minutest detail, on the other hand, as one must with the patient in psychoanalysis, is hardly dazzling but is immensely therapeutic.

This, incidentally, is a central difficulty with reading psychoanalytic publications in order to try to understand what psychoanalytic treatment is all about. It would make it unreadable to reproduce what the work actually consists of: mulling over the same things endlessly in varying contexts, with long silences needed to catch the meaning and manage the emotions aroused, until the pieces of the puzzle finally fall into place. Instead, the publications show how things look after they have fallen into place, which is fascinating but totally misleading. It was easier in my time, when the person in training was not permitted to read any psychoanalytic writings before his own psychoanalytic treatment was completed. By then he knew from his own hard struggles and first-hand experience how such knowledge was acquired, and how different it was from the way it seems when written.

To carry the main responsibility for a mental patient is an awesome task. While it is possible to live up to its demands because of the depth of one's own investment both in the therapeutic task and in the person of the patient, it presents special difficulties. The patient's behavior at times makes it nearly impossible to relate to him fully and genuinely as a person, in which case the main emotional investment of the staff member must immediately be shifted from the relationship to the therapeutic task. But once the patient will permit it at all, the emotional investment must immediately be shifted back to the human relation. Of course, this is all a matter of degree, timing, emphasis. As if this were not sufficiently difficult, there is also all the hard work involved in taking care of the patient's daily needs, complaints, attacks, and ever-present misery. These evoke old unresolved conflicts in the worker, and for them not to interfere with his work he must summon all his strength to master them. Staff members soon realize that if they are to risk themselves in relating to the patient this way, they need the security, the solidarity, and the cohesiveness of the institution; significantly enough, patients recognize this also.

17 | Common Sense Organized

Pouring one's innermost feelings, insight, and highly personalized knowledge into a task which also requires one's most critical intelligence—which milieu therapy demands—makes healing diseased minds more akin to an art than a science. But if it is true that "Science is nothing but organized common sense," as T. H. Huxley declared, then milieu therapy is indeed scientific, because common sense must be the guiding principle of its organizational structure.

Common sense suggests that not professional groups but only individuals can work together. If the well-being of a person is entrusted to many, he will not be well taken care of. If responsibility is divided, nobody will feel very responsible for what happens. If ultimate responsibility and authority rest with somebody else, one will feel little responsibility for what one is doing and have little authority in doing it. Further, unless one feels that his work is important to himself for personal reasons, he will not devote himself deeply to it. If one does as he is ordered by others, he can neither enjoy nor take personal pride in what he is doing. Most important of all: if one does not possess autonomy, he cannot help others to gain it. The organization of a therapeutic milieu must not just reflect such common sense, but be based on it. A therapeutic milieu must provide the right emotional climate for its patients so that they can regain mental health. It will succeed in doing this to the extent that it is able to create a human and social environment which promotes the social solidarity of staff.

An enterprise in which the mainstay is social solidarity is the continuous re-creation of all who at any one time are part of it. Without the staff's participation in the common undertaking at the Orthogenic School, this presentation of our work would not have been possible, since much of it is based on my memories (helped by records) of our working together for a common goal. Various former staff members allowed me to draw on the recollections they had put down at some time, thus enabling me to check my impressions in the light of theirs.

Among the published material, I feel the most important is that of Wright (131, 132), who had been an intimate part of all that went on at the Orthogenic School for seven years, and of Henry (65, 66), who had been its appointed outside observer for two. Henry's background was that of social anthropology. The work for which he first became well known was his pioneering study of the play of children in preliterate societies (67); therefore, his interest in child behavior and what influences it was of long standing.

Henry, coming from the outside to do his study, did not wish to be drawn into the life of the School. He thereby hoped to remain objective, so that his observations and conclusions would not be skewed by a personal bias. But the power or seductiveness of a total therapeutic milieu is such that even a person who carefully tries to avoid being pulled into it, and who is schooled in being an objective observer, cannot entirely avoid getting personally involved to some degree. Still, given Henry's particular background, training, and experience, plus the task he had set for himself, he managed most of the time to avoid becoming a participant.

Before Henry came to the Orthogenic School to study its social organization, he had completed research into the structure of a psychiatric hospital (64); thus he seemed in a particularly good position to evaluate a total therapeutic milieu. Henry's study of a psychiatric hospital came to my attention before its publication. Its severely critical findings—many of which seemed well founded, and which bore out my feelings about what is wrong with even very good psychiatric hospitals—suggested that Henry might be the person best suited to do an equally penetrating evaluation of our enterprise.

At the completion of his study, Henry described the structure of the Orthogenic School as a system of "simple undifferentiated" (SU) subordination, as opposed to "multiple differentiated" (MD) subordination, which he found characteristic of psychiatric hospitals. His schematic statement on these two systems (65) is reproduced on pages 246-7. The Orthogenic School being the model of what he calls the "simple undifferentiated" system, I wish to take exception first to the name he gave it, and second to some of the ways he visualized it. Nevertheless, what he says about it is mostly correct. But this system was not something we first figured out and then set into practice. On the contrary: certain therapeutic and human needs of the patients (seen and understood from the frame of reference of psychoanalysis) seemed to require specific attitudes and procedures which interacted with certain tendencies originating in the staff. Given what we wished to achieve for the patients, we had to organize ourselves in certain ways. These ways were forced on us by both our human and our therapeutic convictions.

I question the name Henry gave our system, probably in trying to contrast the structure of the School with that underlying the work of psychiatric hospitals. Having concentrated on subordination as a main explanatory concept of hospital structure, it seemed reasonable to concentrate also on the nature of subordination in the total therapeutic milieu. Doing this is a good basis for comparisons, but it is already misleading as a description of what is important in the School's organization. Subordination contradicts both autonomy and social solidarity. It is of greatest importance that in the therapeutic milieu, power should not flow in only one direction. The emphasis should not be on power hierarchy or relations but on a dynamic interplay of personal relations and emotional forces, according to the dynamic premises of psychoanalysis.

It must be obvious that I believe the structure of a total therapeutic milieu should be described as one of social solidarity. Such solidarity does not exclude the possibility of one person subordinating himself in some respects to another provided it is done entirely voluntarily; and done only in regard to specific issues to better serve the common enterprise. Whenever desirable this order must be instantaneously replaced by an entirely different order, and the person who in one situation had subordinated himself to another is accorded superiority because it better fits the particulars. For example, which person makes a decision depends not on rank, but on who has the greatest familiarity with or insights into the particular situation. Most important of all in a therapeutic milieu, superordination must depend on the depth and therapeutic validity of a worker's involvement with a patient.

Social solidarity neither requires nor implies that there are no divergencies of opinion, or that there will be no arguments about them. On the contrary, since the solidarity is based on commitment to what the institution stands for, it stipulates defense against those who seem—rightly or wrongly—to act out of line with its ethos. If the battles concern a more therapeutic operation of the institution, they don't threaten solidarity but strengthen it. The open venting of disagreement holds the staff together; avoiding it would slowly erode the staff's trust in the institution.

In describing the School's organization as one of simple undifferentiated subordination, Henry stressed how important the auton-

The Physical Plant

IN THE SU SYSTEM	IN THE MD SYSTEM
Living is packaged around the dormitory.	Living is split up and distributed over the hospital floors.

Task Performance

IN THE SU SYSTEM	IN THE MD SYSTEM
Almost complete responsibility for task execution is in the hands of the workers.	Task responsibility is distributed among several departments and persons.
Most of the workers' time is given over to caring for the patients; no sharp distinction is made between on-the-job time and off-the-job time.	Personnel work on a standard eight-hour day; a sharp distinction is made between on-the-job time and off-the-job time.
One person is with the patient through all phases of the illness.	Different persons pace the patient through different phases of the illness.
The worker has complete autonomy in the execution of the task.	The worker does not have autonomy in the execution of the task.

Worker Personality

IN THE SU SYSTEM	IN THE MD SYSTEM
The large energy output drawn from inner needs is accepted and utilized.	Inner needs are masked under routine and frozen professional competence.
The worker seeks solution of his own problems in work with patients.	The worker's seeking resolution of his own problems in work with patients is not desired.
The worker is possessive of the patient.	Possessiveness is considered an obstacle to work.
The worker is deeply involved in the patient.	Involvement of the worker in the patient is an obstacle to the functioning of the system.
The worker gratifies primary narcissistic needs in task performance.	Such seeking of gratification is not desirable.*

* From the items in this column, it is apparent that the worker in a psychiatric hospital with an MD system is a psychological abstraction that does not exist anywhere—except as an abstraction.

The Director

Over-all Director in the SU System	Department Head in the MD System
The director is limited by his staff because of its autonomy.	The staff is subordinate.
He permits autonomy to the staff.	He governs by "policy decision."
His responsibility, since it is for the total task, is heavy and oppressive.	His responsibility is only for his department task.
He is close to all operations.	He tends to be distant even from his own departmental operations because of the delegation of tasks to executive officers.
He is heavily dependent on autonomous workers, because of the difficulty in replacing their complex training.	His dependence varies: Heads of nursing tend to be less dependent on the nurses than heads of psychiatry are on psychiatrists, because the difficulty of replacement is less in the first case than in the second.
He cannot delegate responsibility for in-service training.	He generally delegates responsibility for in-service training, with a resulting increase in social distance between the worker and the department head.
There is a deep mutual involvement of director and workers.	There is little involvement of the department head in workers.
There is a diminution of *vertical* distance between director and workers and an ethos of equality.	There is a maximization of *vertical* distance and a conscious emphasis on "equality" as a stress-reducing technique. [True equality obtains, by and large, only within each given echelon.] There is an efflorescence of the "you-are-so-right, Master" syndrome.

The Patients

There is a diminution of separation between the patient system and the worker system.	The two systems are strictly separated.
The patient is internalized by the worker.	Internalization of the patient by the worker does not occur.
Status of the worker is dependent on his involvement in the patient.	Status of the worker is dependent on his relative detachment from the patient.

omy of each staff member is for its functioning. He illustrated this by noting "the vigor with which the controversies between [a relatively new worker] and the director were conducted," in which the worker "trades blow for blow with him." Henry continued, "Telling the director off does not occur in the usual psychiatric hospital, not to mention the outspoken resistance to some of the director's decisions." "This," he wrote, "is obviously a function of the autonomous position of the worker." "Expression of the importance of the idea of autonomy, which involves lessening the social distance between worker and director, and giving the worker maximum opportunity to function on her own initiative could be illustrated by many examples."

In fact, it is sometimes necessary to provoke disagreements with the worker when opportunities present themselves. Only through such disagreements will he come to feel sure of his autonomy. Oftentimes, while arguing some question, a new worker proved to himself that he had the courage to defy the director, and that he did not need to hold onto his defenses, though at the time he may not have been conscious that this was what was happening. He would have thought that he could gain security only by pleasing the director, and thus had seen himself only in a specific role. By having taken up cudgels against the director and finding he was accepted in spite of it, he demonstrated to himself that he did not depend on the director's good will for his safety. With beginners it often happened that they rejected the notion that they should take responsibility for a patient and be responsible for their own actions. What the beginner did not recognize, but what was nevertheless most effective, was that by fighting the institution's expectation that he had the strength, knowledge, ability to become autonomous in his work with the patients, he had asserted his autonomy where he felt it most threatened: in his relation to the head of the institution. The director's conviction that even as a beginner a staff member could be important to the patient, not as a worker who could be replaced by another, but as a person in his own right, increased his self-esteem. Such interchange, and others like it in which they fight for their convictions, are steps workers take in becoming more sure of themselves and the work, and thereby a more important part of the common effort.

The very observations Henry selected to characterize the institutional structure of the therapeutic milieu further illustrate that "social solidarity" is a more suitable descriptive term. In the therapeutic milieu, there is no place for submissiveness; on the contrary, it must not be permitted to become a factor so far as the organization's structure and operation are concerned. Henry writes: "The director is limited by his staff because of its autonomy," to which he adds: "He permits autonomy to the staff." This is true when looked at externally, because the director is responsible for the institution to the outside world and staff autonomy seems to be due to his volition; but it is quite misleading when applied to the School's internal structure and operation.

Autonomy which is "permitted" is no autonomy at all.

Far from the director's being limited by the staff's autonomy, this was the institution's and also the director's greatest source of strength. The table counterposing the two systems continues: "He is heavily dependent on autonomous workers, because of the difficulty in replacing their complex training." The first part of the sentence is correct, the second puts the emphasis on the wrong issue. Replacements are shunned unless forced by circumstances, because of the personal relations which have sprung up between staff members, and particularly those between the director and individual staff members. It is the "deep mutual involvement of director and workers"—as Henry puts it a few lines later—around the common task which is the main source of strength in the difficult battle for the patients' mental health. This makes every valuable staff member very nearly irreplaceable, and is increased by the personal involvement of the staff member with patients. It is not the training, valuable as it is, which makes staff members difficult to replace; it is the human relationships that have been formed.

There were those who at the beginning of their association with the School tried to relate mainly to the director, and to rely on this for their security. This would have made them dependent on the director, rather than autonomous. The mutual relation had to be the result of their working together for the patients. A staff member's relation to his patients had to be the basis for his status among the staff, and his security within the institution; not the other way around. It was the nature of his work with the patient, and what it achieved for the worker, which conferred autonomy within the organizational structure. Security as a person was the consequence, and this is what the staff member contributed to the institution.

Without this kind of status conferral, the worker would have had to depend on the senior staff's good will. This would not only have made it most difficult for him to gain autonomy, but would have prevented a relationship based on mutuality, which among adults requires relative equality of the partners. Most of all, if the worker were dependent on his seniors in his work, he could not have "complete autonomy in the execution of the tasks." He could neither give his best to the work nor offer himself as an example of the value of autonomy to the patient. Since the worker's relation to the patient is his very own creation—although all he learns and experiences at the School flows into it—it can confer true status and security to him within the institution. Because the "status of the worker is dependent on his involvement with the patient," whatever hierarchy may exist on paper does not interfere with it.

While there were variations in rank as far as the university was concerned, and differences in salaries, status within the institution was independent of the values of the surrounding world, which were viewed by the staff as empty because based on superficial considerations such as degrees or publications. Within the institution, status depended not on success with a patient, because in some instances this could come relatively easily, but on the nature and depth of the involvement, particularly with the most difficult patients.

The autonomy of each staff member was essential for the institution's success, and the battle had to be waged with almost every new worker against his *not* establishing his autonomy. Autonomy, while one of the highest values and achievements of individual man, also imposes the heaviest burdens, if its responsibilities are taken seriously. *Escape from Freedom* (46) is not just a societal but also very much a personal problem. It is so much simpler to leave decision-making with all its responsibilities and consequences to someone else, even though one is ready to resent any loss of autonomy.

It must be apparent to the worker that there is a very good reason to exercise autonomy; the more so, the greater the risks entailed. As part of my Austrian heritage, I used to tell the staff about the highest award of the ancient Austrian monarchy, the *Maria Theresa Ritter Orden*, which was conferred for only one achievement: a soldier's going in wartime against the explicit order of his superiors because of his conviction that doing so would save the day and risking, if he should have been in error, all the consequences of insubordination. If the soldier turned out to have been right, whatever his rank or background, he would receive this order, which carried with it elevation into the hereditary nobility. The medal entitled its wearer to outrank the highest officers. The purpose of this story is to impress on the workers how important it is not to permit oneself to be limited by the recommendation of those "in authority," if one feels sure he knows better what is required at the moment.

Normally, a person engaged in a task which he considers significant will find it impossible not to exercise autonomy. If the task is not of great personal import, it is easy to follow instructions or do things by routine. Only insofar as the worker exercises autonomy in his work can the patient feel that what the worker does with and for him is important to the worker. But how can the worker feel that what he does is important, if he does it on somebody else's orders? This does not mean that in the worker's behavior and actions, he should disregard the opinions of others who are likely to know more than he. On the contrary, the more serious one's purpose, the more one will seek such help—not to follow it slavishly, but to use it as only one element among many to be considered. There will also be those who are so insecure about their autonomy and feel so threatened by another person's suggestion that they must insist bullheadedly on their own way of doing things no matter what. A person so insecure that he will take advantage of patients even against their best interests to demonstrate his independence has no business working with psychiatric patients.

Beginners had to be warned repeatedly not to permit themselves to be turned into puppets. They were reminded many times of the ancient Roman maxim: "When two do the same thing, it is not the same thing after all" (118).

This same principle had to be taught in many different ways, depending on what manner of explanation would become permanently fixed in a worker's mind. Sometimes it was necessary to convince the worker that if he simply did what somebody else had advised—as opposed to considering the validity of suggestions and forming his own opinions—and it turned out badly, his relation to the patient was damaged even more by the fact that he had only done as he was told. If he made this excuse to the patient, it would demonstrate that their relation was not genuine, did not come from the worker's own feelings and convictions. Thus the loss to the relationship would be double: through the mistake, and then through the announcement that the relation was of so little importance that somebody else controlled what went on in it. This would also imply that the worker cared little about the patient or about himself, since he let others make his decisions for him.

If things go wrong in such a situation, the worker's self-esteem could not be helped by trying to tell himself that on his own he would not have made such an error. Then he would have to ask himself why he was so stupid as to take another person's bad advice, not recognizing that it was wrong! To keep the patient's respect, the worker would have to maintain that he had acted from his own decision; otherwise, the patient could never know whether what the worker did came from his own volition, or because he was following what somebody else had told him. Such lying to the patient always has bad consequences.

On the other hand, if things went well, the worker could not take much pride in what had been achieved—because the credit would then rightly go to the person who had made the wise decision. Thus by following advice given, whether it turned out good or bad, the worker could not gain, and the patient could not gain much.

If the worker made his own decision, after seeking whatever additional advice and information seemed pertinent and available, and all turned out well, his relation to the patient benefited and the worker's self-esteem was enhanced. This is something everybody needs, particularly those who work with psychiatric patients. But when the worker's decision turned out to be in error, then he would be forced to investigate what went wrong, and where and why, and learn a great deal from it, much more than if it had been somebody else's wrong advice.

Explanations such as these finally induce the worker to accept "complete responsibility for task execution" and to assume "complete autonomy" in his work with the patient, autonomy which is naturally limited by the necessity to work together with others, within the framework of the institution.

Henry correctly stresses the importance of the worker being "deeply involved with the patient" and that he "is possessive of the patient." Before the worker can believe that this is not only accepted, but viewed as desirable, he has to test it; and he has to be encouraged to do so. An important feature of the total therapeutic milieu's ethos is that the worker should, whenever appropriate, "fight" for his patient, even against other staff members, whatever their official "rank" may be. A worker cannot feel that a patient is really "his patient" until he has proved it to himself by taking on the whole world in the patient's interest.

This is so true that experience taught me to feel sure about a worker's involvement with a patient only after the worker had on occasion taken a strong stand against me, for what he believed was good either for the patient or for his own relation with him. Sometimes this interfered with the interest of another patient or even with the operation of the institution; therefore, the worker could not always get what he wanted for "his" patient. But what was important was that his fighting for the patient was highly approved of, even if it did not win the day. When, as sometimes happened, one staff member would complain to me that another staff member interfered with what was best for his patient, my answer was always: "If you are not going to fight for your patient, he will never become yours." This meant we had to accept as par for the course that workers sometimes fought over a patient. Since the senior staff respected the workers for fighting for their patients, having the door to my office slammed shut in my face more than once by an angry worker seemed a very small price to pay for his having thus asserted his autonomy, according to what his work for the patient required. But this kind of battle was appropriate and acceptable only if the personal emotions unleashed had concern for the well-being of a patient or for the institution as their conscious source.

It occasionally required not just careful planning, but even some rearrangement of the institution, to enable a worker to activate himself both in becoming autonomous and in making a patient become "his patient." Situations had to be designed to induce the worker to feel strongly enough to draw on the vast pool of his inner energies, and to exercise his autonomy for his own and the patient's benefit— which is considerably more than what is implied in Henry's saying the director "permits autonomy to the staff." Such a situation is described in the recollection of a staff member, looking back many years later on what to her was the crucial event.

She introduced her memories of this event by quoting Kierkegaard: "There are many people who reach their conclusions about life like schoolboys; they cheat their master by copying the answer out of a book without having worked the sum out for themselves" (75). This, she continues, is a good description of most, maybe of

> *all who came to work at the School, certainly of me. The ones who stayed and worked out were the ones who were dissatisfied with this cheating and being cheated. What made me a good staff member and therapist was that the director refused to be cheated, nor allowed me to cheat myself. This is what made life at the School so interesting and exhilarating and creative and painful.*

She then described the turning point in her career as a staff member which forced her to become autonomous in her work.

She had been "floating along on relatively smooth waters." When the director became aware of this, he proposed that a severely disturbed and disturbing new patient be introduced into the group for which she shared responsibility; and that she should take major responsibility for this patient, whose life was actually in serious danger. It was suggested that at this moment in the institution's life some staff, including this particular person, needed an opportunity to prove what they could do under the most trying and serious circumstances. With much trepidation she accepted the challenge. With the acceptance of the major responsibility for this difficult patient, she writes: "I was shaken out of my semistuporous state and it became a matter of sink or swim—life or death." Actually she had been anything but semi-stuporous; it seemed that only in retrospect. But the challenge to try to understand what this patient was all about was in its own way so exciting and challenging that from it she was able to develop her own emotional and intellectual abilities and grow as a staff member and as a human being.

Social solidarity is hardly a new idea, nor does it apply only to the hospital treatment of psychiatric patients. It is difficult to imagine any undertaking in which people somehow work together where it would not apply (99). When the goal of the common enterprise is to restore psychiatric patients to mental health, social solidarity is not just desirable and helpful, but a necessity—it practically guarantees the maximal success possible, assuming that the workers possess the requisite skills and knowledge.

But in psychiatric hospitals the goals of unity and social solidarity are extremely difficult to realize. Cooperation, even social solidarity, is much easier to achieve and maintain if a person's deepest emotions are not continuously aroused by the work itself. Many studies published by sociologists, social anthropologists, psychologists, and psychiatrists, which point out the incorrect ways psychiatric hospitals are organized and operate, fail to sufficiently consider the difficulties inherent in human nature. The patients' behavior, by arousing our most chaotic emotions, makes integration both of oneself and of activities around the common enterprise extremely difficult. And yet this integration is absolutely necessary for the success of the work. That is why working with psychiatric patients is so emotionally demanding and can be so disruptive to staff integration, on both an individual and a group level.

No social organism more requires solidarity among its members than the family, either nuclear or extended. This is especially difficult to achieve in modern times, more so when there is a commitment to the individuality of each of its members. As long as the roles and activities of each family member were bound by tradition—that is, as long as individuation of each member was not considered possible, desirable, or important—social solidarity of the family, while imposing considerable restrictions on the freedom of each individual, was fairly well maintained. This organization was viewed as absolutely necessary, and accepted as the right order of things. But as soon as it was assumed that each person should be permitted to develop his own personality in whatever way he wished—to become primarily a person rather than a member of a tribe, family, or caste—tensions among the members of the family increased, and in extreme cases it became unmanageable.

This doesn't happen because the members don't want to live well together; nor because they no longer love each other. On the contrary, the intensity of the emotions generated by such close living together of persons, each striving for his own autonomy, makes social solidarity within the family so deeply desired and so difficult to achieve that despondent feelings arise when it fails to materialize. Tolstoy said that all happy families resemble one another, while every unhappy family is unhappy in its own fashion. Each unhappy family is different from all others in the very personal sufferings of each of its members. As long as social solidarity prevails within a family, there is hardly anything to say about it except that its members are all happy to live together; because in encountering problems and difficulties, far from blaming them on each other or on themselves, the family members meet them as a unified group. The desperate agonies of those who suffer from not having experienced such social solidarity within their families is what the practice of psychiatry is mainly about.

The greatest psychological difficulties have their origins in the family: possessiveness and jealousy. Whether it is the Oedipal conflict, which inflames the child's jealousy of one of his parents out of his love for the other, or sibling rivalry, the source lies in possessiveness. This is the paradox: while social solidarity alone makes individuation safe, personal uniqueness, which tends to define itself in contrast to others, threatens solidarity. There is only one antidote or cure for this: security. We feel secure to the degree we feel important to those who are significant in our lives.

The more autonomous each staff member is, and the more he wishes to succeed with the patients, the more envy is generated among the staff. To the degree that members help each other in their work, they derive a measure of security. Ideally, it should be proportionate to the jealousy so as to neutralize it. Therefore, to maintain the cohesiveness of a therapeutic milieu, and to safeguard its social solidarity against staff and patient jealousies, one of the main tasks of its inner organization is to provide the requisite security to all of its members. This is easier said than done, but it is a problem which the total therapeutic milieu must face and solve.

Having one person carry major responsibility for the therapeutic work with a patient unifies the patient's world and promotes his integration. Having only a very few other persons take care of all his needs prevents his life from being split into too many (not to mention contradictory) pieces. But this is effective only if all those who work with him are imbued with the same therapeutic convictions and work closely together; not just as caretakers and therapists but also as human beings. On the other hand, if the differences in personality among those who care for him are obliterated by a uniformity in their work, the patient can never believe that the institution wishes to promote personality development.

But workers are different people and the close way in which they must work with the patient leads not only to differences of opinion but to jealousies. Most institutions maintain staff jealousies should not exist; it is not "professional" to be jealous of another worker. Maybe so, but a psychiatric institution that takes psychology seriously as far as the patient is concerned must do the same for the staff. In a therapeutic milieu, what the staff feel must be basic to what they do. Without the right feelings their doing would be an empty shell. But being deeply interested in their work and its success, something would be wrong if the staff members were not also jealous of each other.

There is a rarely mentioned aspect of the mythical story of King Solomon's judgment which ought to be always kept in mind by every staff member. In the story, the false mother was ready to hold onto the infant even if it meant tearing him apart, while the true mother let go of him so that he wouldn't be hurt. This story has also a hidden moral, overshadowed by the obvious one. The true mother relinquishes her child not just to protect him against being dismembered, but because if this were to happen she, too, would be fragmented. Her inner experience of being torn between the wish to keep her child and the desire that he be left inviolate gives her the immediate empathy to insist that under no circumstances, even at the risk of greatest loss to herself, must he be torn between the contending factions. The false mother also desires the child, and wants to take good care of him—not for his sake, but for hers. Because she is so taken up by her own need for the child, the false mother is not torn apart by any inner conflict; this is why she is lacking in empathy about how it feels to be pulled in opposite directions, and thus keeps pulling on the infant.

The story doesn't say that the two mothers should not each wish to have and keep the child. It is a warning that such jealousy, when not controlled by an overarching devotion to the child, will tear him apart. If there were not some possessiveness among those working most closely with the patient, how could the patient believe that these people really want him, that he is very important to them?

A psychiatric patient, moved by and responsive to his primitive emotions, is therefore more impressed than a normal person by what feelings convey, including jealous feelings. The patient knows that as soon as a worker becomes important to him, he is jealous of what others may in actuality or in his imagination receive from that worker. Since the patient's jealousy is often the first sign that he cares, he cannot believe that it is any different for those who work with him. Consequently, he not only wants those around him, who have importance in his life, to be jealous of each other, but he may believe they are much more jealous than they actually are.

Thus any system of organization, even the most cohesive one, has its inherent disruptive forces. If all important tasks performed for a patient are unified by being entrusted to only a very few persons, among whom there is no status and, as far as the work is concerned, no professional differentiation—then interprofessional jealousies are precluded but personal ones are not. The great merit of the therapeutic milieu, for patients and staff alike, is that all problems are put on an appropriate level: the personal one. Theoretical or professional disagreements cannot be used to cloak personal antagonisms, so they may be resolved. When personal animosity is hidden behind professional or theoretical disputes, no resolution of the professional controversy can cure the problem, which is fed by the continuance of personal enmity.

If things go wrong, the temptation is great to reproach somebody for it, and such faultfinding is very destructive to social solidarity. But if one's personal shortcomings or professional errors are accepted as part of our common humanity and treated with generosity, this goes a long way to neutralize jealousies. It is thus the director's task to prevent attribution of blame, and to demonstrate that such blame will not remedy the situation. Whatever the unfortunate situation, it is the patients who become shaken. To fix blame on one person, though the difficulty may have originated with him, would not restore the patients' security. Since all of us are responsible for the organization, we too in varying degrees have contributed to what went wrong and have to work together to correct it. Here again the image of the happy family is evoked to enlighten staff attitudes. A happy family is not one where everything goes right; it is one in which, if and when something does go wrong, the one who caused it is not blamed but is supported in his distress. If a staff member feels downcast and is not uplifted, how can he spend his days in uplifting the downcast patient?

It is hard to maintain feelings of jealousy when the person of whom one is jealous is also the person most likely to help extricate one from a mess. Here the arrangement of two counselors working with one group of about seven patients proved its merit. Naturally the counselors would become envious of each other, as they saw one of their patients showing preference for the other. But if something went wrong in the group for which they shared responsibility, they had to rely on each other to straighten things out. This meant that one had to pick up where the other had erred, or when a patient refused to cooperate with the other one. It is not so much the need to help each other with their patients, as the experience that the other has offered aid, which lessens the feelings of jealousy.

Each of the two counselors had some patients who were particularly important to him, and each had to rely on the other to help him succeed in the task. While jealousy might prompt otherwise, self-interest commands this, since one needs the other counselor to do things for one's very own patients. In the long run, such self-interest always won out over jealousies, but only because jealousy was accepted as something we all have to learn to manage rather than something to deny or suppress.

One staff member wrote:

My co-counselor and I had to steer a middle course between "dividing up our empire,"—the patients for whom we were responsible. This meant that one of us would be mainly interested in and devoted to some of the patients in our group, and the other counselor would concentrate on the others. Occasionally in some group where one counselor walked away with all patients, and the other stopped investing himself in any patient, the uninvested staff member soon left, because he found the work not rewarding; whereupon the other counselor did not receive the help he needed in trying situations, which occurred much too frequently to be able to succeed without the support of one's fellow counselor. The only successful way to handle the various difficulties which were apt to occur—jealousy of other staff members was only one of them—was that each counselor concentrated on using his particular strength. For example, my co-counselor was always better than I in handling the entire group, even several groups, and could provide important therapeutic experiences for several, if not all patients involved. I was better in dealing with patients individually, though through the help of my co-counselor I slowly learned over the years to develop greater skill in handling groups therapeutically. I guess from observing me, and discussing with me what I did, and why, she became more accomplished with individuals. Another difference between the two of us was that she was better with the very active, acting-out patients, and I with the very withdrawn ones. While as beginners we both had been jealous of each other, as we had to work together to help our patients and each other, we tried our hands at each other's skill, which contributed to our development as persons. And what had started out as a very ambivalent, if not outright jealous relationship, after the first year of working together developed into a most intimate and rewarding friendship, so that today, many years after we stopped working at the School, we still are closest friends.

If the feelings of jealousy are denied, it leads to finding fault with the person one is jealous of. But if jealousy is recognized for what it is, then it becomes quite possible to integrate it. One way to do so is through identification: if one admits jealousy to oneself, it is not such a difficult step from "I'm envious that he can do things better" to "I want to do things as well as he." If this wish is supported by the conviction of one's colleagues that this is quite feasible, it takes the sting out of envy. The institution's ethos that doing something the way another person does is an insult to one's individuality also served to reduce the acerbity of jealousy. If several persons perform in a similar manner, comparing themselves to each other is practically unavoidable, and jealousies are thus continuously fed. But knowing that two people do things differently because of the inherent difference in their personalities, it is much easier to look at what the other person achieves without being overwhelmed by feelings of envy.

For all those who remained for some time with the Orthogenic School, personal jealousies were neutralized mainly through identification with the School's values and methods of doing things. Thus social solidarity won out over personal antagonisms. Even when the identification with the institution was not yet a total one, as one staff member put it:

Whenever I was with others who were not committed to the work I was doing, I felt isolated. I felt they could not possibly understand my life, in most cases just didn't want to, as much as I tried to explain it to them; so I gave up trying. Possibly because of the intensity of my feelings about what I was doing, they baited me, so much so I had to bite my tongue; I knew that any defense would give me away and on top be ineffective. Yet I pitied them; I thought their lives were less meaningful—well, their way of life would have been less meaningful for me, though obviously not for them, or they would have done something else. There were times when I felt pretty desperate about ever meeting anybody outside the circle of present and past staff members I could be friends with, who could understand my involvement in what I was doing.

This continued until the process of identification with the institution had run its course; when its values no longer seemed extraordinary but most ordinary to her, and could become fully integrated into her personality. Then "I suddenly found friends outside the staff who seemed not only to understand but appreciate my work at the School, and all it meant to me." A short time thereafter she met her future husband and after their marriage, continued to work at the School for some years, no longer feeling an outsider among non-staff members, and finding her own circle of outside friends.

In order to work through some as yet unresolved problems of her life and fully find herself, this staff member had to direct herself single-mindedly toward the institution as an intermediary step to becoming fully self-directed.

Staff members whom I have known who did not work out at the School are those who, even behind closed doors, or in the dark of the night, could not admit to themselves that if something went wrong between them and a patient it was their fault. I well remember my making the necessary decision for the first time. A pubertal psychotic girl, on first menstruating, noticed some drops of blood on her underwear and said, "Oh, goody, I got my wish." To which I said, with what now seems to me like amusing innocence, "Don't worry about it, you're all right," whereupon she became terribly upset and attacked me. The director tried to help me understand what had happened, but I was bound and determined that her attacking me was her fault, after all, wasn't she psychotic? He asked me to stop worrying whose fault it was and, just for a minute, try to assume that it was not the patient's fault. Instead of figuring who was wrong, he asked me to consider what kind of feelings about menstruation the patient's remark suggested, and what kind of attitude was indicated by my reply. Did not my telling her not to worry communicate to her that I thought there might be something to worry about? What I had said to reassure her might have confused her, who was pleased to menstruate, by implying that what she enjoyed others might find worrisome. It was a lengthy conversation, but it remained not very convincing to me. The director seemed to feel this and ended it by saying about the patient, "Well, she's got the courage of her convictions." This was tremendously inspiring to me, I don't know any other way to put it. If the patient could have the courage of her convictions, so certainly could I. Also I found it very startling that a psychotic patient had made more progress than I in learning to live with herself in respect to accepting her femininity in all of its aspects. There she certainly had the courage of her convictions—something I was conspicuously lacking. Up to then it often had made me angry to continually soul-search myself for the patients' benefit. Here I realized what up to then I had given only lip service, that I, too, benefitted, and by no small amount. And practically immediately I also realized that I gained much more than the patients, because I could do much more with it than they.

The exchange could only have had this consequence because, given her own feelings, she couldn't and shouldn't have said anything other than what she did. Anything else would have come from her head and not from her feelings about femininity. It was much better to have responded with the way she felt and to examine it later, than to give a "correct" reply which would have meant nothing to the patient. It might have prevented the attack, though we could not even be sure of that, since the patient would probably have responded to the emptiness of the reply. But since it had been an honestly felt remark, the patient could respond with honest emotions. Out of this incident came an impasse that permitted a positive solution which would be beneficial to both.

The institution's senior staff could not abdicate the responsibility of teaching. And for the teaching to be effective, it had to benefit the staff not only intellectually but personally, otherwise it would have led to behavior that would be intellectually correct but an emotional sham.

The senior staff had to offer self-direction to each staff member; it had to open up a higher level of understanding of both himself and the patient, the two being inextricably interwoven. Helping patients solve their psychological difficulties activates the staff to master unsolved problems within themselves. The self-direction of the staff is not restricted to what they do with the patients; it also entails what they wish to do about themselves. As Blos (18) has pointed out, even after adolescence infantile conflicts are not necessarily removed from our lives, but by then should have become ego-syntonic—integrated within the ego as life tasks to be met. Every step toward ego-syntonic mastery of such residual conflicts enhances self-esteem, and permanent stabilization of self-esteem is one of the major achievements of adulthood.

Whatever one's role in society, it should help one to stabilize one's self-esteem. Lack of self-esteem comes from a discrepancy between the wishful ideas of what the self is, and the actuality (69). As Wright describes (131), the wishful self-concept of one worker was being a person ready and able to "help these poor souls," and it only led to actions which failed to be useful to the patients. This worker's self-esteem rose when he gave up acting out his wishful thinking of what a good person he was, but gave substance to it in reality. The person who wishes to remain alive to the world of feelings, and in possession of healthy self-esteem, will undertake "a life-long effort of the ego to re-establish this accordance between wishful thought and actual behavior and remove discrepancies by judicious interaction with the environment" (18).

Erikson described this same concept, in more general form, as being true for all life activities which enhance rather than destroy self-esteem. He uses the term "generativity" to characterize the paramount achievements of adulthood, a term denoting "a responsibility toward younger age mates" which has to grow into a "sense of responsibility for the next generation" (35). Psychiatric patients—given the many ways in which their personalities have disintegrated, as well as the ways they have regressed—function as regards their psychological needs as younger age mates of the staff, whatever the chronological age of patient or staff member may be. The School's goal is for the patient eventually to go out into the world and find his rightful place there. The staff's task is to help this process along, which makes their work similar to that of those who guide the younger generation toward maturity.

The main requirement for successful adulthood in Erikson's scheme is integrity, through which the mature person becomes a suitable "figure of identification." The staff must indeed act as such a figure, at least for their patients. Identification with the institution (which its organization facilitates by insisting on the staff's autonomy in the work, and by offering opportunity for higher personal integration) is an intermediary step toward the staff's being able to assume full responsibility for the next generation. This responsibility is met by their becoming suitable persons with whom to identify. Once this integrity has been gained, a staff member is fully trained.

Why is working in a therapeutic milieu such an eminently suitable way to resolve the residues of one's childhood, and to achieve autonomy and integrity? To suggest an answer, we must consider the staff: their personal characteristics and how they develop during this phase of their life.

IV | *Staff*

18 | Staff Selection—In Depth

Everyone who comes into the Orthogenic School enters through two doors. The first is sturdy and normally closed to the outside, so that nobody uninvited can enter, though like all other doors in the School it cannot be locked against leaving. A small hallway separates it from a second door, which, being usually open, invites one to come inside. This door is closed only when it is extremely cold or hot on the outside. It has no lock, is gaily colored in many hues, and decorated in bas-relief with many sculptures of infants, angels, and flowers (Plate 2).

When a prospective staff member comes for an interview, this inner door gives him his first impression of what the institution is like on the inside. Quite a few remark on the door's unexpected design, thus easing the first tense moments of the interview. In all these years, no potential patient has ever made a remark about the door when visiting the institution or during his early stay, but those being considered as possible staff members are much more securely anchored in reality than the patient is. Since the latter cannot trust overt statements, he looks for the hidden meaning and doesn't really know what to make of a door so different from others. If the patient were sufficiently in touch with his feelings, and had the courage of his convictions, he probably would tell us: "Your door lies." But to be able to say so means he trusts himself enough to know the truth about his own reactions, and that he trusts others enough to tell the truth as he sees it. Since he doesn't, he says nothing.

On the other hand, those wishing to join the staff do trust their impressions, and are confident enough in the institution (all their understandable anxieties about it notwithstanding) to mention something that has pleasantly startled them. If they don't remark on it, this suggests to some degree that, like the patients, they don't dare believe their interpretations are correct. So in a way, the door is a test: will the prospective staffer respond openly to something unexpected and pleasant, or is he too inhibited and lacking in spontaneity to do so? Is he unable to respond to nonspoken statements and uninterested in the physical setting where he will work? Of course, the door was not placed there as a test, or for any other reason. It just seemed to convey a specific feeling which we thought appropriate to those entering.

As we developed our method of staff selection, it became very similar to the ways in which we would get to know a prospective patient and decide whether we wished him to become part of our common enterprise. It is entirely possible that there just aren't that many different ways of arriving at whether one wants to work and live closely with another particular human being. Nevertheless, a group whose members believe that mental patients and the rest of us are not different in kind but only in the way we see the world and function in it, will especially feel that there is only one way to really get to know a person.

As a preliminary, the candidate has to know as much as possible about the work of the institution and its philosophy; and we about his background and outlook on life. He is requested to familiarize himself with the philosophy and the work of the School through reading the books that describe them. If on this basis he thinks this type of work and way of life is what he wishes to engage in during the next few years, and that the training he will receive and the experiences he will be subjected to will best serve his interests at the moment, and if, on the basis of the information he has sent us, we believe it likely that he could become a good therapist for our patients, we encourage him to visit us for a few days.

Whether we invite him depends on the impression we receive about the genuineness of his interest in this type of work; whether he is young and flexible enough to develop new views on himself and life, but mature and responsible enough to take on a most demanding task. His intelligence, and ability to learn and to meet demands, is usually indicated by his academic record in college and graduate school, which must be superior. But the most revealing set of data for our evaluation is provided in an autobiography we request him to write. He is to tell what experiences of the past made him the person he sees himself as, and what in particular made him interested in working with psychiatric patients. While his depth of psychological insight is important, we are more interested in his inner honesty in evaluating himself and his past, as well as in his ability to recognize and openly admit to himself (and us) the flaws in his personality, without tearing himself down.

Just as the patient on arrival is shown into the School's "living room," so is the prospective staff member—for much the same reason, so that he can absorb the "feel" this room conveys. He is given enough time to look around at his leisure and, if necessary, compose himself for the interview. But it is not so long an interval that it gives him the impression he is being deliberately kept waiting, or that we are not ready for him. So there he is, tense with anticipation about what this place may turn out to be like; worrying about whether he will like working here, how he will fit in and be received by the staff and patients. He wonders what it will all mean to him. Did he do the right thing in applying for a job at this institution? Might this job change the course of his life, and if so, how? Whether he is fully conscious of it or not, all these thoughts are going around in his head; and he tries to find answers as he looks or walks around this strangely furnished room, absorbing in some measure its unspoken but very definite message. This initial experience permits him later to empathize when a patient comes to the same room for the first time.

This is a most important experience for the prospective staff member. He finds that psychiatric patients don't experience the world all that differently. When subjected to the same predicament—anxiously waiting for something unknown that can have far-reaching consequences in their own lives—their feelings are similar in content though different in degree. Of course, the overt reactions of the potential staff member are bound more by the conventions of society than are the patient's reactions. The applicant may have learned all this in books; he may be able to quote it in his sleep: psychiatric patients and the rest of us have much in common; we are likely to have the same anxieties, and only handle them differently. But for most applicants, it was the first time they had really experienced this. I can't recall a single staff member who turned out to be good at his work who did not in some measure experience his own feelings in this room again when he met a new patient there. The applicant realizes sooner or later that, during his initial visit to the School, an effort was made to teach him what is most important for the success of his work. While we cannot and should not always find ourselves in the same predicament as the patient, it is only by thoroughly projecting ourselves imaginatively that we can truly empathize with what goes on in his mind and, on the basis of this, help him to deal with it.

When interviewing the potential staff member, it was most important to clarify why he wanted to spend the next few years of his life doing this type of work. This was crucial to those who would work directly with the patients, as well as those who would support the institution's work in some other capacity. During the years that I was responsible for the School's operation, I held detailed interviews with everybody who applied for work, whether as a counselor, secretary, janitor, cook, or maid.

An organization which is serious about helping psychiatric patients needs the services of very special people, even as cooks and janitors. It needs people who can understand, accept, and appreciate that this job may require a great deal of patience and extra work— work that in other situations might be considered superfluous, if not offensive. For example, it might be more constructive to let patients break quite a number of windows without interference than to prevent them from doing so; but this is possible only if the janitor, who has to clean up the breakage and replace the panes, is not only able to take it in good humor, but also to appreciate how this extra work may speed the patient's recovery. Only if he can adopt such a view-point—not merely because he is told it is necessary, but because he fully understands its merits—will he not resent the seemingly wanton destruction and unnecessary extra work for him. If he doesn't understand that a patient's rage against objects is preferable to violence against persons, and that accepting his rampage and later using it constructively is so much better than forcefully restraining him, he will not only resent the patient for having created the necessity for his labor but also the professional staff for letting it happen. If a janitor is to maintain an accepting attitude toward patients and staff who make so much additional work for him, he must be carefully selected for his ability to develop this attitude. He must be encouraged all along to understand how and why this helps a patient. Unless he feels that he shares in the institution's achievement of curing mentally sick people this will remain an intellectual acceptance with little impact on his emotional reactions. He must feel appreciated by the staff for his contribution, and view staff and patients as people who play a significant role in his life, whose appreciation of him and his efforts makes a difference to him, and to his work.

In a previous publication I had written briefly about the role of our janitors. When I mentioned that it is sometimes constructive to let a patient act destructively, many persons erroneously concluded that we advocate letting the patients do whatever they want. Some even believed that this was essentially curative in itself. Others believed that we were wrong and that it was deleterious. Most assumed that we believed being able to destroy things was good for the patients. They inferred this, for example, from what I said about a patient breaking many windows without our stopping him. I used this example to point out, as I do above, that an institution which truly wishes to help psychiatric patients requires very special services from its janitors. The reason for letting the patient act so destructively was that the rampage could be a turning point in his life, a behavior explosion that could be part of a therapeutic plan, accepted for what we considered to be excellent reasons. This was totally overlooked by almost all those who heard about it. It was assumed that if such behavior were to be allowed "as a matter of principle," the institution would be one which serves either silly or lofty principles, depending on one's views. On the contrary, such seeming permissiveness is the result of a carefully thought-out plan devised for a specific purpose. Our effort is to understand and meet the specific needs of particular human beings, each of whom requires something different at each moment in his life.

A janitor who would perfunctorily clean up and replace dozens of windows without understanding the importance of this would be a robot—exactly the opposite from the person we needed for doing janitorial work. Awareness of its importance gives dignity to the work the person performs; and when confronted with especially demanding tasks, this alone enables him to respond in the spirit of the institution. In symbolic form, the first interview established a bond between prospective staff members and the institution. The point was made that everyone, from the director to what might be called the lowliest worker, had to be cooperators in a common enterprise, which would not succeed unless each one were convinced of the importance of his contribution.

At the outset of their work, the only demand that could be made of them was to refrain from any overt negative response. There was nothing we could say in a few words or lectures to make them understand and accept the patient's behavior toward them; only they themselves, over a period of time, could develop the ability to do so. Yet mental patients are much too subtle in assessing the staff's inner attitudes to be fooled by a surface acceptance which was contrary to inner feelings. Thus we had to depend on each new staff member to internalize some teaching and guidance and to develop, on his own, a truly positive attitude toward what we were trying to do. Such an attitude had to be his own unique contribution. This is why personnel tended to remain at the School for many years. Staff turnover was a rare occurrence, and it permitted me to spend a sufficient amount of time with a new applicant to explore his attitudes adequately.

Sometimes this kind of staff interviewing had unexpected and most delightful consequences. Neither she nor I shall ever forget when one day a young lady, recently out of college, applied for a typing job. Her reason for wanting to work at the School was that she found working in a large business enterprise unappealing, though much better paying than what we could offer. From talking with her, I got the impression that she was an unusually sensitive person. I told her I thought she would be much more interested in working directly with the patients. It then turned out that in addition to being a music major, as her record indicated, she had also majored in psychology; and that one of her reasons for wanting to work in a psychiatric institution was to learn more about such patients. She had not been able to admit such an interest before, thinking it would be viewed as morbid curiosity, which she knew would be wrong as a motivation for working there. She took my advice and the job with both pleasure and trepidation, and working with very difficult patients she soon became one of our most successful therapists. Eventually, she continued her education toward a Ph.D. and made the treatment of severely disturbed patients her career, which she has pursued with great success.

There were, of course, interviews which went in the opposite direction. Some who applied for jobs as therapists had to be helped to accept some other assignment more suited to their present interests and abilities. One applicant thought that because she had once suffered a breakdown and recovered from it, she would make a good therapist for mental patients. I succeeded in convincing her that this would be too emotionally demanding and hence entail certain risks for her. She accepted working as a seamstress, and for several years we had the privilege of being greatly helped by a most imaginative, truly artistic seamstress, whose work gave her a great deal of satisfaction and was duly appreciated.

With all prospective employees we stressed the demands and emotional difficulties of the work, and told them how much they would have to learn. In the case of those who would be working most directly with the patients—therapists, teachers, and counselors—the depth of the interview and the follow-through were necessarily much more probing. I explained to each applicant that working at the School would probably change his outlook on life and himself. He would have to realize he did it not only for altruistic reasons, but for self-serving ones as well. It came as quite a shock to some that their motives were not accepted as they stated them, but were subjected to scrutiny. As readily as some gave lip service to the idea that working with psychiatric patients might change their ideas—even their personality—none really believed it. While one might feel that he needed or wanted to change himself, the idea that working with severely disturbed patients would do this was entirely unacceptable. Therefore we did not press the point; much like the patients, he would have to find out for himself what to accept and believe. Instead, we would discuss what the applicant was most concerned about in doing this type of work. Even more than with prospective patients, we strongly emphasized how far-reaching a decision it was both for him and us, if he were to join us in what then would be our common enterprise.

The specific problems discussed had to do with the particulars in the applicant's life history and personality. For example, in the past having observed the reaction of religious persons to exposure to psychoanalytic thinking, if an applicant's religion appeared to mean a great deal to him we would warn him that his beliefs could very well be shaken as had happened to others. It was then up to him to decide whether he felt they would be shaken or not.

The desire to work with mental patients has many conscious and unconscious roots—some of which are constructive in the work, and others which aren't. Without strong inner motivation, nobody succeeds in helping mental patients regain their sanity. For example, during the Vietnam War quite a few conscientious objectors wanted to spend their service years at our institution. Hardly any worked out. Their motivation was not helping the patients, but meeting an unwanted obligation that had been imposed on them. When asked what they would choose to do if they did not have their service obligation, many answered quite honestly that they would do something very different. Most of them, some very reluctantly, realized what it would mean to a mental patient if his very existence were entrusted to a person who preferred to be doing something else. When we reached this point, some countered that in other mental hospitals, people worked with patients out of reasons other than helping the patient to get well, such as for money. We agreed and advised them to work in such a place where their help would be welcome; in our institution we didn't expose patients to association with persons who would rather be doing something else if they had the choice.

Very few applicants openly revealed that their motivation was a need to dominate another person. More serious problems were presented by those who felt that, because they were so stable, they were particularly suitable and equipped to help mental patients. On the contrary, some of the most successful workers were those who, right from the beginning, vaguely understood that the work offered a unique opportunity to solve some of their own problems. They knew that they would be forced to work something through in themselves in order to be better able to serve the patients. The most important indicator for success was the deep desire to achieve personal autonomy, and the realization that this can be accomplished by solving specific personal difficulties. The staff member who was deeply committed to becoming more true to himself—to finding out what this might mean, and going about realizing it with determination through constructive work in reality—was the one most capable of developing in patients the ability to do likewise. He would not only have full empathy with the patient's need to achieve autonomy but, because of first-hand experience, he knew how difficult and important it was. Only that staff member who has the courage to look into himself has the moral right to expect a patient to do the same.

Today when there is so much loose talk about having to be a schizophrenic in order to understand one or to help him, it is even more important to make sure that the worker's intent is not to establish a *folie à deux* with the patient. The fact that some people believe this helps psychiatric patients is hardly astonishing since all persons who engage in *folies à deux* are convinced that their disease is its own—and their own—cure. Such people overlook the fact that in all our mental hospitals psychotics live with each other for years without improving their conditions.

For the staff member, self-realization has to be achieved through a deep commitment to the therapeutic task on a rational, realistic basis. He must work hard, not spare himself emotionally, and at all times be subject to the most careful intellectual scrutiny. Every inexperienced person—as well as those who have experience but have failed to extract the most important lesson from it—will become so frightened by the patient's pathology that he either denies it (as do those who maintain that insanity is higher sanity) or fights it (and with it, the patient). Or the worker will be so fascinated by the strangeness, and the primary process thinking and behavior, that he unwittingly encourages the patient's holding onto a pathological and hence destructive defense. This is a crucial error. All of the worker's efforts ought to be directed toward making such a defense unnecessary. For this to happen, he must understand how the defense works, what needs it serves, and find ways to satisfy these needs in constructive ways. Doing this requires deep emotional empathy with the needs, respect for the symptom, and at the same time a realization that it is destructive. Deep and genuine respect for that which is incapacitating is one of the hardest things to learn.

The biggest mistake, often made by even the best-intentioned beginner, was his wish that the patient relinquish his pathology so that a positive relationship could develop between him and his caretaker. In actuality, it can only be the other way around: it is only after this good relation has become established between worker and patient, and has had time to work its curative effect, that the patient can begin slowly to let go of his pathology.

Whether a staff member can learn how to establish this kind of relationship, and everything else the work requires, only experience will tell. But it doesn't take too long to ascertain whether he possesses the most important ingredients for the work—deep respect for the patient as a human being who has been severely hurt by life; sensitivity to his needs; courtesy, even in trying situations; the ability to keep his own needs and anxieties—which are invariably evoked by encountering psychiatric patients—in abeyance for the sake of the patient. These qualities cannot be discerned through interviews, but only through what happens in the actual situation.

A minimum of about three working days—seven or eight hours each day spent visiting with the patients, and many additional hours talking with staff members about this experience—revealed much of the newcomer's inner attitudes about the problems presented by mental sickness. An especially crucial test hinged on what is required to serve the needs of the patients. Some felt they had been degraded to "servants" because of it. Since this was how they felt, it was certainly not a kind of work in which they could maintain (to say nothing of enhance) their self-respect. And without that, the result could only be a fiasco.

Some tried to impress us with their theoretical knowledge or other abilities, using emotional detachment and escape into abstractions for coping with the difficult test to which they had been subjected. Those who could openly admit how terribly exhausting the experience was at least showed that they not only had feelings, but could acknowledge them; and this spoke in favor of their ability to succeed in the work. Of course, much depended on how seriously they wanted to do it. The long hours and the very moderate pay all helped to weed out those who didn't really feel committed to such an undertaking.

During these trial days, various staff members got to know the applicant. Since they would have to live and work with him, it was important whether they wanted to, or felt good about trying. A staff that is given no part in the staff selection process doesn't possess much autonomy, and won't be able to foster it in the patients. Not only did we consider the staff's feelings but both their counselors and I listened to the patients' impressions of the visitor. Of course, the patients had been asked if a visit by the prospective staff member was all right with them. They usually were curious enough to accept him into their group for this short time. If they had any objections because of his behavior, the visit was terminated. While usually only some of the patients committed themselves one way or the other, they all had some very keen observations to contribute: if the visitor was too withdrawn, or intrusive; whether he showed respect for them and their possessions; whether he seemed more involved with himself or the other staff members than in them; whether he tried to force them to be interested in him; whether he had preconceived notions about "psychiatric sickness" or "psychiatric patients"; whether he had wanted to impress them with his experience, or had let them take the initiative in how they wanted to relate, or not relate, to him. Thus while the patients did not make the final decision, they did influence the decision-making process; and this affected the way they felt about themselves, and about living in the institution. More than one patient changed his views about the School after he saw that the patients' negative evaluation led to a prospective staff member's not being employed.

An example may illustrate this. Many years later, a patient recalled that a visitor became terribly upset when he beat him in a game of skill. He asked the visitor why he was so put out when it had been only a game. With some hesitation the patient had reported his observation; in the discussion which followed, we found that other patients had also been aversely affected by the visitor. The next day when he asked whether the visitor would return and was told that he would not, he believed for the first time that the institution was there for him.

While patients had a good deal of influence in decisions, the staff ultimately decided whether they wanted the applicant as a fellow worker. If their decision was negative, we always accepted it. If it was positive, we didn't feel bound by it if we had very strong reservations. We felt we had no right to force somebody on them as this would have run counter to their autonomy, but we also felt we should not have someone working with the patients whom we could not fully trust.

It took easily six months to a year before we could be sure how well a staff member would work out. Thus, while we were rarely disappointed in our initial evaluation of the patients after a few days of getting to know them, this was not equally true for staff members. It is not that psychotics are so much easier to understand and assess as persons; but with a staff member everything depended on how task-oriented he was, a criterion not applicable to the patient. Thus a staff member may have seemed very sensitive, and indeed may have been so, and he may have been deeply involved in what was going on—but he could have been more interested in what he could gain from the patient than in what the patient could gain from him. Or, despite his other qualities, he may have felt that because he was so involved with the patient's unconscious and so helpful to him, somebody else should mop up the messes he and the patient created. Some let their jealousy of other staff members carry them away, or had other reasons for acting out their own problems rather than acting for the patients' and hence the institution's benefit.

It was less important where new staff members stood at the beginning of their association with the institution, than whether they could over a period of time actualize their potential. The ultimate test was how a staff member responded to the extreme demands: emotionally, intellectually, self-critically, and, most of all, in regard to the patience and persistence which the work required. It must be stressed that, as with the patients, respect for the staff's autonomy had to exist at the very beginning of their association with the institution, because for them, too, the end is contained in the beginning.

Any venture into depth psychotherapy has to be a new, demanding, and challenging experience for the therapist, although much less so than for the patient. The difference between therapist and patient is thus one of degree, rather than of kind; what works for the one somehow must also work for the other; what does not work for one cannot work for the other; and if our experience with the patients is not very important for us, it will be even less so for them. Acceptance of this rationale has to permeate the entire life of a psychiatric hospital. In his studies comparing the Orthogenic School with other psychiatric institutions, Henry arrived at the conclusion that the crucial difference from which all others flow is that the Orthogenic School is based on personal commitment, the others on professional detachment (65, 66). Personal commitment can be as fully professional in intent as any other. In the staff's first encounter with the institution this has to be already present in nuclear form as a potentiality; and it must continue to become, with many ups and downs, ever more a reality until the moment of leaving the institution.

19 | Opening Up to the Patient

Once we had succeeded in creating a total therapeutic milieu, it soon became apparent that some of the most intractable functional disturbances could improve when the patient lived in such a setting. While all the thinking and planning that went into the creation of this milieu was based on the insights of psychoanalysis, individual psychoanalytic therapy was only one of the milieu's features. The more psychoanalysis was integrated into the total program as one of its aspects, the more the setting approached the ideal of milieu therapy. Despite our experience, nearly all other psychiatric institutions continue to expect that the truly important therapeutic impact comes from individual therapy alone. The more this theory is upheld, the greater the split between private therapy and the rest of the patient's life—a schism hardly propitious for his becoming able to heal the split in his personality.

The idea of a total therapeutic milieu has also been severely condemned. Goffman (49) and others, relying on studies of the German concentration camp, emphasized the destructive propensities of total institutions (particularly mental hospitals) without recognizing that any institutional setting which can have such far-reaching impacts on personality can do so either for better or for worse. A total institution does have a powerful influence on the personality and behavior of those who live and work within it. This aspect is exemplified by an experiment of Zimbardo's (133), in which college students who volunteered to participate in a psychological experiment on prisons were arbitrarily cast in the role of either prisoners in a jail, or their guards. Within days those play-acting the role of guards began to commit such acts of brutality on their colleagues as prisoners that the latter began to show signs of severe personality disintegration and permanent psychological damage seemed a likely consequence. The experiment, though planned for two weeks, had to be discontinued prematurely after six days.

A total institution, then, has a powerful impact both on staff (in this experiment the guards) and inmates (the prisoners). If the total institution is committed to therapy (the Orthogenic School), as distinguished from one committed to incarceration (the concentration camp, the prison, the "custodial asylum"), this powerful impact on the staff who work there, as well as on the patients who live in it, will be therapeutic. Both staff and patients of a total therapeutic milieu are exposed to its integrating influence from the moment they join it. I have seen some patients respond to it practically immediately, as illustrated by anorexic patients who soon began to drink and eat on their own. It took much longer before a marked change could be observed in some staff members, but then the demands on the staff were great, while those on the patients were minimal. Much more was expected of the staff, even the beginners, and they expected more of themselves, than had been true in their past. The staff member starts from a relatively high level of integration, while the patient begins on the lowest; and to progress from there is easier because there is nowhere to go but up.

Szurek (122) writes:

> *A brief delineation of the "noncontrolling" therapeutic milieu's goal might be formulated somewhat as follows: the aim of every staff person . . . is to help the child to reduce the internal (conflict) disorder, however it manifests itself in the activity in which the particular staff member is concerned. It is postulated that after the child has taken some steps toward the reduction of his internal disorder, the energy freed from symptomatic binding makes it gradually possible for him to learn and to become eager to act with less destructiveness.*

After enumerating a long list of what the staff need to do for the patients, he adds:

> *This means that the satisfactions of the staff are derived from their own technical contribution to the child's achieving reduction of his inner turmoil, and from their own increasing technical development and proficiency. . . . All this requires that kind of technical collaboration with other staff members that could be termed an integration of the entire staff in the work toward the goal defined.*

All this is very true and to the point. But valuable as these and similar remarks are, the emphasis is essentially on what the patients need, as if this were so difficult to recognize in theory or so impossible to meet in practice. I believe that in milieu therapy, the essential problem is how to create a milieu in which the staff will not have to defend themselves against the emotional ravages the patients and their needs inflict on them.

August Aichhorn, the first who tried (for a short time successfully) to create a total therapeutic treatment design on a psychoanalytic basis, recognized that the therapeutic spirit "must proceed from the personnel. . . . It is not enough to comprehend what the child says and does; the worker must be able to 'live' himself into the situation so that those experiences become his own" (1). How utterly true; but the problems which arise are how the worker can do this without being emotionally devastated in the process, and how he can experience what the patient experiences and, unlike the patient, not become disintegrated by it.

We all need defenses to protect us when our integration is threatened. The primitive behavior of mental patients is threatening to those who permit themselves truly to experience it. Therefore, the staff can afford to subject themselves to experiencing the patient in all his terror, hostility, and dependency only when they feel sufficiently secure and know that they will be able to reintegrate themselves. One becomes worried about being drawn into the maelstrom of the patient's anger, anxiety, despair; fear for one's own sanity emerges; one may even begin to question which of their delusions are delusions, and which may be reasonable.

The most "natural" defense against this is a near-automatic response of buttressing one's defenses to avoid the impact of such experiences; and of closing one's heart, if not one's mind, to those who apparently threaten to overwhelm us with the power of their emotions. Yet by doing so, the worker destroys his best chance to help the patients gain mental health. It takes courage and determination not to engage in defensive maneuvers, and to expose oneself to the very dangers one wishes to avoid. If one does open himself, this automatically activates instinctual strivings parallel to those of the patient and awakens, by association, other unconscious pressures which normally are kept under conscious control or unconscious repression. Technically speaking, what happens is that if we respond feelingly to what goes on in the psychotic person by trying to understand it through our own inner experiences, this disintegrates repressions in us, and those thoughts, desires, and anxieties kept from our awareness threaten to inundate the ego. If we truly open ourselves to what goes on in the mind of the psychotic, our ego "experiences such excessive crescendo of the instinctual forces as danger for itself and, independently of any consequences menacing from the outside, a danger to be destroyed and its organization overwhelmed" (126).

How natural, then, for the intelligent, well-educated person (and only he has the resources eventually to become a good therapist) to wish to fall back on his intellectual defenses in the stressful experiences the patients subject him to. He develops the device of viewing the patient as something to be studied rather than as a human being like himself. But the more one comes to "know" intellectually about the patient in abstract form, the less one is in "touch" with him as a human being. While such a worker "sees" much more of the mental and emotional mechanisms at work in the patient, he loses sight of him as a person. The more he concentrates on learning about the paranoid personality, the less he responds to Mr. Jones in the flesh, and the less empathy the worker has with Mr. Jones's conviction that he is helplessly at the mercy of those who misuse him for their nefarious purposes. Mr. Jones is certain that those beyond his reach are out to destroy him. But viewing this only as a figment of his imagination (which it is, but only to a degree, because there is always some psychological truth deeply imbedded in any delusion) and not as an expression of the living hell in which Mr. Jones exists, the worker fails to respond to Mr. Jones's panic fear of being undone by his enemies. The more one knows about the catatonic personality, the less one feelingly accepts that Mrs. Smith must remain unmoving, unseeing, frozen into immobility and insensitivity because only thus can she stop the world in its tracks and prevent the next moment from bringing utter destruction to her and those important to her. Seeing Mr. Jones and Mrs. Smith as paranoiac and catatonic patients gives them the conviction that they are treated as cases, not as persons unique in their needs, desires, and anxieties, as worthwhile human beings like the worker himself.

The scientific study of human psychology can easily become so engrossing that it interferes with one's paying attention to how much one has in common with these suffering persons, and to one's part in any interaction with them. I believe the writings of Laing can be best understood from this perspective. He writes, "The concept of schizophrenia is a straitjacket that restricts psychiatrist and patients" (81). Obviously he has had experience of psychiatrists using their discipline as a device to distance themselves from the patient.

Laing sees the schizophrenic as possessing as important an understanding of the world as we do; possibly even a more penetrating comprehension of some of its aspects. Moreover, Laing believes that only someone who has had, or has come close to having a schizo-phrenic experience, can truly understand the schizophrenic patient. At least this is the way I understand Laing's statement that the treatment of the schizophrenic requires his being guided "by people who have been there and back again. Psychiatrically, this would appear as ex-patients helping future patients to go mad" (80). I have no doubt that ex-patients may contribute to others going mad; but I know also that they are less able to understand what goes on in other mad per-sons than a psychoanalytically well-trained person; and that they are much less able to help them to get well again. True, those who have recovered from a psychiatric disease may have greater and more spon-taneous *sympathy* with the predicament of the psychiatric patient, but (at least in my experience) hardly any *empathy*. They don't have sufficient distance from the psychotic process to see it as any different from what they themselves experienced. But psychosis is an in-dividual's very personal hell, which can be understood only from his own experience, whereas the former schizophrenic sees everybody else's hell as identical with his own. As mentioned before, the schizo-phrenic has uncanny insight into the problems and difficulties of others as long as these relate closely to what concerns him. If they don't relate closely to him, he is much less sensitive than the normal, even psychiatrically untrained person as to what goes on in others. Otherwise psychiatric patients would cure each other; after all, they spend plenty of time together in hospitals.

Contrary to Laing's opinion, experience has shown me that direct therapy of schizophrenics requires therapists with a very strong ego—so strong and well integrated that despite their fears, there is no danger of the ego being overwhelmed either by their own primary processes or by being exposed to the patients', even temporarily. The beginner, subjected to new experiences for which he has been only partially prepared through his studies and casual contacts with psy-chiatric patients (which is different from living and working for days on end with schizophrenics), naturally worries that his ego may give way under the onslaught of the patients' primitive behavior. For the staff member to succeed in his work, there must be no chance that this can possibly occur.

One of the prime qualifications for the direct work with psy-chiatric patients in a total therapeutic milieu is that the staff member must have an ego strong enough to reintegrate after relinquishing de-fenses to achieve empathy with the patient. In this way better forms of mastery are progressively attained. One of the reasons we require that staff members have a four-year college degree from a first-rate university, and an excellent academic record, is that this is an indicator of ego strength. It also suggests a cultural background with which to build as a member works at the institution. Psychoanalysis is, among other things, a historical reconstruction. It helps greatly if the worker is steeped in human history, both individual and of the species. Literary and artistic creations are the expression of unconscious processes that have been worked through and sublimated. Anyone who is not interested in these paramount examples of sublimation will not succeed in helping patients sublimate their primary process thinking and their instinctual drives. While every staff member must familiarize himself with psychoanalytic and psychiatric literature, this alone will not do; he must also devote himself to the understanding and enjoyment of such writers as Shakespeare and Dostoevsky, to mention only two.

An applicant is exposed to several days of direct experience with the patients so that we can have a correct assessment of his ego strength. Occasionally we overestimated it, and as he came into prolonged contact with psychotics, the worker not only feared that his integration might give way, but was in actual danger of this happening. Then the worker had to be removed immediately from direct contact with the patients—both for his sake and theirs—and helped to find a safer occupation. Since such disintegration in a basically healthy ego is due to specific traumatizing experiences, it is reassuring to see such persons fully reintegrated within a few days after direct work with the patients had ceased. In several instances, the persons felt they had been enriched by the experience, but that it had simply been too much for them. They did not regret doing it, but had realized it was not for them. Some of them later became psychiatrists, where seeing patients who were less sick within the structure of office practice provided sufficient protection for them to do a good job.

It is significant that we usually didn't have good results with workers who had recently undergone psychoanalysis. But those who did go into psychoanalysis after having been at the School for a while, and who wanted to find out more about themselves, were often our best workers. Those who sought treatment before they started working had found the normal vagaries of life seemingly too much for their ego to master. Some otherwise quite able college graduates who tried to work at the School had at one time used drugs, though they no longer did so. It seemed reasonable to give them a chance to try, but none of them worked out well. This was not because of any ascertainable aftereffects from drug use, but because of their relative lack of

ego strength, the same weakness which had led them to use drugs as a means of escape. While to the best of my knowledge none reverted to drug use, nor suffered any other psychological impediment, the work was simply too demanding of their ego for them to be really successful at it.

Nevertheless, to come back to Laing's thesis: If we cannot see the schizophrenic as a person very much like ourselves, we cannot come close enough to him to be able to understand or help him. This is true, but I am convinced it is not necessary to believe that he knows more about the world than we do. He certainly knows more about *his* world than we do. Even with the most complete psychiatric knowledge we can only assist him in bringing better order into his world. One does not have to have a touch of schizophrenia to understand and help the psychotic; there is enough of primitive thinking and feeling in all of us for that. It is not that schizophrenics know more about the world as it really is, as Laing and a few others who follow his lines of thinking believe; but by trying to understand them and what they are about, we can "learn from almost every schizophrenic a new aspect of the world" (33).

When we stop anxiously defending ourselves against our awareness, we find that we have a great deal in common with the psychiatric patient; enough so that we can bridge the gap between us. The difference between the patient and the therapist is that the therapist can at will walk back and forth across this bridge. He knows at any one moment how far he can safely venture into the chaotic world across the river that separates sanity from insanity, as he knows when to beat a quick return from this alien territory back into the sane world. The patient, by his very illness, cannot freely cross over this bridge; which is all the more reason why we must make excursions to his side of the river so that we can visit there together. But if we become captives of this particular schizophrenic netherworld, we will never be able to guide the patient back across the bridge into the world of sane living.

Laing is essentially correct when, in a most felicitous statement, he sums up what is also the essence of milieu therapy: "Psychotherapy must remain an obstinate attempt of two people to recover the wholeness of being human through the relationship between them." In milieu therapy, these relationships extend over all of the life of the patient. But we cannot expect obstinate devotion to this task from the patient; on the contrary, one must be prepared for his most determinedly defending himself against it. It is we who must be obstinate in our efforts to restore wholeness of being to the patient.

And while we do not need to recover the wholeness of our personality since we must possess it to begin with, we must try to gain a higher degree of wholeness—or, as I prefer to call it, integration—for ourselves through what we experience in interaction with the patients.

The difficulties the beginner encounters with patients often prevent him from recognizing his own contribution. The patients react negatively to him because they cannot manage their own anxieties and needs, let alone his. The patients are hurt by the worker's underlying attitude that they are "lost souls," while he is not; the beginner has put himself on a higher rung of the ladder. Even if this is true in reality, such an attitude is nevertheless always offensive; but mental patients are much more vulnerable to it, and so more deeply offended. A worker can be made to see how his attitude, which is similar to that of the well-meaning, "unprejudiced" whites toward blacks, has provoked the patients' rejection.

We often encounter serious resistance when showing a worker how his attitude has contributed to creating the undesirable situation, but the difficulty cannot be avoided. This is done gently, one small step at a time, with patience and the greatest respect for the worker's feelings since this will serve as a model when he, in his turn, will assist a reluctant patient to recognize his own contributions to the problems he encounters in life. No matter how painful it may be to acknowledge this, it is the only way the worker will feel hopeful about his eventual success. Because if he is the partial cause of what went wrong, it follows that he can also partially contribute to improving the situation.

Let us consider the experience of one young worker whom I had to confront about the way in which his own unconscious prejudice was affecting the patients. Since this worker was disappointed in himself about his attitude toward the patients, it was both important and helpful for him to see that the patients, too, had experienced defeat. They had approached meeting the new worker with apprehension, but also with some hope that this time their experience with people would be different; that they would gain something from being with him. Since things didn't turn out well, the patients saw this as another demonstration that nothing good would ever happen to them; that people would always be disappointed in them and think they were no use.

Until then, the worker had only been aware of the patients' total indifference, rejection, and disgust with him, or their glee about the defeat they inflicted on him—or whatever defensive maneuver they had used to protect themselves and test the worker. Once they had succeeded in wearing down his veneer of good intentions in wanting to help "these poor souls," they could ascertain his true motives for wanting to work with psychiatric patients.

After exploring what had really happened—as opposed to what seemed to have occurred—many beginners were amazed to see how similar the feelings had been in both worker and patients: they both had been motivated by their anxiety about each other; but given their different positions and personality makeups, the anxiety had expressed itself in very different ways. The worker had tried to be "nicer" than he really felt toward them, given his inner reservations and anxieties; and they, using the opposite defense, had been as ornery and trying as they knew how. They both had had hopes about the experience with each other, they both had been defeated, and become deeply disappointed in themselves because they hadn't managed the situation better. In self-defense, both had sought a way out by blaming the other: the patients deciding the worker was no good, the worker blaming the patients, explaining it all as due to their being insane.

From this analysis it should be obvious how much worker and patients have in common, but this is still beyond the grasp of the beginner. He is still much too insecure, too afraid of accepting that identity. Those who later turned out to be the best workers usually reacted to such an experience with dejection. Where they had hoped to do some good, the result was that the patients were worse off than before. They might respond to such a realization with a desperate cry, or a silently suppressed: "So that's what the patients feel, but what about me?" This response was expected, for whoever represents the institution to the worker must insist on his feelings being treated with as much consideration as those of the patients. As a matter of fact, in line with the institution's philosophy the worker's feelings are in a way more important, because they are the only ones about which *he* can do something. He can remain dejected or even quit, if he wants, or he can pick up his courage and continue his struggle. Only he can decide how he wishes to react.

One worker stated this dilemma succinctly when a patient of hers seemed to need extra time because he was upset, and she had already made plans for spending her free evening. We had discussed the patient's feelings of distress about being deserted. The worker, in a subdued scream, blurted out: "What about *my* feelings?" To which I replied that they were most important; but what *were* they? Years later the worker wrote:

> *Then I was really up against it. Did I really not want to spend a couple of hours of my precious free time to help*

one of my patients? First it was guilt that motivated me, but soon I learned that was no good for anybody. It took a long time, but eventually I came around to not putting it on the patients but really asking myself what kind of person I wanted to be and deciding on that basis; rather than on what the patient needed, because decisions made that way always had the end result that the patient had to somehow pay for them. Did I want to be the kind of person who worked from nine to five and had all weekends free? Did I want to give up all I had gained in understanding and as a person from the work? Of course not! When I began to make decisions not on the basis of what the patient needed, but because of what kind of a person I wanted to be, then it all became so much simpler though the work continued to remain difficult. But it also became so much more personally rewarding.

This is the end of a long development; but in milieu therapy it must be understood from the beginning that nothing is done because the work requires it. That is too impersonal a principle. The beginner will fight the institution around this issue. Because so much work in psychiatric (and other) institutions is performed in line with what the organization expects of the worker, or demands that he do to "perform his duties," these institutions fail those they are supposed to serve. Tragedy awaits the child whose mother feels that since she is a mother, she is required to do certain things to take care of her child, even though she would much prefer to spend her time doing something else.

Some workers survive the first trying months out of a feeling of guilt, a wish to "make up for past sins." Others persist not out of concern about the kind of person they wish to be in their own eyes, but how they might appear to the rest of the staff. Yet even bad reasons, since they *are* the workers' reasons, have to be treated with great respect as the starting point for higher integration, when shallow motivations are replaced by the only truly useful one for staff and patient alike: first doing things to become the person the staff member wants to be; and later to retain his self-respect as the kind of person and therapist which his self-image demands.

In milieu therapy, it must be made clear to the worker that the decisions are his as to what he thinks needs to be done; if he should turn out to be in error, the rest of the institution is there to pick up the pieces so that nothing very harmful will occur. After it has all been talked over, if the worker comes to believe he was mistaken in his views, then he will change. If not, then maybe he was correct in the first place; the next time around, the patients' reactions will prove who was correct.

One worker told me that she had once interpreted some remark I made to her about an attitude toward a patient as meaning, "Well, if you want to be the kind of person who hits a schizophrenic patient below the belt, go right ahead and do it." With that, she was up against herself; but up to then she had thought she was only up against the work. The result was that her attitudes toward the patients, the institution, and herself all changed. Given the freedom to be as bad as *she* wanted to be, she could give the patients their freedom to be the same. Consequently, the patients no longer had any reason to be all that bad, and she no longer had any motivation to act in ways she herself felt were like hitting patients below the belt.

Undoubtedly there are persons who would abuse such freedom by expending little energy on what would be the best way to handle patients. That is why each applicant has to be carefully evaluated; not on the basis of degrees or certificates but as a person, before he is accepted as a worker. It is why we have to get to know this person as an individual and also see him at work with the patients, eliciting his reactions afterwards. Here, too, the end is contained in the beginning. Unless those persons chosen to join the staff are the kind who simply cannot afford to be capable of "hitting mental patients below the belt," the therapeutic milieu will not succeed.

Despite the greatest care, errors occasionally will be made. For example, one worker got carried away by a patient's behavior and hit him; another scratched a patient—not by true chance or accident—but because he became so furious at him. If the setting was to continue as a therapeutic milieu, in each case it was necessary to ask the worker to leave. The patients must be able to feel that their legitimate interests will be protected, not only against dangers coming from the outside, but particularly against those which may originate within the institution. In each case the separation of the worker from the institution to protect the patients had an immediately beneficial impact—not just on the patient directly involved, but also on many others.

Of course, we cannot simply let the worker flounder in situations where he is up against himself. If he is to become the person he wants to be, not carried away by his angry anxiety or his disappointments, he needs help in understanding just what led him to this inability to live up to his own expectations. To establish the connection between something he wishes to integrate within himself, and what is necessary for his success with the patients, considerable knowledge of and empathy with his personality is required. The groundwork for this was laid by studying the autobiography he submitted with his application—what he didn't say about himself is as important as what he did say—and by the conversations during his trial visit and all others since, as well as observing him at work and in interaction with other staff members. But even this is barely the beginning of what is needed, which is the specific connection between his personality and what is happening between him and the patients. A direct approach to the matter is possible only when the worker is already partially aware of something in himself he disapproves of, and when the issue is one which is so universal that his privacy is not invaded when it is brought into the open.

The actual content of such conversations, or of any others designed to help staff members in their personal and professional development, always has to be geared not only to benefiting the patients, but to whatever it is that will help this particular staff member at this moment in his personal and professional development. Let us consider, as is usually the case, that the trouble centers in the relationship between him and one particular patient, with whom he has not been able to do as well as he wishes. Since everything occurred within a specific relation between two unique people, they both have to be considered at all times.

If something is required of the worker that is too difficult or threatening to him, in self-defense he will misunderstand it to protect himself. And if his *own* need for self-protection is not considered an important issue, he will never be able to be truly concerned with the patient's need for protection. He will come to resent being put in such jeopardy because of the patient. This, incidentally, explains why staff training, based on intellectually elucidating the patient's pathology, is often counterproductive. Overwhelmed by all the problems the patient presents, by the severity and complexity of the dynamics at work, the worker feels overcome and frightened by the magnitude of his task. Indeed, if I were asked point-blank what specific steps and in what order were needed to cure a particular schizophrenic patient— even one I knew well—I wouldn't know what to answer, although I have devoted all my professional life to this task. The question becomes immediately answerable when the problem is not how to go about helping the patient restructure his personality in general, but what in a given situation is required to further this goal; such as how to be able to help him fall asleep after a nightmare, to defecate without fear, or to enjoy eating, difficult as each of these may be. It is quite possible to guide a worker toward understanding what was involved in a specific interaction, and how it could be handled better. Although he might not yet be able to see how it all adds up, he will gain from this. Therefore, he must be encouraged to forget about long-term results, to stop worrying about the future, and to concentrate on the day.

When a worker would anxiously ask how what he was doing would help the patient regain sanity, I often quoted something which I believe comes from the Talmud. A wise rabbi was asked what one must do to be saved; his answer was that everybody who obeyed all the laws of the Lord on the day before he died would be saved. Just as the day of death is uncertain, so is the day when a psychiatric patient will be restored to adequate functioning. Since this day is so uncertain, we must do the best we can for him and his needs on the day at hand. If we do this, the days will add up to a cure; just as living the good life on the day before we might die will, of necessity, add up to having lived a good life.

We frequently encountered beginners who believed they could avoid worrying about their specific dealings with a patient because, so they said, the patient knew that they "loved" him, and felt only positively about him. This idea that others "know" and thus react to our good inner feelings is too often used as an excuse to avoid acting in line with them. Never once did I encounter a staff member saying, "It doesn't matter how I acted, because the patient knows how I feel about him," when the action was, in the staff member's opinion, unquestionably positive. Statements of this kind are made only if the worker somehow knows he has shortchanged the patient—possibly for excellent reasons as far as he is concerned, such as momentary exhaustion, or justifiable preoccupation with something else. After a staff member had been with us for some time, it was usually sufficient to bring this strange discrepancy to his attention. The image of the patient "knowing" how we feel about him is never used unless we have doubts about how we acted. I would remind him that psychiatric patients are extremely sensitive to our feelings, but only when they fit into their frame of reference—which never assumes that others are motivated by the best intentions. If they had such a positive outlook on life and people, it would preclude their having to be psychiatric patients. The worker then realizes that the mental patient—more than anybody else—can judge us only by our actions; and if he has any doubt about out intentions, his mental makeup and past experiences permit him to put only a negative interpretation on them. That is even more reason to recognize that having good intentions is not enough. We must act on them. If we do this, eventually our positive actions will win out over the patient's negativism and doubts; but since he *is* a psychiatric patient, this will not happen sooner or later, but only much, much later.

One way to encourage a worker not to feel defeated is to give him a truthful account of having had the same experiences. Nothing provides better support for a self-esteem weakened by recent failure than to be told how those who are now obviously successful had similar bad experiences. Here, as always, everything depends on the spirit in which it is done; if such stories are told with glee that others are no quicker in learning than oneself, or with an attitude of "We all had to learn the hard way," they are not helpful at all. What the beginner needs is not a homily on the difficulties of learning to live up to the great demands of the work, but empathy with his agony over defeat. Only if the senior staff shows a feeling for and an understanding of this will the worker eventually learn to develop a similar attitude toward the patients.

One of the director's major tasks here is to prevent the senior staff from becoming impatient with the beginner and his complaints. The attitude of the worker on being told that other staff members experienced similar defeats is: "So you had to go through it in the past, and now you feel fine, that's just great for you; but my trouble is that I feel miserable right now." Therefore, if one really wishes to help the staff member, one's attitude should be: "Isn't it terrible that although we, too, had to suffer through that, we are unable to do a better job in helping you with it"—because at the moment when the worker is feeling so ineffective, it is not a senior staff member's story about his past failures but only one about his present ineffectiveness (on a different level) which will bridge the gap between the two. This helps the worker do the same for the patients; as we all know, misery wants company not in the past, but in the present.

We thus did everything we could to give the new worker the strength—despite his difficulties—not to give up, or estrange himself emotionally from the patients. Nevertheless, a beginner would report that for a while, when he could possibly do so, he tried "to stand to one side and watch fearfully what they were doing"; whereas "when I had to act, I plunged in, very much like the proverbial bull in the china shop, succeeding only in beating down the patients who had no spirit, and provoking those with some resources to fight back, thus making things worse." When the worker no longer had to defend his integration rigidly at all times, since the institution was always able to help him reintegrate himself on a higher level, then he could open himself to the patients' inner feelings despite the effect this might have on him. "Even then when things got upsetting," he reported, "I could barely control myself, and it was my habit to say, 'Calm down, everything will be all right.' For some time I wondered why this injunction usually led to more, rather than less chaos. Then one day a patient turned to me and said: 'Calm down? How can we calm down when you're the most excited of us all?' " The worker fortunately experienced this admonition not as defiance, nor as a threat to either his position of authority or his self-respect and integration, but as sound advice. Having finally permitted himself to let the patients act on him and his emotions, he could use what they had to offer him to strengthen his ego at the very moment it was endangered by his own chaos.

At this early phase in his becoming a competent staff member, this worker was most surprised by that which, in less than a year, he would be taking for granted: "Strangely enough, the major impact of this experience for me was not the technical realization that I could not hope to calm down a group of patients when I was so excited, but rather the tangible experience that I was an important and influential part of the interaction" (131). At the moment of crisis he had permitted his ego, temporarily weakened and possibly even threatened, to become buttressed by the narcissistic supplies which the patients provided, by implicitly telling him how important his emotional state was for them. Obviously one cannot derive narcissistic supplies from people one thinks of as mentally deranged, or subhuman. By viewing patients in this way, most psychiatric hospital workers, while protecting their egos from being threatened by the patients, also cut themselves off from gaining ego supplies. Only if the patient is fully felt as a person—one in deep distress and in part delusional, unable to cope with the world, but still as important as oneself—can working with him not only threaten but also buttress our integration. Regardless of this particular experience, it would be silly to assume that psychiatric patients are more capable of taking care of themselves and each other than the staff is. But if we listen to what they say or express in other ways, our mental energy is drawn away from being beset by our inability to do something about ourselves to doing something for them. As we all know, undergoing a crisis with a feeling of utter helplessness is a most debilitating experience. This explains why attendants in mental hospitals often immediately sedate or restrain a patient; doing nothing in an emergency is so difficult to bear. While this may momentarily end the crisis it does little for us as workers and is damaging for the patient.

Schizophrenic patients particularly feel as if they are in desperate straits, and this creates a feeling of emergency around them. The staff then becomes very anxious about what they should do, and again and again their inclination, both in emergencies and routine matters, was to depend on me or the staff meetings. Rather than trying to understand the persons involved, attention focused on the particular act. A patient is dangerously assaultive; what should one do about it? Some way has to be found to stop him or divert him. The psychiatric hospital fails as a therapeutic institution if the patient's violence is made the center of deliberation, rather than the patient himself, or the worker's inner reaction to him. It is difficult to decide which of the two—patient or worker—needs more attention at the moment. But such subtle complex judgment is not what the staff usually want of those who teach them; when the chips are down they want direction, not teaching. Yet if the worker's direction comes from the outside, rather than from himself, how can he help the patient to become inner-directed—which is the only lasting cure for whatever emergency he may create at the moment?

Within a professional group, the complex staff hierarchies and the overarching one of the institution are maintained in the fallacious hope that they will do away with the crises. The staff wish to be able to turn to somebody with greater knowledge, power, and status to relieve them of their responsibility for the patient. Sometimes it does seem cruel not to offer them immediate help. But if one does relieve them, it is only momentary, and they are permanently deprived of their autonomy. Of course common sense—and the law—requires that action be immediately taken to safeguard the physical security and well-being of everybody, patients and staff. But this is seldom necessary if one concentrates instead on sorting out the emergency and all that is involved in it. The pieces of the puzzle come together and the emergency evaporates.

To understand the complex ways the psychotic person sees the world, to learn to see what is hidden behind his strange behavior, and sense the terror that is covered up by indifference or displayed by open aggression—for all this, training, experience, expertise, and "insight" are not enough. It demands what Freud correctly viewed as an art of gaining access to the disturbed mind. And helping the patient actually achieve mental health requires a much greater art, demanding a great deal of formal teaching and experience. But as important as all of this is, the greater the emergency, the less formal learning helps. When things must be done right away, careful analysis is too time-consuming. The situation requires spontaneous insight through empathy.

After the event, the expert may be useful by explaining the reasons for the emergency; what lies behind it; why what one did out of spontaneous insight worked so well or failed to achieve desirable results and made things worse. This is useful intelligence, but essentially no more than that. When the next emergency comes around, one has no time to recall it all; only what has entered one's preconscious mind, and through an autonomous act been made part of one's personality, will be available in a flash. To deal with the patient in the present, the worker must be helped to use his own resources, not those borrowed from the specialist.

Were the worker not jealous of the psychiatrist's superior position and overawed by his knowledge, he would be less eager to partake in it. His own rationality tempts him to believe that what he understands, he is able to do without inner reservations. If he would concentrate on asking himself, Why didn't I think of it myself?, he would come to the conclusion that it was not lack of knowledge, but emotional blocking which prevented him from comprehending it. Somehow we are more willing to accept our ignorance or lack of skill, than use the intelligence and information we have. This is why the psychiatrist's opinions are eagerly sought: it permits us to overlook what is really preventing us from using the training, knowledge, and experience we have.

To comprehend the emotional needs of another person is no complex intellectual matter, nor does it require arcane knowledge. True, because of our anxieties, prejudices, defensive maneuvers, we sometimes have to make the most complex intellectual detours to comprehend what is really obvious. The psychiatrist knows from his study of psychoanalysis that once the worker is freed from his blinders, he will be able to use his own judgment and know how to behave in a particular situation. Yet, when the psychiatrist is teaching the staff, more often than not he relies on two methods unrelated to this: he gives suggestions and orders about what should be done, and he engages in theoretical explications of the patient's pathology, both to the neglect of helping the worker see things wholly and clearly himself.

20 | Staff: Joining the Community

A salient feature of the Orthogenic School is its physical and social indivisibility. How can a patient rush to a staff member for help in a crisis, perhaps in the middle of the night, if he doesn't know where the staff member's room is? How can he feel free to do this if he hasn't already been there on occasions other than emergencies?

The more staff members who live within the institution the better. Of course there will always be some who don't want to "live in," but the better the living quarters that are offered, the more likely will people be to choose to do so. All of this requires careful handling. The staff's privacy must be respected, and not unduly infringed upon. But if the staff member is truly concerned with a patient, it will set his mind at rest if he knows that the patient can come to him in a real crisis. If such a crisis does occur, the staff member knows immediately, if he lives in close proximity to the patient. Only after they had been shown where and how the staff members lived were many of the patients assured of their safety and convinced that we cared about them. If the worker on whom he depends is housed far away, or in a separate building, it will be difficult for a patient to believe that the staff member wishes to be close to him. Therefore any attempt by the staff member to make the patients feel closer to him is belied by the distance existing between where patients and staff live. Furthermore, if staff members live in quarters that are drab and uninviting, how can the patient believe that those who live so impersonally will be able to guide him back to an enjoyable personal life?

Married staff members are not expected to live within the institution, and this raises problems when it is difficult to attract unmarried staff. At the Orthogenic School, about half the professional staff lived at the institution at any given time. The burden of taking care of emergencies always rested more heavily on those who lived there, although the others would have to be called in occasionally. Nearly all who lived in were counselors. They took care of the patients in much the same way a good parent takes care of his child, facilitating the patients' living, but in addition helping them therapeutically in all of the big and small events of the day and night (which in their totality make the patient's life).

An institution which is also home for a significant part of the staff, particularly those members most intimately involved with the patients, is much more a home for the patients. It is hard to believe that a patient can ever emotionally accept having to live in a place where *they*—those who take care of him—wouldn't dream of living. If it is not a desirable place for the staff to live, how can it be a good place for the patients? While the patients would prefer that all staff members live at the institution, symbolic expression of intent can in some way make up for the failure totally to conform to this ideal. Because some staff wish and choose to live in the same ambience as the patient does, this seems to guarantee its comparable worthiness for the patient. But since about half of the staff, and particularly most of the senior staff, don't live at the institution, it also indicates to the patient that while temporarily advantageous, living within the institution is not a desirable permanent arrangement.

For patients and staff, it is also important that the Orthogenic School is part of a university. This makes it easier for staff members who are also graduate students to live at the School. According to our experience, graduate students are among the most desirable groups from which to draw counselor-therapists; provided they work on a full-time basis and are ready to remain for several years, and that working there takes precedence over finishing their studies within a particular period of time.

But even within a university community, living at the institution is acceptable for a sizable number of staff members only if doing so carries high prestige and special emotional rewards, beyond just the enhanced importance they have to the patients. For those who do live in, the flow of communication is easier because of many casual meetings during the day, as staff members pass and meet each other. Residence at the institution must offer the staff the advantage of not having to wait to receive consultation or other help for their problems.

One of the most frequent—and justified—complaints of workers in psychiatric institutions is that those workers of high prestige usually have the most convenient working hours, and those of low prestige the least convenient. Staff morale cannot be high wherever this is the case. The only possible arrangement which guarantees both that staff morale will be high and that patients will be well taken care of at all times, is where some member of the senior staff is always at work, and hence readily available to staff and patients. This may obviously create problems in a relatively small institution, since it will not have a great many persons who are clearly in an authoritative position; yet it is the only arrangement which can provide the highly individualized services mental patients require. Crises cannot be scheduled. At the Orthogenic School, a small institution with only a few senior staff people, we managed to overcome this difficulty. On the other hand, many vast institutions with a large number of senior staff fail to do so; this convinces me it has little to do with available numbers, and a great deal to do with what the institution's underlying philosophy is, and how serious the staff is about living up to it.

If, for example, those who direct the institution are not at all times (evenings, weekends, holidays) available to the staff when they need help, then living at the institution will be much less attractive because it doesn't carry special advantages regarding the work, but only the liability of having to help out in emergencies. But it is not only the increased availability of "experts" which adds to the value of living at the institution; there is also the comfort the staff provide for each other in difficult situations, and the companionship at all times.

If living provisions for the staff were inferior to those of the patients, it would arouse unmanageable resentment. But since I have never encountered this, it needs no elaboration. If staff living rooms, bathrooms, and so on, are of about the same quality as those of the patients, another barrier separating staff from patient is removed (Plate 13). The patients at the Orthogenic School were familiar with staff quarters. Every staff member living there occasionally invited the patients with whom he worked, singly or as a group, to visit him where he was "at home." There was also an "open house" a few times a year when all patients who wanted to do so visited all staff members who lived at the School. We all like to know how "the other half" lives, and this went a long way toward satisfying such curiosity. There were always some patients who tried to abuse the privilege and invade staff members' privacy, but with good humor and the conviction that we all need our privacy protected there never was any serious difficulty, and within a few days the problem would be solved.

Usually it took staff members some time before they began to experience their rooms at the School as their real home, a feeling which then always extended to the institution as a whole. A few made a complete accommodation within hours or days after they moved in. Others had to undergo a process of acclimatization. Those who did not manage to settle in within a year or so would leave the institution, and often this field of work. While all staff members tried to help the patients feel that the institution was now their home, and to make their quarters more suitable for attaining this meaning, if the staff member did not view it as his home, too, he would fail to give the patients the feeling that it was theirs. The staff member's inner reservations about living at an institution could not help flavoring what he conveyed to the patients about its being their home. (Luckily, patients could get the proper feeling that this was truly their home from another staff member who did feel that way.)

There is a world of difference in our emotional attitudes to a place—and to what degree we make it our very own by pouring ourselves into it and rendering it a reflection of our personality—which depends on whether we view it as merely a temporary stopover or our real home. It doesn't matter how long we continue to live there. Some people stay in a place for many years and continue viewing it as a provisional arrangement, while others may feel completely settled in although they remain someplace for only a relatively short time.

As a staff member came to think of the School as his home—not just a place where he lived—he would personalize his quarters and arrange them much more to his taste. He would then no longer be satisfied with the pleasant furnishings the institution had provided for him, but would add pieces which made his place more important to him, more a part of himself. As he did so, he became much more effective in making the patients' quarters more of a home for them; his attitude extended beyond his rooms to the entire institution. He became interested in and concerned with everything that went on; wanting all places within the School to have the pleasant, comfortable, "lived-in" quality that makes a place a home. And he would make it his business to see to it that everything sustained this feeling. He no longer automatically called the janitors to change light bulbs; he did it himself. He was more apt to give the patients' room a special cleaning than to ask the maids to do this extra work. He suddenly enjoyed making small repairs, which had previously been fixed by the engineers.

I noted earlier how much the home stands symbolically for our body; the home shelters our innermost being—our soul. It was fascinating to observe that as a staff member reshaped his room to fit his personality, his patients' quarters also took on a different appearance. They began not just to reflect what the patients wanted them to look like, but ever so subtly to express also what the staff member and the patients had in common. Mementos of things they had done together appeared in prominent places, on either the patient's or staff member's initiative; pictures were replaced by others the patients and staff member selected together. Gradually the patients' quarters began to integrate what they and their staff members felt made the most pleasant surroundings in which to live. This happened so consistently that occasionally when some major change took place in the physical arrangements of a dormitory, I would jokingly ask the staff member involved what he had done with his room; it always turned out that as he had reshaped his living area, he had felt compelled to help the patients make theirs more reflective of their own idiosyncrasies.

The kinds of changes that occurred may be illustrated by the following rather extreme example. One particular staff member's room became diagonally divided as if by chance into one area to the north, which was soon furnished with things she bought for herself: a fancy bed, an easy chair, an onyx-topped table, and so on. The southern area was always in complete disarray. The bed and a favorite chair were so placed that from them only the nicely arranged northern expanse of the room could be seen. Now it so happened that this staff member had been born and raised in the Deep South, and had originally come north to Chicago to escape a home that she felt had heavily stifled her personality. She concentrated all her chaotic, unmastered difficulties in the south area, while in the north, where she now lived, things seen were effectively organized, as she was in her work as a staff member. She was seemingly unperturbed by the incredible mess assembled in the south, which remained out of her sight. Occasionally she consciously tried to straighten out the southern half of her room, but the order never lasted, not even for a day. Then she developed an interest in antiques; she acquired some lovely fragments from ancient Greek excavations, and a very nice case to keep them in which she placed in the center of the southern area. It seemed that she understood there were some valuable things in the past; worthy to be unearthed and cherished, which could enrich her life. The case stood in the center of the southern area and its immediate surroundings were also kept in perfect shape; but the rest of this space remained chaotic. Finally, in a fluctuating development that stretched out over more than five years, the southern part of the room was straightened up, but somehow the division between the two areas remained. Both areas were now very nice-looking each in its own way; but the northern area gave one the feeling of very relaxed and comfortable living, and the southern of a strained, unlived-in little museum. At last she became disgusted with the room's arrangement and radically reorganized it, so that there was no longer any separation of the two areas. Now it was a well-integrated room that hung together and reflected excellent taste and comfortable living. Some six months later she decided to move out of the institution into a nearby apartment of her own, while continuing to work with her patients as before.

How could such a staff member be effective in helping very disturbed patients, when her room reflected a severe split in her own personality? The fact is that even before she joined the institution, she had been very accomplished in her work. She had left her parental home to enter college when only sixteen. All her life she had been a top student, largely supporting herself by scholarships and part-time jobs. All through her years of being a staff member she was most successful in her work, taking on responsibility for the operation of some aspects of the School in addition to her work with the patients. True, in her room she acted out a split in her personality—an inner conflict that had beset her for a very long time. But since the total milieu supported her, and because it was required by the nature of work that was so important to her, she could permit herself to thus expose a hidden inner split and still not let it interfere with maintaining integration in her work. The room disintegrated, split wide open, but never she. Working through the split caused by her past life experiences was no easy task; but the total milieu permitted her to do this and at the same time help patients do the same for themselves. What then is the difference between such a staff member and a patient? Not the cleavages in the unconscious—but the strength of the ego to contain it all.

In many ways it is easier for staff members who live in the institution to make it become home for them. But to be truly effective even those who never roomed at the School had to undergo a parallel process of feeling at home there. After about six months or so, usually these staff members would find themselves spending more and more time at the School: taking more of their meals there even during their free time and dropping in at all hours of the day and night. When they started, these extra visits would be explained by some excuse to themselves that the work required it; then they lingered on for hours afterwards. Without doubt the work and all it entailed, including learning about themselves, was fascinating to them or else they could not have remained with us for so long.

To succeed with these disturbed patients, one must really live with them. Learning to do so requires an incredible amount of emotional energy, and a long time. One has to immerse oneself for a considerable stretch of time in the therapeutic milieu so that it becomes a large part of one's own life. It usually takes two years for a staff member to feel he is part of the life of his group and the institution. After this has happened, it then becomes possible for him to considerably reduce the time spent at the institution, though it never can be restricted to a forty-hour work week; but then neither can any work that is really important to oneself. Once the total therapeutic milieu has become part of oneself, one can call on it immediately, no longer needing to live there physically in order to do so. And the patients feel this: they know which of the staff can afford to live outside the institution and have it still remain a significant part of their lives. Naturally, they would like to receive more of the worker's time; but having made himself a part of the milieu, when he is with the patients the worker is truly *with* them, not just working for them. This is what counts. When this point is reached, the staff member usually finds it more agreeable to live elsewhere. But it is never a good idea for him to live too far away from the institution. Full-time staff members at the Orthogenic School always lived within the aura of the institution —that is, in its immediate surroundings—because in this way, though not living within the institution, they were at all times part of its immediate community. Those who lived farther away—consultants, specialists such as dance teachers—skillful though they were in their various professions remained essentially only casual visitors. In the task of effecting recovery from mental illness they did very little, although as consultants they helped the staff in their work, or as specialists in some activity they enriched the lives of the patients.

Quite spontaneously, "traditions" evolved which facilitated a staff member's feeling that the institution could become his home. These traditions increased his empathy for what feels good to patients. For example, it became a custom to give a new staff member some token of welcome when he moved into his quarters: a plant, some flowers, or what not. His appreciation later helped him prepare the welcome for a new patient. Most of the living-in staff arranged for their own private celebrations, such as Christmas parties, birthday celebrations, and other special occasions. Naturally many lifelong friendships were formed, and a few married each other. Quite a number came to feel that they had their nicest Christmases or birthdays at the School. Here is another indivisible aspect of life in a mental institution: if those working there do not profit from and enjoy the work, life for the patients will not be enjoyable. A staff which thoroughly enjoys arranging parties for the patients will be likely to do the same for themselves, or the zest would soon go out of the first. Those who feel that doing it for the patients is an unwelcome burden will not do it for each other either. If one lives closely and willingly together with the patients and other staff members, the "tender loving care" which one extends to the patients will in some measure be automatically transferred to relationships among the staff. There were quite a few "parties" at the School, some for everybody working there, some for various smaller groups. Doing much for others cannot help arousing some resentful feelings in those who thus extend themselves; doing something special for themselves righted the balance somewhat.

Christmas may serve as an example; the more important a holiday, the deeper the emotions it arouses. Christmas always brings back childish longings, memories of both happy and unhappy experiences one has had. The "Christmas depression" is a well-known psychiatric phenomenon, the result of hopes aroused and dashed. Working for others, as staff members of a psychiatric institution have to do if the patients are to have a nice Christmas, takes one's mind off how one feels about working while others celebrate. It permits temporarily forgetting or repressing one's disappointment at no longer being the person who receives; but it does not do away with these feelings—if anything, it makes them more acute. When all the work is done and one can no longer keep oneself busy, it all grows more painfully depressing. So it became customary for the staff at the School to have a Christmas party for themselves at this moment of letdown. It took place after all preparations for the Christmas morning celebration of the patients had been completed, beginning late at night on Christmas Eve. Since the beginner might feel that preparing for this party was only another burden, the senior staff did it; and efforts were made to keep the party secret so that it would be a surprise for the newcomers. While Christmas office parties are almost a universal custom, what made this different was how it was done.

On their first Christmas at the School, new staff members sometimes felt very low and, although invited, would not join the Christmas get-together. But the staff were experienced in helping patients who refused to participate in events which they feared would contribute to their own depressive feelings. So when this happened with a new staff member, a friend or the one who worked closely with him would join him in his room; not to drag him to the party but just to be with him there. The first reaction was as expected; the reluctant staff member would not really want company, and least of all somebody leaving the party to be with him at this time. But the experienced staff member had learned how to break through to patients, and the same skill and desire to reach the lonely one was brought into play. Empathy with the loneliness of a patient which does not extend also to one's colleague is a professional concern that comes with the job, not from the heart, and which is also ineffective on the job. The fact that a senior staff member was willing to spend considerable time away from his friends and their celebration to be with the lonely one never failed to bring the desired response; though sometimes a second or even third staff member had to join in to convince the reluctant one that he was really wanted, and that the others could not enjoy themselves knowing him to be outside the circle. It was experiences such as this which gave some staff members the nicest Christmas they ever had. And in the following years they were able to make it a much better Christmas not only for the patients but also for themselves and the other staff members.

The staff had to form a community. It has been recognized that communal life is of great importance in the treatment of mental patients, and efforts are made to create it through group meetings and trying to let patients, so to say, rule themselves. The merit of this parliamentary palavering is doubtful; that it works at all is due to the patients' need for community. But it is not the patients who can or should form the community and control its life; if they were able to do that effectively, why would they be mental patients? Only the staff can provide the symbol, image, and matrix of the community which alone permits a truly therapeutic feeling of it to exist among the patients.

The relationship between professional and nonprofessional staff is a good example of the value of institutional indivisibility and community. In order to achieve this closeness of shared purpose at the School, some professional staff members volunteered to work together daily with one group of the nonprofessional staff. A counselor would spend an hour or more of his free time with the cleaning staff, letting them know what was particularly important to take care of this day, chatting about the patients as they discussed the work that needed to be done. In doing so, all got to know each other as individuals, becoming interested not only in each other's work but also in some aspects of their private lives. Unless some sort of friendship developed between the individuals it would not work out, and we would have to ask another staff member to volunteer. But we could not rely only on the few staff members who were the official liaisons to the nonprofessional staff. Unless a staff member who was working with a group of patients established some sort of personal relation with those who took care of the patients' rooms, and sometimes dropped in for a chat with those who were cleaning, there would be no sense of community. In short, the rest of the staff could not simply rely on these volunteers to create the feeling of a common enterprise; unless everybody did something to establish it and keep it going, the work suffered.

Other professional staff members spent some time each day working with the kitchen staff, planning the meals and explaining why the patients wanted this or that, while encouraging the kitchen staff to make their own suggestions. Some of the most successful meals were the kitchen staff's ideas, which often required a great deal of extra work and even overtime, resulting in dinners that were much more elaborate than any the professional staff would have dared suggest. Still other staff members interacted similarly with the laundry staff, the seamstress, and others. Of course, relations with the office staff also had to be carefully nurtured. All the minutiae of the innumerable daily needs of the patients and the means for meeting them—for example, buses and all other necessities and niceties for an outing—would not have worked so smoothly if the person arranging them had not known for whom and what purpose the enterprise was being planned, and felt personally gratified by its success. For a time, under pressure from the university administration, an effort was made to have the ordering, bookkeeping, and so on done by the appropriate university departments, such as central purchasing. The central offices were most cooperative; all was very well and efficiently done. But without the special human touch that comes with knowing the people for whom it is done, the results were disastrous. Money would be spent, for example, on an excursion to some distant place; but there would be so much irritation around it, and so many unforeseen hitches, that the excursion was useless. Those who made the arrangements were not personally involved. Before long, all this was handled by staff members who knew the patients and the work of the School, and understood the whys and wherefores of what, without such knowledge, must have often seemed strange undertakings.

The official liaison between professional and nonprofessional staff met at least once a month with all the nonprofessional staff and the director in a formal meeting to talk things over. This would have achieved very little if most issues had not already been settled in informal ways during daily contact through more personal relations. Occasionally, material help with the work of the institution did come from these meetings. For example, when I submitted the plans and blueprints for a new building for criticism, a janitor pointed out a serious oversight in the planning which neither the professional staff, the architects, nor I had discovered. Without the janitor's discovery, a practically irremediable error would have seriously interfered with the operation of this structure. But as with many other formal arrangements, these meetings served as a symbol of the spirit to which the School's whole actual operation gave body and substance.

One example of the close cooperation which grew up centers on a mute schizophrenic patient who for months not only refused to defecate into the toilet, which was all right, but felt the need to stuff up toilets so effectively that not only did they overflow—he saw to that by repeated flushings after the toilet had been obstructed—but many toilets became unworkable. Sometimes for days on end, the pipes had to be rodded out by the engineers; and it often took ingenuity to extract the obstructing objects which the patient selected as suitable for achieving his purpose. If the janitors who had to clean up the mess, and the engineers who had to do the complex work of rodding out (sometimes all the way to the city sewer) had not had a personal interest in the patient and his doings, their resentment sooner or later would have forced us to put restrictions on the patient. But each morning all the toilets were in good working order again. The real payoff came when this up-to-then mute patient not only suddenly commenced defecating into the toilet, but also started to talk. Now all the stuffed-up words overflowed, as the toilets had before. When this patient began all at once to talk, it seemed such a miracle to those who had worked so hard at unplugging the toilets that it was as though through their patient labor they had unplugged the patient which, in a way, they had.

Despite all the hardships, this breakthrough was a great gain for the School. While the other patients naturally resented it when they had to walk to another part of the building, sometimes even to another interconnected building, to find a usable toilet and had to be helped not to take it out on the spoiler, they didn't fail to notice that the institution was willing to go to such lengths when we felt that it would be damaging to a patient to force him to conform. For several other patients it was an experience which permitted them to open up about anxieties and resentments around elimination, which they might not have done if the plugging up of the toilets had not provided the necessary stimulus. Our acceptance of it proved to them that we would be able to do the same for their fantasies. Some of the stories they were then able to tell showed that they too, in some measure, had become unplugged; and this made the whole incident all the more worthwhile. When it was all over, the glee some patients revealed that this patient had dared to do it was much more impressive than any resentment that had been voiced when it was going on.

It also means a great deal to the nonprofessional staff to see that because of their work, a mute creature turns into a human being who can appreciate what they have been doing for him all along. It is not easy to launder the clothes of a soiler; to mend newly torn clothes daily; to put in a zipper ten or twenty times when it is going to be torn out again immediately, unless it is understood that there is a good and meaningful reason for doing so. That one is paid to do such a job is no reason to accept it. How could a maid prepare the bed for a total stranger with care, or serve him his meals with interest, if she knows nothing about him except that he makes work for her? Only when she understands why this new patient needs to smear his food over the dining table, the chair, and the floor, and why he should receive a very special menu only to waste most or all of it, will cleaning it up become a meaningful task. Personal involvement is even more important in those who clean the patients' rooms. If their belongings are strewn all over the place as they are apt to be, these will not be handled with care and the room put into that particular order the patients like, if those who do the cleaning do not have a personal interest in the patients, and feel that through their labor they are helping them to recover.

Many of our patients had special pillows, blankets, and rugs which were very important to them—for example, the rug that has to be placed just right to secure their area, or their stuffed animals— though on leaving their room they may throw all these things carelessly into a heap in a corner. The patients expect and need the reassurance that we will take care and see to it that when they return, they will find these objects in their proper place. It also makes quite a difference in a maid's care of a room if she has a personal relationship with the professional staff who work with this group of patients, and the staff are ready to encourage her feeling of importance in their common undertaking.

Nowhere in the literature on mental hospitals—with the exception of some writings influenced by or based on the work of the Orthogenic School—is there mention of how much success in treatment depends on the personal satisfaction the staff derives from witnessing how they have helped restore a damaged human being to full humanity. And this applies not just to the director and the psychiatrists, but to all the personnel. It was a great pleasure to observe how when former patients returned to the School for a visit, they spontaneously asked to see the nonprofessional staff they remembered so well. As a matter of fact, it was more often members of the nonprofessional group who would still be with the School after many years had passed. These staff members had remained with the institution long enough to experience deep satisfaction in their work, and to behold the fruits of their labor in the restorative task. As they did this over the years they came to enjoy it more, and became more convinced of the importance of what they were doing.

Today there is a considerable desire for greater communality in living. But the reason most so-called communities usually cannot keep their members and exist on the fringes of society, often as its parasites, lies in a crucial misconception about communal life. Most of these communities are formed "to live the communal life," and therefore they concentrate on it. I am convinced communal life can flourish only if it exists for an aim outside itself. Community is viable if it is the outgrowth of a deep involvement in a purpose which is other than, or above, that of being a community.

When speaking of communal life, it is usually tribal life that comes to mind. It is true that in preliterate societies a very active communal life can be found. The origins of society are shrouded in impenetrable mist, and we don't know how our ancestors became human beings living in families and social groups. But it is reasonable to assume that what made them form groups were the tasks—first of all, survival—which required working together communally, rather than any conscious desire for such a life. It is not pure chance that at the Orthogenic School, when talking together as a staff, we often spontaneously remarked that to survive under the onslaught of the patients we had to help each other; that we had to work together as a group, a community, if we wanted to carry out effectively what we considered our task: not controlling patients or making them over according to some preconceived notions, but accepting and using therapeutically what they "dished out" so we all could gain from the experience.

The Israeli kibbutz is possibly the best contemporary example of communality. It was founded not by people who planned to live a communal life, as some of the kibbutz protagonists now want to pretend. The history of the kibbutz proves that it was the particular and inescapable conditions surrounding the founding of agricultural settlements in Israel by immigrant Jews that led to the formation of viable settings for communal living (3, 15, 110). Were these conditions no longer existent, I am convinced the kibbutz would not survive, regardless of whether some of its members might like to continue communal living. The fact is that when very serious efforts were made to create kibbutzim in urban settings, where the members worked at different tasks, the communities fell apart.

The staff of a mental institution will be more effective, and find the work more rewarding, to the degree that they are able to form a community for a purpose. It is not necessary that all live together as members of a community; but during working hours they must function as one, though each person must retain his own private life. This allows for both community at work and privacy elsewhere, which I believe is the only way modern Western man can incorporate part of his life into a community without damage to the individuality we all cherish.

The staff's ability to function as a community is greatly aided by the fact that most of the staff members, whatever the role in which they later function—counselor, teacher, psychologist, psychotherapist—began their training as counselors. As counselors they all learned about becoming part of the community and what is involved in helping psychiatric patients. This is also the reason why in discussing the staff this report concentrates on the counselors. On many occasions during the year, every staff member functions in this capacity, whatever his main assignment may be. For example, all staff members participate as equals in the big events of the community, a birthday celebration, a major outing, Thanksgiving dinner. Every staff member is present on these special occasions, and often, for example, director, psychotherapist, teacher, or counselor alike serve the patients their meals, or in many other ways function as equals not only in theory but in practice.

Only because of this common background, and the many common experiences, can the staff, as workers, form a community of equals, whatever their level of training, knowledge, or experience may be. As they work together for the patients, they are all equal members of this community, which they create for the sake of the patients; the patients are living in this created community. If all goes well, at the end of their stay the patients should be ready and able to become members of the large and very diffuse community which is the outside world. It is a mistake to think that they could simply move from being in the community, which is the therapeutic milieu, to becoming part of it. Of course the staff, while forming the matrix for the life within the community which is the institution, must also simultaneously be members of that larger community, our common world; while the patients must live entirely within the therapeutic community until they are ready to join the wider community of everyday life.

21 | *The Total Involvement of Staff Members*

All important decisions concerning the patient are made by those who work most closely with him. Once he has been admitted, the decisions affecting the patient's life and well-being are made with the same concern that went into his acceptance into the institution. In an emergency situation, when there isn't time to discuss a problem with a senior staff member and the patient's therapist (in individual sessions), then those who are most involved with him make the decisions. The rest of the staff are informed of this as soon as they get together, which is usually the following day or before.

Whenever time permits, the entire staff are invited to express their opinions on important matters—such as whether or not the patient should have a visit with relatives and for how long; whether the time has come for him to go outside the institution by himself, and if so, where to, and for how long; whether he should move to another group, and with this to other workers; and the most far-reaching decisions of all: whether the time has come to think about his leaving the institution and how to help him plan for his future life. But in all these decisions, after everybody has been heard and his views considered, the judgment that prevails is that of those who have become most deeply attached to the patient, and he to them. Unless they have the decisive say, after such full discussion, how else could they, for example, prepare him to go for a walk alone with such a good inner attitude that the patient feels secure because of it, and desires to return?

Naturally, these larger decisions are not arrived at in one sitting, nor on the basis of a presentation of facts followed by a vote. Discussing the reasons why one staff member thinks a proposed course is best for the patient, even when everybody agrees, is a lengthy process. It is an occasion for gaining deeper understanding not just of the patient, but also of what motivates us to prefer one course of action over another. And reaching a common understanding where initially there was some disagreement is even more helpful, not just for those who are involved, but also for all others who by observing their co-workers gain a better understanding of what motivates themselves.

This cannot be done as a routine or as good practice to enhance the staff's efficiency in speeding the patient's recovery. That merely would be the application of a particular method, and would not necessarily lead to a different approach to each human being, depending on the specifics of his situation at the moment. Everything a staff member says or does must be taken with the utmost seriousness, otherwise these meetings will deteriorate into a purely utilitarian practice.

For example, it is simple for a staff member to think that it isn't time for a patient to visit with his family, because of his relation to them, his underlying pathology, and overt behavior. It is somewhat more difficult to acknowledge to oneself that one would prefer the patient not to visit his family because one feels one's relation to the patient is still too tenuous. Then the problem becomes: Should the visit not take place, so the patient will relate to the staff member, when he doesn't already feel inclined to do so? What, then, is lacking in their relation? Or, why does the staff member feel that the impact of the visit will give the parents so much power over the patient that it will threaten the worker's relationship with him? Once this point has been reached, it is relatively easy for the staff member to recognize why he feels so insecure about the patient's attachment to him, and what can be done to strengthen it. It requires a major emotional and intellectual effort to recognize that one's feelings about one's own family—the hopes and disappointments surrounding one's own visits with relatives—may tend to influence a decision about the patient's visiting with his family. Particularly to the inexperienced staff worker, a whole world opens up when he sees how what seemed a simple management decision may have the most deeply rooted sources in his own attitudes and life history, and in his very personal relation to the patient.

If, on the other hand, the staff member has decided in favor of a visit, it might seem unproblematic to prepare the patient for it. It is agreed that the patient, though ambivalently, looks forward to the visit, so it is just a technicality to pack his overnight case for him. Or so the beginner might conclude, thinking he has little feelings about doing this. But a discussion of what a worker packed for a patient in one instance revealed that he had sent the patient on an overnight visit with enough clothes to last a week or more; while in another case, there was hardly enough contained in the bag to last the patient a day. When this was brought out, it was hard for the worker in the first case to maintain that there was not some ambivalence involved which led to his wanting the patient to stay away for a much longer time; while for the second worker, it was difficult to deny that he had some resentment at the patient's preferring to leave him even for a short while.

Difficult as it is, it is nevertheless easier for a staff member to understand the origins and consequences of ambivalence or even negative feelings than to acknowledge feelings of a definite positive attachment. Many staff members, particularly at the beginning of their work, are much more ready to explore and even acknowledge why they shortchanged a patient, than what in them has helped the patient. For example, they would be quite ready to report with obvious delight some new thing the patient had done, but they were most hesitant to investigate what they had thought, felt, and wished for the patient immediately before he became able to do it. The patient had done it, that was great; what more was there to talk about? Why should they turn themselves inside out when all had gone so well? Until the staff members can see the results of their positive attitudes, they will never really be able to accept how deep an impact their negative feelings can make on the patient.

All of us seem to feel and react in much the same way. If we have made a mistake, we regret it, and we will try to do better next time. But that doesn't commit us deeply to the other person involved. Yet if things we do have far-reaching positive consequences, this implies to all people of good will—and those who are not have no business working with mental patients—a terrible obligation. This proves that staff members can make the patient get better; and if this is so, how can they shirk the responsibility? In my experience every new staff member defended himself against recognizing how terribly important he could be to a patient. Each felt it much easier to admit to having made a mistake (convinced that he wouldn't repeat it) than to accept the commitment which comes from realizing his importance to others. We all can live quite easily knowing we've made an error, or that we've been lazy or inattentive; but it's not that easy to realize that we are able to break, or have broken, another person's heart. Going through this realization makes a patient become a staff member's very personal, very own project. Having had a decisive vote about his admission only sets the stage. Without recognizing this commitment, a relationship of this sort would never take place.

An example may illustrate this. A staff member had been working very hard for several months with a most difficult patient who, largely because of these efforts, had begun to make considerable progress. Another staff member joined her for a day, interested in learning how she managed to survive under the onslaught of the patient's violent outbursts. The patient had been told that this staff member was only visiting. Suddenly he reverted to his original behavior, becoming totally unreachable. Distraught, his worker asked a senior staff member for help. Being less involved, he immediately understood the patient's behavior. He sensed that despite what he had been told, the patient feared that the visiting staff member might take the place of his worker. When the senior staff member explained this to the worker and she appreciated the patient's fears, unwarranted as they were, he immediately got back into contact.

As devoted as his worker was to the patient, later discussions revealed that she had some reservations about exposing herself at all times to behavior which was so difficult to take. Unconsciously she didn't want to feel deeply obliged to continue working with him indefinitely; to prevent this, she had not permitted herself to recognize how terribly important she had become to the patient. This incident gave her confidence in how much she meant to the patient, how desperate was his anxiety about losing her. Because of the better understanding of what she already had achieved with him, she no longer worried about whether she would have the emotional strength to continue to work with him.

In every staff meeting all suggestions, whether from the senior psychiatrist or the newest staff members, had to be viewed as equally important. Unless the staff member has a deep feeling that the senior's opinions are correct, he will never be able to implement them in his daily life with the patient. How the staff member *feels* about what he has learned has a much greater impact on his work with the patient than what he now *knows* should be done. The patient understandably often reacts more to the tone in which something is said, or the inner emotional intent behind what is done, than to the obvious, overt content.

No intellectual understanding of how important it is to give a patient a long and pleasant bath, to play with him in the tub, even to encourage him to defecate into the tub (which in the case of a psychotic boy broke the lifelong inability to move his bowels without the help of enemas) will do if the staff member hasn't really examined his own feelings about the body and its excretions. The patient knows how the staff members feel about him, and about his body, by the way in which he is approached in all the innumerable daily encounters: how they wake him up and put him to bed, feed him, hold his hand when he tries to hurt himself or others. But these underlying feelings are most clearly revealed when a staff member is physically or psychologically attacked, slapped or kicked, held up to ridicule, lied to, spit upon; how he reacts when the patient smears his stools on himself, the furniture, or the staff member.

It is useless—worse, counterproductive—to tell a staff member he should be able to view such symptomatic behavior in the same way he would view another patient who always needs to be best on the playing field, or needs to please and ingratiate himself to the staff. Until a staff member has experienced a number of deep insights into his own unconscious motivations, through searching discussions with others of the staff, however much the individual worker knows about the patients it is not likely to enable him to be an effective therapist. In addition to realizing that the patient is expressing his view of his place in the order of things, regardless of how strange or upsetting the behavior might be, and understanding this on an intellectual level, the staff member must also feel further empathy, which stems from becoming truly aware of his own motivating emotions.

But if a worker has gained this insight through similar experiences, while the patient's behavior may still worry him greatly, it will no longer be personally upsetting.

It is impossible to teach this kind of empathetic sensitivity. Staff members learn it only through experiencing their own attitudes; if one is vomited upon it is "natural" that one is disgusted, but rather than seeing this reaction as "right" or "wrong," it should be understood and respected as an important indication of one's own feelings. Only then can workers accept that these are important messages about inner attitudes (though not necessarily the best or the only way human beings can react to situations, or to each other).

A staff member must understand how terrorized a patient would have to be to hold onto his stools for weeks on end. He must realize how this would force him to think continuously about avoiding defecation, a preoccupation which would consume all of his time. Then when he holds the patient's hand for hours while he is sitting on the toilet, empathy with the patient's panic anxiety about letting go, or dirtying himself, becomes the staff member's dominant emotion. There is no place left for disgust. It was this direct empathy with the panic about letting go that permitted the patient mentioned earlier to finally eliminate in the bathtub.

Unresolved remnants of one's past can either be the most serious impediments to working with psychiatric patients or the greatest of assets. They are impediments when they are *acted out*; assets when they are judiciously *acted upon*. Those who work with psychiatric patients are often expected to refrain from acting on the basis of their own emotional preoccupations. Since we all have emotional problems, this is impossible. Without these emotional preoccupations, the therapist could not do the work; they are the main incentive for him to help psychiatric patients on their incredibly difficult road to recovery. *Without this source for empathy with the patient*, psychotherapeutic work could never succeed. Everybody who wants to work with psychiatric patients must have some ability to develop empathy. One of the main reasons for a worker's trial visit was to ascertain whether he did have this ability.

Empathy is very different from sympathy. Sympathy, too, is important, but much less so. With compassion we feel deeply *for* the other, with feelings of sympathy, *with* him. For example, if we think he is distressed, we feel sorry for him that he feels so badly. In empathy, we experience for brief periods the feelings of the other—that is, we feel *the same way* he does. There can be no empathy without compassion and sympathy, but for empathy to occur, another experience must implement them: an introspection which, on the basis of our experience, permits us to feel as the other person does. If we can't find within ourselves something closely akin to what is going on in the other person through introspection, then we can't empathically understand him. This may be illustrated by a simple example presented by Kohut (78):

> *We see a person who is unusually tall. It is not to be disputed that this person's unusual size is an important fact for our psychological assessment—without introspection and empathy, however, his size remains simply a physical attribute. Only when we think ourselves into his place by vicarious introspection; begin to feel his unusual size as if it were our own, and thus revive inner experiences in which we had been unusual or conspicuous—only then there begins for us an appreciation of the meaning the unusual size may have for this person. . . .*

Unfortunately, in English there is very little literature on empathy. Were there greater understanding and appreciation of the important role of empathy in all good human relations, behavior modification could not enjoy such favor among psychologists as it does at the moment. Anybody who could have empathy with the object of behavioral manipulations—including the inner experience of how degrading it is to permit oneself to be bought off by candies or tokens by somebody who claims to "know" how one should behave— would feel a revulsion when thus manipulating another person. The dominant traits of our culture and its pragmatic and behavioristic temper are mirrored in its tendency not only to manipulate things but persons as if they were objects, as opposed to merely understanding them and allowing them to work matters out in their own way.

There is considerable German philosophical and psychological literature on the problem of empathy, and many different words to designate its various forms (104, 130). When translated in accordance with its original Greek meaning, the word "sympathy" is best rendered as "feeling with" somebody; empathy requires in addition a "feeling oneself into" somebody. The word "empathy" became part of the English language only as a translation of the German *Einfuehlung*, "feeling in," to which it hardly does justice. As a matter of fact, the Webster dictionary definition of 1966 is outright misleading. It states that empathy is "the projection of one's own personality into the personality of another in order to understand him better."

Empathy is not anything that can be done "in order to," that is, for a purpose; as a matter of fact, nothing interferes more with empathy than a person's being goal-directed in any way. To understand something, one must call on his intellectual resources, such as scientific knowledge or his realized experiences; in short, understanding is a rational process. Freud does not specifically discuss empathy, but relies instead on his explanation of what is going on when it occurs. He speaks of what he calls "the sympathy of one unconscious to another," thus making it clear that this can never be a rational process. On the contrary, he warns that conscious rationality interferes with it (42).

Projection is entirely different from that definition of empathy. *Projection is essentially self-centered, while empathy, though drawing on one's inner experiences, is centered on the other.* In projection, one sees oneself in the other; in empathy, one feels the other in oneself, not as a totality as in introjection, but only as the other is feeling at this very moment, and without going beyond the boundaries of the self, which remain intact.

Everybody who comes to work at the Orthogenic School comes because of inner motivations which might best be described as compassion. While he may only be aware of his compassion for the unfortunate patients, a staff member also hopes for sympathy and consideration for his own difficulties, which are a strong factor in his desire to help others. This compassion motivates the worker to try to relieve the patient's distress, to make him more comfortable. But it still comes from something extraneous to the situation, as well meant and profoundly felt as it may be. So while compassion motivates one to do something for the patient, believing that it will be good for him, it can still lead one severely astray. Approaching the work scientifically, and understanding exactly what the patient's psychological problems are, results in decisions which are based on what he may need in the long run, rather than what he needs at the moment.

Useful as scientific knowledge about pathology and psychological problems and mechanisms is, it can only tell us about man in general, not about a specific man at that precise moment in his life, in a very specific relation to a particular person.

For example, in an incident in which a relatively new staff member encouraged patients to throw water around (described in some detail in the following chapter), the worker thought it would be a relief to let go of self-control; he even thought that the patients in general might benefit if they could unleash their frustration and act out their violent feelings. But he hadn't really considered his relationship with them at the moment. Thinking that the worker had relinquished his ego-supporting role and had temporarily suspended his ability to control expressions of anger, they became carried away by their own anxieties. Because the worker acted out of sympathy, and projected his own feelings onto them, he wasn't able to move freely with them as the situation developed. He was carried away by his own desire to act out of anger. But, had he felt empathy, he would have been able to see at just what point the patients became frightened by the lack of control and needed help in re-establishing control over their aggressions; he would have "felt into" their fear of being swept away by their feelings.

Only empathy gives us this immediate recognition to which, in the therapeutic work, knowledge is then brought to bear. A major task of the therapeutic milieu, therefore, is to develop empathy out of compassion and sympathy. The worker will then be able to respond to the patient, not only out of general knowledge of what's involved in therapy, but with compassion for what the patient needs at this unique moment.

Most of us have experienced "empathy" with the grief of a person who has lost a loved one. Yet while we feel with him, we don't really understand all that moves him. This depends on what the departed person meant to him, including all of the complexities of their relationship. A complete understanding of the other person would require our comprehension of all this and more; yet such an intellectual preoccupation would seriously deplete our "feeling into" the other person, which can only come from our own experience. From our own experiences with separation, we can feel how bleak the world appears to him at the moment.

Olden (89), by a telling story, elucidates the nature of empathy. Shortly after she began psychoanalytic treatment of an eight-year-old boy, he dictated a statement to her which was to be shown to her housekeeper—whom he had encountered only once and by chance, and who knew nothing about him except that he was a patient. He asked that this housekeeper be called in to read the story, which she did silently. It went as follows: "My mother is a stinker. My father is a stinker. My mother is ugly and has wrinkles. Christine's [the analyst's] hair is horrible. . . etc." When the housekeeper had finished reading, the boy, after waiting for a reply that was not forthcoming, said, "That's quite a story, isn't it?", to which the housekeeper answered, "This is a very sad story." The comment bowled over the little boy, for as he had seen it, he had written not a sad but a bitterly angry story. Therefore he asked the housekeeper why she called it a sad story. "Because," she replied, "it tells how little you like yourself." "To know the child, his background, his fears, his recent experiences, will not help the adult to feel as the child feels in this or that situation, if he lacks the capacity for genuine empathy . . . [which] has the capacity to trespass the object's screens of defenses, behind which the real feelings may hide."

In a way, empathy is a back-and-forth, oscillating process; in the "back" swing, one goes back into one's own primary process thinking and feeling; in the "forth," one returns to one's adult integration of these same processes and uses them to come closer to the core of the other's experience of the moment. Since these primary processes all go back to the time before our personality was fully formed and became controlled by the ego, empathy requires that "the adult [be able to] allow himself to live with the sufferings of his childhood and reach a degree of reconciliation with them" (18).

All this is theoretical. The problem is how the therapeutic milieu can help staff members reconcile their childhood sufferings and thus enable themselves to feel empathy, to feel into those primitive basic emotional experiences which characterized our world when we were children—and which, if we have not integrated them into our personality, continue to interfere with our ability to cope in the present. Only the staff's ability to achieve such reconciliation can form the basis from which they can help the patients do the same.

In line with our views on the importance of forming relations based on empathy, patient and worker mutually selected each other.

The selection was usually unconscious. The patient sensed something about the worker which made him or her feel that this particular staff member would be better than any other. And the worker thought that the patient was particularly interesting and appealing. Then as the work progressed, the worker would find that unconscious pressures coming from crucial but unresolved childhood residues resounded to complementary ones in the patient. This may be illustrated by Dana and her worker.

Dana, an anorexic girl, had spent three prolonged periods in the psychiatric ward of a university hospital to save her life. During the first two hospitalizations, the friendly and accepting attitudes of a nurse—the opposite of the extreme rejection she had experienced with her mother—had soon permitted her to gain weight and be out of danger. But within months after each return home she was again dangerously anorexic, leading to the next hospitalization. The third time nothing seemed to help; nothing could induce her to eat, and artificial feedings failed to improve the situation. In addition, she became openly schizophrenic: she would stand catatonically stock still, unable to move, at the window, looking at the sky.

After her transfer to the Orthogenic School she soon began to eat, within a few months becoming obese, but without change in her catatonic rigidity. One way we induced her to eat was to place her bed by the window so that she could look out, watching the sky, as much as she wished. Otherwise we were as stuck with her as she was with herself, despite all we tried. Then a new worker took to her, and Dana in turn seemed more ready to be approached by this worker than she had by anyone else. Dana's behavior did not change toward others; but, as became known much later, she viciously assaulted this worker, beating her up each time the two were alone. It was amazing how they managed to keep it a secret.

The worker, by now deeply devoted to Dana but as yet unsure of her position within the staff and of what was expected of her in such a situation, kept these beatings hidden, as did Dana. The worker revealed later that she had kept Dana's attacks a secret partly because she felt she did not merit anything better, since she did not know how to help this wretched girl; but mostly because she feared that if she admitted her incompetence, she would no longer be considered suitable to remain on the staff and to work with Dana. The relation had become so vitally important to the worker that she was ready to protect it at all cost—even that of enduring almost daily beatings, severe pinchings, kicking, and other mistreatments. Interestingly enough, Dana always managed to hit or kick her when nobody could see it, and to hurt her in places on her body which the worker could hide, so that others did not become aware of what went on.

Eventually, after more than a year, Dana became obviously less rigid though not any less schizophrenic. The rest of the staff believed that things were progressing with Dana and the worker, however slowly. But the bruises could no longer always be hidden; and the worker's explanations that they were due to her clumsiness and other chance circumstances began to wear thin.

The staff, concerned with the worker's well-being, refused to accept her excuses and guessed the truth. Eventually the worker admitted that because she felt inadequate in helping Dana, she had accepted being punished by her. By letting herself be pummeled, she was at least of some use to Dana.

The worker's "confession" of deserving punishment permitted others to argue that her failure to do better with Dana was not a sufficient explanation—particularly given the obvious fact that she had done better with Dana than anybody else, small though the progress was. The worker's belief was a bit shaken when the others, whose devotion to their patients she knew, told her they would not accept such abuse, because to do so would be demeaning to both the patient and themselves. Yet for quite some time, the worker insisted there were no other reasons but her deep involvement with Dana. Finally, when asked whether Dana, or her relation to Dana, resembled or reminded her of any other person or relationship she had known, the worker came to the startling realization that her relation to Dana reminded her of that to her next younger sister, though she could not understand why—because this sister had never attacked her, but on the contrary, had always been very much dependent on her.

To summarize what took hard work and considerable time to unravel: the worker, as eldest of several sisters, had had to play the "mother" role with her younger siblings from an early age. Their mother claimed to be incapacitated by illness, and while the worker had accepted this consciously, unconsciously she had never believed it and thus had resented taking full responsibility for her sisters, which seriously interfered with her own life. One afternoon, seemingly without reason—but in fact exasperated by the too heavy burden of responsibility—she had run after the oldest of her sisters with a butcher knife, with murderous intent. Unconsciously she was outraged by this sister, who not only didn't help with the younger sisters but continued to expect to be taken care of by the worker, when her mother continued to demand that she take responsibility for all her sisters, irrespective of their age. She had entirely "forgotten" this event all these years, remembering only how much she had loved all her sisters, and her pride in having effectively mothered them. When she had gone after her sister with the knife, she had been so "out of it" that she did not know what might have happened if her sister had not been able to elude her, giving her a chance to get hold of herself. Though the entire event was repressed, she had somehow continued to feel like a murderer who deserved severe punishment.

Until she met the worker, Dana could not give up her catatonic immobility, since any move—given the inner rage that consumed her—would have meant attack. As it later turned out, Dana had somehow guessed that with this person she might dare act with open violence without being destroyed in retaliation. It began with Dana's kicking the worker under the table as if by chance. When the worker accepted it—consciously pleased because Dana had begun to move her body, unconsciously encouraging her to continue the mistreatment so as to relieve her own guilt—Dana became more vicious in her attacks. Full of violent anger against her mother, she had found in her worker a mother figure who was ready to accept her fury.

Thus each had sensed in the other a strong psychological attitude, or constellation of motives, in which they could derive satisfaction for an unconscious need. The worker's need to be punished for what she had wanted to do to her sister was satisfied, and so was Dana's need to discharge rage, so that she no longer had to store it catatonically. The attraction was based on complementary needs rather than on identification. This is true in most cases where patient and worker spontaneously select each other, rather than the worker alone preferring a particular patient.

Some students of the problem of staff members' spontaneous selection of patients—Rosen, for example (100)—too facilely adduced identification as its only cause. Later she extended her findings to take in the age group of children that teachers preferred to work with, and found identification a causative factor here, too (101). No doubt identification is a frequent basis for object choice, but such relationships remain static and restricting if the identification is with qualities one already possesses. From a dynamic point of view, identification is acceptable only as a temporary phase. For their own development the young certainly need to identify with suitable adults. But to grow toward maturity, even they must identify with characteristics they don't yet possess, but wish to acquire. The story is very different when the mature person, who should provide leadership, identifies with the immature; this will then fix the immature one to his immaturity, since he cannot relinquish that which forms the essence of the mature person's attachment to him. Thus, while

Rosen's findings are correct, the identifications she describes represent an immature object choice on the part of adults, narcissistically pleasing but not suitable for a constructive relation; because instead of promoting growth, it retards or prevents it. Even in education the best teacher, while he behaves so that the students can identify with him, does not himself identify with the student. This is even more true in therapy, and workers at the School who identified with patients never worked out. Only those whose commitment was to supply the patient with something that was missing in his life succeeded in helping the patient toward his autonomy. Sometimes the worker would find some ego ability to be missing in himself, and thus had to develop this aspect of his personality to be able to provide it for the patient. This led to the challenge the worker needed to become more mature himself.

The patient, on the other hand, may benefit greatly from identifying with a staff member's emotional maturity. While it was sometimes necessary and good for patient and worker to carry on this spontaneous self-selection on the basis of unmet childhood residues, it was not good for the relationship to remain pegged to this level. If it did, it often resulted in a *folie à deux,* as strong mutual identifications do. These are narcissistic choices, because if one wishes to relate to what is most strongly developed in oneself, one tries mainly to relate to one's own image (as did Narcissus) and not to the other person. Only those relations that are based on complementing each other in respect to something mature in one but less well-developed in the other can foster greater maturity. While relationships based on complementing one another's childhood residues, or each other's neurotic needs, offer relief from pressure, they don't lead to higher integration. It is the ethos of growth—the opposite of the continuance of sameness—which in the therapeutic milieu militates against object choices based on neurotic identifications, and promotes those based on complementary needs without permitting them to get stuck there.

Such a relation may be cathartic, as Dana's beating up her worker was cathartic for both; but not therapeutic. Still, an object choice based on complementary neurotic needs is at least dynamic insofar as it permits the relief of pressures and the satisfaction of needs which would otherwise remain unmet, thus making repressions, fixations, and all defensive mechanisms less necessary. Such complementary choices, when well handled, may permit the partners to move on to higher levels of integration through the relief thus provided, thereby freeing energy for other endeavors. Everything then depends on how this energy is invested.

Because the satisfaction of complementary needs can be so rewarding, the partners may get fixated to it, as Dana and her worker did. Only the staff's continuous scrutiny of motives as a deliberate device for achieving higher integration—which is the most essential characteristic of a therapeutic milieu—safeguards against this fixation. Without it, worker and patient probably would develop rigid and unchanging closed systems of interaction which would prevent the progress toward integration of either. Since in the total therapeutic milieu all relationships—those of staff members to patients, those of patients to each other, and those of the staff to each other in their work situation—are under constant scrutiny, potentially closed systems are forced to remain or become open systems which move toward higher levels of organization and integration. The example of Dana's worker may illustrate how this works in general, though each case is unique.

The worker's self-examination began in earnest when she was asked why, if she thought it was good for Dana to thus unleash her rage against her mother, she had kept Dana's attacks secret. Wasn't it expected that a worker would report such an important move in a patient to the rest of the staff? She said she was convinced that Dana's behavior had been fully justified because of the way she had been rejected by her mother; but that she had not reported it because she didn't know where to go from there. But that being so, wouldn't there have been all the more reason to seek help about what to do next? If the worker were only insecure about how she was doing with Dana—a feeling which she correctly stated—this would be even more reason to report that with her, Dana could unfreeze and cathartically attack a mother figure.

Eventually the worker realized that she had kept it a secret because to her it was something very precious that only the two of them had together, which would lose much of its meaning if others were to know about it. From there it was an easy step to realize she was also afraid that if it became known, the senior staff would in some way stop her being beaten up. So she really had not wanted it to stop. Was she then so much of a masochist that she would misuse a patient to satisfy her masochistic need? The worker responded with righteous indignation to the accusation, which was exaggerated inasmuch as she had not just used Dana to meet some of her own unconscious needs, but had offered Dana the same opportunity. But being the conscientious person the worker was, it troubled her to think that she might have taken advantage of Dana to satisfy her own needs. So with this, she began asking for help in understanding what it was all about. She asserted that she was not masochistic; she had truly been joyous that Dana had come to life, and for some time she remained convinced that she did not mind the suffering, because Dana now also did other things with her. But perhaps, certain as she was that Dana had excellent reasons to beat up a mother figure, there was also something in the worker's own past which suggested to her that she deserved such punishment? It was this line of inquiry that had the entirely unexpected result of permitting recall of the knife incident with her sister.

Such scrutiny of staff members' attitudes and behavior with patients often produces similar positive results. It is almost impossible to know what are the inner motivations of another person. But one can make shrewd guesses; and if they are correct in assessing what the psychological constellation and emotional pressures may have been, although in error about the specifics, such hitting close to the emotional truth permits the person to recall what actually did happen.

Even with this new knowledge available to the worker, it became necessary to hark back to why she had wished the injuries to remain unrecognized. As long as she was not aware that she accepted them as deserved punishment, there may have been reason to keep them a secret; but why was she still accepting them and trying to make little of them? The answer was the old one: she accepted the punishment because since this was all she could do for Dana, she deserved it. But if this were so, then she must think there were better ways to help her; what were they? She claimed she was just too inexperienced to know them; the senior staff should tell her what to do.

So we then tried an approach we always found most useful. How had she felt about herself when she had tried to harm her sister? What a stupid question—had we not together arrived at the understanding that she still felt so miserable about herself, that she welcomed being punished for it? So then, how did Dana feel about hurting her? Obviously, she replied, it felt good to Dana to finally be able to do to a mother, at least vicariously, what she always had wanted to do. Well, if it was good to be able to express such anger in attack, why did the worker feel she deserved to be punished for having attempted the same thing? She answered that any moral person would feel that way. We pointed out that by her reasoning she obviously felt that Dana—so important to her—was not a moral person; otherwise Dana too would feel miserable for venting so violently what basically was also justified anger.

This development took months to achieve. After each question, the purpose of which is to have the worker find out more about herself, she must be given ample time and opportunity to work on what it arouses in her. Sometimes a week, sometimes a month, has to elapse before the next step can be taken. In the meantime, the daily meetings of the staff where other problems are ventilated, the discussions with other workers on this patient and others, all assume a different meaning to the worker because of what she has understood about herself. She participates in, or at least is present during, many conversations dealing with complex psychological problems which do not directly refer to the one she is struggling with. She understands more about herself, and she knows it. She also has more understanding of what goes on in the others, and why. This in turn makes it much more difficult for her to repress what is coming to awareness; to prevent it from continuing to occupy her conscious mind. When they are ready, most workers, after the problem has had time to germinate in their minds, will take up where they had left off. If not, a correctly timed question about what has been going on between worker and patient since she made the discovery about herself will lead to the next step in self-understanding.

For Dana's worker, the biggest step was made when she finally understood that the basic flaw in her relation to Dana up to then had been her viewing Dana as somehow less human than herself. She felt terrible about her own destructive wishes toward her sister. But she had been convinced that Dana felt just fine about such actually violent behavior. It comes as the greatest shock to a worker who is emotionally deeply involved with a patient to have to realize that—contrary to his conscious conviction of what he thought about the patient—he actually, unconsciously, had held a very low opinion of him. This more than anything induces the worker to change his view; not only of the patient but also of himself. Up to that moment, this worker had been convinced that it was good for Dana vicariously to beat a mother. While she knew she was supposed to help Dana understand herself, and thus often asked Dana why she did it, the worker had accepted Dana's saying that she was just so angry she would explode or return to catatonic immobility if she could not thus get rid of some of her inner violence. Up to now she had never asked Dana how she felt about herself, when she thus abused the person closest and dearest to her.

Only after the worker had realized that in her own mind she had done a great injustice to Dana by believing that she could unambivalently enjoy her open acts of violence, was she able to approach Dana with the thought that she would have felt guilty if she hurt somebody of great importance to her—regardless of how much anger she might feel. Now Dana really exploded. More viciously than ever before she attacked the worker, screaming: "Your letting me beat you up made me think you too saw me as a savage animal; which I believed of myself anyway," and then she broke down sobbing for the first time in her life that she could recall.

Still and all, we cannot be certain whether Dana would have moved out of her catatonic rigidity had things progressed differently. The worker's acceptance of her violence—fully approving for her own emotional reasons of the only move toward the world that Dana could then make, and taking pleasure in her doing so—was probably of greatest importance for Dana's being able to unfreeze a bit. It had proved to her how important she was to the worker, despite what she viewed as the worker's low opinion of her. By keeping it all secret, the worker had proved herself utterly trustworthy. She had accepted the savage in Dana, and perhaps this had been necessary, before Dana could believe anybody could accept her also as a moral person, with guilt feelings about her misbehavior.

A direct consequence of the worker's having convinced Dana that she did not see her as an inferior human being, or believe she had attitudes different from her own, was that Dana let her in on her deepest secret: she had stood motionless in the hospital at the window because of her need to watch the sky, to understand the changes in weather. Why this had been and was still so important, she could not tell. But around the weather Dana began to overcome her intellectual blocking, and became even physically agile, as she began running out of doors innumerable times to get a better view of the sky and clouds than she could from her window, to which she had restricted herself up to then. During the next two years, she accumulated an incredible amount of knowledge about the weather. While she was seemingly engrossed in other activities, she would without so much as looking tell how the wind had shifted and how its velocity had altered. Seemingly fully occupied, she would suddenly rush to study the cloud formations because they had changed. From the variations in temperature, humidity, and so on, all of which she "knew" as soon as they occurred, she was much better able to predict the weather than the Chicago Weather Bureau.

It is feats such as this which have led some to think that schizophrenics experience an expansion of their minds. They do show extraordinary abilities at times. But far from having experienced an expansion of his mind, the schizophrenic has concentrated it with the most minute focus, as the solution of the riddle of Dana's startling weather predictions shows.

For the next couple of years we explored Dana's past and her reactions to it, and helped her to understand herself and to meet the world and people. Repeatedly the worker and Dana had to go over what had happened in the early days of their relationship, how it had started to go wrong at first because the worker had been too caught up in her own needs to understand how she enticed Dana to act out on her what she needed, instead, to integrate. One day when the worker again spoke with Dana about how sorry she was that she had failed to comprehend all this, the old anger and violence emerged again, but this time only in words, as Dana savagely told the worker: "You are still stupid. You still don't know what weather means to me." The worker repeated that she regretted her past and her other still present limitations in understanding, and begged her to enlighten her. At which Dana went to a blackboard and wrote in large letters, "We eat her," saying, "That's all there is to weather." She had to be able to predict the weather to know how, from where and whom the ultimate danger of oral destruction was likely to come.

Dana's anorexia had been due all along to her anxiety that she, another Gretel, would be devoured by the witch, her mother. One way to forestall this danger, and not an unusual dynamic of anorexia, was to have as little body as possible, so that it would not be attractive—to be eaten up in childhood, to be used sexually in adolescence. Of this possibility we had been cognizant all along, as well as that her obesity had been her response to the security she felt that at the School no such danger existed. But we had been in error in believing that the anxiety which had caused anorexia was no longer with her in its old and most primitive form. Somehow we failed to connect the two symptoms, the old one of anorexia, and the newer one of monomanic preoccupation with weather. She could let us in on her secret when she finally believed that the worker did not just devote herself to her because she was a patient; that the worker did not only like her, but also respected her as a person.

After this admission she was through with the fixation on weather. All her good intelligence, which had gone into being a weather expert, now became freed for other interests; her rage against the world had subsided because she felt she could have a good life. Within a year she could have left the School, but she preferred to remain to give her newly won mental health a chance to become better established and secure, wishing to take advantage for a while longer of what the therapeutic milieu had to offer until a year later, when she left to enter college. She decided to become a teacher because she liked the idea that, on the basis of her experience, she would be better able than others to teach children how important words are, and to know what they really mean. In summing it up she said, "Not the crazy way I thought what weather meant."

One might think from this little case history that the unraveling of the intricacies and complexities of the schizophrenic mind require consummate psychoanalytic skill and knowledge. These are needed; but as this story shows, and as every staff member must learn, even they are easier to come by than common sense. As in Dana's preoccupation with weather, what seems totally incomprehensible is due to the patient's inability—because of his anxiety, the depth of his repressions, and the disorganization of his higher mental functions—to recognize the usually simple and primitive derivation of symptoms. The constructs he continues to weave around their origins hide their very nature from himself and others, making them ever more elaborate and confusing. These constructs are to prevent others from comprehending how unacceptable the meanings of the symptom are; to forestall the expected destructive consequences if anybody should recognize its true nature.

What a staff member thus needs most to learn is how to respond as the specific situation requires. An incident that happened once during a night staff meeting illustrates this. We were interrupted by a message that a patient had woken up and needed to be comforted. The staff member working most closely with the patient left the meeting to take care of him. When he returned a half hour later, I interrupted what we had been talking about to ask him what had happened with the patient. The reply was an account of the dream the patient claimed had scared him, with appropriate interpretations. I asked why the staff member had engaged in dream interpretation. What else could he have done? was the astonished reply. I wondered what other possibilities there might have been; so I asked how the staff member had approached the patient. The patient had said he could not get back to sleep, so the staff member had pulled up a chair to his bed and asked him to discuss what he had dreamed.

The dream had been an interesting one from which things could be learned about the patient, and the staff member had cleverly interpreted for the patient some of this meaning. I gave the worker credit for how well he had understood the dream. But I asked him: If he were to wake up in the middle of the night, feeling lonely and deserted, what did he think would have been most reassuring to him? He first tried to say, help in understanding what the dream was all about. But when I asked what was really most upsetting at the moment—the feeling of anxiety or loneliness, or the dream?—he was no longer so sure. But, he said, his efforts at interpretation had been meant to show his concern. Of course, I replied, and it obviously had worked; since he had returned to the meeting, and the patient was now asleep. But can we be certain that it was the interpretation that had worked? If an infant cries because he is hungry, is it sufficient for the mother just to give him a bottle, or would a good mother not also soothe the infant by cuddling him and rocking him? The worker readily saw that both were needed—dealing with the anxiety by rocking the child, and with the anxiety's source, by feeding him.

The staff member now could see that when he had been with the patient, he had been concerned mainly with the possible source of the discomfort and not with the discomfort itself. And since the patient, as revealed by his own remarks, had felt so lonely, would it not have been equally or even more reassuring to comfort him; by bringing him some food or by holding him? The staff member then asked why, if this had been required, had talking about the dream helped the patient to feel comforted? My reply was, how do we know that it was the content of their conversation that comforted the patient, and not the worker's willingness to spend some time with him after his regular, on-duty hours? Perhaps what the patient desired and needed, even more than understanding the dream, was for the worker to spend time with him. Perhaps the dream was even invented, as we quite easily can do in the hypnagogic stage of being barely awake, to keep the worker interested so that he doesn't go off in a hurry. The patient knew the worker was attending a staff meeting. Maybe what the patient wished most was to find out whether he was more important to his worker than the meeting. Maybe the feeling of excruciating loneliness was due to the patient's fear that the meeting was more important than he. Well, had that been the patient's anxiety? asked the worker. We could never be certain.

If he had been in the patient's situation, I asked the worker, what would he have liked best? The worker could now see that he probably would have preferred somebody being emotionally close to him; perhaps putting his arm around him, assuring him that he liked being with him when he was in distress, that he was much more important than the old staff meeting, rather than questioning him about the content of his dream. Exactly so; and would he not have liked it even better if this person, after somehow soothing him, had offered him something to eat or drink? Would it not have been even more reassuring to talk about the dream as they were eating together, if that was what he wanted to talk about? Conveying to the patient that he was now safe was more effective than dream interpretation, since together they could fight off all possible dangers lurking in the dark.

As it had happened, while the dream had been appropriately analyzed, the patient was left with the question of whether the worker's response was due to his professional obligation to provide what seemed needed, or whether it was the result of a relation so strong that it could negate the feeling of loneliness and desertion. Had the worker immediately shown the patient through his behavior that his separation anxiety was unjustified, the lasting effect of such spontaneous reassurance would have been much greater than reassurances coming from intellectual understanding of anxiety. Since the worker was devoted to the patient, why had he been lacking in empathy, and why had he detoured through intellectual understanding to re-establish it?

It eventually became clear that while the staff member was willing to extend himself intellectually to the patient, he had some inner reluctance to extend himself emotionally to him at this moment. The worker had been ready to support the patient's ego, overwhelmed by id anxieties, by strengthening its rational understanding and control over the unconscious. But he had not taken into account that the patient's waking up and requesting company was also—probably mainly—a cry for emotional closeness from a parental figure. As it was, the way the staff member handled the incident left the patient with the feeling that he could not master his discomfort all by himself; whereas cradling him, if meant emotionally, might have given the patient the conviction that he alone had mastered the impasse of his insecurity about how important he was to the worker.

This incident may suggest the shortcomings of a merely intellectual approach, as compared to one which takes the total situation into account, and approaches the patient's problem not on the basis of what the therapist knows and can do best, but of what the patient needs most at the moment. The patient did not need understanding of his unconscious, but the feeling that he could sleep safely and soundly at the institution because of the strength it has to offer him in an emergency, which he can borrow and use as his own.

It had opened up to the staff member a fuller comprehension of the difference between an uncovering of unconscious material and a directly ego-strengthening approach—what was the right time and setting for each one. It also gave him a more direct feeling for the importance of the so-called countertransference. As the discussion of the incident continued, we discovered that while the staff member knew he had to leave because one of his patients was in distress, he'd been very interested in what we had been talking about and was very reluctant to leave. Therefore, his pursuing the content of the dream was in some way a punishing of the patient.

By interrupting what I had been talking about on his return to concentrate on the staff member's experience, I showed my recognition of his having extended himself to the patient, and that I didn't mind dropping what I was doing to respond to the situation created by his return. My doing this for the staff member would later allow him to be more spontaneous and emotionally involved with the patient. When the staff member left the staff meeting he had been only randomly involved; when he returned he was the center of interest; everyone wanted to help him further understand what he had done, why he had done it, and the consequences to both himself and the patient.

The depth of understanding and empathy which milieu therapy demands does not come mainly from insight into what the patient requires for restructuring—or, as in the case of extremely disturbed individuals, often for structuring—his personality. It comes from the realization of what the staff member would want to have done for and with himself, should he suffer the kind of anxiety, anger, and despair that would drive him to act and feel as the patient does at the moment. Perhaps there is no better touchstone for the humanistic principles in which milieu therapy must be grounded than the great philosopher Immanuel Kant's categorical imperative: we must always act as though the principles underlying each of our actions were to become universal principles.

In most psychiatric institutions the patients live by routines, which vary from the daily scheduling of therapy or recreational sessions to a complete regulation of all they do. This regimentation, as well as the institution's relative lack of sensitivity to the patients' hopes and sufferings, its view of the afflicted as somehow subhuman, comes mainly from the staff's need to defend themselves against the onslaught of emotions which originate with the patients. The staff do so by building a diaphanous but essentially impenetrable wall that, emotionally, separates them from the patients. The nurses' stations in psychiatric wards epitomize this attitude. They are glass-enclosed—in common parlance often called cages—so that those within can observe what is going on outside and vice versa, but only by means of the most distant of our receptors: sight. For the patients to see the nurses talking there—be it on the telephone, or to attendants, the doctor, or other nurses—shows them that they are felt to be less important. This increases their paranoia, since they are convinced they are being talked about, which is often true. Records and medications could be kept safely under lock and key in a cabinet and hence are no excuse for the "cage." In their stations, the nurses are truly "out of touch" with the patients; they can neither hear nor "feel" nor "smell" what goes on with them. Typically, the nurse emerges from her seclusion when she thinks something needs to be done, or when called by the patient. The nurse acts on the patient, or he on her; the physical separateness of the nurse's station expresses the desire that they should not act on each other in a continuous process.

From the chief of staff to its lowliest member, from the psychiatrist to the ward attendant, there is an overwhelming tendency to assure smoothness of operation, which of course runs counter to the ever-changing needs of the patients. Certainly chaos does not help them, and some order and regularity is needed to facilitate their coping with their inner disorganization. But a truly human organization of life never runs "smoothly."

Psychiatric hospital arrangements can best be understood as designed for the purpose of precluding or minimizing the patient's *acting* on the staff, since this may create disorder. Even his *acting out* on the worker is preferred; staff members know what to do if a patient becomes assaultive, as opposed to being able to respond spontaneously on the basis of their inner feelings, in a nevertheless therapeutic way. Depending on the institution's philosophy, if the patient becomes violent he is either restrained (physically, chemically, or through words), or, rarely, the staff member is expected to "take it." Psychologically speaking, it is equally devastating to a patient to be restrained for something like spitting or hitting, or for it to be accepted as if nothing had happened. While the first is physically more unpleasant, the second proves to the patient that he is viewed as being of such little account that his actions do not provoke any reaction.

I don't presume to know what Jesus had in mind when he advised us to turn the other cheek. But if all he was after was for us to make ourselves the butt of the other person's aggression, he would have said we should offer our cheek to be slapped in the first place, whereas he only advised turning the other cheek after the attack has happened. He certainly tells us we should not retaliate in kind, that is, with counter-aggression, even should it be camouflaged as restraining the assaultive patient "for his own good," so that "he will not need to feel guilty afterward." But from my experience it would seem obvious that if we slap somebody we want a reaction, and if it is not forthcoming we are defeated in our intention of beating down the other person. The psychological consequence of offering the other cheek is really either humiliation or outrage in the aggressor, because we act as if his violent effort had no effect, or not the desired one. If I read Scripture correctly, the advice is to demonstrate to the aggressor how totally ineffective aggression is, because it defeats him more than it does the person attacked, not physically but psychologically. If my interpretation is valid, then the psychology underlying this scriptural passage is widely misunderstood. Far from teaching that we should invite further aggression and accept it because the meek shall inherit the earth, it gives advice on how most effectively we can defeat the aggressor; though in the process we might be hurt once more physically, we win out psychologically. Hence if we respond to physical aggression by inviting its continuation, we may teach something of importance about violence, but we do it in a way that is psychologically devasting to the aggressor. If he is our patient, then this is certainly not the way we should teach him. Hence I do not believe that if we are attacked we should offer the other cheek—not, that is, if our intention is therapeutic.

Redl writes: "I have run into people who really love 'crazy youngsters' and are quite willing to sacrifice a lot. Only they simply cannot stand more than half a pound of spittle in their faces a day, professional attitude or no" (94). Unfortunately, he does not tell us what they do until the amount of insult which is their limit has been reached. Do they at first pretend it doesn't matter, and then suddenly act as if it matters a great deal? Or does it really not matter to them at first but only later, and if so, why? Is the message the patient is trying to convey in barely disguised symbolic form any different after the half pound of spittle has accumulated?

Wouldn't the worker's reaction be different if he thought the patient did it to express his hate and low opinion of him; or that he is so important to the patient, that the patient must find out whether he is acceptable even when abusive; or that at this moment the worker has come to be identified with early experiences with a mother who never permitted the patient to spit out his food, and even forced it back down his throat when he did so?—to mention only three of practically limitless possibilities. If the worker has been helped to react to the patient simultaneously as a person and as a therapist—rather than just trying to accept or control the patient's behavior, neither of which is therapeutic—then he will make some judgment about the meaning of the patient's behavior, and respond on this basis. Even though he may be wrong in his initial evaluation of what it all signifies, if he does respond thus, his personal response (as opposed to an institutionalized one) will usually provoke the patient to react in a way which will permit arriving at a more correct assessment of the meaning of it all.

If it is wondered how one can respond in a positive way when he has just been made the butt of aggressive behavior, the simple answer that doing so is the only therapeutic attitude, while true, largely begs the question. We may come closer by drawing a parallel with the good mother who doesn't mind her child's spilling everything down his highchair—maybe even himself—since she realizes he does so because the world has just become too difficult for him to manage. Therefore her child needs her more now than at other times, and she likes it because he relies on her to mediate between him and the difficulties of living. The bad mother, because she does not understand what is going on, believes that it is all directed against her, which is much harder to take calmly.

A considerable amount of staff training must be directed toward teaching this lesson: that everything a patient does can be easy to take, or very difficult, depending on what interpretation one puts on it. If, like the good mother, one understands that the patient needs one so much, especially in an emergency, this makes it all more acceptable. If one reacts like the bad mother, then instead of feeling one has been given an important message, one feels manipulated, put upon, even abused, and things can only go from bad to worse, ending up with the patient's suffering more and with the staff member's feeling that he is doing a bad job. All of this could be put into theoretical language, but I find such language to be much less effective.

The staff also has to be taught that the crucial phase in any psychoanalytic therapy is reached when the patient is in the negative transference; that is, when he projects his negative feeling on the therapist. Any therapist can bask in the sun of the positive transference, when the patient views him as wonderful and as unable to do any wrong. This is pleasant enough, but it has never yet helped anybody to get well. But how the therapist handles the negative transference—when he is seen as the sum and source of all evil, the most selfish, vile person in the world—how he reacts to this attitude of the patient, is the decisive factor.

It is easy to understand, but very difficult to accept, that violent action against a staff member may also be a demonstration of how important he has become in the life of the patient. This is the responsibility which the inexperienced worker tries to shy away from, although essentially it is the greatest reward he can expect to derive from his efforts. It seems so obvious that nobody is going to vent his anger against someone he is indifferent to; yet it is very hard in our society to accept that if we heavily invest our positive emotions in a person, we are also apt to do the same for our negative ones. All too many people think it is possible to be the recipient of only the first, and not also the latter. If the patient is going to be helped, this is a lesson the staff has to be able to learn well.

The staff member who has made such thinking his own will respond to the patient's sweeping the plates off the table with: "His throwing them down is unimportant; the only thing that counts is his distress and how I react to it." If he feels thus, then the action of throwing becomes indeed unimportant. It becomes better to concentrate on what will make a difference, namely, one's response. Knowing this, a staff member can handle himself and the situation so that what seemed a destructive act turns into a constructive experience. Seeing it this way makes doing it easier. What we are convinced is important, we try to do well.

Further, nobody can develop full empathy for the misery which forced the patient's violent actions, if he is worrying about whether his colleagues will be critical of him when a patient for whom he is responsible acts out this way; or whether they will resent it if they have to interrupt their meal to help clean up the mess. To eliminate the need for such worry, all staff must have made the institution's philosophy their own: that protecting property can be and often is counterproductive; not because we like seeing it destroyed, but because our obligation is to promote the mental health of the patients, whatever reasonable expense is involved.

It is the task of the director to convince every staff member that not only the patient's feelings but also those of the staff member (including how he felt when the dishes were broken, or food was spilt over his clothes) are of much greater importance than the inconvenience or expense of the damage. If only the emotions of the patients are viewed as worthy of concerned consideration, the staff member will not be able to keep from becoming annoyed that his feelings count for so little; and he will end up being resentful of the patient. Neither staff nor patients will be able to believe that the institution takes its own philosophy seriously, if one person's feelings—the patient's—are valued, while those of another—the staff member—are neglected. The ethos of an institution, if it has one, must be indivisible. It is all-important how both patient and staff feel about things; the difference is that much more command of himself is expected from the staff member. He must realize what his feelings are before they explode into uncontrolled behavior, and he must do something constructive about them on his own. The patient, on the other hand, often does not know what his feelings are before and while he acts them out; he needs the staff member's help to recognize their nature and origins, before he can begin to control them. If a staff member's saying, "I felt like dropping a dish myself," is not taken seriously just because he only *said* it, he will be in a poor position to act with compassion the next time the patient does it. But if expression of the staff member's emotions is given full attention—not criticized as "immature," or "unprofessional," but seen as a valid reason to examine what went wrong to make *him* feel this way, if it engenders a response which helps him to decide what he and the institution can do to improve matters to prevent this in the future—then the staff member will be able to go on dealing constructively with situations as they arise.

The trouble with the staff in most psychiatric institutions is that they are not prepared and don't know how to react to a patient who arouses deep emotions in them; as he is apt to do if they open themselves to him, rather than retiring into an attitude of "professionalism" which inhibits, and hence protects against, their own emotional response. It isn't so much the patient's actions or feelings against which the staff need to protect themselves, but mainly their own. If, for example, I believe that things have to be done at a certain moment and in unalterable ways, then this conviction—irrespective of whether anything else in reality justifies it—protects me against being devastated by what I inflict on others when I force them to submit to these routines. If I view some others as subhuman, then when I do what I believe is necessary, I cannot be shaken by their discomfort.

The mental hospital worker's nonresponse to what goes on in the patients on whom he imposes certain living conditions originates in the belief that unless the worker makes himself nonfeeling, he cannot meet his tasks. He is additionally convinced that his actions are required by what is best for the patient. But if the psychiatric hospital worker were truly to experience the patient as a person, he could not continue to maintain insensitive attitudes or unresponsive behavior. And it is the fear that his own integration might be threatened which prevents him from responding as a person, as opposed to reacting as a nurse, attendant, psychologist, or whatever his position is in the hierarchy.

On his trial visit to the Orthogenic School, every prospective staff member who eventually became a successful worker was completely exhausted after a few hours with the patients. There were those others who had automatically protected themselves by a wall of "professionalism" ("These are mentally deranged patients, and therefore what they do, feel, and say does not touch me"), in whose case it was clear that both they and we would be better off without each other. But those who could permit themselves to be open to the patient and his experiences to some degree were immediately drained of all emotional energy. Nobody could afford to open himself beyond a very limited degree until he felt assured of the support of the institution, which took at the very least several weeks. After joining the staff, new workers would be in a state of complete exhaustion for many weeks or months, because of what the work demanded of them: facing themselves, recognizing what the patients aroused in them, opening aspects of their personality they never knew existed and didn't want to realize were part of them. This didn't come from understanding the patients' pathology, or "observing" their primitive behavior, but from experiencing it. That is why nearly all psychiatric hospitals are organized to permit the staff to protect themselves against experiencing the patient. Therapeutic sessions are sometimes exceptions to this. But in individual therapeutic sessions the patient's behavior is controlled by the setting, and the therapist knows it will be over in fifty minutes, usually less, and he still often protects himself by means of a "professional" attitude.

The therapeutic milieu must support the worker, so that he doesn't need to withdraw behind the protective wall of insensitivity; and at the same time help him to reintegrate his own personality, not just at the pre-working level but at a higher one. There are many ways for the staff member to do this, all of which must be made use of. One is to open himself to the patients, and thereby give them a chance to act on him as much as he acts on them. This may be illustrated by a sequence of recollections from a former staff member who, looking back and comprehending what had happened, wrote:

> I had entered into the work full of the usual ideas about being understanding of, and nice to patients. I wanted to see myself as a good fellow doing an admirable job on behalf of those poor lost souls. Instead I found myself exasperated, ineffective, and losing my temper. . . . I explained [this] as the result of the patients being basically different from me. I was sane, an adult, taking care of them. The gist of these efforts was to protect myself by maintaining a gap between me and them . . . it was their fault for being different. (131)

It made this worker angry that the patients' behavior and his reaction to it prevented him from seeing himself the way he wanted to be: understanding, helpful, in short, some kind of saviour. When the psychiatric hospital worker needs to appear thus to himself, the frustration of his wish and consequent anger explain his making himself insensitive to patients. These feelings can be neither understood nor positively dealt with unless they are recognized as the worker's desperate effort to maintain his integration—which is indeed threatened, not by the patients and what they do, but by the feelings they evoke in him.

Just because the intentions of the new staff member are so good and still do not achieve anything for the patients (or do not seem to, which is a possibility he as a beginner is not aware of), the worker reasons it must be the fault of the patients, who then are viewed as so unresponsive that they hardly deserve further efforts. Most workers in psychiatric institutions do indeed begin with good intentions, having long forgotten where the path thus paved leads. Intentions alone will not save the day, much less the year; only the persistent acting on them will. Unfortunately, the story of the ordinary psychiatric hospital worker is that when these good intentions do not succeed right away, he becomes disappointed over his inability to make them work; he feels himself a failure and defends against this by erecting a wall of "professionalism" between himself and the patients.

In milieu therapy, at this point, the staff must be helped not to wish to give up; or at least be prevented from doing so, by encouraging them to believe that hard work based on good intentions will eventually win the day, as it did for the staff member cited above. There is no universal way of assisting staff members with the problem of their narcissism and self-esteem being badly damaged by lack of success in their early efforts. But in many instances, it was sufficient to ask the staff member to project himself into somebody else who for years had all his hopes disappointed, and was therefore unable to believe in anybody's good intentions. After then reminding him of some of his patient's specific traumatic experiences, we asked him how *he* would react to having to contend with all this past, even if somebody approached him with the best of motives. The beginner's answer often was that he would be delighted, because it would be such a desired and hoped-for relief. The worker was surprised when we pointed out his apparent belief that neither he nor the patient had ever learned anything from past experiences—since the worker stated that despite all, he would still approach any new experience with such naïveté. This led to the realization that indeed it would take months or maybe years of experiencing an entirely different approach before the patient could believe in its sincerity.

Another quite effective way to evoke empathy is to remind a worker how long, and how much, a mother must do for her infant before he can feel sure of her love and does not respond to any frustration with a fit of screaming. This happens even though the infant has not yet had any bad experiences; and it happens in one of the best, least ambivalent relations known to man.

If none of this convinces the staff member that the patient's negative response to his positive efforts, far from proving him ineffective, is just what should be expected—then it may be effective to ask him how many positive things he has done, and for how long, to counteract all the bad experiences the patient has had. In his imagination, the worker should try to put the patient's unending series of bad experiences on one side of the scale, and the good experiences he has tried to provide on the other, and decide what the balance or imbalance was likely to be.

Such homespun appeals to common sense are much more constructive in developing empathy for the patient's predicament than the elaborate technical explications the beginner craves, pertinent as these may be from a scientific point of view. There are several reasons why the beginner seeks theoretical explanations about the nature of a particular patient's psychiatric disturbance, its origins, the psychoanalytic meaning of his symptoms, and similar information he thinks will help him "understand" the patient. One reason is that practically everyone genuinely interested in this type of work wants to learn about human beings, but in abstract form; that is, in ways that will not hit home. Whether or not they are aware of it or can admit it, they fear knowledge that does not apply exclusively to the patient; because such knowledge may have unfathomable consequences for themselves and thus is best avoided. Yet unconsciously, they do want to find out about themselves, they may even wish to find themselves through working with psychiatric patients, and at the same time they consciously feel that this is a bad, selfish motive which would invalidate their belief that they want to help these unfortunate people. Thus, studying the patients, working hard at scientifically understanding them, "proves" that they are in the enterprise for the patient, and not for themselves.

Then, too, they are convinced that the psychoanalyst possesses arcane knowledge, which they wish to make their own. If he does not talk about mental mechanisms or the diseased mind of the patient, but instead talks about what we all have in common, they tend to feel cheated, and talked down to. This happens until they realize that they learn more important things in this way than from even the most erudite scientific discussion. But by then they are no longer beginners.

22 | Reintegration: The Staff Member Against Himself

Experiences which arouse unsolved emotional impasses in us can project us into such states of disintegration that we cannot deal with them when they occur in the patient. Most psychiatric workers defend themselves by declaring such experiences to be of no significance to them, and taking place only because the patient is insane; a conviction which powerfully reinforces their defense against recognizing the same impasse in themselves, since this would imply they are insane, too. Or they may view such experiences as things that must not be permitted to happen again for the sake of the patient's well-being, whereas they are actually worried about their own well-being; thus they may punitively restrain the patient physically, through threats or with drugs. All these and many more defensive maneuvers which characterize the staff in psychiatric hospitals suggest how many unresolved inner conflicts we all have; otherwise a defensive response to the patients' primitive behavior would not be so prevalent.

The senior staff must not permit themselves or others to hide behind the professional language of pathology, or to explain patients' behavior as being the result of insanity. No patient actually engages in "primary process behavior," or acts "insane." He does concrete things: he spits or throws up, he strikes something or somebody, he gorges himself, he cowers unmovingly in a corner with his back to the world. Our reaction to particular types of behavior can bring to awareness the likelihood of our specific problems. Why is it so upsetting and degrading to be spit upon, for example, given the fact that we all as infants spit up on those who fed us? Why, we may begin to wonder, has spitting up—once probably an expression either of affection, of feeling well fed, or of something that disagreed with us—become one of the worst offenses in our society? Why should we react with such strong emotion? It is easy to maintain that a patient's primary process behavior does not affect one; it is impossible to believe that one has no reaction to his spitting on us, his screaming out at us his anger or distress, or to his utter lack of response when we try to reach him.

On reaching that point in his development where he could use his experiences with the patients to further his own integration as well as theirs, one worker wrote:

> Working with the patients was having a profound effect on me, one with which I was trying to come to grips. I wanted to understand what I was going through. I was particularly impressed with the overwhelming complexity of my experience as a worker when I approached it intellectually or mechanically; but the comparative simplicity of the basic emotional issue. That issue was the nature of my feeling about, and facility for, emotional involvement with the patients.

It took a few years more for this worker to understand fully what was going on; that in his experiences with the patients phases of his own childhood which had remained, as he put it, "unfulfilled" became threateningly activated.

This same worker reported feelings that would overwhelm him on the occasion of birthday parties for the patients. During his first year he had participated in many such celebrations, and always tried to help make them as nice as he could for the one whose birthday was being celebrated. But on the day of the party, each time as the moment approached for the birthday cake to be brought in he would become terribly impatient, feeling such stress that he wanted to leave immediately to escape the mounting tension. Only his feelings of obligation to the patient would force him to contain himself. He reports:

> When the cake finally came I was in a frenzy. When at last a piece was served to me I would stuff myself and want more, whether I liked the cake or not. Usually these cakes were too sweet and sticky for my taste, but despite the fact that they were cakes I didn't like and would never eat on my own, I stuffed every last morsel in my mouth. (131)

The worker finally began to wonder whether he could possibly be jealous of somebody; perhaps even of a patient who had become very important to him. As he began to question what was going on inside him, he remembered something he had long forgotten. His younger brother, of whom he had been intensely jealous, had his birthday five days after his own; and the brother's celebration always seemed to wipe out his own. The brother's birthday had come to stand symbolically for how the brother's arrival had wiped out the worker's privileged role as the first and only child. All this had been long forgotten and repressed, because it had been too painful to recall how the brother had seemed to replace and "dethrone" him in everything, even stealing the glory of his birthday celebration. As long as he had denied his jealousy of his brother and the childish way it had affected him, birthdays had made no emotional impact. But once he had opened himself to the jealousy the patients experienced watching another's birthday being celebrated, he became swamped by the old and unresolved sibling jealousies of his own. Re-experiencing these feelings in a childish form in the present, when he had by now achieved much more in life than his brother, permitted him to put one of his unresolved childhood phases to rest since he had not only relived it, but worked it through.

This is, of course, hard work; and since the staff member can never be sure what repressed archaic problems may be activated, he approaches every encounter with the patients with considerable anxiety for quite some time. As another worker put it:

The first months of working with the patients were really terrifying. The only thing that sustained me was that the director assured me I could become a good counselor, and that he would help me become one. I was terribly scared most of the time about what I still didn't know, about the patients, about myself. As time went on I felt changes in myself; I felt better. I felt more successful than at anything else I had done in my life; not that I didn't have successes before, but they meant little to me by comparison to how important it became to me that I could do things for the patients, understand the hidden meaning of what they did, and understand better why I did what I did.

At first, I guess like all other workers I resented it; it scared me when I was asked what I had been up to, in something I did. This really upset me, until I got in the habit of asking myself this question. What a relief when I was able to understand what makes me tick, though I didn't exactly like what I found out. But if I did, I never repeated the same mistake. What a revelation it was to realize not

*just that I had the same problems as some of the patients,
but that I am so much better able to deal with them in myself; so much so that I can help them do it a bit better too.*

She went on to describe an experience she had in her association with the School: one of her patients sat on her lap and suddenly
she felt slightly damp.

*I put the girl down as I jumped up, crying "Oh, Dorothy!"
wanting to continue "how could you," but I stopped myself before it left my mouth, because I knew I would sound
just like my mother, and I didn't want that. As I realized
it, for some reason the whole thing struck me so funny I
laughed out loud. All the other patients gathered around,
Dorothy looked at me, mouth wide open—she was as surprised at my reaction as I was. Now the whole thing seemed
so ridiculous—all I had to do was wash out the damn skirt
—why did people get in such uproars about things like this;
why had my immediate reaction before I caught myself
been as if something terrible had happened? Thereafter I
was careful to wear easily washable things at work, which
helped when some others wet on me, but it was not necessary for Dorothy, because she didn't do it anymore.*

The experience, as it turned out, was so freeing that the worker
spontaneously broke out laughing, with such deep feeling that the
patients realized that something important and very positive had
happened. In that instant the worker realized how much she still
carried feelings in herself that were derived from her infantile relationship with her mother, an inner beholdenness she detested; and
at the same time she suddenly knew that there was no longer any
need for her to act in accordance with it. As she recognized the
remnants of the archaic "bad mother" in herself, she exorcised them
with her laughter, and with it could become the "good mother."
In an instant a potentially disintegrating experience: *I am somebody
on whom people urinate and I have to defend myself against it by
becoming punitive toward the offender,* had been turned into the
integrating one: *I no longer need to act as my mother had forced
me to, I am free of that. From now on I'll be able to do things my
way and what others do to me (my mother's criticism of me,
Dorothy's urinating on me) will not give me a bad feeling because
I have become more sure of myself.* Since the patient's regressed behavior had suddenly become the source of an integrative experience

for the worker, it lost its regressive meaning for the patient and attained a progressive connotation—thus making this regressed behavior no longer necessary.

Nothing would have come from this event but a soiled skirt if the worker had "taken it" with the professional attitude that this poor soul had to act out her regressive behavior. Only bad things could have ensued had the worker responded negatively, as her first impulse prompted; in retaliation for the rejection, the patient would have continued trying to wet on her, or would have engaged in even more hostile behavior, or withdrawn from all meaningful contact with her. The worker permitted herself to respond spontaneously, though it led to a momentary regression—the "criticizing mother" in her took over, but as this happened, she also became conscious of it—because by then deep down she felt sure she would somehow be able to reintegrate herself on a higher level. In this instance the reintegration happened immediately; often it may take much longer, even weeks or months. But if what was aroused is not again repressed, this longer process can be sustained.

Professional development, no more than one important aspect of the worker's striving for his own higher integration, can become a cancerous growth if it is pursued at the expense of his integration as a total person. While desire for professional growth, which is present among many workers in psychiatric hospitals, can serve as a momentum for personal integration; the crucial difference is whether it is only incidentally related to the actual work he is doing, or whether it is a direct result of a commitment to the ethos of the therapeutic milieu and to particular patients. Everything here depends on whether the institution is built around the conviction that it must do everything possible to promote such integration of the staff, with the patients' integration as the ultimate goal.

The difference between personal and professional growth may be illustrated by the example of Marcia's counselor. Working with and for Marcia, a mute autistic pubertal girl, her counselor gained professional understanding and technical skill in handling Marcia and her problems. For example, she learned to understand how important Marcia's daily flooding the floors with water over an inch high was, and also that it was Marcia's effort to set things right—to inundate as she had been inundated by enemas being forced on her all her life (13).

The worker gained in professional and technical skill as she learned how to make this flooding possible for Marcia despite her anxiety about it; even more, the worker became able to accept without inner reservations and with good feelings, not only the flooding but being drenched and having her clothes damaged in the process. In short, the counselor fully understood the importance of the water play for her patient. As ever more psychological ramifications of all this became clear to her, she became more skillful in constructively using what Marcia acted out. The worker gained considerable satisfaction for herself and approbation from the staff from this as her technical skills increased, and she became better able to help Marcia reduce her inner emotional turmoil.

As meaningful as all this was to the worker, she actually integrated herself around an experience which required little intellectual or professional knowledge, but demanded quite a bit of her morally. This came about when the janitors objected to the extra work involved in the continual mopping of the floors. The counselor asked me to persuade the janitors to go on with the mopping; this succeeded for a while, but eventually an impasse was reached. Asked by the counselor to insist on continued mopping, I objected that if it was done with resentment, Marcia would be exposed to negative feelings, which had undone her in the first place. But Marcia had to be given the chance to do what she craved, the counselor insisted, and I agreed. How could she do this if the floors were not dried? My guess was that the floors would have to remain flooded. This could not happen, the counselor said, since the water seeped under the door into the corridor and people could slip and hurt themselves; then they all would insist the flooding had to stop. This was indeed a problem, but the counselor just could not see stopping the all-important water play. I agreed, but returned to the problem of the mopping up. She asked if I expected her to do it. I did not; but it seemed that unless somebody mopped up afterwards, the water play would have to be restricted to the sink. The counselor felt that restricting the play would threaten all Marcia had gained.

It seemed the only solution was that the counselor would have to do the cleaning up, though nobody expected this of her, with the possible exception of herself. With that, the counselor was up against it. Could she permit herself—irrespective of what others thought her work for Marcia required—to take a different attitude to the floor being flooded, depending on who would have to do the cleaning up? Posing the question to herself of whether it should be she who mopped the floor implied some disintegration of her image of herself as a highly responsible, moral person. Asking it revealed that up to this moment, contrary to her beliefs, she had not done the very best for her patient, since she had done things without suffering the hardships involved, and considered not doing them as soon as she was the one who would have to do the unpleasant labor. She reached a higher level of reintegration when she decided that who did the mopping must make no difference when Marcia's getting better was at stake, and that therefore she would do it.

In order for a worker to be able to relate closely enough to the patient to reintegrate herself for the patient's sake, she must feel that whatever happens to and with the patient is conditioned more by her than by any other person (except the patient, of course). Only this makes the patient so important that one is willing to take all the risks involved in reintegrating oneself; a serious venture which requires partial disintegration as a first step. Such reintegration around the patient seems to have a near miraculous effect. Actually, what is involved in the process makes understanding it quite readily comprehensible: the worker's integration often induces a parallel process in the patient.

As her worker thus integrated herself on a higher level, Marcia did the same; she spontaneously began restricting her flooding to the sink within a few days after her counselor began mopping the floors—which Marcia did not consciously know about, since it was never done when she could observe it, and of course she was not told about it. She used the sink without any loss in what the water play meant to her and did for her.

This example illustrates what has to be a common occurrence in a total therapeutic milieu. Of course, opening oneself up to the patient and subjecting oneself to the disintegrating impact this might have does not always lead directly to positive results; it can also have some dangerous effects. The milieu that invites staff members to risk such experiences must remain alert and stand ready to protect staff and patients against possible bad consequences. It is natural for all of us when we "let down our defenses" to avoid engaging in the difficult process of reintegrating the primitive behavior which has emerged. The initial unconscious desire is to "get even" with what forced us to repress by acting it all out, by repeating a difficult early experience without any untoward consequences. If we as adults could live out safely and successfully that which we kept repressed all these years, how much simpler and satisfying it would be than having to integrate it all through a process of sublimation; how much less energy this would require! Such acting out behavior on the part of the staff—which is fed by the omnipresent tendency of mental patients to act openly, immediately, and radically, based on the pressure of their primitive drives—is sometimes easily arrested and the process directed toward sublimation. At other times the stopping has to be done much more forcefully, and even then it may take a long time before reintegration is achieved. An example may illustrate this.

Looking back on something that happened some three years earlier, a staff member reported:

> *Working with a group of patients who had a hard time controlling themselves, in a moment when I was frustrated by my inability to redirect their acting-out behavior into more constructive channels, I encouraged them to throw water all over each other, at me, and at the walls and furniture, to express their anger. I felt I was acting in line with what I had been taught: to give the patients freedom to express themselves, and felt very smart that I had directed them to use water which, after all, could not hurt anybody. To my utter dismay, they went to pieces and started breaking up the furniture, even their own prized possessions. One of the patients, fortunately at the moment more sensible than I, went for help. (131)*

(Such capability of psychiatric patients to know when things go wrong and to seek help occurs in any mental hospital because, as already noted, each patient retains large areas of rationality, particularly around phenomena which do not directly relate to his personal pressures, anxieties, defensive needs, or delusional preoccupations. The more an institution succeeds in creating a total therapeutic milieu, the better patients are able to act autonomously: partly because their acting this way is encouraged all along; partly because they feel that the milieu is there to protect them, even if one of its elements —this particular staff member at this moment—fails them; and they basically like the setting sufficiently to want to protect it. In addition, they could sense that even in acting out, the staff member was motivated by something he erroneously believed was good for the patients. All this gives them a chance to take the initiative in helping so that things do not get entirely out of hand.)

To continue the incident: the worker wrote,

> *When the havoc was immediately stopped, and I was asked what I was up to, I was so upset about how it had turned out, I in tears complained to Bettelheim that I had been only trying to do exactly what I had learned from his books —to give children freedom to express themselves. At that time, I was unable to appreciate the vital importance, or even meaning, of real self-regulation (as opposed to chaotic and destructive acting out), nor how I had used these*

poorly integrated and hence vulnerable patients to act out
emotion for me, which I was unable to act out for myself.

The problem was that this worker could not yet integrate anger, so he had to keep it repressed. But when a situation with the patients seemed to him to permit or even require letting anger break out into action, this did not lead to a removal of the anger's source or even to its being constructively neutralized through positive action; it evoked uncontrolled behavior. Far from helping the patients with their anger, his inability to recognize and deal with his own anger had increased their anxiety to an unmanageable degree. My response at the time was to give the worker a great deal of credit for having been wise enough to suggest water as a medium for acting out destructive tendencies; this showed that despite the utter chaos that resulted, his ego nevertheless had been at work to the extent that worse things had been avoided. This reaction permitted him to accept reluctantly that he had played the role either of the agent-provocateur or the sorcerer's apprentice, who could activate incredible powers based on unconscious motivation but not yet control them, not to mention use them constructively to achieve sublimation. He could then take the advice to wait a while longer, before encouraging patients to act out their anger. In time he would learn to unleash it only when he could be sure this would lead not to uncontrolled acting out, but to its integration.

Everyone who chooses to work with mental patients because doing so is attractive to him (as opposed to those who merely seek a livelihood) is motivated by the unconscious hope of also gaining something for himself. It might be to prove oneself a good person or to expiate a guilt; but even then a hope of gaining something further for himself is mixed in, although his moral code may not permit this to surface. Actually, man can do his best only if he feels a personal necessity to engage in this particular work. Somehow when we only work for wages, we feel we don't get enough out of it for ourselves, even though we depend on and enjoy what the money can buy. Work becomes meaningful only as we are convinced we gain something very special from it for ourselves. The skill demanded of the senior staff is the prime requirement for making the institution into a therapeutic milieu: they must be able to demonstrate to the rest of the staff how much they can gain for themselves from this work, and help them to do so.

In the case of this particular worker, some of his reasons were quite clear. He had been outstandingly successful in his studies in mathematics and physics; he had done significant research for which he was awarded a fellowship to work for his Ph.D. But while his work in this field progressed very satisfactorily, he became dissatisfied because he wanted to get closer to people; having taken a course in the field of human psychology, and become vaguely acquainted with the work of the School, he decided this was a good way to achieve this end. Getting closer to people was the conscious gain he hoped for.

As we can see, there were also unconscious hopes that the uncontrolled behavior of the patients would permit him to let down his defenses against acting out his unconscious pressures. His tears, and his statement that he had only done what he thought was expected of him, had the same source: his frustrated hopes that the work would not only permit but require him to "let go." Thus, uncontrolled behavior in this particular setting would conform with the demands of his ego and superego: the task of helping others made it necessary. His inner motivation was to put one over on his ego and superego, by working in a situation which would force them to side with the id. This can be a constructive impulse, if the institution knows how to use it; that is, if it helps the worker to channel the energy thus freed toward sublimation.

The prime task of staff members as executed for each other—usually by the senior staff for the junior members, but sometimes a new staff member can by chance render this service to a much more experienced one—is to foster the process of personality reintegration by guaranteeing it will not get out of kilter. At all times the effort must be that any dissolution of ego structure will not only go hand in hand with a more adequate formation of it; but that this will proceed in a process which is both appropriate and optimally balanced between dissolution and new formation for this particular individual.

Therefore, the dejection of the worker which made him break out in tears was due not to the fact that he had made such a mess of things, but to the sudden realization that, for all his hard efforts, he would not gain anything for himself—which in his case was the chance to act out openly and violently what he had painfully and rigidly controlled for so long. He had yet to learn that there were much better ways to deal with his anger: namely, to recognize its origin and do something about it. But to tell him that at the time would have only made him feel immature; whereas my task was to convince him that a higher maturity was within easy reach, and could be plucked from this defeat.

Essentially the only way the staff can feel they have gained something for themselves is if each time they make an error (which when dealing with psychiatric patients always means they have gotten themselves in some kind of psychological mess), they are helped to learn something of importance to them about themselves and about the patients. The fact that a mistake made in working with patients leads to the feeling that the worker, patients, or both have landed in a psychological mess makes learning about it all much more pressing, and much more rewarding.

It was of the greatest importance that what the worker experienced as a double defeat—since the patients had suffered, and he himself could no longer look forward to acting out his own repression through the work—should have turned out to be something from which he gained. Otherwise he would have been left with the feeling that the work was only hardship, and had little to offer which he could not gain more easily elsewhere. The first positive experience which counteracted the defeat and turned it into victory was that despite the havoc he had created and its criticism, his acceptance as a person did not alter. Thus he actually had a corrective emotional experience, though at the time he didn't realize it. His past experiences had been that when he did something wrong, he was rejected for it; this time his actions had led to a special effort to help him understand himself better.

Finally, whenever the patients feel that the staff member has learned something of importance to him, through them, it is a great experience. This builds their egos more than anything else. Just because a total therapeutic institution does so much for the patients, they must be able to feel that they, in turn, do something for the staff. What they can and do indeed do for the staff is to help them grow in self-awareness, and thereby increase their ability to help the patients. Patients would often throw this very fact in the staff's face: "You are here to learn on us." What was shown openly in this remark was anger, because it was made only when the patients felt that the worker was amiss in something. But the anger was only passing; the patients' pride in being able to make such a significant contribution was continuous, though it usually was not directly expressed. Unless the patients feel they are making such a contribution and that the staff member in fact does become a much better worker and person through working with them, they are losing out on one of the most effective ingredients toward their getting well.

A hard lesson which every worker must learn is that he has to give up childish fantasies that some great and unique event will cure the patient and prove his own worth. Such dreams of glory die hard. It is difficult to accept that those occurrences which hit us to the core are usually so complex, so beset by ambivalences, have so many different and far-reaching ramifications, that it is almost impossible to extract only positive meaning from them. These big events are flashy, much talked about, visible to everybody. But the elements out of which human relations are forged are not these big events, but the small, day-by-day incidents. We must give up our image of the knight-beyond-reproach who rides out and slays the dragon Insanity, and accept that we are nothing but humble workers. Our plucking a few weeds or planting some little flowers will not create the beautiful and everlasting rose garden the patient—and maybe we too—has unrealistically wished for. Yet if we keep working hard, although we cannot create the magnificent park of our hopes and dreams, eventually where previously grew an impenetrable and thorny thicket of weeds, there will be a nice little garden in which it will be pleasant to walk with a friend to whom, when he says, "The two of us have cultivated this together," one can answer: "Oh, I did pluck out some weeds, but the flowers are your doing; together we made them grow."

Through empathy a worker can avert a suicidal crisis or even use it constructively; he can turn what could have been a destructive experience into something that restores the patient's faith in life in an instant. While such crisis intervention can save a life, it cannot make it worth living. Strangely enough, we all are so afraid of catastrophic events, so fascinated and desirous of "peak" experiences which seem to lift us suddenly to a higher plane, since they are so remarkable, unforgettable, easily talked about, that we tend to believe it is these experiences which make us what we are. Psychoanalysis as popularly conceived adds credence to this view, by emphasizing the consequences on personality of traumatizing experiences. But this is not so; Hartmann, Kris, and Loewenstein (59) have pointed out that it is not so much the traumatic event per se which is crucial, as how the person responds to it day after day. The process of psychoanalysis teaches how often the neglected minutiae of life are what reveal most, and how frequently the same experience has to be repeated in manifold forms before it is mastered. Of course, we all can activate ourselves around a big event; but it is not the big birthday celebration or the visit to the circus (while these stand out in the memory) which make for a child's positive outlook in life. That is not shaped by the fancy birthday cake he got once a year, but by how he was held and fed by his mother on each of his feedings, and with what emotions.

At the Orthogenic School, at the beginning the worker would try to rely on, and spend most of his energy on, such special events as a birthday or a big outing. These are not unimportant; they do have a role in therapy, but only if they are pleasant corroborations of what has been happening all along, around all the small events of the day. These small matters don't make for exciting conversation or reading in publications. But tiny piece by tiny piece adds up—how a patient is helped to meet the day morning after morning—and these are much more important than the special occasion.

Moreover, it is undesirable from the standpoint of therapy for the patient to feel that he needs us to be able to overcome some great crisis of his life. If the task of the institution is to help the patient to become master of himself, develop self-respect, then it is particularly important that we help him to recognize his own contribution in dealing with the crucial impasse, with only minimal help from the worker. If the patient were led to feel that he needs his worker to overcome any major difficulty, then he would simply have exchanged bondage to his chaotic tendencies for one to a reasonable and supportive human being of good will. Thus the patient would never believe in his ability to meet life successfully on his own. One of the disappointments the beginner must face is that he must not claim what are possibly his greatest contributions; otherwise they would not be therapeutically effective.

Any good mother intuitively knows that as she guides her infant's first steps, carefully holding him by his hands, she must tell her child with delight, "You walked all by yourself." And if at the moment she is not sufficiently carried away by his great achievement and her pleasure in it emotionally to forget that without her hand he could never have done it, the child is cheated of one important experience which could have guided him toward autonomy. Of course, intellectually the mother knows very well that she is the guiding hand in the child's experience of mastery, but any credit she would claim for it would take that much away from the child. Therefore, without thought, the good mother will tell others with pride and happiness: "Today my child took his first steps all by himself." Only when questioned: "Did he really?" might she add as an afterthought, "Well, of course, he held onto me."

To be able to feel good about giving the patient the credit for an accomplishment which may largely be due to the worker, he must feel confident of his importance to the patient and to his colleagues. Once the worker's empathy has become a full and operative part of his personality in his dealings with the patients, the sudden or gradual achievements and new ego strength of the patient will give him pleasure. Not only can he take partial credit for them, knowing his has been a real contribution (whether or not outwardly recognized by his colleagues or the patient) but he will also feel empathic delight, knowing the added emotional comfort the patient is feeling. Once this is established, then without much jealousy the worker can give recognition to the others who help the patient's progress along. The worker can feel this way, and his co-workers go along with it, only if the institution is a total milieu of which he is an integral part. Not claiming the patient's accomplishment as his own is acceptable to him only if he knows this will not take away recognition of what he did achieve for the patient; and the credit given must not take any away from all the others who have contributed. An institution which is split into competing departments is ipso facto unable to give most of the credit to the patient, since the departments will clamor for credits to defend their vested interests and justify their importance. And if the entire staff do not feel they are together in the work, they will not implicitly give credit to the worker when he himself ascribes the achievement to the patient. So in a roundabout way, only a total therapeutic milieu can afford to give the patient the feeling he did it all by himself, or nearly so; and this is the most potent way to help him get better.

The psychiatric patient who is convinced that he cannot do anything right, or on his own, needs even more than the small child to feel he can now do important things all by himself. This is true even for the megalomaniac who claims his superiority to one and all, which is a very tough defense against reality but barely a paper-thin protection against his conviction that he is a nothing. The therapeutic milieu must be so constructed and sustained that his experiences with life will lead him to feel, contrary to all his own doubts, that he can do a great deal—much more than he ever believed was possible. Around relatively unimportant accomplishments, the patient can give credence to the help he receives without damage to his self-respect, but only if this is never expected of him. The more we can convey to him: "You did it all by yourself," at least the most difficult part, the more he will eventually be able freely to acknowledge the help given him. Although it may seem at first glance to be an exaggeration or outright distortion, it is deeply true that the patient "did it all by himself." Milieu therapy consists of creating and maintaining an environment safe enough to free the patient's inherent maturational potential to achieve balance within his own psyche and realistic relations to the outer world. Simultaneously with working through and mastering of past traumas, milieu therapy must permit development to proceed as it would have but for the original trauma. Were it not for the innate developmental drive toward growth and normal functioning, no amount of tender loving care from the environment could bring about the vast changes we have observed in our patients.

To lead the patient to believe in his own achievements, we must accept and be satisfied with the role to which Freud likened psychoanalysis: that of the midwife, whose task is to see that the child the woman has conceived and grown in her body may safely enter this world, without any damage to him and his mother in the often difficult and painful process of being born. We are indeed midwives in the sense that we do not create this new person who has found his wholeness; our pride and satisfaction must come from having helped its coming into being.

The worker can do this only if he doesn't have to struggle to gain recognition, which must be freely given by those from whom receiving it counts most. The senior staff in particular must serve as such midwives to the beginners, as much as all staff must function in this capacity in their relations to the patients. Here, too, the attitudes of the senior staff to junior staff and patients must serve as images in the likeness of which the beginners form themselves.

A major task of the therapeutic milieu is to be set up so that the worker does not need to depend on recognition from the patients, who cannot give anything, though what he helps them to achieve is his greatest satisfaction. But while there is great fulfillment inherent in the positive consequences of one's work, this is still not the same as receiving recognition from those whom one respects, and who one believes are best able to judge whether it is deserved. This requires that praise not be given for trifles, of course, because then it is of no value. As a matter of fact, just because the worker knows that his greatest reward comes from the patient's achievement, his self-interest induces him to believe that the patient did do it himself. After all, the satisfaction a mother gains from the fact that her child can walk when holding her hands is not comparable to the pleasure that comes from his walking on his own.

The worker who has gained confidence in the importance of what he does will be full of the great things his patient has done today—he will tell about them and not about his own contribution, which by comparison will seem to him unimportant. The worker is able to give the patient all the credit so necessary to successful therapy when he feels secure that by doing so he will not be cheated of his due. This security is wholly different from the attitude of the self-effacing worker, who thinks so little of his significance within the institution that he gains no satisfaction from working there. In the latter case, the patient will lose from the worker's presence, rather than gain from it.

I have found that praising a worker in the presence of others tends to create jealousies even among a well-integrated staff. If the relation between director or senior workers and the rest of the staff is the right one, the worker gains more satisfaction from a private understanding of how much he contributed, expressed in some casual appreciatory remark, than from a laudatory speech. I have seen workers more satisfied when a senior staff member listened with deep interest as they told what their patient had achieved, and then remarked, "Yes, and we all know he did it all by himself, and you just sat by and did nothing." A big laudatory speech somehow implies that one is astonished that the worker was able to do it, as if one had not trusted him all along to perform the difficult deed. It also somehow suggests a lack of genuine pleasure in the worker's achievement, this being hidden behind too many words.

I have mentioned this mainly to make the point that it must be possible to convey deep appreciation in ways that are not offensive to other staff members, who might resent too little being made of their contribution, if it seems to them too much is made of a colleague's. How this is done naturally depends on the persons involved and their relations to each other; and it has a great deal to do with how the institution is organized.

But there is still another reason I feel wary about elaborate praise. If the director praises too loudly, it cannot help creating a vague feeling that what the worker did was done to gain recognition from superiors, rather than for the patient, because the patient is his personal project. One cannot do one's best in order to satisfy somebody else; one can do it only to please oneself. If one has done his best, then it is nice indeed to be praised. But if the praise becomes excessive, one may begin to wonder who one really wanted to please in the first place.

23 | *Personal Change and Professional Growth*

The success of a therapeutic milieu depends on the soundness of its view of man, and the realm of experiences it offers to the patient to restore him to mental health; in short, on its philosophy. Yet even the best theoretical understanding of what is involved in such restoration will be ineffective if it is not developed into the right practice. Only individual persons can do this, though they can be aided (or impeded) by the organizational structure. Whether or not the institution achieves its purposes depends on whether it is staffed by the right persons, working within the right organizational setting.

What motivates members of a therapeutic milieu to achieve those intellectual, attitudinal, and personal skills which they need to serve the patients well and become contributing partners in the common enterprise? What is it that engages them in the more difficult venture of changing themselves into the people who not only can do this demanding work, but find it more rewarding than anything else they could do at this moment in their lives?

The senior staff, who have already acquired these characteristics through previous experience and development, don't concern us here, although they too continue to grow as persons and workers. But since they already have achieved maturity, no further deep-reaching changes are necessary. As persons, they have gained that mature integration which, for example, Erikson describes as generativity, Goldstein and Maslow as self-actualization, and others in different terms. As therapists, they have reached a familiarity with their own unconscious, both its content and processes, which permits ready empathy with the patients; while their grip on reality is so firm that they no longer fear whatever the closest relation to a patient may evoke in them. That is, the senior staff apply in their participation in the therapeutic milieu what the others are still struggling to achieve. No longer faced with the problem of becoming what they already are, the senior staff can provide leadership for those who are still in the process of becoming.

A personal psychoanalysis does not necessarily equip a person to become a successful staff member; sometimes it helps, sometimes it hinders the process. A person ordinarily undergoes psychoanalysis because of some serious difficulty he encounters in living. If the outcome is favorable, he will have overcome what stood in the way of his creating the life he desires; most likely it also helps him understand his own unconscious better, thus giving him greater readiness to comprehend that of others. There is no reason to assume that psychoanalysis makes him ready to become part of an enterprise that makes so many emotional demands. For others, participating in a therapeutic community is the best way of achieving higher integration for themselves; though they, too, may profit from a personal analysis.

A former professor of social group work and a former director of nursing in a university hospital serve as examples. In their professions they had been recognized leaders, but on coming to the School they were, of course, just part of the group. They didn't know why they felt so much better about this, yet somehow in their previous occupations things had not been done the way they had wanted them. Successful as they had been in the eyes of the world, they nevertheless had felt they were failures; neither their private nor their professional lives had been what they had wanted for themselves. After some five or more years as staff members, these two, as has been true for others, returned to the professions they had left and did even better in them than before. To find true satisfaction in their first-chosen professions, they had to solve problems of inner integration, difficulties which even personal analysis had failed to remove sufficiently. The challenge of working with psychiatric patients, not as supervisors as they both had done before but in direct contact, activated and permitted resolution of childhood residues which had stood in the way of finding their old professional activities satisfactory. In order to find themselves, they needed to work with others as equals, in a situation where so much emotional give-and-take was unavoidable. When they had done so, their original professions could prove fully rewarding.

While these workers had been projected into a mid-career crisis, most staff members found themselves in similar confusion at an earlier age. Maybe this is why working with psychiatric patients was attractive to them, since they dimly felt that if they were able to help the patients to find the answer to the question of what they wanted to do with their lives, then they too would be able to do the same. Helping others in order to help oneself, if one is sincere about helping oneself, is not such a bad motive for therapeutic work.

Most staff members were considerably younger than Dante when he found himself seeking the right way out of temporary darkness; roughly in their early twenties to early thirties. But, like Dante, circling with understanding and compassion among those condemned to live in their private hells was what they needed to find their own way to a higher realm of clarity. Perhaps the conviction of their own importance to others and the realization of how much they could do for them was what these young people most needed to find themselves and their rightful place in the order of things, including their chosen profession.

Not everybody who is attracted to the idea of helping psychotic patients can live up to the demands, both of devoting oneself to others and of changing oneself. Those who wish to do this type of work are mainly persons of good will, and the rock on which they run aground is that of frozen defenses of which they don't dare let go. Though we tried to prevent this from happening, for each worker who was willing and successfully able to restructure his personality through his work experiences, some two others failed and left the School, under the impact of a challenge to personality growth they felt unable to meet.

What usually happened was that despite his best and genuine intention to work with psychotics, the worker became repelled, or beset by terrifying anxiety. He would leave, giving a variety of reasons which served as rationalizations for not recognizing that his inner integration had been threatened. Among such rationalizations were the difficulties of the work, the inconvenient hours, the offer of better pay elsewhere, and so on. Contrary to his conscious desire to get close to such patients, these claims prevented the individual from realizing that he was disgusted or upset by their behavior or afraid of them. Such workers were unable to state openly that because of the nature of the experience they were fearful for their integration, or that they had begun to hate the patients or the psychological demands of the work.

A characteristic example is that of a young woman who, because of her unusual abilities, had been given a special fellowship to train in the education of blind children. For more than a year she had lived with such children in an institution, working with the most emotionally disturbed ones there, and in terms of what this institution expected of her had been very successful at it. In a prolonged correspondence, she expressed her desire to use the training the School had to offer. When she finally joined the staff, and the difficulty of working with these unintegrated persons was pointed out, she said with much conviction that she could accept all of it and repeated that ours were exactly the type of patients she wished to work with. She was a well-educated and well-brought-up young woman, successful in her adjustment to life and in her profession. At first the children didn't respond badly to her, and her work showed promise.

One day, after about six weeks of work, an autistic girl bit her. She took this with a certain spartan attitude and resisted efforts to help her uncover her own feelings about the injury. When offered the opportunity to rest for a day or two, she insisted she did not mind and wished to continue, despite the localized pain. The next time she was with the autistic child the child suddenly ran away to escape the anger she felt in the worker because of the injury she had inflicted. Our efforts to show the worker this connection were again to no avail. The next time worker and child were together the child began to hurt herself severely, biting herself worse than she had bitten the worker a few days before. Obviously, for the safety of the child and her eventual improvement, we could not permit the situation to continue. The worker could no longer deny that the child's behavior had become quite different from what it formerly had been with her and still was with the child's other counselors. The new worker now seemed to become dimly aware that, contrary to her self-image of a person who loved emotionally disturbed children and was not afraid of their hostility, she had been repelled by the child's unintegrated behavior all along, a repulsion that may very well have led to the child's biting her. Since the injury, she had been very much afraid of the child. She could not at all accept what seemed obvious to those who were observing her: that she had also begun to hate the child. This was probably caused much less by the injury sustained than by the fact that her inner response to the child's action came to threaten her self-image. In her work she now became emotionally frozen, and another group of children who had tentatively accepted her before this series of events now began to reject her because she could no longer respond to them spontaneously.

Obviously, at this point the worker would have had to realize that her self-image of accepting emotionally disturbed children, no matter what their behavior, did not stand up under stress. To continue her work, she would have to recognize that on occasion she was rejecting of children, and, in reaction to their attacks, was afraid of them, perhaps even hated them. Such realization could and probably would have led her to become conscious of her own hostility, which until then had been so well controlled that she could remain unaware of it. Such recognition would have presented her with the immediate task of achieving better integration in certain respects. Later, starting with this or other experiences, such efforts at integration would also have had to extend to other aspects of her personality as yet not fully integrated.

The worker, unwilling or unable to undergo this process despite the help other staff members offered, suddenly decided the remuneration was not adequate. In an attempt to show that she was denying her true motives for wanting to leave, an offer was made to increase her salary. She did not accept, left the School, and stopped working with emotionally disturbed children. Being a person with a healthy, normal personality, excellent training and abilities, and realizing that her present level of integration was perfectly adequate for average living, she immediately secured a teaching position in a school for normal children.

In doing so she protected herself against the further disintegration of her personality that might have resulted from continued experiences with psychotics. It should be stressed that such disintegration of personality is definitely a reaction to the impact of the unintegrated behavior of the patients, and to the requirement inherent in the therapeutic milieu not to meet it defensively but acceptingly, with therapeutic intent and action. This kind of personality disintegration is not a pathological process, but a temporary and appropriate response to the pressure not only to meet the work task but also to live up to the ethos of the milieu.

Other new workers, whose motivation for devoting themselves to these patients is much stronger, try harder. While able to accept extremely primitive behavior in the patients, they still may not be ready to face what it activates in themselves. The patient's physical, verbal, and sexual assaults awaken deep anxieties and doubts in these hitherto secure and adjusted young adults, and their integration is threatened. Their response to this challenge to their values and way of life depends, in part, upon what is most threatening to their own integration. For most, it is the reactivation of primitive tendencies in themselves as they watch them being acted out by others. The worker may then resort to defensive efforts at suppressing the patients' expression of uncontrolled instinctual behavior and try to force them to conform to more acceptable standards of conduct. If the worker's personality or therapeutic convictions (the latter strongly supported by the mores of the institution) do not permit him to try suppressing the patients, then the worker will try to reinforce his wall of defenses against his own instinctual tendencies, and become more rigid and frozen in his emotions.

These normal, well-adjusted individuals, who had sufficient ego strength to enter and do well in graduate school and in working with people, after living and working intimately with these unintegrated patients sooner or later appear to develop quite serious neurotic behavior. Some become hostile, or even punitive to the patients, and hostile and unmannerly to other members of the staff. They are very uncomfortable and resent the institution and its mores, and the other staff members, who expect them to be able to accept the patients' threatening behavior without undesirable counter-reaction. Other new workers defend themselves by feeling nothing, or by other forms of emotional withdrawing. Still others try to erect new, stronger defenses against the new and violently activated inner pressures—through intellectualization, for example.

For a worker to succeed in the task that now confronts him of restructuring his personality, all other members of the therapeutic milieu must understand and accept that such developments, though seemingly quite neurotic, are normal reactions to particular stress situations. These are emergency reactions. They spring from the realization that a system of defenses and a level of inner integration which until now in the world outside were considered fully adequate are suddenly insufficient. Matters are made even more difficult because what has broken down this level of integration and system of defenses is a professional activity chosen freely by the adult as his preferred vocation. To work successfully with these patients, it has become obvious that an infinitely higher level of personal integration is necessary. It is also necessary to be familiar with and have a greater acceptance of one's own unconscious mental life, as well as the unconscious mental life of other people. Disillusionment with oneself, and occasionally even despair, is one of the reactions to realizing that one's defensive system and level of integration (once apparently so adequate) have suddenly, under the very special conditions of working with psychotics, turned out to be wanting.

This is the critical moment in the development of a staff member. It takes varying periods of time for different persons to reach it; usually more than six months and rarely as much as two years. Once this point is reached, the successful staff member begins the process of slowly giving up his old defenses and any newly erected ones. He proceeds to gain greater tolerance of primitive impulses in himself.

With this, he can accept and deal constructively with the patients' expression or acting out of the same impulses.

From then on, having the need and desire to achieve mature personal integration, and dimly realizing that his work will be a continuous challenge to higher integration, the worker experiences the discomfort inflicted by the patients as a relatively small price to pay for very considerable benefits.

Many have remarked on the "dedication" of these young members of the therapeutic milieu. Dedicated they undoubtedly are, but not merely to the patients under their care. They are dedicated also to achieving their own integration. No longer needing or wishing to put a barrier of emotional distance between themselves and the problems the patient's behavior poses for them—actually being prevented from so doing by the ethos of the milieu—they have to find ways to integrate the emotions aroused by their experiences.

Whereas initially they had to defend themselves against what their experiences with the patients evoked in them, these are accepted later as difficult but nonetheless desirable challenges to solve problems within themselves. Such challenges are not eagerly sought; self-protection militates against this. Personality integration is just too difficult a task, recognition of the latent unsolved problems within oneself too painful, awareness of the need for sublimation too demanding, for anybody to wish to seek such experiences. But now, when situations that unavoidably occur as part of the work with patients present these tasks, their implications for oneself are no longer denied; instead, serious efforts are made to meet them straightforwardly.

To recognize the extremely simple needs, hopes, anxieties, and exasperations behind elaborate psychotic constructs, and to assess their true nature from overt behavior and fantasy productions, demands training, knowledge, insight, experience, and most of all application. But underlying this skill are experiences common to us all. To be able to see through patients' myriad defensive screens takes considerable knowledge of oneself, and acceptance of how simple one's own psychology really is, despite the elaborate contraptions we erect to hide this fact from ourselves. It requires that we accept how obvious we all really are. To succeed in therapeutic work, every worker has to struggle through to this realization; it is a task of varying difficulty depending on the particular worker. Still, as they develop in their competence as staff members, they and their lives become simpler—because they learn that the most basic feelings and experiences are what counts, in the patients' lives as in their own.

A worker, in the autobiography she had written when applying for a staff position, stated that she came from a very happy, closely knit family, and the photo she was asked to enclose was one of herself and her mother, the two closely entwined. After a year of being part of the therapeutic milieu, she saw her family relationships differently. On returning from a visit home she wrote in her diary:

> I feel as though I never got enough of anything from my parents. This goes for food, as well as less conspicuous necessities like caring for what I wanted. Mother had once mentioned to me that I was a good baby, never cried, ate well. I know that I was a very fat baby and for some reason when I was home this month I asked if I had gotten enough food. She said yes, but added that they were afraid that I was too fat and had put me on a diet. . . . This is very much in line with my feelings of deprivation. I can remember when I was seven or so saving food from parties I went to as if I never got enough candy. My mother had many ideas about the badness of candy, cokes, and so on, for teeth, and my teeth were always full of cavities. But after the first year I worked with the patients, and ate with them much candy and drank many cokes for the first time in my life, I had no cavities.

After having been part of the therapeutic milieu for two years, this same worker wrote:

> As anyone who looks at me can see, I have even in the relatively short time I have been working here undergone changes towards becoming a calmer, softer, more peaceful person. I am aware there are other areas which are also changing. Just the fact that I can believe in the changes in me is something new to me.

This change was in part the result of her helping the patients become "calmer, softer, more peaceful" persons, and her observations that such changes are possible in a residential setting, of which she was then very much a part.

> I feel more settled; knowing that I will be some place for many years is very satisfying to me. It's as if I have found a place which I can keep if I try, which is stable and yet which I am sure will grow more satisfying as time passes. . . . I

feel the comfort in many substantial ways, too. When I had a cold and took a whole big can of juice from the storeroom I offered to pay for it. I was told, no, that the workers' wants were to be satisfied, as those of the patients; only it was said in different words. This pleased me. So does being able to get food out of the storerooms or kitchen whenever I want it, at night if I want it. I sometimes stand in the storeroom; just looking at the amounts of food is wonderful. I have been eating less, but I feel as if I can get what I want when and if I want it. This business of getting what I want has spread, for I now buy myself things, like a skirt or some chocolates, which I've wanted before but was unable to buy for myself. I guess this can be summed up by saying that I seem to be treating myself more in line with my needs, without employing any semiexternal criticism, such as that I shouldn't have too much when others are starving.

Staff members acquire a new personal dignity because of their work. Though they may continue to doubt at moments that they are welcome or important in the world, they soon become convinced that at least one human relationship—that with the patient—is of great importance. In order to understand better the process of change which takes place in those who attempt and succeed in becoming part of a therapeutic milieu, we also engaged in more objective studies of staff development. Wright (131, 132) and I specifically devised a drawing test for this purpose. First let us consider four drawings: two examples by beginners; one by a senior staff member; and one by a worker who was just beginning to feel the desire to commit himself to the therapeutic milieu and had hopes he might succeed in doing so. All were asked to draw what to them would be a typical dormitory situation.

While these drawings reveal many aspects of the workers' personalities and attitudes toward those they worked with, particularly important were the degree of emotional closeness or distance revealed between the children and worker, his conception of the patterns of interactions between himself and the children, and those between the children themselves. When the drawing shows emotional distance between worker and children, it also suggests something about the nature of the worker's defenses.

Drawing 1 (p. 366) is that of an experienced and skillful staff member. The children are shown as interacting freely with each other and with her. She is playing with one child, while the others are pleasantly occupied; the games the children are playing are both active and quiet, according to what they happen to like best. The adult's size is not accentuated in the drawing, and she participates in the most childish activity, "pat-a-cake." There is no evidence of a defensive distance between worker and children, nor of any preference on her part as to the children's activities. There is neither emptiness nor crowding.

Drawing 2 shows the worker who is no longer a beginner, having spent approximately one year at the institution, and who shows promise but as yet is by no means an accomplished worker. In this drawing three of the children are playing by themselves. Another has withdrawn and is reading on his bed. Two children and the worker . are playing at a table, but one child is precariously balanced on his chair and may "fall out" of this interaction at any moment. As a whole, the picture is less well organized than Drawing 1. The single elements seem to float in the air and are basically unrelated. All figures are relatively small in size, surrounded by much empty, unorganized space, as if they might be swallowed up in it. The figures are drawn with heavy, uncertain lines. There is shading around the periphery and to some extent within the figures.

Previous studies of drawings suggest that such shading and uncertainty of lines represent anxiety and ambivalence (22, 85, 87). This is borne out in the case of the worker who made Drawing 2. He still experiences anxiety and ambivalence about the children, although he is reaching out to them. The picture seems to express this since he is in contact with some of the children. No particular defense system is suggested. Even more important, when compared with the following two examples of beginners' drawings, this worker views the situation from the inside and in close perspective. While in the drawing some children remain unrelated to him or to each other, they are involved in different activities of their own devising, not activities dictated by the worker's desires.

A danger sign is the worker's apparent feeling that the children can form a group only around him. This was confirmed by his self-observations. He stated that he feared children relating to each other or to other workers would be lost to him forever. His anxiety was felt by the children, who when with him were either involved in an activity with him or tended to play by themselves; with other workers the same children also autonomously engaged in group activities with each other.

Drawings 3 and 4 were typical for new and relatively unskilled workers. In *Drawing* 3 all the children are lying in bed, and the worker is set apart from them. She is doing something *for* rather than *with* them, and this on a very adult intellectual level: reading to the children. There is great physical (representative of emotional) distance between adult and child and between child and child. More important, the worker does something different from the children; while she is active (reading), they listen passively. The whole scene is drawn as if seen from afar and above (possibly as she sees herself as an adult, distant from and above the children). It may also be significant that the worker chose to picture the end of the day, shortly before she will be leaving the children.

The suggested defense mechanisms against emotional closeness in this drawing are neatness and orderliness in external arrangement; physical distance and the children's inactivity; passivity and escape into intellect or fantasy (reading stories). Possibly the drawing also expresses a compensatory feeling of superiority to the children. The fact that all the children are doing the same thing and are drawn alike may express the worker's inability to view them as distinct individuals.

Drawing 4 differs in that the worker is not shown. Since he was asked to draw a typical dormitory situation, one has to assume that he is situated in the dormitory, looking out through its window. Interest in playing (not an absence or rejection of lively interaction) is depicted, but only among the children. As in Drawing 3, all the children are doing the same thing—this time playing ball. Again there is no individuation, no recognition that different children like to do different things. They are seen not only from a distance, but separated from the worker. He does nothing for or with the children, who play actively only with one another.

This worker's defense is also distance; but since he removes himself from the situation entirely, putting a wall between himself and the children, he doesn't need to impose his defensive pattern on them (as in Drawing 3). While he does not allow himself to come close to them physically or emotionally, he views the children in freer terms. Secure against direct personal involvement through distance, he can conceive of them acting in a relatively free, expressive way. This drawing fitted with what was known about this worker, who originally had wanted to do psychological research rather than clinical work, and became a therapist only after considerable inner struggle.

At the time staff members were asked to draw a typical dormitory situation, they were also asked to draw a person, whatever person they wished. A group of beginners were asked to do this about seven to twelve weeks after they began working, and then again in intervals of about six months. The development during these crucial first two years is illustrated by the drawings made by two workers who did

DRAWING 1

DRAWING 2

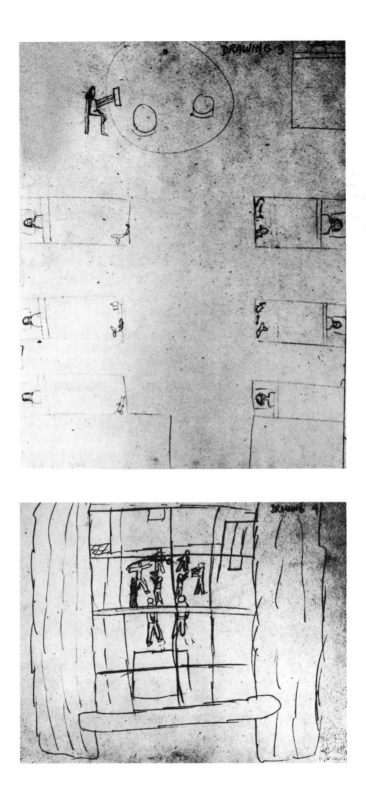

not work out, one who became a good worker although he never reached the senior level of accomplishment, and two who did succeed in reaching the senior level.

First the two failures: June's drawings are shown on page 369. They are quite remarkable for their sameness; nothing seems to have changed over time in her view of the dormitory scene or her place in it throughout. In each drawing, she is sitting down playing a game.

In Drawing A, June identified herself as the figure sitting to the right at the center table; in Drawing B, as the figure farthest to the left, sitting at the card table; in Drawing C, as the figure sitting right center at the table looking out of the picture. Drawing B is the most promising, since she seems to be doing something with the three children sitting with her at the table. But in Drawings A and C, she sits at the table in somewhat isolated activity. Her drawings of a person (herself) are also strikingly similar except in size. The decrease in the size of the person in her drawings between Time A and Time B suggests that during that six months' period, she did relinquish some of her interest in herself. That this interest was then accorded to the children is suggested by her drawings of the dormitory situation at Time B, in which she seems more in contact with them. This is the kind of growth process to be striven for; but June did not maintain her movement in that direction, as her drawings at Time C reflect. Thus, while her defensive isolation from the children and her concentration on herself weakened (Time B), she was not strong enough at this crucial moment to let her defenses be further softened by the impact of the milieu. On the contrary, she realized the weakness in her defensive armor and instead of reaching for higher integration, began to reinforce her defensive position. By Time C she was back to her initial position and soon thereafter left the School of her own volition.

Page 371 shows George's drawings. He also depicted a scene looked at from the distance in his first dormitory drawing. All his drawings reveal the great emotional pressure he experienced in working with severely disturbed children. Before he came to the institution, he had been an outstanding student in the Ph.D. program of clinical psychology. After leaving in the middle of his second year, he resumed his studies. Following my suggestion, he changed to medical school, where he did extremely well and eventually became a deservedly well-known research psychiatrist. But under continuous, intimate exposure to the pathology of the children he was unable to maintain his otherwise successful integration, and gradually fell to

A

B

C

pieces. The increasing disorganization and eccentricity of his drawings reflect this.

Morton's drawings are shown on page 372. At first he drew a
stereotyped figure sitting down, while his dormitory scene is but an
architectural plan. Six months later, his person has gained life,
becoming more active and less stereotyped. The dormitory scene
pictures him and the children, not just an empty plan. Although he
is not yet with the children, he is doing something *for* them. The
change from drawing a dormitory floor plan to depicting interacting
children is most dramatic.

Perhaps such progress was too fast, overreaching his ability to
integrate. Six months later (Time C), Morton is again more self-
protective. While his drawing of a person retains its action, it has
again become stereotyped. In the dormitory scene he sees himself
among the children, but in a self-depreciating way—they are making
fun of him. By Time D, his drawing of a person reflects the essence
of the change he was undergoing. The figure is younger, active, optimistic; he has gained more freedom. With a child, he is still the
passive participant; but the child is depicted as full of life.

It should be noted that Morton had completed his psychoanalysis while working in another children's institution about a year
before he joined the School's staff. Shortly after Time B, he began
to realize that the integration achieved through his analysis was
sufficient for normal activities, but not adequate for working with
psychotic children, and that it was beginning to give way. Unlike the
failures discussed above, he did not reinforce his defenses or fall
apart in such a predicament. Instead he decided to undergo a second
analysis. This decision to reach for higher integration, and his
greater ability to accept unconscious processes, began to yield results,
as can be seen from his drawings at Time D. Still, the need for two
experiences with psychoanalysis suggests an inherent ego weakness,
which prevented him from reaching optimal success in the therapeutic
milieu. He eventually left to direct a social agency.

Mary's drawings are reproduced on page 374. Mary begins with a
small female figure somewhat off balance. Her children are stick
figures; while she is pursuing them in this drawing, they have nothing
to do with her. Six months later (B), Mary draws a man. Her stick
figures of children have become wilder, but she is still essentially in
the same relation to them.

At the end of a year (Time C), she indicates for the first time
the identity of the man she is drawing; it is the director with whom
she has become strongly identified. Her drawing of a typical dormitory scene has "thawed" from stick figures to figures with bodies.

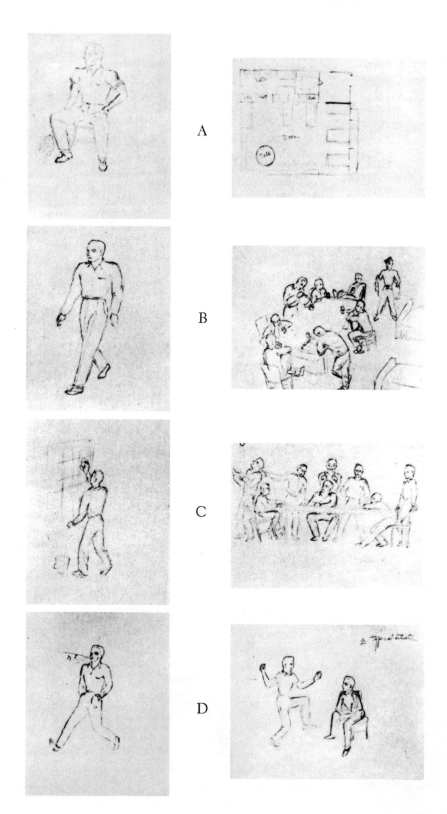

A

B

C

D

She is no longer pursuing the children but is now among them, doing something with at least one of them.

In the last pair of her drawings (Time D), she has returned to herself as a woman. The figure is a much larger, happier, and more open one than she drew eighteen months before (Time A). The figures in her drawing of the dormitory scene are closer to her and more detailed. Now three children, instead of only one, are doing something with her. The fact that she chose to draw herself from the back suggests there are still some issues in her view of herself as a worker she is uncomfortable with; but while her back is shown, she herself has turned her face to the children. Her growth then was still far from finished; yet the sequence of the drawings reflects the considerable development that took place in her and which continued unabated, though with many ups and downs, until she became secure in herself and her work—a senior member of the milieu.

Elizabeth's drawings are shown on page 375. Her first drawing of a person (A), while presenting a good appearance, is actually quite self-centered. Her interest is in the woman, not in the children. In the dormitory scene there is more emphasis on the furniture than on the children.

Six months later (B), things begin to change. In the drawing of a person, the baby has somewhat more substance and is close to the woman. Still, the picture is so pretty as to suggest an element of make-believe. The dormitory scene is much closer to the viewer and more active. The worker is doing something *for* the children, instead of just standing by and watching; more significant, the children are now more important than the furnishings. She is not yet doing something *with* them, however; each child is preoccupied with himself or with another child.

Another six months pass (Time C), and the make-believe element becomes frank; the picture could be Cinderella at the ball. But in the dormitory scene, Elizabeth draws the counselor in close contact with the child, feeding him while he is looking at her. Unlike either of the previous drawings of a dormitory scene, both figures give the impression that they are aware of, and relating to, each other.

Finally, eighteen months after the first drawings (Time D), Elizabeth has transferred her interest entirely to the children. The person she draws is one of the patients under her care. Since observations of workers suggest that in their work they identify with the children for a time, this pictorial development is of interest. In her drawing of a dormitory scene, she is *among* the children. The scene is close to the worker and gives an impression of active mutual awareness between her and the children, of something going on between

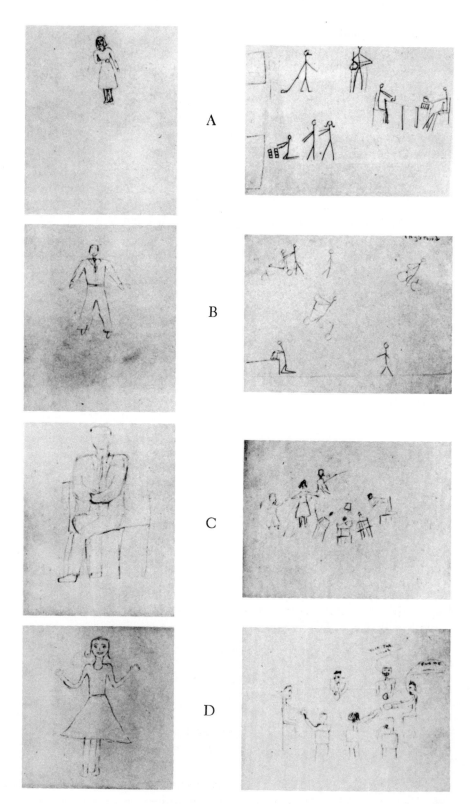

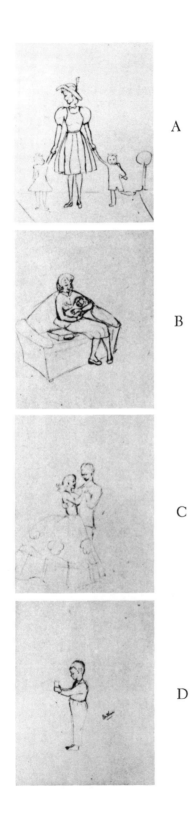

A

B

C

D

them. Like Mary, she developed into one of the most valuable senior staff members.

To further understand the process of change which takes place in those who make themselves become part of a therapeutic milieu, Wright and I also developed a variety of other projective tests. One of them consisted of asking staff members to write down questions or problems they wished to have discussed in the next staff meeting, assuming that the answers would be helpful to them in their work at the moment. (The problems they mentioned formed the topic of the next staff meeting.)

The following three questions were asked by a worker who was relatively unsuccessful while with the School. Despite excellent academic training, he could never get himself to become part of the therapeutic milieu but remained a mostly uninvolved outsider, even though he tried conscientiously to apply himself to his work. He left the therapeutic milieu after about a year; if he had not gone voluntarily, it would have become necessary to ask him to do so. After some nine months at the School he wanted to know:

> *What does it mean for a patient to be cured? Or to put it another way, what is the therapeutic goal of our institution? How does it differ from other methods of therapy or does the difference lie primarily in the methods used?*
>
> *What are the important things to consider in charting a course of therapy for an individual patient?*
>
> *What are some important principles which a worker could use in planning a program for a heterogeneous group such as those I am working with?*

This worker spoke of the work at the School in terms of overall theory, and of the patients in impersonal generalities. He wanted to come to grips with the problems therapy presented to him by acquiring a well-organized, theoretical, intellectual understanding of his task. There was no direct relation to action, to his or the patients' feelings, or to any specific problem. The question closest to the reality of his work was that referring to his group as "heterogeneous," but he still envisioned treating his group in terms of planning principles, rather than as distinct individuals. The worker's preoccupation was essentially with himself, in terms of his wish to understand intellectually. Even in the first question, where he began by asking what it means for a patient to be cured, he immediately left this relatively personal ground by explaining that he was not concerned with a particular patient, but about the therapeutic goals of the institution (as if there could be such generalized goals independent of the particular personality and life history of an individual). The final elaboration of that question took it even out of the realm of work in the Orthogenic School, into a general comparison with other therapeutic methods.

The questions were quite characteristic of this worker's approach to the patients. He wanted to become emotionally close to them; but as soon as he made some positive step in this direction, he would become afraid and withdraw into intellectual speculations about their "problems." Along with his desire for a carefully preplanned program, this suggests compulsive defenses and fear of spontaneous living together with the patients. The questions showed this worker as basically unrelated to, and distant from, the patients he worked with. There was no indication of a wish for immediate interaction with them.

The next three questions were asked by a beginner who had been with the institution three months and who had no previous experience in this type of work. She later developed into a successful staff member:

> How can I handle the anger, resentment and consequential acts of hostility of the older girls toward the younger ones when acts are done before I come to be with them in the morning?
>
> When a child is screaming at you for something that you can't immediately do anything about so far as preventing it from happening again, what is the most effective way of pacifying the child? Child is not concerned with "What can I do now" idea, but rather what can be done or should have been done.
>
> What can be done about directly announced or implied spite, such as delaying of the group in retaliation for being delayed themselves at other times?

This worker asked questions about things that were happening with the patients. She differentiated among them as individuals (older and younger girls), and spoke of both children and one individual. She wanted to know "what can be done" and was primarily preoccupied with what she could do. Although she did not mention her own feelings, she recognized the importance of emotions such as anger, spite, resentment. She seemed to feel a desire to become more active and effective; her first question suggests a feeling of responsibility. To some degree it contains ideas of omnipresence; but also the wish to be relieved of blame for hostility which takes place when she is not there. On the other hand, the questions suggest that she was preoccupied with negative emotions only, and with efforts to bind them. The value of expressing these negative emotions was not recognized, nor was there yet concern with positive emotional closeness to the patients.

The following questions were asked by a worker who was considerably further along in growth but not yet a senior staff member (some two years later she achieved the requisite competence to become one):

> The difficulty in feeling toward the patients that they are emotionally like babies, are emotionally disturbed—without degrading them.
>
> Seduction—by them and me. What physical contact means. I think I'm too defensive about it to gain much from a staff meeting—or to think realistically about it.
>
> Hitting—of all kinds. What it means to them to hit me or each other. Again I think a lot of me is involved.
>
> Talking—when am I just falling into their verbalization and when is it good. It's obviously one of my own difficulties.

A sense of closeness and close interest is conveyed by these questions. This worker asks about specific situations, and her interaction around them with the patient; her feelings about the patients and what they do to her. At the same time, the identification with and interest in what is going on suggest a fusion in fantasy with the patients: we "seduce" each other; they "hit" her as they hit each other. But she is beginning to recognize the influence of her own feelings on her behavior with the patients, and that she is defensive about them. The variety in content of these questions and the dealing with essential problems, the self-recognition, and the intense interest in the patients all suggest the potential for further development.

Finally, two questions asked by a senior staff member to exemplify her attitudes and concerns:

> In her doll play Mary portrays the mischievous, active, hiding youngster—in other words herself. I am to act out the roles of the ineffective adults who can never understand her; prevent her acting out, or be of any help. While playing this out may be less threatening for Mary, it makes me anx-

*ious and uncomfortable. Have you any suggestions for how
I can handle my feelings and/or what I can do in the play?*

*Pat has been "playfully" hitting at me. She often uses it
to get my attention away from the other girls and then when
I am with her will try to get me to hit her. I have talked
with her about her jealousy of others—that everyone has
these feelings—that I like her. Have also approached it from
the angle of her father and beatings he used to give her.
Nothing has made any impression yet. Any suggestions?*

This senior staff member referred to the patients by name and
discussed, both in detail and in terms of the total situations, particular problems of her interaction with these children. She showed concern both for the behavior and feelings of the child, and for her own
behavior and feelings in the situation. She revealed an understanding
of the basic dynamics of human relations in the events described. She
both plays with the patients and interferes constructively. The full-
ness of her description is evidence that her actions are based on careful thought, observation, and empathy.

In terms of the classification we developed, she and the worker
just previously referred to might be viewed as persons whose participation is based both on an empathic understanding of what goes on in
the patient, and on bringing to it a critically evaluated comprehension of pertinent issues in the patient's past (the beatings by the
father) and present (jealousy of others). At the same time, this
worker recognized the nature and impact of her own emotions (it
made her anxious). Thus while the main essence of her participation
was empathy with the patient at the moment, it was an empathy informed by aspects and motives of which the patient herself was
unaware, though she was moved by them. What goes on at the
moment was recognized as only a particular but very specific expression of the consequences of the patient's past and her general problems. Therapeutic participation must recognize simultaneously what
the patient's permanent problems are, and what the specifics of the
situation are (she acts this way only when the worker's attention is
focused on others).

These two competent workers took that so much for granted
that they no longer mentioned any of it. The first one presented as
her main concern how to protect the dignity of the patient despite
his regressed behavior. She concentrated on herself because she had
been fully convinced that she could use only herself; that she could
change her own inner attitudes but not those of the patient—which
only he could do in resonance from what comes across from her to

him. But she did not yet know quite how to do it. She was more concerned with her own shortcomings as a therapist than with presenting the problems of the patient, convinced she could handle these well, once she had straightened herself. She recognizes what she is able to learn right now. She is aware that she is still too much in need of defending herself against the recognition of what is involved in seduction, and states that she cannot yet think realistically about it; and this was the necessary awareness which led her to do exactly that.

The more mature of the two, the senior staff member, relies largely on the type of empathy that is tempered and enlightened by what one knows about a patient, on her relation to him, and what she has learned from her work with other patients and from theoretical knowledge. This empathy at all times carefully scrutinizes what is currently going on in the patient and in herself, what is inherent in the situation, and what both the patient and the staff member bring to it. The difference between the two workers is that while the first concentrated on what was going on in her in connection with the patients, the latter recognized this but was not carried away by it. Instead, she concentrated on the work she had to do on herself and with the patient.

Observer—Intruder—Participant Observer

To further assess the development of staff members from beginning to senior, Wright (131) used Stephenson's Q-technique (115) to assess the changes in values which a worker underwent during his professional growth. Each worker was asked at various stages of his development to state his image of the ideal staff member, by arranging eighty statements on a continuum from those describing attitudes and behavior most appropriate for therapeutic work with patients in residential treatment, to those least applicable or pertinent. The eighty statements sampled four typical attitudes or approaches to patients, which on the basis of preliminary studies had been found most crucial and discriminating: (1) observation, (2) intrusion, (3) participation, and (4) participation-observation revolving around care. These statements on the questionnaire dealt with five areas of interacting: eating, bodily care and contact, sex, the patients' self-respect, and anxiety.

These findings suggested that, independent of his "basic personality," the worker as he grows professionally changes from an initial approach characterized by too much self-protection, intrusion, or observation to one characterized by participation strongly tinged by personal needs, culminating in an empathic participation based on self-scrutiny and a judicious evaluation of how the patient's underlying difficulties can best be ameliorated in the specific situation he finds himself in at present. We called this latter attitude "participant-observation" for short, hoping the term will suggest that therapeutic attitudes and actions are based on an empathic understanding of the patient's past and his needs of the moment, as well as his long-range rational and realistic therapeutic goals for himself—irrespective of whether he is aware of them. The empathy of participant-observation is derived from an understanding of the patient's past and what it has meant and done to him, from the worker's introspection, and from careful observation of what is going on in and around the patient.

This development doesn't proceed evenly or uniformly. A worker may be an observer at one moment in one activity with one particular patient, and a participant or intruder in another setting, or with another patient. The general course of change is generally unidirectional, though it proceeds with many ups and downs, returning to attitudes that were given up only temporarily; with appearances and reappearances of neurotic involvements after others have long been integrated; and with temporary breakdowns under stress of not yet fully or permanently achieved integrations.

The findings were consistent with the workers' experiences as we observed them. The new worker—as a stranger to the institution, the staff, and the patients—undergoes a brief period of confusion and increasing anxiety. The job before him suddenly appears much more difficult, and he finds himself less prepared than he anticipated. Long-latent childhood residues that he thought he had overcome are stirred up, and others are precipitously intensified beyond his expectations. His self-concept, as an adult desirous and able to help psychiatric patients, is suddenly threatened, and he finds himself wanting. He is propelled into a parental role by part of his work and the resulting emotions are usually profoundly surprising and unexpectedly frightening. Within a few days, or at the most a few weeks, he tends to react in some such ways as these:

> —He may preserve his defense against the threatening reality of his new job and subsequently resign. His typical and truthful explanation is: "It is too much for me."
> —He may act out against the patients without knowing that he is doing so—actively, by punitively restraining them, for example, or passively, by letting them hurt each other.

*This is an often unconscious but successful effort to force
the institution to ask him to resign for the protection of
the patients; what he is after, unconsciously, is his own protection against the danger of personal disintegration.*

*—He may try to rise to the challenge of that most diffi-
cult task of inner integration. He may throw himself into
the work of helping the patients, deciding to continue and
to give the task the best he has to offer. More often than
not he helps himself by helping the patients, usually without realizing that this is his goal.*

After the initial shock has worn off and the worker has decided
to continue, despite his anxieties and the hardships the work entails,
he usually enters probably the most crucial phase leading to his
eventual success. His childhood residues become increasingly more
activated by the work, he finds himself in an ever-growing emotional
turmoil, and the effect of this on his work with the patients can be
serious. (Needless to say, this is the period when the senior staff
must give the new worker the most support; otherwise he will fail.)

At this point, the worker may show an intense neurotic identification with some of the patients under his immediate care, or with
some of their symptoms, often to the detriment of staff relations, the
institution's philosophy, and other patients' interests. On an unconscious level, he tends to confuse the patient's motives and
interpret the patient's behavior on the basis of his own rather than
the patient's needs. He is dimly aware of this and, at once conscientious in his desire to help the patients and fearful of losing his
own ego boundaries and failing in his job, he precariously and
defensively tries to maintain what he considers mature attitudes.
The consequence is that he may try to widen the distance between
himself, as "normal" adult, and the patient. This prevents the close
interaction that makes his work rewarding and which could lead to
his higher integration, as well as the patient's.

At this stage, projections are frequent and extensive, and the
worker derives vicarious neurotic satisfaction through the patient's
behavior—at the expense of the patient's (and the institution's)
actual needs. Often the worker offers subtle permissions and induce-
ments that the patient experiences as temptations, particularly along
asocial lines. The unconscious aim of this is to cause behavior in the
patient that will satisfy some aspect of the worker's suddenly and
violently pressing childhood residues. Fortunately, such tendencies
of the beginner have no untoward effects on the patients, because

he has not yet become important enough to them. All major responsibilities for the patients are still those of the senior staff, who are able to see to it that such temporary tendencies to act out with or on the patients are kept under safe control, and have no bad effects.

During this period the worker experiences his responsibility mainly as an almost unbearable burden, exhaustingly difficult and with few, if any, rewards. Even playing with the patients, in what could be easy situations, is not experienced as enjoyable. The worker is drained of all his emotional energy by his efforts to repress ever stronger and more insurgent, largely unconscious processes. His intellectual and other neurotic defenses become more and more activated, complicating all his activities. Under such conditions the worker may feel temporarily exhausted and deeply dissatisfied with himself and his job.

In this period the typical approaches of observer and intruder are used defensively. The role of *observer* permits the worker to become minimally emotionally involved, in his attempt to preserve his dwindling emotional resources. By merely watching and waiting passively, he hopes to maintain his endangered integration. He tends to emphasize knowing, rather than doing—a passivity that is mostly a defense against the emotions aroused by situations with the patients. He denies the effects on him of working with the patients by belittling, ignoring, or not "seeing" them, or what goes on in and with them. Attention to the minute and unimportant is another typical defense. The worker's anxiety about emotional involvement will not even permit him to take advantage of situations that could offer vicarious gratification.

Skillful workers may also be observers in certain situations, but only temporarily and for an entirely different purpose; they observe to understand, so that it may evoke in them pertinent introspection. That is, they observe in pursuit of empathic understanding, to better help the patient. The defensive observer's approach is used to achieve immunity from human relations.

The *intruder*, on the other hand, defends himself against his emotions or emotional involvement with the patient by activity. Into each situation he introduces a frame of reference external to the unique and individual needs of the patient at that moment; and he does it as a protection against his own emotional problems. A typical example is the worker who pushes the patients to engage in activities, preferably those which do not allow for personal relations. His ideal is to see to it that something is always "cooking," so that the patients have no time to evaluate him, nor he to scrutinize what he is doing and why. By "running the show," he tries to give himself the feeling that he is and will remain in control of himself. He tries to avoid real emotional contact—the only experience that could help him in integrating his difficulties—by controlling those phases of his relationship with the patient which seem to threaten his psychic equilibrium.

Again, this must not be equated with the protective or constructive interference which is often necessary and characteristic of the skillful worker, who may also encourage patients to become active —but only in their interest, and within a growing relation to him and to others. The competent worker interferes only in accordance with the particular needs of the patient at a given moment, not to combat his own anxieties or to avoid emotional contact with the patient's reality.

Newcomers who stay on to become either observers or intruders seem to divide into two general groups: those whose defenses tend to be somewhat rigid and intellectual; and those who act out, are impulse-motivated, emotional, and somewhat disorganized. Paradoxically, although higher academic training tends to place a newcomer in a better position to grow professionally, it also tends to reinforce rigid intellectual tendencies. The impulsive, emotional, somewhat disorganized person, if he survives the first six months and works hard on "getting organized," seems to develop more rapidly into a successful worker. Perhaps the intellectual inclinations of the rigid-intellectual group create a defensive shell more resistant to the emotional effect of actual work with psychiatric patients, and permit development of rationalizations that are hard to penetrate. Disintegration and simultaneous reintegration of their childhood residues seem to proceed very slowly.

Moving out of this stage is the most difficult step in the professional development of the worker. Unsuccessful staff members in most respects remain stuck as observers or intruders. Though they may master the techniques of their work, they do so with their heads, not with their hearts. What they say and do seems to be therapeutic but fails to be fully effective because while they give of themselves to the "therapeutic task," they withhold themselves from the person who is the patient. They fail to make him *their* patient. They are unable to risk themselves, so that he may win his life.

Development of optimal therapeutic interpersonal relations, even in the case of successful workers, seldom happens sooner than a year after they have begun to leave the initial stage. It occurs when, through the influence of the total therapeutic setting and its special mores, and through the guidance of senior staff, increasingly large areas of the worker's interaction with the patients become experiences integrating some of his childhood residues. The resultant greater freedom from inner pressures allows him to give more of himself to the work in general, to some patient in particular, and he typically becomes a participant.

The *participant:* As his integration proceeds, in one area after another, the worker gradually can permit himself to participate in the patient's behavior with empathic understanding of his needs at the moment. Before this phase of development was reached, the worker had erected a barrier between himself as a "normal" person and the patient as one who is "out of it," in an effort to protect his threatened self-conception; now he no longer needs such defensive self-protection. In the participant stage, the ego boundaries between worker and patient are greatly reduced. While before there was too little "sympathy of the unconscious" between them, now there is not only uncritical sympathy between their unconscious thought, their ids; but often also a shared disrespect for their superegos and the mores of society. The newcomer tends to coerce or seduce the patients to act out his childhood residues for him; the danger for the participant is that he may act them out directly for himself.

Competition with patients and other staff members begins to come out in the open, and may cause serious staff conflicts. In this period, intellectual pursuits often are temporarily abandoned and all considerations beyond the immediate work with the patients disregarded, at least in comparison to the worker's former emphasis on them. The worker may even go so far as to act out irresponsible impulses with the patients, always under the guise of being close to them, "a boy among the boys." Unexamined "gut" reactions stand in the place of well-thought-out actions which, while based on an empathic understanding, give id, ego, and superego their rightful due.

Nevertheless, there is an intrinsic logic in this development. Once the worker has become a participant in most aspects of his work, the pressure of the therapeutic environment and its mores almost inevitably leads him in a slow movement toward integration of his childhood residues. So far, no worker has remained permanently at this level, although it may take up to two years for him to become a participant-observer in the best sense, and thus part of the senior staff. Very few workers leave the institution at this stage; the pressure for higher integration that hinges on continuing their work is too great, the goal too attractive.

As his experiences of participation become steps toward higher integration, the worker's own need to participate is increasingly reduced. Eventually he participates for the patient's benefit only, and not his own. He once again becomes an adult, now fully mature. For it is not rigid adherence to an empty self-image, but confident flexibility that permits true interpersonal relations. The worker now feels secure that he will be able to help the patients, and do the right things at the right moment.

Thus the worker becomes a *participant-observer* as he succeeds in fulfilling and integrating his childhood residues. He can now be an adult who is fully accepting, understanding, and sympathetic to even the most disturbed patient; who can have full empathy with the patient's behavior and unconscious, without losing his own adult integration. The worker will then participate more and more freely with the patient, actively using this participation to help the patient toward his own higher integration. No longer needing to act on the basis of his childhood residues, the worker does not need to assert his status as normal adult. He has become an adult therapist, interacting therapeutically with the patient.

After this finally occurs, some workers may become restless and even leave the profession. In this final integration they have lost a prime motivation for working with psychiatric patients: the need to resolve their own emotional problems through their profession. Fortunately, for the majority the old intensive neurotic motivation is replaced by the desire for the inner rewards and satisfactions offered by working successfully with psychiatric patients. These workers continue to gain experience and proficiency in the field as valuable and mature members of the profession, while they provide leadership and, most important, empathic help for those who have not yet reached their level of achievement.

24 | The Inward Journey

Many varied experiences, and easily three, four, five, or more years of hard application, are required for a beginner to develop into a senior staff member. No experience is more important and effective in aiding this development than the long and often difficult hours the staff spend together, trying to understand themselves and the patients, to find out what makes them and us "tick," to search for what can be done to set things right for them and for us.

Personal development, different as it is for each staff member, is a long and perilous journey which many find too demanding. When the worker is with a patient, the exigencies of the moment don't allow for much self-scrutiny. Observing what goes on in the patient, trying to understand what it all means and what must be done right now while interacting with him, is so all-engrossing and demanding that only fleeting introspection is possible. Sometimes what emerges out of one's own unconscious into conscious awareness at such moments can constitute a deep insight into oneself. But even when this occurs, the exigencies of the moment do not permit following it up and working it through immediately. This has to wait until the pressures of active doing are no longer there. Yet a worker cannot significantly help psychiatric patients if he is not able, and does not find it deeply rewarding, to reach for greater self-awareness despite the agonies this entails. Certainly the sudden insight realized with a patient doesn't come from just anywhere; though it may seem like an inspiration, it is actually the final result of a very long battle for clarity. The pieces of the intricate psychological puzzle which each person is (and which the patient presents), don't suddenly fall into place unless one has pondered their meaning at great length and turned them around many times in one's mind.

But self-scrutiny can only go so far. As one psychoanalyst

(Bernfeld) waggishly remarked, the trouble with self-analysis is that the positive countertransference is just too overpowering and misleading. Even Freud failed to recognize some meanings of his own dreams, because he did not wish to see what they told about himself; but these meanings were quite readily recognized by others (34). Thus every worker needs to be both challenged and supported in his self-scrutiny by his colleagues. This is as true for the least experienced as it is for the most experienced staff member, and it must apply also to the director, who could not achieve certain insights into himself, his co-workers, and the patients if he did not invite and subject himself freely to the criticisms of others, and if he did not feel secure that any resulting narcissistic deficit would immediately or eventually be compensated—either directly by emotional supplies coming to him from other staff members, or indirectly by the success of the institution's efforts.

> When a group of us who are counselors at the Orthogenic School congregate for our midnight snack and coffee, we nearly always chat about the children whom we have just put safely to sleep; about the funny, unusual, or exasperating things that happened during the day. We talk to each other to unwind, to understand better what occurred during the day, and to bring each other up-to-date on what is going on in the rest of the institution. As we relax, we also gradually become more serious about our problems; our talk is more intimate as we search within ourselves, with each other's help, for likely reasons for the difficulties we encountered during the day, and for the possible solutions to them. (97)

These remarks suggest how mutual support and reassurance enable one to master disintegrating experiences one had while with the patients. As the workers relax, they are able to become emotionally more daring and more serious. That is why the conversation begins with the "funny" events and moves on to "unusual" things, as the workers unconsciously test out how safe it will be to open up about the "exasperating" ones. Most important, this shows how as one falls back on intimacy with colleagues, some of whom also are friends, coming to rely on their emotional backing one becomes able to search within oneself, as opposed to exploring only what has happened with the patients.

But communication is by no means enough. Much discussion in the literature about the shortcomings of psychiatric hospitals stresses the insufficiency or breakdown of communication; yet even complete communication, if it were possible, would not be enough for the requirements of a therapeutic milieu. Great as may be each staff member's need to "know" what goes on with the patients and the rest of the staff, when compared with the importance and beneficial effects (for staff members and patients too) of engaging in the "search within ourselves, with each other's help," its significance fades. This crucial endeavor motivates the many staff discussions, and it cannot help but spread knowledge most effectively about everything that goes on.

Important information may fail to be transmitted when a worker has not yet become intimate with other staff members and thus cannot accept (not to mention seek) their help. This happens not because he doesn't want to convey information, but because of his uncertainty whether he will receive the emotional support of others. Withholding information is therefore often neither callous nor negligent, but the result of repression which the worker fails to recognize by having "forgotten all about it," or having been convinced that "it was not important," or that "nobody would be interested in what I have to say."

Criticizing the worker for not having told others something of relevance will not help him to repress less the next time, nor will it aid him in overcoming the repression. Sympathy for the worker's predicament will be much more likely to create an emotional matrix in which he can accept the assistance of others in unraveling what was repressed and what forced him to repress it. The aid that workers received at the Orthogenic School in understanding why they forgot to tell something was often the first experience that gave them the courage to believe they would be helped with—rather than condemned for—difficulties residing within them. It convinced them that they were finally at a place where they, as persons, were as important as what they did.

Another source of information and tacit communication, as well as a means of self-learning and for guidance by the senior staff, were the workers' reports, occasionally written but usually dictated and transcribed. Everyone who had regular contact with the patients was expected to report (usually from notes) on his observations of and experiences with the patients, what he thought these told about the patients as persons and about his interactions with them, and what his reactions to it all had been. These were called "anecdotal reports" to stress their informal nature; and, since completeness could not possibly be the goal, effort was directed toward selecting vignettes which seemed resonant with meaning.

Since three or four staff members regularly reported on each patient (his two counselors, his teacher, the person who saw him in individual therapeutic sessions—as well as any others who happened to observe or experience something that seemed worthwhile remembering or considering), the reports revealed not only how different the same patient appeared to different persons, but also how stereotyped or varied his relations to them were. The reports also attested to what one staff member found worthy of his attention, as compared to another member. What a worker felt or did not feel to be of interest about a patient's behavior was often quite revealing of his view of himself. How much was reported varied from staff member to staff member, but the goal was a minimum of some two to three hours of dictation a week; some did much more, and others less. Each contributing staff member in a year's time would then have easily spent a hundred hours on such reporting and many more on thinking about it; and each worker's reports were read by the others who worked intimately with the same patient. All reports were read by the director—which required a considerable segment of his time, many hours each week. Anybody else who was interested in learning more about a particular patient, or how a worker handled events as they occurred and why, would study the appropriate parts of these reports.

With the exception of direct personal contact, the reports were the single most important source of knowledge about patients and workers. Much staff discussion and learning was based on them. The value of the anecdotal form of reporting, as opposed to a summary type, is that an account striving for completeness does not reveal what the worker found of special interest to him, and thus is comparatively devoid of personal flavor. Particularly when the person is lacking in literary talent, efforts to tell the whole story tend to lead to an empty enumeration of events. An anecdote is more apt to contain implicit information about the patient and worker—things the worker might not have been aware of and which can be deduced from the report.

Perhaps the most valuable aspect of the reports was the learning they practically forced on the worker. In dictating, the worker had to rethink his day with the patients. How had it gone? Whom did he pay attention to, and which could he remember hardly anything at all about? Why did this little story about something that had happened seem significant enough to report on? Why did he want somebody else to learn about it? Just because it revealed something about the patient? If that was so, what did the story show? In retrospect, what did he think about what he had done or said? How could he explain his motives, if not to others, at least to himself? What problem required help in understanding from the staff?

Dictating these reports was very hard work, and the motivations for it varied from worker to worker. Among beginners, some reports were cries for help in understanding; others were a sort of display of how well one had done, or understood. Yet within months the beginner who reported consistently could not help observing how much keener his ability to recollect, observe, select significant events, and understand their meaning had become; how much more he comprehended about the patient, himself, and himself in relation to the patient. Had he not been forced to rethink certain things which had seemed insignificant when they happened, the worker might never have become aware of them and their meaning. Other matters, which had upset him at the time, now seemed trivial, and he had to figure out exactly why he had been so disturbed by them. Sitting in front of the dictating machine and ruminating was often the worker's first experience of scrutinizing the meaning of a patient's behavior, as well as his own.

As the worker recalled the patient—his speech habits, his expressive movements, the ways in which he put himself across or withdrew, his compulsive rituals, his slips of the tongue—and as he speculated at leisure but with concentration about what it might all mean, he learned to pay attention to phenomena and surmise meaning which before had no particular importance to him. He began to see how a person unconsciously reveals a great deal about himself. And he couldn't help realizing that, when examined, he too probably revealed himself in a great many ways. Though he may not have been aware of it at the moment, as he would begin to convey his understanding of the patient's behavior and what it revealed about his unconscious motivations, the worker, by also reporting his part of the interchange, started to grasp what had gone on within himself at the time.

These reports were not kept a secret from the patients. Of course, at first the patients were sure that it was just another form of spying on them. Since counselors stayed with a group until everybody was asleep, some workers used this time when all was quiet to think about what happened during the hours they had been with the patients, and jotted down some notes to be used later to refresh their memory when dictating. This was one of the many ways we used to let those patients who wanted to know become aware on their own of how the staff proceeded; while those who didn't want to know could either not observe what the staff member did, or give it any interpretation they wished.

Like all other aspects of the staff's work, except that which was needed to protect the privacy of patients, these reports were freely discussed with patients who wished to find out more about them. Occasionally, at his request, parts of the reports on him were shown to a patient. Since he could see reports on himself at random, no patient was interested in reading more than a few pages, because he soon found out that there was nothing in these anecdotes that he didn't know, though he encountered events he had forgotten. All patients were pleased about the interest and concern. Once reassured, the content of these reports became a matter of indifference to the patient, and not a single one wanted to see them a second time. Quite a few took them very seriously, and were incensed when some staff member failed to know about some occurrence. Had the worker with whom it happened not considered it important enough to report on? Had the staff member not been interested enough to read the reports? This was one of the innumerable ways in which the patients, as part of the therapeutic community, exercised influence and improved its operations; here by adding further incentives to improve the flow of communication.

Psychological observation and in-depth investigation usually begins with other people. The student of psychology particularly restricts himself at first to trying to understand others, although deep down he is motivated to find out more about himself, but is still usually afraid to do so. But such exploration always has its implications for oneself. As a worker becomes more involved with his patients and with the institution, such contemplation about another person's behavior is no longer restricted to the time when he is with the patients, or is reporting on it. It fills many odd moments of his day, as does speculation about himself. But at no time (short of that he may spend in his own psychoanalysis) is this contemplation as intense as when the worker is participating in a meeting with other staff members, whatever the setting and format may be—seeking guidance from senior workers, bull session, chance encounter, planning events, or formal meeting. And in these gatherings the positive view of oneself and the wish to have been right (which leads one to overlook some phenomena and to overemphasize others, thus skewing self-scrutiny even when reporting) is controlled and corrected by others.

In many ways, the informal meetings are the most interesting of all because they are never planned but are the spontaneous consequence of felt needs. Within days of the reorganization of the Orthogenic School in 1944, the staff began to congregate late every night after work, because we were all so full of what had happened during the day that we just had to talk about it. Strange as it may seem, these meetings late at night were the highlights of the day for us. Largely they were so rewarding because, by then, we were freed of the pressures and anxieties of the day; and they were instituted at a period when we were not quite sure whether our new methods would work. When we got together at night we knew they had worked, at least for this one day; and so we could look back on it—our anxieties, the patients' difficulties, and all that had happened—with the feeling that it had not totally overwhelmed us. We would lay the day to rest, as w˙ gained reassurance from each other. And on the basis of what had happened during this day, and what we had learned from it, we would plan what to do tomorrow. Knowing what we were going to do in broad outline helped us to sleep more easily. While such intense reacting to what had happened might seem physically tiring after a long and exhausting day, it actually restored us emotionally.

One staff member would burst into such a gathering, full of the remarkable events of his day which he could no longer postpone sharing with others. Before he had finished telling about all the good things that had happened, another staff member might enter, barely able to drag himself to the next chair, totally dejected about all that had gone wrong. No longer having to keep a grip on himself and his misery for the patient's sake, he could finally let loose. A woman, particularly, might soon break down crying (not that the men felt any differently, they were just less able to let go in this manner). She could not go on another day; could not take the patients' rejection, which made her feel she was no good. It wasn't only that she needed all the support those present could give her, but also everybody *wanted* to give it, even the worker who had to stop telling about the glories of his day. For he remembered only too well the nights he had felt just as miserable as his colleague did at the moment. Because others who had gone through the same experiences did everything possible to help her regain her perspective on what had happened— showing her how much she was needed and appreciated by those who had had a good day—she soon got out of her doldrums and was ready to listen to all the good things that had happened around the institution while things had been going wrong in her group.

Identification with the institution permitted the worker to balance his bad experiences with the successes of others; to get comfort from the realization that while some things had gone wrong (as they invariably did every single day), all in all as a therapeutic community we had neither failed our purposes, nor the patients, nor ourselves, though at moments it seemed to one or the other of us that we had wrecked everything. When we felt that our shortcomings and even our unavoidable failures *had* wrecked everything, the patients also felt this and were convinced how important they were to us—a conviction that could not help having a curative effect.

After a while the dejected worker might be followed by another worker, who needed to tell about her experiences of the day and also wanted to hear what had been described earlier. Not surprisingly, as the excitement decreased, by the second and third retelling new ideas about what it all meant came to mind. In the first account of the story, the desire to convey the personal meaning it had had for the worker was so great that any question or suggestion only annoyed him. At the second or third retelling, all interruptions were not only accepted as a sign of interest, but were now wanted. The psychological phenomena occurring during a day's work were so varied and so rich in meaning that they had to be gone over several times to get a better intellectual grasp of them, to gain control over the emotions they had aroused. As it became clearer what had been involved in both the good and the bad things, questions would come to mind which would put them in a somewhat different light. The unfavorable events might suggest important things the worker could do the next time she was with the patient. So there was excellent reason for her not just to continue but to look forward to doing her work, to try out some ideas suggested by others or, even better, ideas she got from their telling about parallel experiences.

While at first the morrow held only promise of more defeats, now it offered hope for an entirely different experience with the patients. The ethos of the institution demanded that the downcast worker must not be permitted to leave before she had regained her spirits. If she was unable to do so while still with the group, some colleagues would follow her into her room to stay with her until the crisis was over. Thus practically every night everyone had the experience either that he was needed by the institution—not just for the patient's sake but because of what he contributed also to the staff —or that he needed the institution for the help it gave him. The roles were so often reversed that everybody had ample experience with both; and this was true for even the most senior staff member.

Even the best therapeutic milieu probably cannot maintain for a quarter of a century the same enthusiasm that surrounded its creation. Looking back over the years, it seems astonishing that the Orthogenic School managed to do so for almost two decades. As things got easier, the amazement that we had fairly successfully weathered the vagaries of the day slowly wore off, and these meetings became more "organized" without any intention that this should be so. Things weren't as exciting to everybody; maybe some of the senior staff just got older. But even at the end of my connection with the School, the nightly get-togethers remained for some the most rewarding part of their day—exciting for some, unhappy for others—until things got settled for them.

There were other times of the day when some staff members would gather informally. One was when a group of workers ended the period they spent with the patients; for example, the teachers got off at three o'clock, and on weekends and holidays so did those who had worked during the first half of the day with the patients. This situation was similar to that at night, but somehow not quite so satisfying. There just seemed to be a difference between the feelings one experienced when the day was really over, and those when one knew there were still quite a few things to attend to. While at these afternoon get-togethers there was much talk about what had happened, it never went as deep or became as personal as at night. But if there were unresolved problems, things that needed to be tied together for the sake of the patients or the peace of one's own mind, here was a chance to do so with one's colleagues.

Before beginning to take care of the patients, early in the morning and again before three o'clock, something of what each group would be doing had to be planned. This was also the time to receive the latest news about what had happened with various patients, or within the institution in general. And it was a great emotional help to get in touch with the milieu, so to speak, before one met the patients and the arduous tasks of caring for them. It gave the feeling that one was not alone; that at any moment one could count on the help of one's colleagues, physically when needed but more important, in spirit.

It was reassuring to tell one's fellow workers, "Well, it's time to start working, good luck!" or at least "So long!", with the implication that we'll all get together again at night when this is over. As deeply involved in the work as each staff member was, and as fascinated as he was by it all, as much as he truly liked his patients and looked forward in many ways to being with them, there could be no doubt about the emotional demands that would be made on him. Along with many pleasant and some very exciting moments, there would be others which would try him to the core of his ability to meet and master the emotional demands made of him. That is why the implied assurance, "We're in it together," offered so much emotional support.

Then there were special occasions, both good and bad, when without any planning or arrangements nearly the entire staff—again with the exception of those who were taking care of the patients at the moment—spontaneously drifted together to share what had moved them. When a patient had just left there were always feelings of loss, however good his leaving may have been. One would no longer be able to enjoy the close relations with that person, and this marred the pleasure in our achievement, as well as the patient's. But this pleasure was also to be shared with those others who had made it possible. On the rare occasions when a patient left improved, but not as much as we had hoped, now that the chance to do better was over, we had to ruminate together about his future. We felt the need emotionally to close ranks; to find comfort in what may be likened to a mourning, a first working-through of what the loss meant. As in any other case of mourning, we felt a need to recall many events in the life of the patient which had been significant to him and to ourselves.

Whether the patient had left cured or not, we pondered on whether he had understood the message we had tried to convey to him through the gift we gave him, as a remembrance of our good feelings for him. (A party and a special gift celebrated each patient's leaving as it had his coming.)

Happy feelings also seemed to demand sharing. After a celebration (not necessarily one of the great events of the year, such as Thanksgiving, Halloween, Christmas, or Easter), whatever the special event may have been, most of the staff felt a need to get together and go over what the event had meant to them before each one went on his way. How had one patient reacted to the festivities, how another? What feelings did it arouse in the staff and why? How did others deal with their feelings around such a holiday? How could it be improved on for next time? This could not all be settled right after the event, but a beginning could be made before the freshness of the feelings dissipated.

All this is not so different from how any intact family would respond to such occasions; where the good feelings for each other after the Thanksgiving meal, for example, were the highlight of the event. Since thoughts were centered on the patients at these and other moments, one's feelings about them, and what theirs had been around what had happened, and what it all meant to oneself and why, all this made it even more a therapeutic community.

This description cannot fully convey our continuity of effort at struggling for greater clarity about the work and ourselves. The diversity of the settings in which we worked at gaining understanding forced the staff to deal with the same problem in a variety of ways. A difficulty one had had with a patient, or in understanding his behavior or one's own behavior around him, could be talked about in one way in a regular staff meeting, to be followed immediately by a lunch conversation where the mood was entirely different. Or, since twice a week lunch preceded a staff meeting, something that began as a more or less chance remark while eating could be followed up in a much more serious vein in the staff meeting. Any feelings aroused at the staff meeting could be laid to rest again very differently, at the nightly get-together. Once a week, the regular daily staff meeting took place late in the evening. When it broke up after eleven, most people would remain together for a small supper. After this, the staff would break up in many small groups, some moving to other rooms, to consider in a yet different spirit what had happened in staff: to react to it, or enlarge on what it had brought to mind.

In addition, three to five times each week, beginning at three o'clock, there was a meeting of all patients and most of the staff for about half an hour, to mark and ease the transition for the patients from the morning group of staff to those of the afternoon and evening. Here, usually one staff member spoke about some topical issue: something that had happened during the day within the institution, or events on the outside, or about some of his personal interests which might also be of interest to others. But occasionally, when the entire community met, the patients conducted the meetings. Matters which the patients brought up were discussed, such as how things should be done at the institution, or what they wanted to know about it and the staff. For example, for several months each year during one meeting weekly I explained to the patients the workings of the institution, and was told that some staff members got a better understanding of what the milieu was all about from these remarks than from the many other meetings. Often the questions or issues raised by the patients in these meetings forced the staff to reconsider the way we did things.

With all this going on, it is safe to say that most staff members had direct contact with at least several other members four or five times a day, not even counting the hours those working together with one group devoted to talking with each other about their patients.

These informal get-togethers would not have led toward higher integration if that had been their conscious purpose; in some measure this was what the regular staff meetings were for. All casual gatherings of staff had free-floating purposes, those which the persons congregating felt most appropriate. That is, they had no other conscious goal but to exchange thought and to gain security from emotional rapport with each other. Sometimes the direct confrontation of a staff member with what he was "up to" with the patients could be most effective in bringing about a change in attitudes and values—but this worked only if it was done rarely, and then in the appropriate situation and manner. Freud said that an interpretation, psychologically correct as it might be, will be effective and hence purposeful only when made at the right moment, in the right way, with the right feelings, in the right tone of voice, and by using exactly the particular wording that is required. But for the confrontation to be successful, even when all of this applies the person must have ample time and leisure to decide whether he wishes to respond to the challenge at all.

It usually took a new staff member some time before he realized that the many meetings he sat through—where matters were discussed which seemed only of peripheral concern to him—nevertheless in their aggregate gradually altered his views of himself and changed the quality of his work, as well as his life. There were those who at first didn't see how they benefited from spending time listening to, and only occasionally participating in, what was of concern to others. They couldn't recognize that as they took part in their colleagues' struggles vicariously, they became much more involved in the milieu, as individuals and as staff members.

At first, when a beginner was asked whether he got anything out of one of these staff meetings, the answer was usually an honest "Not much." When he had learned something of interest it was more often academic, since he did not yet know how he could apply it to his work, much less to himself. If he had a reaction, it was that the meeting had failed to give him clear instructions on how to behave in a specific situation. If he was not told how to handle things, how could he ever know? After all, he had come here to learn how to do the work, and now he was told to rely on his own resources. If he had them, there would be no need for him to apprentice himself to the institution.

Or, if the worker was more convinced of his sophistication, after having attended a meeting (such as the one where we discussed a worker's reaction to a patient calling him in the night and telling a dream; see pp. 409–15), he would assert, with some superiority, that he knew one had to listen to a patient's dream. He even knew what its manifest content told about some of the latent aspects hidden behind it. He expected to gain some fine points in dream interpretation, so that he would be better prepared when dreams were told to him. His implication was that he could have done a more competent job than these fumbling fools, not realizing that what was at stake was not the worker's understanding of a dream, but the emotions with which he approached the task. If one is familiar with psychoanalysis it is easy to extract latent content from a manifest dream. But the worker's problem had not been with the intellectual feat of dream analysis, but how to behave emotionally so that the interpersonal experience would become meaningful and therapeutic to the patient. The beginner cannot yet realize this.

The staff meetings gradually direct the beginner away from his attempts to master the problems the work presents to him through intellectual understanding alone. For comprehension to be effective, emotional rapport is needed. Helping the patient requires very personal involvement, geared toward what the moment and the patient need. The meetings achieve this end just because what emerges may mean academic learning for one staff member, guidance to self-understanding for another, a deeply corrective, emotional, and therapeutic experience for a third, and a mixture of all these and other experience for a fourth. For others, what goes on in a particular meeting may be neither learning, nor guidance, nor a corrective emotional experience, but just something that is stored away somewhere in the mind, perhaps for future reference. Another staff member might have to defend himself against the impact of what is going on in the meeting by dreaming off. But days later the fact that he had dreamed off when a certain interaction between patient and staff member was being discussed may, for one reason or another, become the starting point for significant spontaneous insights. Or the worker may suddenly recall the content of his dreaming off and understand that it had a great deal to do with what was going on at the time among his colleagues. But for the first six months or so, the beginner derives mainly intellectual stimulation from the meetings. Only in time do meetings begin to achieve some of their more important goals for him.

In order for staff conferences invariably to achieve such deep meaning for at least some of the participants, one must consider the frequency of the meetings, the number of participants, and the continuity of staff participation.

As far as frequency is concerned, we found that attendance in four of the five regular weekly staff meetings will do. Further, if fewer than about seven to ten workers participate in the staff meeting, it either tends to take the form of individual supervision (which is only impeded by the additional persons present, who are experienced as bothersome spectators) or it becomes like one of the casual get-togethers, such as the nightly ones; and since there are enough of those, there is no need to duplicate them. On the other hand, if the number present exceeds twenty, much gets lost. On the average, the professional staff numbered around thirty. At any one time a minimum of about six had to be with the patients, and a few were absent because of vacations, or some other reason, so that at the most twenty-four members of the professional staff participated in a meeting, at which they were joined by several of the office staff, which numbered five or six. Several times each month part of the supporting technical staff (cooks, maids, janitors, laundresses, etc.), numbering altogether about twenty, met with members of the professional staff to learn what the work was all about and to exercise an important influence on the School's operation.

Participation was not always easy. As one staff member put it:

> *At first I dreaded staff meetings and informal discussions much more than I dreaded working with the patients, which too was an ordeal because of what they seemed to need, and what I seemed unable to offer to them. I felt I was making nothing but mistakes, because at the end of the day they stood out so glaringly that they overshadowed the positive things I know I must also have done. Still, when with the patients I was perfectly content to go on in my merry ways, not looking at what I was doing; but in staff meetings this is impossible, at least it was for me. At first and for a while it made me angry to continually soul-search for the patients' benefit—that is, until I recognized that I too benefited, and by no small amount. I find it very difficult to write about what the meetings meant to me because a lot of what I was able to do with and for my patients was directly related to what these meetings taught me about myself as an individual; as a human being not different from the patients, and in regard to what I wanted and hoped to be in the future. The ethos of the staff meeting had the effect of making it impossible for me not to examine what I was up to—both in terms of myself and in relation to the patients. I cannot write any more about it, because I feel it would be too much like a confessional.*

She is absolutely correct; the important insights gained about oneself had to remain implied and covert, while understanding what one did with the patients, and why, had to be made explicit. What the staff member might do with what he thus learned regarding himself was his private affair; a privacy which had to be carefully protected or staff meetings would have deteriorated into encounter groups, which tend to be cathartic rather than curative.

For the senior staff to bring up problems of others—unless these were definitely also their own, in which case their situation was no different from everybody else's—would have been extremely intrusive, and contrary to the School's steadfast insistence on the autonomy of the staff. Occasionally a staff member felt he had to get help with a problem that he viewed as personal, not as one related to the patient. Then he was encouraged to try to work it out himself, or if it seemed he could not do so, he was advised to seek personal help. Staff get-togethers were not the place to ask for help on personal problems except if they were connected with patients. Had this principle not been most strictly and carefully adhered to, there would have been danger that the meetings might have deteriorated into group psycho-analytic sessions, each staff member "doing his own thing" rather than working together for the common weal.

No doubt the line between what pertained to the work and what to the worker was sometimes quite thin. It was the task of senior staff members to see that it was never crossed. Many methods were appropriate: the simplest was a remark such as "That's as far as we can go with this problem at the moment," or, "I guess that's all we can do now, maybe you want to think some more about it and if you like, we can take it up at some other time." More reassuring was "Don't try to solve it all at once; don't worry. Something like it will come up again and by then, because of what we understood today, you'll be much better able to handle it." Sometimes it was best to quite abruptly cut the discussion short with "I guess we have to give other staff members a chance to talk about what interests them." Each senior staff member had his own way of getting the one who felt on the spot off the hook, in the most gentle way possible. I preferred to tell an anecdote which only suggested a possible solution to the personal impasse in which the staff member found himself, and leave it at that. Sometimes junior staff members, out of inex-perience or carried away by their understandable wish to learn more or penetrate more deeply, wanted to stress a point. Then the senior staff had to cut them short with, "This is the worker's private affair, and if you were in his place you would not wish others to pry into your private affairs."

Even quite new staff members soon learned which of the senior staff would not press personal matters beyond a certain point. Thus with some they would open up more, certain that they would be pro-tected from revealing themselves too far. With others they would bring up only those matters which, while important, would not take them into sensitive areas. Something that was opened up in a public get-together would frequently be continued later, in a private con-versation with a close friend or a senior staff member in whom the person put great trust. While such private interchanges were beyond the milieu's control, senior staff members were careful, even then, not to go beyond what the other could integrate.

Here, as in all other respects, the nature or depth of the worker's emotional difficulties of the moment was not of the utmost importance, nor was the seriousness of neurotic fixations or defenses which might come out in the open; but rather, the ego's strength in re-establishing its dominance after being temporarily threatened by unconscious material coming to the fore. The necessities of the work were often a great help. Sometimes I was amazed how in an instant a staff member who I feared at the moment had come to a precarious state could put himself together if one of his patients needed him, or if he was scheduled to go and take care of the group. Sometimes if a rather loaded discussion were to take place just before a worker was to meet with his patients, he would seem so shaken that I worried how he would manage the requirements of his tasks. In all my years at the School, there were fewer than a dozen times when a worker was not fully able to re-establish complete ego control when necessary. The emphasis in staff selection on ego strength, rather than on the absence of pathology, paid off beautifully.

There were other meetings of staff members which also furthered staff development. There were the talks in which a junior worker received help with the problems he encountered, including some aspects of his own difficulties, by talking things over with an experienced staff member—which are typical of all institutions that are serious about giving patients the best possible psychiatric help. At the School these talks were regularly scheduled once or twice a week, rarely more often. While usually a very meaningful working relation was thus established, it was most often of a specific and limited nature. In a therapeutic milieu, what is usually called supervision takes on a different perspective. The term "supervision," while a widely known concept and practice in psychotherapeutic work, doesn't fit the reality of the therapeutic milieu because it assumes that one person knows more than another, and therefore can direct his work; as if in psychotherapy this direction would not have to come from the worker's inner convictions and his very personal feelings about the situation, his relation to a particular patient, and what these require. Thus while these talks were learning experiences, it was understood that both the senior and junior worker were at the same time teaching one another and learning from each other, as is unavoidable if two persons struggle to better understand what is at stake. True, one person brings a greater backlog of experience and knowledge, but the other brings a much more direct feeling for the situation that concerns him.

Since the presumption is that both partners bring unique knowledge to their talking things over, neither is felt to be superior or inferior. The way this was experienced, and sometimes discursively explained, was that two heads are often better than one; without this necessarily implying that one of the heads, or brains, was therefore superior to the other. Applying two different viewpoints, based on two different persons' past and present experiences, to the same situation or problem often permits a better comprehension of what one is trying to understand.

Staff Meetings

What follows is for a simple reason drawn only from the general staff meetings, although I have already said that the informal staff meetings were more interesting and many times more effective and valuable. But the five-times-a-week formal staff meetings were tape-recorded and typed, so that staff members could go over them at leisure, while to have transcribed the many more casual get-togethers would have destroyed the very informality which was their greatest asset.

Before concentrating on these meetings as instruments for challenging staff members to confront themselves, I should say something about the way I conducted them, as background for what emerges from the material itself. Again I shall rely on something a former staff member wrote:

> When people hear that I worked for many years at the Orthogenic School, the first question usually is, "Is it true that the director is as authoritarian as he appears?" In most cases this is a rhetorical question, because they are not at all interested in what my answer might be; all they want to hear is that he is. However, when I feel it is a sincere question, I tend to give a qualified yes. It is based on his, when necessary, authoritative insistence on questioning. This unwavering insistence on a questioning attitude is one of the basic tenets of the School: to take nothing for granted or at face value, and to regard everything, whoever does it including the director, as worthy of consideration and exploration, however trivial or unimportant it may seem.
>
> At the School everybody learns that questioning must start with himself; without an active self-scrutiny of what makes one tick, one is usually not terribly interested in what

makes others tick. As long as I worked there it was very important that I be in touch with myself and most especially my feelings, otherwise I certainly would not be in a position to help the patients with their feelings.

Being in touch with my feelings was not something that happened overnight, but was a gradual process that occurred simultaneously with a growing investment in, and attachment to the patients. Naturally, working with such very disturbed girls (I worked with a group of adolescent girls) stirred up a great deal of unresolved feelings and conflicts within myself. More often than not, these feelings and conflicts were rather a startling revelation to me, since I was unaware of their existence. These often unpleasant revelations were the source of a great deal of pain, but what kept me going despite the pain or perhaps sometimes because of it, was the knowledge that not only was I helping myself to become a better, more thoughtful and serious person; but that I was also helping others to grow into insightful, mature and responsible people. The combination of the tremendous growth I felt within myself and in my girls was the basis of a very strong and important attachment between us. Seeing the changes in me in my first two years was a powerful incentive to my girls, who reasoned that if I could change the course and direction of my life, then perhaps there was some hope for them to do the same. Just as a little girl strongly identifies with her mother, so did my girls with me.

I believe that the value of questioning is that it opens doors which otherwise would remain closed. Being open and accessible to the various clues which a patient presents is of crucial importance in this work. The issue of dealing with a patient on his terms, and the need to understand him from his frame of reference was also discussed many times in staff meetings.

The following is an excerpt from the tape of a general staff meeting which centered on this difficult and important issue of understanding the patient from his frame of reference. A novice worker asked about Ralph's compulsion to touch which, he said, was a source of great difficulty to Ralph.

B.B.: Is it a source of difficulty, or what is it a source of?
Worker: Well, it's also a source of protection to him.

B.B.: That's right. Why, then, did you say it's a source of difficulty?

Worker: Because it prevents him from doing other things.

B.B.: True. Let's say somebody opens an umbrella because it pours. Sometimes it's difficult to open it or to hold it and it prevents one from doing some other things with the hand that holds it, but would you call the umbrella a source of difficulties? If it were, why would you open it?

Worker: Because as he sees the world, he needs it.

B.B.: Exactly. Would that be called a source of difficulty?

Worker: Well, it's a protection.

B.B.: That's right. So, what is your attitude now to his touching compulsion?

Worker: To let him use the protection he needs, that it's O.K.

B.B.: "O.K." can be said in many different ways and in a variety of intonations. Suppose you had told one of your teachers in college that you wanted to study psychology and suppose he had said, "I guess it's O.K." What would you have deduced from his answer?

Worker: That he really didn't think it was such a good idea.

B.B.: So now I would like to know the emotional content the "O.K." you just said has for you.

Worker: I'm afraid it varies, depending on how much difficulty the symptom poses.

I had hoped that my first question would permit the worker to recognize that while the touching compulsion was indeed a source of difficulty, it was not, as he assumed, one for the patient, but for the worker. Had I phrased my question differently, asking: "Tell me, for whom is it a difficulty?", the worker probably would have seen right away that the difficulties he was concerned with were his own and not those of the patient. But at the same time, he would have felt that this realization had been forced on him; it would have prevented his understanding all on his own that what he had viewed as a difficulty was really a protective device for the patient. Thus while the worker didn't understand what I was trying to get across, he nevertheless learned something of importance which he was ready for at this moment, which was directly useful to him, and would be indirectly to the patient.

What the worker had wanted to begin with was for me to suggest how this "source of difficulty" could be removed, without any reference to himself; to bring this to his attention I had asked quite directly: "What is your attitude?" The worker had learned by now that he should respect the patient's symptom; but his "O.K." revealed he had no positive feeling for it, nor about how much the patient needed it and how totally exposed he would feel without it. I used the example of the umbrella to suggest that without it we would be exposed to the vagaries of the elements, hoping that this would evoke appropriate associations in the mind of the worker; but it did not. When I finally brought it down to his own experiences as a graduate student in psychology, he was able to realize he still hadn't emotionally accepted the patient's symptom, though he had understood its value intellectually. To ask him why he had such difficulty in viewing a touching compulsion positively would have been too intrusive, and would have shifted the issue from the patient to the worker. As a beginner, all this worker was able to do was make some progress toward getting a feeling of how important this symptom was for the patient, and how little he, the worker, could accept it. I carried the idea a bit further on a less personal level:

B.B.: The non-therapist is the one who wants the patient to give up the symptoms which are his only protection. If you call Ralph's touching compulsion a difficulty when it is his only protection in life, then he fears you want him, deep down, to be exposed to the vagaries of life without any protection. This demand is unbearable. Somebody is a good therapist when he deeply appreciates and protects the symptomatic behavior of the patient. That's the first step. Only after you have given a full measure of recognition to the validity of this touching compulsion, and if that really has gotten across to Ralph, then he might be willing to consider your thoughts on the matter. But only after you have given full recognition to *his* thoughts and feelings.

Another worker describes how she applied what she had learned from this staff discussion the next day to one of her patients with whom she had been stalemated:

> I heard some singing emanating from the bathroom, or perhaps I should say resounding. In the past when this had happened I had been very apprehensive about it, because it is one of Betty's most flagrant presenting symptoms, and the one which finally got her parents to realize there was something very wrong with their daughter. She would listen to her rock and roll records sometimes for all twenty-four hours of the day; during which time she would be in a

trance-like state, unable to eat, hear or speak. Knowing how destructive these records were for her, I had tried to prevent her from playing them. I had no doubt that she was addicted to them, and I thought I must first withdraw this poison before I could reach her.

Under the impact of the staff meeting, I changed my beliefs and I went in the bathroom and listened to this particular song. As I paid attention to the words, I realized I had made a very serious mistake. The song tells the story of a girl who runs away from home and the chorus tells the parents' reaction to their daughter's rejection, which is one of total bewilderment since, as they say, they have given her everything that money can buy. Superficially, this is very much the story of Betty's life, or at least part of it. It now occurred to me that in all probability many of the songs I had so cavalierly outlawed contained important messages and clues to her various preoccupations which she could more easily state through these songs, since such expressions are less direct and therefore less threatening.

Along with the realization of my original mistake came others. Since my mind had been closed to the entire issue of the records, I had not realized there was another alternative as to what to do about the collection when she first came. That was to listen to the records with her, since the destructive element was not in the records themselves, but in the way they had been used. Rather than attempting to understand this very important "symptom" of Betty's, I had tried to get rid of it. I had thought that my motive for outlawing the records was to protect Betty. Stimulated by the staff meeting, I realized that I was trying to protect myself —after all, I didn't want to have a catatonic on my hands! Up to that point, I had found Betty quite resistant to my efforts to get to know her, since I was trying to get to know her on my terms rather than hers. In effect, with her resistance to me she was saying, "If you aren't interested in me and the things (record collection) which are important to me, then why should I have anything to do with you?"

From then on, this worker regularly set some time aside when she and Betty listened to records together; she prevented Betty from falling into her trancelike state by talking about the messages she got from the records. Soon Betty was correcting her, saying she got many of them all wrong; in this way telling more of the personal meaning a song had for her. Betty so much enjoyed setting the worker right that eventually most of their time was taken up with talking about what the records meant, with hardly any time being left for listening to them. This by no means cured Betty, but for ever longer periods of time she was in contact and not catatonically withdrawn.

One of the maxims I tried to have every worker make his own was that how we approach a situation defines how it will evolve; hence the end is always in the beginning. A senior staff member provided an illustration of how, in her ninth year, she used this principle to promote understanding in a worker who was then at the end of her second year.

For two weeks Laura, an adolescent girl, had either been late when meeting this junior worker or avoiding her altogether, refusing to discuss her reasons for it. The senior worker asked Erica, the junior worker, to talk about their most recent time together.

Erica: Laura came in and sat down—didn't say anything for about ten minutes. Finally when she started talking it was about how furious she was at Julie [her other regular counselor], and she went on and on about something that Julie had promised to get her the day before and had forgotten. After a tirade of about fifteen minutes she stopped talking. After awhile I asked her what she was thinking about and at that point she got up and walked out.

Senior: Why do you suppose Laura tells *you* about how angry she is with Julie?

Erica: Maybe she's afraid to tell Julie.

Senior: There might be other possibilities.

Erica: I just don't know.

Senior: Well, how did she first come into the room and what were your feelings when she entered?

Erica: As I said, she didn't say anything at all in the beginning. Oh! but before that, now I remember when she first came in she looked very angry and sat in such a way that her rear end was facing me and I remember having the fleeting thought that by doing so it was as if she was saying "Shit on you," but then when she started talking so hard and fast about being mad at Julie, I lost track of my thought. It occurs to me, now that we're talking, that it was probably more comfortable for me to hear about her anger at Julie rather than at me.

Senior: Right, and I think that Laura is reading you correctly—

she comes in and says, not in so many words, but more strongly and clearly than that, "Shit on you," and when she "sees" that it is not acceptable to you, she then talks about her anger at Julie, which she knows will be acceptable to you [there was a great deal of competition between Erica and Julie]. But this just makes Laura angrier, and since the real source of her anger is not acceptable to you she has no choice but to walk out.

From this exchange Erica learned that if she had begun the meeting differently, the outcome would have been quite different as well; hence, the end is in the beginning. Again, it was the underlying attitude of the worker (in this case, Erica's glossing over Laura's anger at her and her readiness to see it passed on to Julie) that was of the utmost importance. As long as Laura's feeling toward Erica was ignored, very little if any progress or understanding could be achieved.

It would be easy and by no means incorrect to conclude from these and the following examples that in staff education, the emphasis is on exploring the countertransference. But this is such a highly technical term that it tends to serve as a barrier against recognizing the simple emotional experiences that are involved. Much of the teaching of psychopathology and psychotherapy concentrates on the patient: why he became the person he now is, why he developed his pathological defenses, what the pathogenic influences were in his life, what anxieties he defends himself against—as if this knowledge would automatically suggest how to approach him, and the best ways to help him. The following excerpts from a staff meeting show how a very well-intentioned, highly intelligent beginning worker, who had some years of experience as a teacher and had been in psychoanalysis for a couple of years, got carried away just because she knew so much about dreams and their interpretation from her own analytic experience, and from what she had learned in theory.

Lena: I was visiting and playing with the Pathfinders [a group of adolescent boys] and toward bedtime David said, "I have a scary dream I want to tell you." He talked at the top of his voice and so I said, "Do you really want to tell me?" And when he said he did, I suggested we go outside. If it was scary I didn't see any reason why everybody in the dormitory should listen and get anxious. I didn't know what was best to do. I didn't really know if he should tell me a dream. He doesn't know me very well and I don't know him very well. So we went outside and he said every night he has this dream of a giant who's chasing him and he's running and there's a rope that he's trying to climb but he can't get the rope, and it's disappearing. I was pretty sure it was an oedipal dream, the giant his father, and possibly also one based on castration fear, but I didn't know what to do with it. I listened and didn't say anything because I didn't know what to say. Then he became very anxious and he said, "Would you tell Alan?" [one of his counselors]. And I said, "Well, what do you want me to do?" And he said, "Tell him." And I said, "Well, it's your dream and if you want Alan to know you should tell him." And he said, "No, you tell him." And I said, "Well, if you want me to tell him, I'll tell him, it's all right." He insisted: "Will you tell him right now?" And I said, "Well, I'll talk with him later." But I was caught in my own anxieties, not knowing whether I should have let him tell me the dream in the first place. As we went back into the dormitory he was just about pulling on me to "Tell him now." So I felt that I had mishandled something. I left the dormitory shortly after this. I had the feeling that he was extremely upset.

B.B.: This is a very good example of a beginning counselor not knowing how to react. My advice is that unless there is good reason not to and unless one is quite sure of one's grounds, the first way to react would be to respond the way one would to one's friends. If a friend of yours were to say to you, "I had a scary dream I want to tell you" what would your reaction be?

Lena: It might be, why do you want to tell me a scary dream?

B.B.: No, I don't think so.

Lena: Sort of a "What do you want me to do about it?" or "What can I do?"

B.B.: So you see, you already started with some uneasiness— "What do you want me to do about it?" David wasn't asking you to do anything about it. All he asked was—what?

Lena: Can I tell you a scary dream.

B.B.: So what did he ask you to do?

Lena: To answer his question.

B.B.: Exactly. But what action on your part is required for this interaction to take place? What have you got to do?

Lena: Be there.

B.B.: Correct, what else?

Lena: To listen.

B.B.: To listen. Exactly. From your own experience, what is the prime task of a psychoanalyst?

Lena: To listen.

B.B.: So when he said, "I want to tell you a scary dream," what would the natural reaction be?

Lena: I would listen.

B.B.: Sure. But because it's David, a homicidal schizophrenic, right away the wheels started to turn in your head.

Lena: Then, as you said, I should react the way I would if a friend of mine asked to tell me a scary dream.

B.B.: Yes. And what would you say? Now if in all eagerness I were to tell you, "I want to tell you something very important to me" and you said, "Well, if you want to tell me . . ."

Lena: That kills it right there.

B.B.: That's right. And this is particularly true for David, who is continually all eagerness to have somebody listen to him, and from whose history we know that his parents, whenever he was eager, always threw cold water on it.

Lena: So I did, too.

B.B.: But if you did, you must have had good reasons for reacting this way. The question is, why? As I have told you many times, you must know how to respond because you couldn't have survived so long without knowing. For if you want to make or keep a friend, whatever nonsense he produces, the best way is to listen to him, all eagerness. The poor guy is sunk if you don't do that.

Unfortunately, many young people are so full of their own need to tell, to get something for themselves, that they cannot give the other person what he needs, though if he gets it he's hooked. I don't want to imply that you want to hook more friends. You may have more fish on your lines than you know what to do with. But you want to hook David. Maybe his continuous, eager demandingness is more than anybody can stand. On the other hand, I don't know but that it might subside if and when he were to get the right type of response.

Let's look at this particular situation. There he is, all eagerness to tell you something and you ask him whether he really wants to, questioning whether he knows what he wants to do. And then you say, "Yes, you can tell me the dream, but only after I have found a safe place for it." As if to impress him further with your need for emotional distance, you say, "Let's go outside." Now that would help you greatly with your boy friend if you said, "Yes, Johnny, I would like to listen to you, but there are some other people here and I first want to make sure that they don't get bored or anxious by what you might tell." By then, if Johnny has any mind of his own, he says the hell with you. Well, to put it in psychoanalytic terms, listening to a dream after you have put an emotional distance between yourself and the dreamer, or the dream content—you might as well not listen to it. Because, you see, this is the most dangerous thing we can do: to fool the youngsters. They have been fooled all their lives; somebody pretended to be helpful who really wasn't; somebody pretended to be dutifully interested, but was really preoccupied with his own needs. And if you repeat that here, going through the motions of interest when actually you are preoccupied with your own defensive maneuvers . . .

Lena: I was speculating what David would have done if I hadn't put this distance . . .

B.B.: You see, you are again speculating about David and not about yourself. The issue now is not what David might have done because that we can never know. But we might get to know why you have the need to put this distance between yourself and him.

Lena: I do know that he can in a second arouse my anxieties.

B.B.: That's right. Now that's the real issue. Why can he arouse your anxieties?

Lena: I've been thinking about this but I haven't gotten much closer than that he is constantly at me. I mean, he just doesn't let up for a second, asking, demanding.

B.B.: Well, I don't know whether this discussion is at all fruitful.

With the last remark, I tried to give Lena an easy way out. If she didn't want to explore her anxiety, all she had to do was not reply, or to agree with me, and matters would end there. For my purposes it was sufficient that she recognized it had not been David and his dream that had created the impasse, but her anxiety. Aware of this, she sooner or later—alone in her thought, in her psychoanalysis, in talking in private with some senior staff member, or by bringing it up again in some future meeting—would have continued to explore the origin and nature of her anxiety and what she wanted to do about it. But she chose to continue the exploration immediately.

Lena: I think I missed something.

B.B.: Well, what do you want to know?

Lena: I want to know why I get so anxious.

B.B.: That's exactly right. Now, what makes you so anxious? This is an issue that comes up at least once a year.

Staff: Once a year? Seven times a day.

B.B.: Well, same difference. Let's go back to our example. In what tone of voice did you say it, please repeat.

Lena: If you want to tell me, it's all right.

B.B.: You all have listened to this interchange. What impression of her attitude has Lena's tone of voice and reaction given you?

Alan: Blasé. There's nothing.

Staff: Fear.

B.B.: Possibly, but I would have been hard-pressed to hear it in the way it was said.

Staff: Not very excited about it. Extremely cautious.

B.B.: That's right—extremely cautious. When are we cautious?

Lena: When we are unsure? When we feel danger?

B.B.: Correct. If we are sure, we don't feel danger. So while it is true that you could say we are cautious when we are unsure, just to take that one step further shows that behind this uncertainty is the fear of a danger. All right, what is the danger involved here? Or to put it differently, about what are you unsure?

Lena: About what I should do.

B.B.: That's right. So the anxiety is about what?

Lena: Me.

B.B.: That's right. The anxiety is not about David but about yourself. I think it is now quite clear that when you worried about whether it was all right for David to tell you the dream because you didn't know each other very well, and about where he should tell it to you, it was not as you originally thought, due to uncertainty about these issues having to do with David—but with anxiety which he activated in you. Your worry that others might get anxious when listening to the dream, though possibly true, was largely a projection of your own anxiety. Since the idea of listening to the dream made you anxious, you naturally expected that it would also make others anxious.

If you had been aware of this, you could have told David, "Look, I am not comfortable with your telling me your dream, and since I am not, telling it to me won't do you much good. Why don't you tell it to somebody you know better, like Alan, your counselor?" David obviously contemplated this possibility after you had expressed your lack of interest, since he asked you to tell Alan about it. Or you could have shown your pleasure that he was willing to take you into his confidence, by telling him how much it meant to you that he trusted you with his dreams. You might even, with some self-humor, have wondered what was so special about you, that he told you in preference to others whom he knew much better.

If you had done this, you might have got an answer which, while less flattering, might have surprised you and taught you something. Because it probably would have shown that he really didn't expect you to help him with his dreams. Given his anxiety—particularly about any female who entered or might enter his life, because of his mother's murderous rage against him—he may have felt he had to appease you for his own safety.

Lena: So he found out that I'm as bad as his mother.

B.B.: No, if you make things worse than they are, you'll have a miserable life here. Things are difficult enough, without us putting the worst possible interpretation on them. As a matter of fact, that David dared to approach you at all shows the progress he has made in not immediately assuming all mother figures are out to get him. He gave you the benefit of the doubt, and tried to find out what kind of a person you are. Why do you think he wanted to tell you about his nightmare?

Lena: Perhaps he thought as a psychologist I'd be interested in it.

B.B.: Quite probably. Now he didn't do it to be specially nice to you; he did it out of his anxiety, to get you on his side, as if telling you: look how badly off I am, don't think you need to be afraid of me, I am nothing but a helpless creature chased by giants. Because while you had correctly understood some of the meaning of the dream, you paid no attention to the message for which he used it, when he told it to you. Because you see, it's not just the dream and its manifest or latent content that's important. For your relationship, for understanding what goes on at the moment, it is much more important *why* it is told *to you.* If you had recognized this, you would have seen how important you are as a person—because for his present view of the world, all depended on whether you'll scare him like his mother, or will comfort him as only you can—so he told you the dream to get something positive from you.

If you had told David honestly what was going on in you, which you could not since you were not aware of it, then at least he would have experienced that here we are open about our feelings, and don't pretend we do something to protect him or the others against getting anxious, when we are actually out to protect ourselves. That's why we have to try to understand what is motivating us; so that we don't blame it on things which have little or nothing to do with it. If we can't permit ourselves to recognize when it is our own anxiety that motivates our actions, then we must blame it on others, such as David, by believing it is he who makes us anxious, as if any other person would have such power over us.

Believing another person has power over us to make us feel anxious about what he may do to us forces us to defend ourselves against such possible impact, by distancing ourselves from the situation. We cannot help resenting those who seem to have such power over us. It is natural to want to blame our difficulties on others, for then we don't have to feel responsible for them. What we don't realize is that when we do this, we make it appear that those others have power over us, and this debilitates us. Out of their anxieties, their need to test us, to find out what our weaknesses are, schizophrenics have an uncanny ability to discover our Achilles' heel, our specific vulnerability. Feeling that she was not competent enough to help David, this worker experienced their interchange as his power to make her anxious. But David was only the incidental catalyst which made her aware of a feeling that resided within herself. He could not create her anxiety; all he could do was bring to her consciousness what up to then had remained preconscious.

Nothing will do the patient any good unless it happens within a personal relation. Interpreting a dream outside such a relationship only convinces the patient of the superior knowledge the staff member possesses; this makes him feel inferior, because another person knows more about him than he himself. An attitude of "We know better what's good for you, understand better what's going on within you," is most injurious to the patient's self-respect, and destructive to him and to the possibility of his forming anything but a dependent relation, if any at all.

Every staff member must create an "I–Thou" relation, in

which what counts is not what is transacted, but very much that it is transacted between the two of us. If a patient says, "I want to tell you a dream," the issue is not the dream but that he wants to tell it to a particular person, at a specific moment, in a unique situation. Instead of accepting this obvious fact, the worker was dubious about her appropriateness as the person he should tell it to, and the place; she doubted him. If she had asked openly, or silently to herself, "Why me, of all people," she could not have avoided also wondering, "Well, maybe he thinks I am the right person," which would have flattered her, despite her worry as to whether she was up to doing it correctly. Feeling flattered, she would not have been anxious, or less so, and could not have helped feeling more positive to a person who thought so well of her. This would have made it all the easier for her to relate to him.

So interpreted, her experience with David should help the worker not to look at what takes place coldly, abstractly, distantly, as something that happens; but always as something very personal which occurs between two people because they are these two persons. This view strengthens her feeling of importance and responsibility, and thus provides the emotional supplies she needs for dealing with the situation. Only when she views this as a personal interaction can she feel that she can do something important about what goes on, because she is at least half of what is happening. Obvious as this is, it takes many such attempts at teaching before a beginner learns it.

Anyone who is attracted to this type of work wants to do something for the patients. But it becomes very hard to learn that the most effective way to achieve this goal is by doing something about oneself; and that trying to do something only about the patient is more often than not counterproductive. An example:

Joan [*A counselor who had been with the institution just a few months, hence still very much a beginner*]: One thing that bothers me is the fact that I'm pushing Agnes around.

B.B.: I would never insinuate that you do any such thing.

Joan: But I do. I want her to do things and then we sort of meet in a head-on clash—that is, she doesn't want to do them.

B.B.: From what you say, nobody would know what is really going on. Could you give an example of a situation where you feel you push her around?

Joan: Eating at the table. She still eats only with her hands. Forks and knives and spoons were just never invented as far as she is concerned. [Agnes was fifteen at the time.]

B.B.: If it bothers you so much that she doesn't use the silverware we provide, why don't you see to it that they are not put by her plate at the table? [My purpose in so deliberately misunderstanding what upset the worker, was to bring to her attention that the issue was not the non-use of silverware which she had stressed, but that Agnes preferred to eat with her fingers. This is what annoyed the worker, and not the avoidance of forks and spoons.]

Joan: She'd feel terribly deprived. [This remark showed that the worker could recognize deprivation if a person was not provided with what the worker valued. She couldn't see that she wanted to impose a much more severe deprivation; namely, that Agnes should give up eating with her fingers. That is, this beginner viewed gratification and deprivation only from her frame of reference. Nor could she see that my suggestion, if done correctly, would give Agnes the feeling that her non-use of silverware was quite acceptable to us. But the worker was right; if she had taken the silverware away, given her feelings about it, for Agnes it would have had the connotation of taking something away, rather than of accepting highly individual behavior.]

B.B.: But why should she feel deprived since she doesn't use these utensils? After all, they are not put on the table for decoration. They're placed there so that those who want to use them can easily do so. For those who don't, they are pointless.

Joan: I still think that would be pushing her around.

B.B.: If you say so, I'm sure you're right. But so far you've told us only that she eats with her hands. This hardly constitutes your pushing her around.

Joan: I thought everybody understood that I tell her not to use her hands, and that we have a fight over it.

B.B.: If you think that her eating with her hands is something that leads to head-on clashes, then you should do something about it.

Joan: I guess that's what I don't know, because first of all I don't know why she doesn't use any utensils.

B.B.: Well, maybe that's what we should have started our deliberation with. But tell me: How does she eat applesauce?

Edda [*Agnes's other counselor, and the more experienced of the two*]: She eats stuff like that with a spoon.

B.B.: All right, then let her have a spoon.

Inge: I don't know how much it means, but she uses chopsticks better than anyone I've ever seen. [This senior worker wanted to bring to Joan's attention how selective Agnes's non-use of eating utensils was. The intention was to help Joan recognize on her own that there must be very strong reasons for Agnes to refuse to use knife and fork, since she was quite ready to use chopsticks and spoons. Agnes had never been accepted by her parents. All they had been interested in from the time she was an infant was that she act the perfect lady. Her eating manners became one of her ways of fighting back against being pushed unbearably to perform, without any regard to her feelings.]

B.B.: So let's give her spoons and chopsticks.

Joan: She might like that, she might think it's kind of funny; but I still would feel I'm pushing her around.

B.B.: Which takes us back where we started, which is only natural, because we haven't made any progress in understanding what is involved. Agnes's is a very complex series of behavior to which you have a very strong reaction. Before I know what it all means to you, I can't have any suggestions. One thing I certainly would never do, and that is, if a behavior irritates me, do nothing about it.

Joan: Why should she change for me?

B.B.: I haven't said that she should.

Joan: Then what can I do about it?

B.B.: That's a most sensible question. Why didn't you ask it in the first place?

Joan: Because when I do something because it irritates me I feel I'm pushing her around. [This, incidentally, exemplifies a quality that must be present in the beginner even before she starts her training: a deep commitment not to push others around. That is why Joan was able to avoid projecting something in herself (irritation) into the patient; she knew that it was her problem and not the patient's. Although she thought it wrong for Agnes to eat with her fingers, she knew that forcing her to use knives and forks would be pushing Agnes around. Joan's approach thus showed a readiness to question her own attitudes; and what is much more important, a strong desire to be fair to Agnes, even when she found her behavior irritating. Though deep down Joan wished to force her values regarding eating behavior on Agnes, her conscience did not permit her to do so without feeling guilty.]

B.B.: This is an important observation. But what did I say?

Joan: That if there is something that was bothering you, you would do something about it.

B.B.: That's right. Although it was you who asked: "What can I do about it?" and all I did was to heartily agree.

Joan: That is, if there was something that was bothering you, you would do something about it?

B.B.: Right.

Joan: You mean about you?

B.B.: It might just have been that's what I had in mind, but what's in my mind doesn't do you any good, only what is in yours.

Joan: It did occur to me.

B.B.: So why didn't you say so. If some behavior irritates you . . .

Joan: All you can do is ignore it.

B.B.: I was afraid you might think that. If somebody's behavior irritates me and it's not a therapeutic relationship, I might decide to have nothing to do with this person—which is very much doing something, and neither ignoring him nor his behavior. But if we have entered a therapeutic relationship, then this common response to irritating behavior is no longer open to us, nor is it in circumstances where we are forced to live with the irritating person. Yet if behavior irritates me, the relationship will go from bad to worse, according to the intensity of the feeling aroused. Why wait till it has become unmanageable? Better to do something before this point has been reached.

Then the next decision is: Do I want to do something about myself so that it won't irritate me any longer, or do I want to do something about the person who irritates me? This is a crucial decision we all have to make many times in our lives. So the next question is: Do I do something about my irritation, or about the behavior which causes my reaction?

Believe me, this institution wouldn't have continued long if most of the time I didn't conclude I'd better do something about my irritation. The problem is the sort of narrow dichotomy you presented: ignore her, or push her around. The first is no good because how can we ignore a patient's symptomatic behavior, which is one of the most obvious ways he can tell us something of importance about himself? Ignoring what a person does means also disregarding him to a considerable degree. I need say nothing about the second, pushing Agnes around, because you are quite clear that that is wrong.

But there is one thing to be said about your suggestion of ignoring Agnes's eating manners. Ignoring them implies ignoring your own irritation, which you won't be able to do as long as you haven't freed yourself of its sources. It was you who spoke of pushing Agnes around. That suggests that you must have thought of stopping her behavior rather than of developing a course of action appropriate to remedy the impasse between the two of you; a course of action either in yourself, or in her, or in both of you together, which might reduce the irritation to nil.

Joan: I guess with eating and table behavior I just can't fool around.

B.B.: Did I say you should fool around?

Joan: Giving her chopsticks or taking her silverware away is fooling around. I still react to it as pushing her around, but maybe it isn't.

B.B.: Maybe it depends on what kind of attitude you do it with. I suggested it mainly because you haven't tried any other course of action.

Joan: No, I haven't. I am really completely at a loss. I just cannot do anything about it.

[This was said in a very upset tone of voice.]

B.B.: You seem distressed just by thinking about it. Why?

Joan: I was thinking before staff meeting that I wanted to talk about it. Now I suddenly realized that her getting fat was bothering me. I can't do anything about it.

Joan had an obvious problem with obesity. While not badly overweight, she tended to overeat. During her childhood and adolescence her parents had tried to have her keep on a diet, which she had deeply resented as nonacceptance of her body, and herself. It had been quite clear from the beginning that her feeling of helplessness in regard to Agnes's table manners was due to her own difficulties around eating. She had wanted to assert her wishes about eating against those of her parents, but never could permit herself to do so. Her remark that she just could not fool around with eating was the beginning of the breaking into her consciousness that it wasn't Agnes's behavior that caused the worker's difficulties, but her own inability to feel free about eating.

The discourse about the need to do something about ourselves had taken some effect. Joan was beginning to think about herself.

At first she tried to push it away by attempting to reduce it to an issue of silverware versus no silverware. But when her emotional reaction was brought to her attention, she became aware of what was really upsetting her: the issue of obesity. Joan's "I can't do anything about it," while ostensibly referring to Agnes, was so spoken that it was ambiguous whether it referred to Agnes's getting fat, or Joan's reaction to it. One may guess that unconsciously it referred as much to Joan's own problem with overeating.

Having established that what had upset her was a problem in her own life, Joan's mind was freed to the degree that, as her next remarks show, she could afford to speculate about the meaning and purpose of the symptom (such as the tactile pleasures and the safety Agnes might derive from handling her food), ideas which would have meant very little to Joan had they been suggested by somebody else, but which opened up an entirely new way of experiencing psychological phenomena because they occurred to her on her own.

B.B.: Are we talking about her getting fat, or about her eating with her fingers?

Joan: They seem to be the same to me.

B.B.: Eating with one's fingers doesn't make people fat.

Joan: No, but I think she eats with her fingers because she wants to feel the food, know what you've got in your hand, then you don't have to worry about it.

B.B.: Well, we don't talk about table manners any more, do we?

Joan: Well, in a way not. I have difficulty separating them, because when I think about Agnes, how she eats, I get all messed up.

B.B: Now we've got three possible sources of your irritation: Agnes's table manners, your anxiety about pushing her around, and your reaction to her gaining weight. What is it that irritates you? Her gaining weight?

Joan: Yes, the gaining weight. But instead of seeing the three things separate, I think it all has to do with eating.

B.B.: True. So let's start with what you started with: her not using a knife and fork. This can mainly be defiance of her parents, while eating the food with her fingers may have to do with other needs or anxieties. So maybe many psychological problems account for this one symptom.

Joan: She's been here already three years.

B.B: So?

Joan: She's still defying her parents?

B.B.: How long has it been that you stopped living with your parents?

Joan: O.K. More than three years.

B.B.: How come what they think about you still bothers you so much?

Joan: But it isn't them any more that I'm defying. It's something right here.

[She was referring to her difficulties in relating to some of the senior staff, in particular to the relish with which she picked arguments with me. She knew she defied the senior staff, and didn't fool herself into believing her attempts to provoke them had no emotional underpinning but was objectively justified behavior.]

B.B.: All right, so you re-create parents wherever you go.

Joan: So Agnes is defying me, and it has nothing to do with her parents.

[Here the worker defended herself against the realization that her enjoyment in being able to tell off the senior staff had its source in wishing she could have done this with her parents; she was trying to assert this had nothing to do with her past, but only with the persons the senior staff were. She could maintain this belief only if Agnes was no longer reacting to her parents, but only to Joan as a real person.]

B.B.: I don't think so. While something in you activates her need to defy her parents, she is fighting back against them and hardly at all against you, or so I think.

Joan: Can you deal with me in terms that I'm defying my parents, or that I'm defying you?

B.B.: That's an easy one. Sometimes I wonder how long you'll have to keep it up, because while you enjoy it at the moment, you feel bad about it afterwards, otherwise there wouldn't be anything wrong with it, at least as far as you are concerned. But the reason your defying me doesn't faze me at all is that I know it has nothing to do with me as a person. I know how I feel about you, and on this basis I know I give you little reason to be defiant. That's why it doesn't bother me or interfere with my relation to you. But since you brought it up, there is something childish in the way you go about defying me, quite out of line with the maturity of your judgment and behavior in all other situations. So that alone shows it goes back to childhood experiences.

Joan: I'll have to find a better way to do it then.

> [This remark showed how secure this worker had already become within the therapeutic milieu. She knew that nobody would force her to give up her defying behavior; this would only happen when she had reached the point where she was able and wanted to relinquish it. As long as she tried to do her best with the patients, her own idiosyncrasies would be accepted as something she still needed. The staff were ready to give her time to work them out the way she wanted, provided it didn't seriously reflect on her work with the patients. But the remark at the same time showed she knew she would have to find better ways to meet her needs.]

B.B.: Yes, for example, you might try defying me in an adult way. If you do, you might possibly feel much better about it; or you might find it unattractive.

Joan: Maybe then there wouldn't be any longer any need to defy you.

B.B.: Exactly, but only you can find this out.

Joan: I'm totally confused now. What do I do about Agnes?

B.B.: Your confusion is my fault, because I deliberately slanted the discussion so that you can see how much you and Agnes have in common. I wanted to show you the irritation resides much more in you, and little in what Agnes does.

I said this hoping Joan would recognize how invested she herself was in Agnes's continuing to defy her parents around eating. While consciously Joan wanted Agnes to eat nicely at the table, unconsciously she enjoyed Agnes's defiance of parental authority. As long as this ambivalence between her conscious and unconscious desires continued, there was no way to resolve the impasse in her and Agnes's relation *vis-à-vis* table manners.

While the effort to bring this to the worker's consciousness fell flat, it would not hinder other attempts in the same direction. If the point were not pressed (and it was fully accepted as legitimate that the worker did not wish to recognize its thrust at this juncture), there was always the chance that at some other more propitious time it might reappear in her mind. Many such hints about possible connections between what goes on in the worker's mind and in the patient's are necessary before one of them will be constructively applied. Nothing would be more destructive to the worker's development than trying to drive such a point home. The subtle allusion, casually dropped, is more effective in the long run. Telling her what it is all about doesn't change the worker's attitude. Telling her what she should do—though that is precisely what most psychiatric institutions do—won't help either.

Joan: I know it's my irritation.
B.B.: True, but if so, why did you start talking about Agnes?
Joan: Because the other day when I complained about her, you told me that I don't care about her.
B.B.: I didn't say that, I said you didn't care deeply enough about her in those ways which would be most helpful to her. Because if you did, you would not have talked about her in the kind of flippant way you did then.
Joan: But that's the way I talk about myself, too. I do care a lot about her.
B.B.: Sure, you should talk more respectfully about yourself too.
Joan: So I have to understand something about myself first.
B.B.: Not necessarily first. Why isn't it possible that you understand something about Agnes first, and then about yourself, or both at the same time?
Joan: I don't want to push her. And yet every time I do something it feels as if I would.
B.B.: What does it mean that you say, "I don't want to push her"?
Joan: That I *do* push her.
B.B.: Maybe there are two different sources of irritation in you: That about her table manners, and your feeling about children being pushed around.
Joan: Yes.
B.B.: So do you want to talk about Agnes, or what shall we talk about now?
Joan: Let's not talk.

And with this, the staff meeting addressed itself to other workers and their patients. Joan's desire not to pursue the matter was quite in line with her determination not to accept what it represented to her adult maturity. My acceptance of her statement, "Let's not talk," was the best I could do at the time to convince her that she would not be pushed around.

But the next time when eating with Agnes Joan talked with her, not about using silverware, but about how it feels if you touch the food you are eating. That is, she pursued an idea that had spontaneously occurred to her during the staff meeting, not suggested by a senior staff member. This eventually led to Agnes's being able to reveal to Joan her cannibalistic desires and poisoning fears, which were combined in the symptom: by feeling the food, she tried to make sure it was safe, while at the same time this evoked cannibalistic wishes for which she feared retaliation, such as the food being poisoned.

Just as the patients have to learn that they possess all the necessary resources within themselves to get well, staff members must become able to comprehend that within them resides all the knowledge necessary to understand the patient. Their inner resources are their only reliable guidance on how to proceed with the patients. If they aren't convinced of the value of what they carry within themselves, then they won't be able to convince the patient of the value within him.

In the staff meeting transcripts which are presented next, two main principles which we found most useful in helping workers to approach and master their difficult tasks are illustrated. In constantly variable form, these principles were the essence of many staff discussions. The first is that "The patient is always right"—that is, nonsensical as his behavior may seem to us, it makes excellent sense to him—and the second, that an understanding of what this meaning to him may be can best be approached or directly derived from our own inner experiences. What we have to do is ask ourselves the question: What conditions would induce me to engage in exactly the type of behavior which seems irrational or otherwise deviate in the patient? While this hardly ever reveals what is going on in the patient, it will be close enough for most practical purposes; particularly when this basic empathic understanding is enlightened by a thorough grounding in human behavior, whether based on art, anthropology, psychopathology, or psychoanalysis. This particular episode also illustrates the use of intellectualization as a defense against a direct emotional experiencing of what is going on. By pure chance, one of the participants in this meeting was a third-year psychiatric resident (Charles) and the other (Sophie) a Ph.D. candidate and intern in clinical psychology. Both of them had completed their own psychoanalysis and were planning to become analysts, but they were not staff members. However, very similar discourses took place with workers of different background.

The incident which the initial question refers to concerned a paranoiac schizophrenic adolescent boy, John, who needed to maintain his self-image of being the most accomplished ball player around, though his actual ability was inferior to that of many other patients with whom he played. His favorite way of maintaining his self-image was to throw the ball onto an inaccessible roof, to run away with it, or in some other way interrupt the game whenever it didn't go in his favor. The other players became very annoyed and didn't want to have him in on the game. He couldn't accept this because he needed to hold onto his view of himself as a superior athlete. He explained their criticisms of his actions as nothing but their jealousy, because he was so much better than they. Alan, the group's counselor, had told him that since he had thrown a ball on the roof three times already he wouldn't be able to continue in the game if he did it again. This threw John into a terrible rage. The other patients, understandably annoyed at John's behavior, were very critical of the counselor for accepting the outburst of violent rage against him without retaliation. That night at the staff meeting, as the incident was being discussed, the psychiatric resident posed a question.

Charles: After all the turmoil on the playing field, as soon as everyone came in, John asked Alan for a favor and he went out of his way to comply. I would like to know how this resolved the incident; and if so, why this way of resolving it was appropriate?

B.B.: I don't know whether it was really resolved, but let's assume that it was. What do you think was the merit of handling it in this way?

Charles: It was obvious that the amount of rage experienced by John on the playing field was inappropriate to the situation.

B.B.: On what basis do you judge that?

Charles: On the basis of any standard.

B.B.: I don't know. I wish I could feel so certain about things.

Charles: Maybe it wasn't inappropriate for John.

B.B.: Let's not put it on John by saying he is a schizophrenic boy. Let's rather look at your statement that a certain amount of rage is inappropriate. I wish you would pursue it.

Charles: All I can say is that I wouldn't have expected anybody to react with that amount of feeling to an incident like that.

B.B.: What was this incident?

Charles: When he was throwing the balls on the roof.

B.B.: Oh, yes. But we all remember the *facts*.

Charles: And that he got in a towering rage because he felt it unjust that he would be put out of the game if he did it again, and that Alan accepted this rage.

B.B.: All right. So far so good. But what started our talking was that you called it an inappropriate amount of rage, or feelings. When somebody speaks about inappropriate amounts there is an assumption that there is an appropriate amount.

Charles: Maybe "inappropriate" is the wrong word.

B.B.: All right, then let's find the right one.

Charles: Unexpected.

B.B.: That's right. What does it tell us about ourselves? If someone—instead of the correct term "unexpected"—uses the incorrect term, "inappropriate" . . .

Charles: That means they're using a value judgment.

B.B.: *Both* are value judgments in a way, but . . .

Charles: But in the one you decide what is correct, or right or wrong . . .

B.B.: For?

Charles: For another person.

B.B.: Correct. And in the second?

Charles: What you say in the second is that *you* would not have reacted in that way.

B.B.: Maybe. Now, between a person who knows what to expect, and another who doesn't know what to expect, how would you differentiate between them? What would you call the first, and what the second?

Charles: Informed, and the other is uninformed.

B.B.: That's right. Or smart and less smart. Therefore, when you said: "John's behavior is inappropriate," actually what happened was that this kind of behavior was unexpected to you. What's the difference between the two statements?

Charles: When I said it was inappropriate, I assumed that I knew what should have been appropriate—or I assumed that I knew how John was feeling.

B.B.: That's right. You assumed that you knew what the appropriate feeling for John is. When you say his behavior "was unexpected to me," what do you say?

Charles: That I don't know what it should be.

B.B.: That's right. You said it was inappropriate because you wanted to put the burden of your lack of understanding on John and not face up to it, while facing it would permit you to really understand what's going on. Because if you say, "That was unexpected to me," and you want to be a therapist, you have to continue and wonder, "Why *was* that unexpected? What am I lacking in understanding of other human beings that I didn't expect that?" So you see, to say a person's behavior is inappropriate, or wrong, is the end of psychological understanding. To say, "This is unexpected to me," is the beginning of psychological interest and investigation. Do you follow?

Charles: You clear yourself to further exploration.

B.B.: That's right. This is why diagnosis is so often the undoing of psychotherapy. Because in diagnosis you evaluate and judge a situation; and after you've made it, you tend to stop the investigation because no further inquiry is necessary.

Charles: But I did not make a diagnostic study of John.

B.B.: Not a study; but by stating with conviction, as you did, that some behavior is inappropriate, you made a diagnosis. A diagnostic study consists of nothing but many such little diagnoses. Good psychotherapy, contrary to the public image in movies and stories, consists of the therapist's ability to be continuously surprised. He has to be. Each step the patient makes is a move away from where he was before, which could be known. But the next step is unknown until he makes it. Do you follow?

Charles: Yes.

B.B.: All right, now let's go back to John. If you say his rage was inappropriate to the situation, that's the end of it. He's just a schizy boy and that's it. If, on the other hand, you say that this amount of feeling was unexpected to you, then you have to ask, "Where does it come from?" What do you think?

Charles: Well, I don't know. Maybe one would have to know him better . . .

B.B.: No, I don't think so. Now you are making the opposite mistake, but for the same reasons. In either case, you avoid relating to John and finding out through him. In the first case you say his behavior is inappropriate, and matters end there. In the second, you say, "I can't react, because I have to know more about the patient," and that stops your spontaneous relating to him. What would you know as a therapist?

Kathy: That you *can* know.

B.B.: That's right, but how?

Alan: You can know, with his help.

B.B.: Yes and no.

Charles: Because he's different than you are.

Worker: Is John so different from the rest of us?

B.B.: That's right. If you say his behavior is inappropriate you imply that there is something wrong with him; that is, somehow you believe he is different from the rest of us. In saying, "I have to know him better," you also assume that he is quite different from you, and that's why you need greater knowledge of him. In either case the underlying attitude is the same: John is an animal of a different species. So both approaches reflect very similar underlying attitudes. True, knowing more about another person may help us realize that he isn't so strange, after all. But I have rarely seen this happen with an investigation started in the spirit with which John has been approached here. Usually such "knowing more about him," as opposed to an "understanding him better" leads to the same distancing: it results in an accumulation of evidence on how strange a person he is.

On the other hand, if we try to understand ourselves better, then we find much in us that is similar to what is going on in the other person; so what really helps is an elaboration of the "understanding him better," by adding "through understanding myself better." What is required is that we understand ourselves better around what upset John at the moment.

This leads me to what I consider the all-important attitude which practically guarantees being a good therapist: to be able to ask oneself, "When would I react in this way?" and to come up with a truthful answer. This answer resides only in ourselves; it cannot be gained from even the best understanding of John, and it will be the best way for getting a feeling of what went on in John—without which we are at a total loss in deciding how to respond to him in this particular situation. If, looking at John and his behavior, you start out by asking yourself, "When would I react in this way?" then you start out with the conviction, "John and I are made out of the same stuff."

So, now comes the question: When would *you*—not "rage," as John did; you are, after all, a well-educated person, in control of yourself—but when would *you* be flooded by such an amount of emotion? What kind of experience would be required for that; what would another person have to do to you to stir up such an amount of anger?

Charles: When you feel an injustice has been done to you.

B.B.: Yes, but not just an injustice. Injustices happen to us all the time. What would somebody else, like Alan, have to do (though Alan probably couldn't do it to you) to arouse in you such unmanageable rage?

Charles: A rejection.

B.B.: A rejection. Of course. A rejection by whom?

Charles: Someone that you love.

B.B.: Exactly. So you see, it has little to do with the ball game. You wouldn't fly into such rage when just anybody said to you, "You have to stop throwing on the roof. If you do it once more, you'll have to leave the game." Because if the person who said it to you were of no importance, you would say, "Of course, I won't throw the ball on the roof, don't give it another thought." You might figure that this guy was treating you kind of low, but you wouldn't have such an outburst. So John's outburst of feelings shows that he must have experienced it as a tremendous rejection.

Alan: Could it have been that he felt he was being pushed around? I would react just as much as he did if I were pushed around.

B.B.: Exactly. Therefore, trying to correct him would be all wrong. Now, if on such a basis you were to think that in this situation John felt terribly rejected by someone he likes, objectively speaking you might be correct or incorrect. From his experience, Alan would have thought that only somebody who is pushed around would react like this. So he would arrive at a different interpretation from that of Charles. This is important for the understanding of how psychotherapy works. If you are going to try to understand exactly what's going on in John, you have to know more, as you suggested. The two of you could argue until Doomsday about it, each one upholding and supporting his position with plenty of evidence.

But let's look at it in a different way for a moment. Supposedly, Charles, from your inner experience of what would cause such rage in you, you would say John's behavior comes from the feeling that you are terribly important to him, he likes you very much, and feels rejected by you. How would you then react to John?

Charles: Show him that I *don't* reject him.

B.B.: That's right. You would react extremely accepting. And so did Alan, acting from his premise that John's rage was due to feeling pushed around. What I'm trying to show is that the correct diagnosis is often immaterial for correct treatment.

Charles: That is why Jungian patients have Jungian dreams, and Freudian patients have Freudian dreams.

B.B.: That's right, and they both can get well, if their therapist is a good therapist. Now you will see why staking therapy on understanding the patient can lead you astray. Because there is no way to really know with certainty what's going on in any other person. But we can always find the right reaction in ourselves.

Alan: Yes, I can understand now, and I can see that his reaction was to feeling rejected rather than to being pushed around, because he had to test it out shortly after by asking for punch, trying to find out whether I was going to reject him.

B.B.: That's right. And that's why I think that Charles's interpretation of John's inner feelings was correct in terms of his oral cravings. But you did the right thing, although you might have had the wrong interpretation. You have much more empathy with a person who feels pushed around than with one who feels rejected. Therefore, your misinterpretation was much more useful in guiding you to the right action. If you had arrived at the correct interpretation, you might not have been induced, given the person you are, to accept his rage equally well.

Worker: On the chance that I could learn a little something: I was thinking about trying not to outguess the patient. It's inappropriate, to want to know more about him than he knows; it's *defensive*, and any time we react defensively, we don't do anything for him. Or we do the wrong things for him out of our own defensive needs.

B.B.: That's right. Basically this goes back to the principles "Look at Your Own Feelings"—when would I do such things, and for what reasons?—and "The Patient Is Always Right." Therefore, John never can do anything inappropriate. But if we look at the event, throwing the ball on the roof, rather than the emotion, we will be led astray. Because what matters is John's deep feeling of rejection. Any external event can trigger that; and the event that did it is really immaterial. Let me add one more observation: If the event had been appropriate to the emotion, we would have learned nothing from it. For example, if Alan had screamed back at John, we would have said, of course anybody who is screamed at is going to be in a rage.

Sophie [*the psychology intern*]: I won't ask a question, but I want to tell you what happened to me last week. Ida came up and said, "You have new glasses on." Which I didn't.

B.B.: But you do, if she says so.

Sophie: I said, "No, Ida, I have no new glasses. I have been away for a while on vacation and I had a rest." Then she smiled and walked away.

B.B.: Now, let's look at that.

Sophie: I'm just telling you my observations. It seems to me that these children need to make contact with somebody who has absented himself.

B.B. [*to Charles*]: Do you see the mistakes?

Charles: That's a large assumption.

B.B.: Of course. We just finished talking about the patient always being right; that means we must assume that he has very good reasons for saying what he does, and that he knows what it means, even if we don't. We cannot know for sure *why* he does what he does, but the best way is to assume he does it for the same reasons we would.

Here we can observe the defensive mechanisms, I am tempted to say, working overtime. Ida says, "You have new glasses on." Sophie knows that this is not so, and that Ida says it out of her need to make contact with Sophie who has been away. Knowing all that, there is no need for any investigation. If Ida were to come up to me and say the same thing, I, too—that is, if I have my marbles all together, which I don't always—certainly would be very much astonished and might say, "So?"

Senior Worker: Is that accepting what she said?

B.B.: Not quite, because knowing that my glasses are not new for me, I can't quite do so yet. Therefore the less I say, the fewer words I use, the less I commit myself to any position —the more open the exchange remains. I invite this by putting the "So?" as a question.

Charles: You want her to explain why she said it.

B.B.: Exactly. Since I believe the patient is right in what he says, and since I as yet do not see how he is right, I have got to find out. But actually it's very simple. Let me try. Whom shall I pick on? Any lady volunteers? All right, Bea; you have a new hairdo.

Bea: That's what the kids told me every day, as a matter of fact.

B.B.: Fine, what are the possibilities?

Bea: That I really do.

B.B.: That's right, it is a decided possibility. But in Sophie's case this was eliminated, because she knew she didn't. So what is the other possibility?

Bea: That they see me differently.

B.B.: That's right. Now what is more important information to the therapist than that the patient suddenly sees him differently? So the issue was that Ida saw you entirely differently.

Sophie: This is what I understood.

B.B.: Yes, but what did you do with it?

Sophie: I told her why I thought I looked different to her, "I have been away on vacation"; whether it was the correct reason or not, I don't know.

B.B.: Yes, that's what you did. But if you tell her what you think is her reason, what does that mean to Ida?

Sophie: That I told her why I looked different to her.

B.B.: All right, let me try it: Kathy, why do you get yourself such a seductive hairdo?

Kathy: Because I want to be seductive.

B.B.: That was your immediate reaction?

Kathy: No, my immediate reaction was . . .

B.B.: It's all right if you don't want to tell us. I had hoped my remark was outrageous enough to provoke a gut reaction, but you are too polite to state it, which I appreciate. Anyway, it shows Sophie that she is not the only one who has difficulty being in contact with herself. What would be your reaction, Kay, if I said that to you?

Kay: I would probably say, politely, "Who the hell do you think you are?"

B.B.: That's right. So what would be your main emotional reaction to being told why you do something?

Kay: Anger.

B.B.: Of course. So why do you, Sophie, want to arouse anger in Ida? Anybody who is told why he does something, reacts with anger. Sometimes it might be true, and sometimes it might be wrong, that is beside the point. I made my statement about Kathy's hairdo as provocative as I could, because I wanted you, Sophie, to feel what it does to us if somebody tells us the reason why we do some things. It is felt as intrusive, aggressive behavior to which there is only one normal reaction possible: anger. The reaction human beings have, when somebody takes it on himself to tell the other person why he does something, is Kay's spontaneous, "Who the hell do you think you are?"

Since you, Kathy, didn't permit yourself to react openly to a statement that can evoke nothing but anger, you have to ask yourself the why, how, and wherefore of it. You see, if Alan had told John: "You are in a rage because you feel pushed around," or if Charles had told John: "You are in a fury because you feel rejected," nothing good could have come from the interaction. The idea that this might be the cause of his rage is a kind of knowledge you have to keep to yourself, though you have to proceed from it.

Those of us who have participated in previous conversations on Ida know what a tremendous change has taken place in her in regard to glasses. Therefore, all glasses now look very differently to her than they used to, and therefore new. Sophie, you could really have gotten some very fascinating answers from Ida, if you had encouraged her to talk about her remark. But by saying, "No, my glasses aren't changed," you tell her, "Ida, you don't know what you are talking about, because nothing has changed." Because Ida is really not interested in your glasses, and the so-called objective reality thereof; she is only interested in the change that has taken place in herself around glasses.

Ida, though a small girl, had been a real terror, attacking everybody who wore glasses, tearing them off and breaking them, while also demanding to wear glasses herself, which she also broke. Letting her do both—by not fighting back against the attacks and by providing her with innumerable (cheap) glasses, all of which she broke—and in many other ways, we gained her confidence. During Sophie's absence, she had let us in, to some degree, on what her symptomatic behavior meant. Her mother was extremely nearsighted; Ida had tried to protect herself against what she believed to be her mother's destructive anger against her, by making it impossible for the mother to see anything, including Ida, by tearing off her glasses and breaking them. From there her anger had extended to everybody who wore glasses. Glasses also came to stand for dangerous power, of which she wanted to have a part, thus her demand for glasses. But as she tried them on and they didn't give her new power, she felt cheated and broke the glasses, crying out for more in the hope that the next pair would give this power to her. Having made us part of her secret, and with her worker having joined Ida in her efforts to protect herself against the danger emanating from those who wore glasses, she no longer needed the power residing in glasses; thus her attitude to glasses had changed, and now all glasses were "new" glasses.

Sophie: I think if I had responded that it was true, that I wore new glasses, my response may not have been a helpful one. If I responded by saying that it was a change in her attitude about glasses, I don't think this would have been helpful, either.

B.B.: No! Have I suggested either of the two? All I suggested was a statement of astonished ignorance, because this might induce her to enlighten us. If you were to have asked, "How so?" Ida might have explained to you what exactly changed in your glasses. What your glasses were before, and what your glasses are now. I wouldn't be at all astonished if she had come up with a statement such as "They are not scary." It probably would have been confusing to you, but you would have immediately seen that here is a problem. Seemingly everyday events—the ball on the roof, "You have new glasses"—turn us off from being psychologists. A statement about glasses no longer being dangerous would have startled us. Do patients really have to act more psychotic than they are to get our interest? This, my friends, is one of the reasons for psychotic disturbances. If we don't see the problem behind the statement, "These are new glasses," the patient has to come up with psychotic strategies. He has to exaggerate and exaggerate until we finally understand that there is a big problem, but through these exaggerations he gets totally out of touch with the world.

At this staff meeting, those who participated were exposed to some of the most basic principles of milieu therapy. Also highlighted was the difference in the two young therapists' ability to learn; both were at the same level of training to become psychoanalysts. But to avoid the conclusion that Charles is a fast learner and Sophie particularly obtuse, it must be remembered that Charles only observed an interaction, while Sophie was at the center of one. Sophie therefore could have learned much more from it; although doing so was incredibly more difficult for her than for Charles. Learning is so much easier for those watching others go astray in their thinking; but such learning usually does not penetrate as deep. This meeting also suggested how some persons with considerable training felt they *ought to know*; and by this expectation of themselves were prevented from accepting their ignorance in regard to what another person's behavior might mean; they therefore judged instead of investigating.

Subconsciously Sophie understood what I had tried to teach Charles, but her emotional investment in becoming a therapist made it unacceptable. Contrary to what I discussed with Charles, she had to demonstrate to herself that she knew what was a fitting reply to Ida's remark about her wearing new glasses. That explains why she asserted, by means of her initial statement, that she would not ask a question but would offer an interesting observation, suggesting that she could report something of importance about a child without any need to ponder its possible meaning.

Had Sophie been a staff member, I would have given the discussion a different slant: stressing her narcissistic need to believe that she as a person and what she did (her vacation) was more important to the patient than the patient's inner processes. It was this feeling of self-importance which had originally led her astray. Convinced that her absence was the event triggering Ida's strange remark about her wearing new glasses, she felt no need to further examine its possible origin in Ida. Had Sophie been a staff member, I would have tried to get across that while we are very important to the patients and that what we can do can be most significant to the patients, we are not all *that* important, at least not as the person we actually are. Sophie's response could have made a great difference to Ida, because Ida needed to gain some verification that glasses had in fact changed their meaning for her. She felt they had, but was still unsure within herself about whether they were indeed "new," that is, no longer dangerous. But to teach Sophie that all at once would have been more than she could have digested in one meeting. Since these two residents (Charles and Sophie) would not relate to the patients in any therapeutic way—as residents usually spent only six months to a year at the School, much too short a time for that permanency which I believe to be a most essential ingredient in a therapeutic relation—I could afford to be more concerned with teaching them general principles than with what immediately or in the long run would benefit one of the patients, in addition to enlarging the staff's understanding.

In some ways, the staff learned more from the short exchange between Kathy, a new staff member, and Kay, who had been with the institution for over a year, and me, than from the interchange between Charles, Sophie, and me. Sophie could never have become a successful staff member, because her narcissistic and intellectual defenses were too strong. But even at the very beginning of her association with the milieu, Kathy was ready to consider, if not to accept, an accusation of acting-out behavior, namely, of being seductive. Rather than rejecting what I said as wrong, she was willing to agree tentatively; convinced that by doing so clarification would be facilitated. It would have been very easy for her to answer that she did not think the hairdo seductive—true to objective fact, as was Sophie's answer that her glasses were not new—or that seduction was not the reason for it, but only that she thought the hairdo becoming; all perfectly polite replies to a totally unjustified attack. Rather than deny the validity of the attack outright, she took me seriously enough to first search into herself whether or not there might be some justification for it, and then to try to figure out why I said it. She eventually developed into a most valuable staff member.

Kay's answer showed Kathy that it was perfectly all right to tell the director to go to hell, provided it was how one felt, and that it was done politely. Sophie, too, had tried to find the reason for Ida's statement; but her narcissism had led her to overevaluate her personal importance. Kathy also searched in herself, and so did Kay; neither came up with the answer that I was wrong, which they could easily have done, or said, "It's something in you that makes you think this hairdo is seductive." They rejected the latter as too intrusive. Since neither Kathy nor Kay arrogated to themselves the right to intrude into my mind, they could tell me not to intrude into theirs.

How much Kathy had learned from the few minutes in the meeting during which I addressed myself to her was indicated by her reply when, after the staff meeting, I apologized and asked what she thought had been my reasons for using such an aggressive example to make a point. "You probably felt that Sophie's telling Ida that she was wrong in anything she said about glasses was much more upsetting to her than even the worst thing you could say to me about me." Kathy's reasoning was right; I had searched for a remark that would hit a staff member to the quick, so that he would wish to break off all further interchange, as Ida had done. Because Kathy was involved with Ida, and because of the person she was, she understood the purpose of what I said; I could not be sure that all of the other staff members would to the same degree. The explanation to them had to wait until the next staff meeting, which Sophie did not attend; but I could not let Kathy keep guessing until then.

People generally find it difficult to relate to nonverbal patients and to understand their behavior, though the principles which should guide us are exactly the same as those which apply to the most verbal and intellectual ones. Beginners had to struggle with this:

Steve: When you came around this afternoon, little Louis, as always, was behaving in his characteristic way, jumping across the room while clapping his hands. You had us all clap our hands. I wasn't quite sure why you did it, nor what was the significance for him. [Louis, who used to be a mute autistic boy, had after a year acquired a few words, mainly exclamations which he used most sparingly and only with a few favored persons. Steve, though having earned a doctor's degree in clinical psychology, was a beginner at the Orthogenic School. Had he been more secure about being accepted and supported by the staff, as he was a few months later, he would have simply asked: "Why did you ask us to clap our hands?" without any pretense that he had some good idea why.]

B.B.: What do you think?

Steve: My feeling was he's doing this to attract attention. [Steve thus shifted away from the question of what I had had in mind and his wondering about my behavior, to what seemed to him much safer—the behavior of the patient. It is always much easier to talk about a third person not present, than about those directly involved.]

B.B.: I don't know whether the staff can stand another of my harangues about "attracting attention." It's a favorite topic of mine, so I have to be careful not to overdo it. We are all hounds for attention. The fact that somebody does something to attract attention fools us into believing we have understood his behavior, while actually all it means is that we try to convince ourselves there is no need to give thought to its possible meaning because we know what it is about. What makes for the differences among us is not that one person wishes to attract attention and another does not, because we all do in many situations; but what kind of attention we want, and how we go about getting it. Thinking or speaking in such generalities as saying somebody does something to attract attention prevents us from searching for the unique meaning such behavior has for a particular person. In nonspeaking patients, we have to be specially careful not to generalize about their behavior;

because it is the only clue we have for understanding them and what they try to convey to us.

Steve: The main reason I wondered about it is that he does it almost continuously. Why respond in one instance, by getting everyone to clap their hands, and then for the remainder of the time ignore it? That's why I wasn't exactly sure why you did it.

B.B.: We couldn't very well clap our hands all day long as he does; quite literally this would kill us.

Steve: I agree. But why, then, do it just once?

B.B.: Your point is well taken. I did it, and you trust that I did it for a reason. I think you will gain much more if you try to figure it out than if I tell you.

Steve: I've been pondering it and haven't come up with an explanation.

B.B.: Why do you think Louis does it? Can we really say he does it to attract attention? Does such a statement stand up under scrutiny?

Steve: I agree that to say "He does it for attention" doesn't mean much; it's vague. Maybe this is just his way of relating to people.

B.B.: Possibly. But let's go back to this attracting attention. What would you do if you wanted to gain somebody's attention?

Steve: Call his name.

B.B.: Is this the only way we can gain attention? How at this moment did Susie get my attention? [This remark showed he had difficulty recognizing nonverbal communication to be as effective as verbal. Since he appeared not to realize how frequently we all engage in nonverbal communication, I tried to bring to his attention that we all do and quite effectively.]

Steve: I didn't notice what she did.

B.B.: Probably because you were concentrating on me, which is understandable. But a psychologist should also always have his eyes open for nonverbal communication. So let's ask Susie what she did, since you didn't see it.

Susie: I moved, and did a specific activity.

B.B.: True, but those of us who didn't see it don't know what you are calling a specific activity.

Susie: I put my sweater around myself.

B.B.: Yes, but before you did that you made a very disgusted face. What conclusion do you think I drew from Susie's effort to attract my attention, which wasn't difficult at all?

Steve: That the temperature of the room was not to her liking.

B.B.: Of course. She was cold, and disgusted that the room was so cold. Now many of us were glad that the air conditioner cooled off the room on such a hot day, but different people feel differently. Besides putting on her sweater and making a disgusted face, what else could Susie have done?

Steve: She could have adjusted the thermostat.

B.B.: That's right. What else could she have done?

Steve: She could have walked out.

B.B.: That's correct again. And what else could she have done?

Steve: She could have asked somebody else to adjust the thermostat.

B.B.: As you can see, we could go on almost indefinitely, so many courses of action are available to us. And if the first thing Susie chose hadn't worked, she being an intelligent girl, what would she have done?

Steve: Tried the second.

B.B.: So if somebody tries to gain a goal, or tries to attract attention and he doesn't get what he wants, in the normal course of events he would try something else, and again something else, until it works. Does Louis's hand-clapping usually get him attention?

Steve: No.

B.B.: Now, if all he were after was to get attention, he would find other means. Extremely limited as his repertoire is compared to ours, even he has some other ways. He says, "Hi," he puts himself in front of a person, pulls at people's sleeves, or shows something saying "Look." So his hand-clapping which is so ineffective in gaining him attention must also have some other meanings to him. Do we know why he does it?

Steve: I don't know.

B.B.: Suppose somebody does something as repetitiously and for such a length of time as Louis claps his hands. Can you think of something like that somebody might do in front of others? It's hard to imagine, but maybe you can.

Steve: You mean some sort of habit? Some habitual gesture?

B.B.: I'm not driving in any particular direction. I'm trying to induce you to do your own thinking. As a matter of fact, I can't think of any particular example at the moment. Can you, Jacqui? [Addressed to a senior staff member who was playing with a piece of jewelry she was wearing.]

Jacqui: I can think of something like that right now, because I'm doing it.

B.B.: What about it?

Jacqui: I frequently play with something with my hands. It's kind of binding; slowing myself down when I have a tendency to push ahead making some remark I don't want to make, so as not to interrupt things.

B.B.: I'm sure Louis is not afraid of interrupting things, but on the other hand it is a fair guess that he claps his hands to bind some of his discomfort. Whatever it may be, if someone engages in an activity which is as obvious as handclapping in front of other people, and he doesn't get any reaction—as if whatever he does is of no interest to anybody—this is terribly frustrating and degrading. When I saw that this was going on, I was both astonished and annoyed by all these, what my friend Edda calls . . .

Edda: Lunkheads.

B.B.: . . . all these lunkheads sitting around and no one paying any attention to what Louis was so obviously doing. Nobody asked: "Why do you do it?" Instead, he was surrounded by what I felt as a total denial that he was doing something obviously annoying, or at least interrupting to the others, and equally obviously very important to him. I wanted to make all those present at least interested in him and what he was doing; to pay him some attention, though I didn't think he did it to attract attention. I also wanted to show them and him that, after all, what he was doing was not out of this world; that we all can do that quite easily, too. He was not fighting invisible giants or spiders, but doing something we all do on occasion. We clap our hands if something has taken place that we liked. I don't know why Louis does it, but as a possibility it occured to me he might pretend that what's going on around him is something that happens because he approves of it. We know this is not so, that he feels totally without power over his life, totally defeated by it. This may be more reason for him to pretend to himself that this is not so, and that we do all the strange things we do, because we think he wants us to do them. I admit what I am saying is farfetched, just to show it's possible to find some meaning in his clapping. Be this as it may, our clapping our hands might have told him that we approve of what he was doing, or at least that we are interested in it, and that what he does is something that we, too, might occasionally do.

Louis is convinced he is crazy. He had been told this often enough before he came here, and the looks people give him on the street or beach reinforce this conviction, as much as we try to combat it here. That means to him that he is totally different from anybody else, and so is what he is doing. So I tried to show him—not through words which he does not trust, that's why he avoids using them—but through our action: "No, you aren't all that different from the rest of us, we all can do what you are doing. True, we don't do it with your persistence, but this does not mean it is all that extraordinary." This is what motivated my suggestion in part.

On another level, the reason for what I did might be put something like this: If somebody can talk only French, and everybody around him speaks only English, no communication is possible. But if one other person in the group knows just a couple of French words, even if he pronounces them badly, and he tries to speak to this stranger in his language much as he may murder it, in this situation it is an indication of good will; of trying to make this foreigner feel less an outsider. If this is true for language, it is also true for gestures. Does that answer your question?

Steve: It does.

B.B.: Maybe it does, and maybe it raises a lot more.

Steve: Sure, it does. What is he trying to convey through it? I can see now that's his way to make himself feel more comfortable.

It was Jacqui's telling us why she engaged in repetitious gestural behavior that made it possible for Steve to realize this, though he was probably not aware of it, and believed he learned it from our discussion of Louis. We all have a much easier time learning from each other, and from ourselves, than from the patients directly. Since Jacqui, a senior and highly respected staff member, used herself as an example, this made it much easier for Steve to recognize, either in himself or in others like him, some mannerism used to bind discomfort. Had he tried to derive such understanding from Louis's behavior, it would have been much more difficult because of the connotation "Maybe I have some craziness in me, too"—an admission which requires a great deal of inner security. If a type of behavior comes to our awareness first in ourselves, or even better, in somebody we approve of, when we subsequently recognize it in a psychiatric patient it becomes a quality that brings him closer to us. This, incidentally, may serve as a small example of an important principle. It is extremely difficult to learn true understanding from the study of psychiatric patients, though this is the method practically universally used in training staff; and it is frequently painful to learn from oneself. While it's not easy to learn from other staff members like oneself, it is still the most acceptable way. If they reveal traits in themselves in rudimentary form, which are characteristic of the patients in an exaggerated form, then it is much more acceptable and much less threatening to find the same thing occurring within oneself. Much as I tried to show parallels between my psyche and that of the patients, the head of the institution is less effective in this respect because there is always the suspicion that the director is doing this to induce the staff member to do the same; that is, he does it for the institution's benefit rather than that of the staff member.

B.B.: How are you going to convey to Louis that you understand he claps his hands because it gives him some measure of security if you don't use his means of communication to do so? We are years away from his being able to tell us in so many words what hand-clapping means to him, and we might never get there unless we show him how hard we try to understand his behavior in his terms. Even I can only occasionally devise such methods to try to convey to a patient that we are on his wavelength; or at least trying to get on it. I also have to consider how the staff and the other patients will react to such methods, whether they are willing to cooperate with me.

Alan: There is something I don't understand yet. If I were he, doing what he is doing, clapping my hands, and everybody started doing the same thing at the same time, I would be mad as hell.

B.B.: All right. You might, and another might not be angry but only rather startled by what it's all about. The possibility that he might get good and mad was a risk I had to take; you're absolutely correct. But let's go on with your assumption. What do you think is going on in Louis's mind? Do you think he loves us, his fellow man, mankind? Is he, as some of us are, worried about world peace?

You shake your head saying "No." So what do you think is going on in his head at this point?

Alan: Fantasies.

B.B.: What kind of fantasies?

Alan: Fantasies about himself.

B.B.: I really wouldn't know.

Alan: I was trying to think what my fantasies might be if I were to clap my hands.

B.B.: Fine, but don't get away from the very good point you were making, that it would make you very angry. At whom would you be angry?

Alan: At the other people.

B.B.: That's right. And at whom do you think he is angry most of the time?

Alan: At everybody.

B.B.: Do you mean at something vague?

Alan: I mean there is nothing specific about his hating.

B.B.: Exactly. If he were to know about whom he is so angry, if he could afford to recognize it, he would be much more of a person; life would be much more concrete for him, and things would be much more tangible and not such a vague morass of despair. But let's suppose he is cognizant of what the source of his fury and mortal anxiety is: his mother, his brother. What can he do about them, who are so powerful that they were able to destroy him as a human being; made him, or forced him to make himself, into a vegetable. He is stewing in his anger, he is smashing them up between his clapping hands. But it is all so vague, and distant, so unspecific. But if my action does make him angry, what is the advantage?

Alan: That you're here, he can do something about it.

B.B.: That's right. His anger is now caused by somebody who is a real person; at least something specific that happened right here and at this moment made him angry. Vague fury, obscure, nonspecific anxiety, is always much more devastating than a concrete experience of it. If you are angry at the whole world, what can you do about it? Maybe you beat your wife, if she lets you. [Alan had recently married another staff member, also present.] And don't tell me that if you were to feel this way it wouldn't give you relief, at least at the moment. Now this is not advice on what to do, only an example I made up.

Alan: But Louis just looked angry as hell and clapped with more intensity than before.

B.B.: Maybe because now he knew whom or what he was smashing between his hands, and this was the advantage. Frankly, I think that if he had been startled into stopping, then my interference would have been all wrong; it would have been a step toward driving a symptom underground before he and we understood what it signified, something very dangerous for our therapeutic efforts. But I wanted to convince him that his clapping had also to do with us right here, and kind of tell him, "If you are angry now and want to kill us, you have good reasons, and reasons you can know." It is so much better to be angry at something we know we're angry at, or afraid of—because sooner or later we will then get the idea that since it's something concrete, we can do something about it.

Bill: I keep wondering what Don did during this?

Alan: I watched him and he was all aglow, perfectly delighted.

B.B.: I thought so, too. [Don is a boy who used to be autistic and among whose symptoms was a continuous but very different hand-clapping accompanied by jumping across the room, which he had given up along with most of his other autistic symptoms about two years earlier. Still schizophrenic, for most of the time he was in good contact and managing quite well, though only at great cost to himself.] This performance of ours convinced him how far he has progressed from such "crazy behavior." He felt very pleased with himself and very superior to Louis.

Alan: You could just see it in him, a kind of: "Look at that nut!"

Karen: Would this explain why Martha now, after all these years, is afraid of things here?

B.B.: Exactly. As long as it was those other nonspecific people who were pulling her skin off her body, we couldn't reach her.

Karen: So that's progress.

B.B. Certainly. In classical psychoanalysis we speak of getting the problem, the neurosis or whatever it is, into the treatment situation. It becomes analyzable as transference neurosis. Since our patients here are much sicker and so inaccessible to others, we have to get them into a living situation, as opposed to a transference situation. Through the living situation, we can eventually induce them to transfer into it what is ailing them. That's why, within reason, we have to offer them a chance to get mad at us, or even to permit themselves to become afraid of us. We do this not by *making* them mad, or provoking them—my purpose was not to provoke Louis. On the contrary, by convincing him it is safe to be mad at us, I tried to make him feel less alien from us; as in my example, which was in bad taste, that it would be safer for Alan to beat his poor wife than to beat up on a stranger who might be stronger than he, or carry a knife. Because, you see, as long as Martha was afraid that somebody out there was bent on pulling off her skin, whatever reassurance we might be able to give her that the world isn't that much interested in pulling off her skin doesn't do much good. But if patients become afraid that it is we who are trying to do it to them, we can slowly show them what we are really like, and how little scary we really are.

Karen: Well, for instance, Martha said recently that Diane and Ann look like her sister. It just bowled me over. Never before had she said such a complete sentence, in such good contact, a perfectly articulate statement. I didn't say anything, but my emotional reaction was, "But they're not. You don't have to be so angry at them, because they're not your sister."

B.B.: That's much too rational. Of course, such an inner reaction comes very naturally, and you should congratulate yourself that you had sufficient empathy with what was going on in Martha not to say it, because it wouldn't have been any good. You see, her real sister was so overpowering and destructive that she couldn't deal with her at all.

Karen: So if Diane becomes her sister, then she can do something with it. And something very similar happened with Monica in regard to her twin sister. Out of the blue she suddenly decided that Pat is like her twin sister, and she now hates her with a vengeance.

B.B.: As you know, there was something that led up to this. Monica hates and loves Inge, her worker. She has made her into her mother, whom she thinks she murdered, because she kicked her when she was pregnant and she died while still pregnant. Monica had hated her mother so much because she wanted so much to be loved by her, and felt her twin got all the affection and she got none. We got nowhere with her until she began to love and hate Inge as she did her mother. Only now her love was not rejected; nor did her hatred lead to devastating results. Her hate did not provoke counter-rejection, nor was her love continuously frustrated. As a matter of fact, we cannot help these patients until they view some of us as if we were a member of their original family, or at least those who caused them the greatest difficulties. It's among the hardest things we have to learn; because if they can finally afford to get so angry at us, it hurts our feelings. Look at all the hard work we put into them, how wonderful we are to them, all the cook-outs and cook-ins we arrange for them, how we run errands for them, sit up all night with them, do this and the other, much more than anybody ever did for us, and now . . .

Inge: Now Monica says I am her awful mother.

B.B.: That's right. But only by becoming her awful mother can you eventually show her that you're not so awful, after all. This is a most difficult thing for the beginner to learn: that the patients are apt to make the best progress if they can afford to be good and angry at us. The problem this acting out presents is that it threatens to shatter our self-image and yet if it does, then we are no longer any use to them. Our self-image must be so secure that when we finally become their awful mother we can be pleased. Then they can test how awful we really are, and eventually come to the conclusion that there are, even for them in this world, good substitute mothers.

The next and final excerpt from a staff meeting will again concentrate on a beginner's work. What milieu therapy is all about can be shown most vividly by what the beginner has to experience to grow into a senior worker rather than by the innumerable problems even the most experienced staff member encounters daily.

The initial phase of this meeting illustrates how difficult it can be for even a very intelligent and, in all other situations, a most astute person to recognize what one inflicts on others and what is inflicted on oneself as identical behavior. The young lady, whom we will call Eileen, had won highest honors in philosophy before she joined the staff. Within a few years after leaving the Orthogenic School, she was appointed professor of philosophy in one of the great universities. Having the worker undergo exactly what he had caused the patient to experience can be, when not overwhelming, most revealing to him; because he cannot then help feeling the way the patient did. Such experiences guide him in the future to consider foremost what feelings his behavior will arouse in the patient, and convince him of how similar our emotional reactions are.

Eileen: Marc always asks when something was invented, or who invented it, like who invented the White House, and when was it invented? And I'll ask, "Why do you want to know?" and all he'll say is "I'm curious."

B.B.: Why do you want to know why Marc does that?

Eileen: Because he does it so frequently.

B.B.: Yes, but why do you want to know?

Eileen: Because it's a question that would never occur to me to ask.

B.B.: Isn't that curious that it would never occur to you? To ask who invented the White House?

Eileen: Yes. Well, it's true. It's a valid question. But he doesn't really want to know about the White House.

B.B.: Well, why do you want to know about Marc? Aren't you curious?

Eileen: Yes.

B.B.: So why should Marc not be curious?

Eileen: Because I'm not "just curious."

B.B.: Maybe he isn't just curious.

Eileen: Well, that's it. I'm sure he isn't "just curious," but this is all he'll say, and when I ask him, "Why do you ask?" he'll answer, "I don't know." So I wonder how I could find out more about what he's interested in.

B.B.: What else about Marc? Let's go on.

Eileen: Go on to what?

B.B.: I don't know.

Eileen: Well, I don't know what to say. Because the repetitiveness of his questions is mostly what our conversation consists of. Because he asks things like this so often.

B.B.: I think it's beside the point how often he does it.

Eileen: Because I want to know what is important to him . . .

B.B.: Why do you want to know? Ask me a question. Just a simple English question. The first that comes to your mind.

Eileen: Why is grass green?

B.B.: "Why do you want to know?" What is your reaction to such an answer?

Eileen: Don't give me that, just tell me why.

B.B.: That's right. The normal emotional reaction to "Why do you want to know?" is "To hell with you." Either you know who invented the White House, or you don't know. Both are perfectly honorable answers. But you choose to tell Marc, "Why do you want to know?" You do something to him which you would, and should, most strenuously object to if anybody did it to you.

Eileen: Well, if I asked you, why is grass green?

B.B.: Well, why don't you try it?

Eileen: O.K. Why are sheep black and white and not red, or why are swans white and sometimes black, but not red?

B.B.: I really don't know. Do you?

Eileen: Why are clouds white?

B.B.: Well, there are some explanations for that. Shall we get a book and study it together?

Visitor: [This visitor was spending a few days at the institution to get acquainted so that both she and we could decide whether she should join the staff.] Yesterday he asked me who invented "Grandfather," and I said, "Well, I really couldn't tell you; it's such an old word, and people just started using it a long time ago." And I don't remember who mentioned using the dictionary—I think it was right at lunch—and he said, "All right, after lunch let's look it up in the dictionary." We talked about it further, and he knew that grandfather is a father's father, or a mother's father. We then looked it up in the dictionary, and all it said there was, "Father's father or mother's father." The dictionary didn't tell him anything he didn't know. I guess he really wasn't interested in who invented "Grandpa."

B.B.: I believe he was very much interested in who invented Grandfather. Who invented Grandfather? That's an easy one.

Visitor: I wouldn't know what to say.

B.B.: You are an intelligent girl; use your imagination. Who creates a grandfather?

Visitor: The fact that his son has children.

B.B.: No, who creates the grandfather?

Visitor: The grandchildren.

B.B.: Yes, But since you do not know his family history, let me tell you that there there is only one grandchild, Marc, in his family. So it was Marc who created his grandfather. Who invented the White House, Eileen? All right, Who invented this white house?

Eileen: You did . . . the children . . . you mean, this house?

B.B.: This white house.

Eileen: What white house?

B.B.: All right, so then, what would be an answer you could give him?

Eileen: What White House? Or no answer?

B.B.: I don't know whether you have to give him an answer. But the point is there are many white houses, aren't there?

Eileen: Yes.

B.B.: All right. So what's the difference between the many white houses, and the White House?

Eileen: The President lives in the White House.

B.B.: So who invented the White House?

Eileen: The President?

B.B.: Well, in a fashion. At least you might find out whether the issue is the President in the White House. You see, when you say, "Why do you want to know?", this shows Marc that you don't go to any trouble to think his question through. Marc isn't here to suffer from our intellectual laziness, if I may call it that. Even you who are only visiting, through a short process of reasoning, could have told Marc who, if not invented, surely is the person who creates a grandfather. When he asks, "Who invented the White House?" this is a perfectly intelligent question. There are many white houses, so why do people talk about "the White House"? What is special about it? But you are right, it is true that his questions are not asked to get an obvious answer, he is much too subtle for this. So what does he ask for? What is the purpose of his question?

Eileen: To find out something about . . .

B.B.: To find out something. Don't rush it by adding about what; because trying to figure something out in a hurry leads us astray. Now if I ask a question to which I don't know the answer, it's simple: I want information. But if I ask, "Who invented Grandfather?" or "Who invented the White House?"—questions to which I know the answers— what do I want to find out?

Eileen: What the other person will say?

B.B.: That's right. If I ask a question to which I don't know the answer, you can have no certainty whether I'm after a piece of information, or only interested in your reaction. This makes things confusing. So, if I don't want to make things confusing, what questions could I ask?

Eileen: Ones to which you know the answer.

B.B.: Why does that permit me greater clarity? What equation is easier to solve: one with several unknowns or with only one?

Eileen: Only one. But do you mean clarity for him, or my understanding of what he wants, by being able to separate whether he wants to know my reaction, or the answer to the question?

B.B.: Suppose I'm asking a question, and the answer is one I'm vitally interested in. When I get the answer, what will I concentrate on?

Eileen: On the answer.

B.B.: On the information. If I concentrate on the information, will I be well able to take in the intention of the person who answers me?

Eileen: No.

B.B.: So if I'm interested in the intention of the person, and don't want to be sidetracked by my concentration on the information, what kind of questions will I ask?

Eileen: Ones about which you don't care, or ones where you already know the answer.

B.B.: Exactly. And one that has nothing to do with Marc, or Eileen, or me, or anybody else. So when Marc asks, "Why is the grass green?" or "Who invented the White House?"—

Eileen: He wants to know my reaction.

B.B.: That's right. And what might he be interested in?

Eileen: If I'll take what he asks me seriously?

B.B.: That's right. Whether you are going to put out some effort to help him with his distress.

Eileen: Because if you listen and consider it, and give the patient credit, he will know you care; and then other things will come out too.

B.B.: But what happens to Marc when he asks you this question: "Who invented the White House?" What answer does he get?

Eileen: "Why do you want to know?"

B.B.: That's right. If he gets such answers all the time, what might happen to his questioning?

Eileen: It might stop.

B.B.: That's right. But let him come to the Orthogenic School, and let's hope that he meets up with people who will show greater understanding than the two of you have done, what might happen? And actually did happen?

Eileen: He'll ask other kinds of questions.

B.B.: No, he will ask exactly this kind of question! But if he is going to get answers like, "Let's go to the dictionary," or "Why do you ask that?", then pretty soon the questions will disappear again, because he has found out what he wanted to know—that you are not interested in his distress. Now let's get back to the grandfather business. Talking to a philosopher, is that not one of the most difficult philosophical questions he raises: "How come, when it is I who create my grandfather, how can my grandfather have created me?"

Eileen: One needs the other?

B.B.: Yes, but on the level of Marc's ruminations, it's the grandfather who played such a great role in his life that it is a difficult concept for him to handle. If he created the grandfather, and his birth indeed did, but if the grandfather also in a way created him, because without him Marc would not exist, then when the grandfather died, as he recently did, would not the grandson also have to die? What Marc actually asks is, "Am I alive," or, "How come I can still be alive? I was a grandson and now I have no grandfather, how can I be a grandson without a grandfather?" So the grandson died, but Marc is still alive.

Senior Worker: Isn't this also related to his turning his anger immediately back on himself? He so often wants to kill somebody, but he feels that then *he* will get killed. This is his constant dilemma and why he can't move, is so afraid to let us know what he really thinks.

B.B.: That's right. This is behind his constant going back and forth on all issues, his back and forth to hide his need behind seemingly pointless questioning, to ferret out what we think, what we are all about. So my question then to you, Eileen, is, If you are asked a question, why don't you give him an answer?

Eileen: Well, it had to do with what my attitude toward Marc was.

B.B.: That's right. And this is exactly what he found out, and this is exactly what he *wanted* to find out by his questions in the first place. And when you have good contact with Marc, he will rarely ask such questions. So when he asks them, he really raises the question, "How do you feel about me right now?" But unfortunately he got it in the neck. Because if you had answered him, "I really don't know, Marc," and had followed it with the question, "Do *you* know?"—then he would have said either "Yes" or "No."

And if he had said "No," you could have said, "Fine, then we are both in the same boat."

The anxious world of these questions he asks are exactly the world in which Marc dwells; and we have to join him there, because that's where we can help him. Most of all, you have no right to ask any child a question in reply to his, unless you have made a sincere effort to understand what his question is all about. If then you can't figure it out, all right; you might question him. But *your* inner attitude to the question of who invented the White House was, "What a stupid question," or inane, or crazy, or whatever you might have called it in your mind. And I believe the purpose of his question was to find out whether you think he is a sensitive person, struggling with problems of greatest difficulty, or somebody you view as not worth your energy to figure out what he may have on his mind, and hence simply ask him: "Why do you want to know?" Now where does the use of the White House as a symbol really come from? Did you ever give that any thought?

Eileen: The President lives in the White House?

B.B.: So why should that be? You see, if you had given Marc's question the serious attention it deserves, you, all on your own, would have gotten further than that. Now in England there is the royal house of Windsor. Long before there was a White House, how did people distinguish themselves from each other?

Eileen: As from such-and-such a manor house.

B.B.: That's right, or Mr. Jones from the Red Farm on the Cross Road. Why was it this way? Because people were designated by something which symbolized the family. And the house symbolized the family, because it had greater permanency than the individuals.

Senior Worker: That's what Marc was talking with me about today, whether a house makes a family.

B.B.: That's why he was talking about the White House. Who invented the White House? That is, who created families? And how? It's the same question. And he worries about it because he has no place in his family. So how come he is out in the lonely cold world when others, even in his own family, have a white house? He's ruminating about these same things, in all possible ways.

The only way not to get annoyed with these difficult and taxing patients is by taking them seriously in all that they do. If you come right down to it, they're all so trying that unless we concentrate on what their aggravating behavior is all about, of necessity we are going to be annoyed by it, and by them. But if we devote ourselves to them, we'll find out that not only they but we too, in our own much more sophisticated ways, are all miserable sinners, as the Scriptures have told us all along. So how can God, in his mercy, not be annoyed with all of us? Because he looks down on us and says to himself, "My god, I created them! And so I'm responsible for them!" Only in this way can he accept all of us.

By taking them and whatever they do very seriously, by speculating what all these annoying, confusing, crazy things they do are all about, we prevent ourselves from getting impatient with them. We've got to try to understand them; and if we do, we cannot avoid accepting them and wishing to help them out of their misery. And in so doing, we end up understanding and accepting ourselves that much more.

It is on this note that the staff meeting ended. And on this note I wish to end my account of milieu therapy.

We can no longer devote ourselves to the most miserable of our fellow human beings on the grounds that this is the best way to serve God. But if we do wish to so devote ourselves to them, we can do it much more successfully than any previous generation, because we know so much more about the hidden workings of the mind. If, out of a desire to help them, we penetrate the darkness of their souls, we cannot help shedding light into the hidden recesses of our own minds. Each generation has to wage anew the struggle against the darkness in our soul. Milieu therapy is not such a bad way of doing it, either for psychiatric patients, or for those of us who choose to join them as their helpers. If we devote ourselves to making sense out of their endlessly repetitive behavior, out of the eternal ruminations in which through their fear they entrap themselves, then to paraphrase the ending of Thomas Mann's Doctor Faustus, the most recent rendering of this great myth of the Western world: "Out of uttermost hopelessness—a miracle beyond the power of belief—the light of hope will dawn."

Bibliography

1. Aichhorn, A. *Wayward Youth*, New York, Viking, 1939.
2. Baker, A., R. L. Davies, and P. Sivadon. *Psychiatric Services and Architecture*, World Health Organization Public Papers, No. 1, Geneva, 1959.
3. Baratz, G. *A Village by the Jordan*, London, Harville Press, 1954.
4. Bateson, G., D. D. Jackson, J. Haley, and J. Weakland. "Toward a Theory of Schizophrenia," *Behavioral Science*, 1, 1956.
5. Belknap, I. *Human Problems of a State Mental Hospital*, New York, McGraw-Hill, 1956.
6. Bettelheim, B. "Milieu Therapy—Indications and Illustrations," *The Psychoanalytic Review*, 36, 1949.
7. ———. *Love Is Not Enough—The Treatment of Emotionally Disturbed Children*, Glencoe, Ill., The Free Press, 1950.
8. ———. *Truants From Life*, Glencoe, Ill., The Free Press, 1955.
9. ———. "Childhood Schizophrenia," *The American Journal of Orthopsychiatry*, 26, 1956.
10. ———. "Psychiatric Consultation in Residential Treatment," The Director's View, *The American Journal of Orthopsychiatry*, 28, 1958.
11. ———. *The Informed Heart*, Glencoe, Ill., The Free Press, 1960.
12. ———. "Training the Child-Care Worker in a Residential Center," *The American Journal of Orthopsychiatry*, 36, 1966.
13. ———. *The Empty Fortress*, New York, The Free Press, 1967.
14. ———. "The Ultimate Limit," *Midway*, 9, 1968.
15. ———. *The Children of the Dream*, New York, Macmillan, 1969.
16. Bettelheim, B., and E. Sylvester. "A Therapeutic Milieu," *The American Journal of Orthopsychiatry*, 18, 1948.
17. Bettelheim, B., and B. Wright. "Staff Development in a Treatment Institution," *The American Journal of Orthopsychiatry*, 25, 1955.
18. Blos, P. *On Adolescence*, New York, The Free Press, 1962.

19. Bowlby, J. *Maternal Care and Mental Health*, Geneva, World Health Organization, 1952.
20. ———. "The Nature of the Child's Tie to His Mother," *International Journal of Psychoanalysis*, 39, 1958.
21. Braginsky, B. M., D. D. Braginsky, and K. Ring. *Methods of Madness, The Mental Hospital as a Last Resort*, New York, Holt, Rinehart and Winston, 1969.
22. Buck, J. N. "The H-T-P Technique," *Journal of Clinical Psychology*, Monograph Supplement 5, 1948.
23. Calhoun, J. B. "Population Density and Social Patterns," *Scientific American*, 206, 1962.
24. Caudill, W. *The Psychiatric Hospital as a Small Society*, Boston, Harvard University Press, 1958.
25. ———. "Around the Clock Patient Care in Japanese Psychiatric Hospitals: The Role of the Tsukisoi," *American Sociological Review*, 26, 1961.
26. Caudill, W., and H. Weinstein. "Maternal Care and Infant Behavior in Japan and America," *Psychiatry*, 32, 1969.
27. Chombard de Lauwe, P. *Famille et Habitation*, Paris, Information Sociales, 2, 1959.
28. Christian, J. J. "Factors in Mass Mortality of a Herd of Sika Deer," *Chesapeake Science*, 6, 1960.
29. Chu, F. D., and S. Trotter. *The Mental Health Complex, Part I: Community Mental Health Centers; Part I of the Task Force Report on the National Institute of Mental Health*, Washington, D.C., Center for Study of Responsive Law, 1972.
30. Cumming, J., and E. Cumming. *Ego and Milieu*, New York, Atherton Press, 1962.
31. Deane, W. N. "The Reactions of a Non-Patient to a Stay in a Mental Hospital Ward," *Psychiatry*, 24, 1961.
32. de Tocqueville, A. *The Old Regime and the French Revolution*, Garden City, N.Y., Doubleday, 1955.
33. Eissler, K. R. *Goethe*, Detroit, Wayne State University Press, 1963.
34. Erikson, E. "The Dream Specimen of Psychoanalysis," *Journal of the American Psychoanalytic Association*, 2, 1954.
35. ———. *Identity and the Life Cycle*, New York, International Universities Press, 1959.
36. Fant, R. S. "Use of Groups in Residential Treatment," in *Healing Through Living*, ed. by M. F. Mayer and A. Blum, Springfield, Ill., Charles C. Thomas, 1971.
37. Fenichel, O. *The Psychoanalytic Theory of Neurosis*, New York, Norton, 1945.
38. Foucault, M. *Madness and Civilization*, New York, Random House, 1965.
39. Freud, A. "The Widening Scope of Indications for Psychoanalysis," *Journal of the American Psychoanalytic Association*, 2, 1954.

40. Freud, S. "Fragment of an Analysis of a Case of Hysteria," 1905 [1901], *The Standard Edition of the Complete Psychological Works of Sigmund Freud*, Vol. 7, London, The Hogarth Press.

41. ———. "Recommendations to Physicians Practicing Psycho-Analysis," 1912, *ibid.*, Vol. 12.

42. ———. "The Loss of Reality in Neurosis and Psychosis," 1924, *ibid.*, Vol. 19.

43. ———. "Civilization and Its Discontents," 1930, *ibid.*, Vol. 21.

44. Freund, W. "Ueber den Hospitalismus der Saeuglinge," *Ergebnisse der Inneren Medizin und Kinderheilkunde*, 6, 1910.

45. *From Chaos to Order*, A Collective View of the Residential Treatment of Children. Compiled by Members of the American Association of Children's Residential Centers. Child Welfare League of America, New York, 1972.

46. Fromm, E. *Escape From Freedom*, New York, Rinehard & Co., 1941.

47. Gibson, W. *The Cobweb*, New York, Knopf, 1954.

48. Glazer, N. "America's Race Paradox," *Encounter*, 1967.

49. Goffman, E. *Asylums*, Garden City, N.Y., Doubleday, 1961.

50. Goldstein, K. *The Organism*, New York, American Book Co., 1939.

51. ———. "The Effect of Brain Damage on the Personality," *Psychiatry*, 15, 1952.

52. Goshen, C. E., ed. *Psychiatric Architecture*, Washington, D.C., The American Psychiatric Association, 1959.

53. Green, H. *I Never Promised You a Rose Garden*, New York, Holt, Rinehart and Winston, 1964.

54. Greenblatt, M., R. H. York, and E. L. Brown, in collaboration with R. W. Hyde. *From Custodial to Therapeutic Patient Care in Mental Hospitals*, New York, Russell Sage Foundation, 1955.

55. Levinson, D. J., and R. H. Williams, eds. *The Patient and the Mental Hospital*, Glencoe, Ill., The Free Press, 1957.

56. Grosser, Maurice. *The Painter's Eye*, New York, Rinehard & Co., 1951.

57. Gulick, H., and L. Urwick, eds. *Papers on the Science of Administration*, New York, Institute of Public Administration, 1937.

58. Hall, E. T. *The Hidden Dimension*, New York, Doubleday, 1966.

59. Hartmann, H., E. Kris, and R. Loewenstein. "Comments on the Formation of Psychic Structure," *The Psychoanalytic Study of the Child*, 2, New York, International Universities Press, 1946.

60. Hartmann, E. "The 90-Minute Sleep-Dream Cycle," *Archive of General Psychiatry*, 18, 1968.

61. Hasek, J. *Good Soldier Schweik*, New York, Frederick Ungar, 1930.

62. Hediger, H. "Freiheit und Gefangenschaft im Leben des Tieres," *Ciba Zeitschrift*, 5, No. 54, 1938.

63. ———. *Studies of the Psychology and Behavior of Captive Animals in Zoos and Circuses*, New York, Criterion Books, 1955.

64. Henry, J. "The Formal Social Structure of a Psychiatric Hospital," *Psychiatry*, 17, 1954.

65. ———. "Types of Institutional Structure," *Psychiatry*, 20, 1957.

66. ———. "The Culture of Interpersonal Relations in a Therapeutic Institution for Emotionally Disturbed Children," *The American Journal of Orthopsychiatry*, 27, 1957.

67. Henry, J., and Z. Henry, *Doll Play of Pilaga Indian Children*, Research Monograph No. 4, New York, American Orthopsychiatric Association, 1944.

68. Hyde, R. W. *Experiencing the Patient's Day*, New York, Putnam's Sons, 1955.

69. Jacobson, E. "Contributions to the Metapsychology of Cyclothymic Depression," *Affective Disorders*, ed. by P. Greenacre, New York, International Universities Press, 1953.

70. Jahoda, M., P. Lazarsfeld, and H. Zeisel. *Marienthal: The Sociography of an Unemployed Community*, Chicago, Aldine-Atherton, 1971.

71. Johnson, D. McI., and N. Dodds, eds. *The Plea for the Silent*, London, Christopher Johnson, 1957.

72. Jones, M. *The Therapeutic Community*, New York, Basic Books, 1953.

73. Kanner, Leo. "Autistic Disturbance of Affective Contact," *Nervous Child*, 2, 1943.

74. Kesey, Ken. *One Flew Over the Cuckoo's Nest*, New York, The Viking Press, 1962.

75. *A Kierkegaard Anthology*, ed. by Robert Bretall, Princeton, N.J., Princeton University Press, 1946.

76. Kiev, A., ed. *Magic Faith and Healing: Studies in Primitive Psychiatry Today*, Glencoe, Ill., The Free Press, 1964.

77. Kleitman, N. "Basic Rest-Activity Cycle in Relation to Sleep and Wakefulness," in *Sleep: Physiology and Pathology*, ed. A. Kales, Philadelphia, Lippincott, 1969.

78. Kohut, H. "Introspection, Empathy, and Psychoanalysis," *Journal of the American Psychoanalytic Association*, 7, 1959.

79. Kris, E. *Psychoanalytic Explorations in Art*, New York, International Universities Press, 1952.

80. Laing, R. D. *The Politics of Experience*, New York, Pantheon Books, 1967.

81. ———. *The Politics of the Family and Other Essays*, New York, Pantheon Books, 1971.

82. Laslett, P. *The World We Have Lost*, New York, Scribner's, 1965.

83. Lazarsfeld, P., and M. Jahoda. *Die Arbeitslosen von Marienthal*, Oesterreichische Wirtschaftpsychologische Forschungsstelle, 1933.

84. Lessing, D. *The Fourgated City*, New York, Knopf, 1971.

85. Levy, S. "Figure Drawing as a Projective Test," in *Projective Psy-*

    chology, ed. by L. E. Abt and L. Bellak, New York, Knopf, 1950.

86. Lifton, R. J. *Death in Life: Survivors of Hiroshima*, New York, Random House, 1967.

87. Machover, K. *Personality Projections in the Drawing of the Human Figure*, Springfield, Ill., Charles C. Thomas, 1949.

88. Noshpitz, J. D. "Notes on the Theory of Residential Treatment," *Journal of the American Academy of Child Psychiatry*, 1, 1962.

89. Olden, C. "On Adult Empathy with Children," *The Psychoanalytic Study of the Child*, 8, 1953.

90. Osmond, H. "The Historical and Sociological Development of Mental Hospitals," in *Psychiatric Architecture*, ed. by C. E. Goshen.

91. Pirandello, L. *Three Plays*, New York, Dutton, 1922.

92. Redl, F. "Strategy and Techniques of the Life Space Interview," *The American Journal of Orthopsychiatry*, 29, 1959.

93. ———. "The Concept of a 'Therapeutic Milieu,' " *The American Journal of Orthopsychiatry*, 29, 1959.

94. ———. *When We Deal with Children*, New York, The Free Press, 1966.

95. Redl, F., and D. Wineman. *Children Who Hate*, Glencoe, Ill., The Free Press, 1951.

96. ———. *Controls from Within: Techniques for the Treatment of the Aggressive Child*, Glencoe, Ill., The Free Press, 1952.

97. Riley, M. J. "Psychiatric Consultation in Residential Treatment. The Child Care Worker's View," *The American Journal of Orthopsychiatry*, 28, 1958.

98. Rockwell, D. A. "Some Observations on 'Living In,' " *Psychiatry*, 34, 1971.

99. Roethlisberger, F. J., and W. J. Dickson. *Management and the Worker*, Cambridge, Harvard University Press, 1939.

100. Rosen, J. L. "Personality Factors in the Reactions of Child-Care Workers to Emotionally Disturbed Children," *Psychiatry*, 26, 1963.

101. ———. "Matching Teachers with Children," *School Review*, 80, 1972.

102. Rothman, D. *The Discovery of the Asylum*, Boston, Little, Brown, 1971.

103. Ryan, W., ed. *Distress in the City—Essays on the Design and Administration of Urban Mental Health Services*, Cleveland, Ohio, The Press of Case Western Reserve University, 1969.

104. Scheler, M. *Zur Phaenomenologie und Theorie der Sympathiegefuehle*, Halle, 1913.

105. Schwartz, M. S. "What Is a Therapeutic Milieu?" in *The Patient and the Mental Hospital*, ed. by Greenblatt, Levinson, and Williams.

106. Searles, H. F. *The Nonhuman Environment in Normal Development and in Schizophrenia*, New York, International Universities Press, 1960.

107. Sechehaye, M. A. *Symbolic Realization*, New York, International Universities Press, 1951.

108. Sommer, R. "The Distance for Comfortable Conversation," *Sociometry*, 25, 1962.

109. Sommer, R., and H. Ross, "Social Interaction on a Geriatric Ward," *International Journal of Social Psychology*, 4, 1958.

110. Spiro, M. E. *Kibbutz: Venture in Utopia*, Cambridge, Harvard University Press, 1956.

111. ———. *The Children of the Kibbutz*, Cambridge, Harvard University Press, 1958.

112. Spitz, R. A. "Hospitalism," *The Psychoanalytic Study of the Child*, New York, International Universities Press, Vol. 1, 1945.

113. ———. "Anaclitic Depression," *ibid.*, Vol. 2, 1946.

114. Stanton, A. H., and M. S. Schwartz. *The Mental Hospital; A Study of Institutional Participation in Psychiatric Illness and Treatment*, New York, Basic Books, 1954.

115. Stephenson, W. *Study of Behavior: Q-Technique and Its Methodology*, Chicago, University of Chicago Press, 1953.

116. Stotland, E., and A. L. Kobler. *Life and Death of a Mental Hospital*, Seattle, University of Washington Press, 1965.

117. Sullivan, H. S. *Clinical Studies in Psychiatry*, New York, Norton, 1956.

118. Syrus, Publilius, Roman Author, *ca.* 42 B.C.

119. Szasz, T. S. *The Myth of Mental Illness*, New York, Hoeber-Harper, 1961.

120. Szurek, S. A. "Dynamics of Staff Interaction in Hospital Psychiatric Treatment of Children," *The American Journal of Orthopsychiatry*, 17, 1947.

121. ———. *Training in Psychiatric Work with Children*, Vol. 2, The Langley Porter Child Psychiatry Series, Palo Alto, Calif., Science and Behavior Books, 1967.

122. Szurek, S. A., I. N. Berlin, and M. J. Boatman, eds. *Inpatient Care for the Psychotic Child*, Vol. 5, The Langley Porter Child Psychiatry Series, Palo Alto, Calif., Science and Behavior Books, 1971.

123. Trieschman, A. E., J. K. Wittaker, and L. K. Brendo. *The Other 23 Hours*, Chicago, Aldine, 1969.

124. Tuke, S. *Description of the Retreat, an Institution near York for Insane Persons of the Society of Friends*, York, 1813.

125. United States Senate Ninety-second Congress, First Session, April 2, 1971, p. 1106. Hearings on "Trends in Long-Term Care," Special Committee on Aging.

126. Waelder, R. "The Principle of Multiple Function," *Psychoanalytic Quarterly*, 5, 1936.

127. *Otto Wagner*, ed. by H. Geretsegger and M. Peintner. Salzburg, Residenz Verlag, 1964.
128. Ward, M. J. *The Snake Pit*, New York, Random House, 1946.
129. Wohlstetter, A., and R. Wohlstetter, "Third Worlds Abroad and at Home," *The Public Interest*, No. 14 (Winter), 1969.
130. Worringer, W. *Abstraction and Empathy*, New York, International Universities Press, 1967.
131. Wright, B., "Attitudes Toward Emotional Involvement and Professional Development in Residential Child Care," Chicago, University of Chicago, Doctoral Dissertation, 1957.
132. ———. "Psychiatric Consultation in Residential Treatment; The Psychologist's View," *The American Journal of Orthopsychiatry*, 28, 1958.
133. Zimbardo, P. G. Hearings before Subcommittee on the Judiciary, House of Representatives, Washington, D.C., U.S. Government Printing Office, Serial No. 15, 1971.

A NOTE ON THE TYPE

The text of this book is set in Electra, a typeface designed
by W. A. Dwiggins for the Mergenthaler Linotype Company and first made available in 1935. Electra cannot be
classified as either "modern" or "old style." It is not
based on any historical model, and hence does not echo
any particular period or style of type design. It avoids the
extreme contrast between "thick" and "thin" elements
that marks most modern faces, and is without eccentricities
which catch the eye and interfere with reading. In
general, Electra is a simple, readable typeface which
attempts to give a feeling of fluidity, power, and speed.

The book was composed, printed, and bound by
Kingsport Press, Inc., Kingsport, Tenn.

Typography and binding design by Carole Lowenstein.